Why Not Parties in Russia?

Democracy, Federalism, and the State

Russia poses a major puzzle for comparative theorists of party development: Virtually every classic work takes parties to be inevitable and essential to electoral competition, but Russia remains highly nonpartisan more than fifteen years after Gorbachev first launched his democratizing reforms. The problem is that theories of party development lack a "control case," almost always focusing on cases where parties have already developed and almost never examining countries where independent politicians are the norm. This book focuses on Russia as just such a control case. It mobilizes fresh public opinion surveys, interviews with leading Russian politicians, careful tracking of multiple campaigns, and analysis of national and regional voting patterns to show why Russia stands out. Russia's historically influenced combination of federalism and "superpresidentialism," coupled with a postcommunist redistribution of resources to regional political machines and "oligarchic" financial-industrial groups, produced and sustained powerful "party substitutes" that have largely squeezed Russia's real parties out of the "electoral market," damaging Russia's democratic development.

Henry E. Hale (Ph.D. Harvard 1998, A.B. Duke 1988) is an assistant professor of political science at the George Washington University, where he researches and writes about issues related to democracy, federalism, and ethnic politics with a focus on the cases of the former Soviet region, especially Russia, Ukraine, and Uzbekistan. Many of the leading journals in comparative politics and postcommunist studies have published his work, including the *British Journal of Political Science*, *Comparative Politics*, *Comparative Political Studies*, *Europe-Asia Studies*, *Perspectives on Politics*, *Post-Soviet Affairs*, and *World Politics*. His research has been funded by the National Science Foundation, the Carnegie Corporation of New York, and the National Council for Eurasian and East European Research. Before moving to the George Washington University, he taught at Indiana University from fall 2000 to spring 2005. From 1998 to 2000, as research associate at Harvard's Strengthening Democratic Institutions (SDI) Project, he managed a program that studied political party development in Russia and brought Russian party leaders to meet with counterparts in the United States. During the 2003–4 and 1999–2000 rounds of Russian national elections, he was chief editor and writer for *Russian Election Watch*, a monthly electronic publication circulating updates and analysis to readers in the policymaking, business, nonprofit, and academic communities. Hale has held a Davis Center for Russian Studies Post-Doctoral Fellowship (1998) and a Peace Scholarship from the U.S. Institute of Peace (1995–6). His other teaching experience includes adjunct or visiting professorships at the European University in St. Petersburg, Russia (Spring 1999), and Tufts University's Fletcher School of Law and Diplomacy (1997–8). He travels frequently to the post-Soviet region and has interviewed many leading Russian politicians. Active in numerous professional organizations, Hale is a member of the Program on New Approaches to Russian Security and has been a visiting scholar at the Carnegie Moscow Center, the East-West Institute's Policy Studies Program, the Harvard Ukrainian Research Institute, and Columbia University's Harriman Institute.

Why Not Parties in Russia?

Democracy, Federalism, and the State

HENRY E. HALE
The George Washington University

CAMBRIDGE
UNIVERSITY PRESS

CAMBRIDGE UNIVERSITY PRESS
Cambridge, New York, Melbourne, Madrid, Cape Town, Singapore, São Paulo, Delhi

Cambridge University Press
32 Avenue of the Americas, New York, NY 10013-2473, USA

www.cambridge.org
Information on this title: www.cambridge.org/9780521844093

First published 2006
First paperback edition 2007

Printed in the United States of America

A catalog record for this publication is available from the British Library.

Library of Congress Cataloging in Publication Data

Hale,Henry E., 1966–
Why not parties in Russia? : Democracy, federalism, and the state / Henry E. Hale.
p. cm.
Includes bibliographical references and index.
ISBN 0-521-84409-6 (hardback)
1. Russia (Federation) – Politics and government – 1991 –
2. Democracy – Russia (Federation) 3. Political parties – Russia (Federation)
4. Post-communism – Russia (Federation) I. Title.
JN6695.H35 2006
320.947'09'049–dc22 2005008106

ISBN 978-0-521-84409-3 hardback
ISBN 978-0-521-71803-5 paperback

To Isabelle Kaplan

Contents

Acknowledgments

I am very grateful to the multitude of people who helped make this book possible. It would only be appropriate to begin by thanking my colleagues at Indiana University, where I found boundless personal and professional support both through the Political Science Department (chaired by Jeff Hart and then Jeff Isaac) and the Russian and East European Institute (directed by David Ransel). Scott Feickert, Denise Gardiner, James Russell, Steve Flinn, Loretta Heyen, and Margaret Anderson deserve special thanks for all manner of practical support. Perhaps my longest-term professional debts, however, are owed to Timothy Colton and Jerry Hough, who launched me on the path to researching party development in Russia by including me in the research project they quickly organized to study Russia's first post-Soviet multiparty parliamentary elections in 1993. Jerry, in fact, first got me interested in Russian politics when I took his undergraduate courses at Duke University, and Tim provided invaluable guidance and support as the chair of my dissertation committee at Harvard University. Much of my early thinking about party development was shaped by them and by the truly outstanding team they assembled to make sense of the 1993 elections.

I owe another large debt to Graham Allison, who not only gave me a job researching Russian parties as part of his project at Harvard's Kennedy School of Government between 1998 and 2000, but who allowed me to spend much of the spring of 1999 on the ground in Russia and to make repeated additional research trips there during the 1999–2000 campaign season. Among others working for Graham at the time, I am particularly grateful to Fiona Hill, who recruited me for this job, and to my colleagues there who provided me with so much support and intellectual stimulation, including Vladimir Boxer, Melissa Carr, Ben Dunlap, Sergei Grigoriev, Alena Kostritsyna, Matthew Lantz, John Reppert, Emily Van Buskirk, and many others. The European University at St. Petersburg kindly gave me a teaching position during that spring of 1999 as well as an opportunity to discuss my early ideas with some of the world's top social scientists working on Russian politics, including Vladimir Gel'man, Grigorii Golosov, Oleg Kharkhordin, Eduard Ponarin, Vadim Volkov, and David Woodruff. Stephen Hanson, Michael McFaul, and Peter Rutland have also provided valuable assistance in numerous ways, both intellectual and practical. Andrew Kuchins and his outstanding colleagues at the Carnegie Moscow Center, especially Nikolai Petrov and Aleksei Titkov, supplied me with a terrific opportunity to study the 2003–4 election at one of Moscow's premier scholarly think tanks. Valuable summer institutional support was provided by John Tedstrom, Robert Orttung, and Steve Massey at the East-West Institute when I served as a Policy Studies Program Fellow in 2002.

Seemingly countless people provided feedback on various pieces of this project in many different forums. Alongside those already mentioned, I would particularly like to thank George Breslauer, Herbert Kitschelt, Steven Wilkinson, Raymond Duch, Mikhail Filippov, Marc Howard, Debra Javeline, Kelly McMann, Mikhail Myagkov, Sarah Mendelson, Peter Reddaway, Thomas Remington, Robert Rohrschneider, Darrell Slider, Regina Smyth, Randall Stone, Joshua Tucker, anonymous manuscript reviewers, and participants in Harvard's postcommunist politics seminar and the Program on New Approaches to Russian Security (PONARS), where some of these ideas were presented in early stages. I also remain grateful to Celeste Wallander for support through PONARS, including circulating some of my first musings on the subject as a PONARS working paper. Invaluable research assistance was provided by Dan Epstein, Marcy McCullaugh, Scott Nissen, and Naomi Wachs, and Jonathan Winburn supplied excellent help with some graphics. Isabelle Kaplan also lent me great support in both developing the ideas and putting them down on paper in a form that I hope readers will find intelligible.

A number of organizations contributed funding to different elements of this book, including the Carnegie Corporation of New York, the National Council for Eurasian and East European Research (NCEEER) (under authority of a Title VIII grant from the U.S. Department of State), the U.S. Department of State, the National Science Foundation (NSF), and Indiana University's Russian and East European Institute through its Andrew M. Mellon Foundation Endowment. The statements made and views expressed within this text are solely the responsibility of the author, however, and not of the U.S. government, the NCEEER, the NSF, the Carnegie Corporation, REEI, or any other organization or person.

I am also grateful to several publishers for permission to reprint parts of some of my journal articles in this volume. While none of these are reprinted in their entirety here, substantial portions of text from the following pieces were woven into certain chapters. Some material from "Why Not Parties? Supply and Demand on Russia's Electoral Market," *Comparative Politics* 37, no. 2 (January 2005): 147–66, was included in Chapters 1 and 4. Parts of "Yabloko and the Challenge of Building a Liberal Party in Russia," *Europe-Asia Studies* 56, no. 7 (November 2004): 993–1020, are reproduced in Chapters 1 and 2 (see http://www.tandf.co.uk/journals). Portions of "The Origins of United Russia and the Putin Presidency: The Role of Contingency in Party-System Development," *Demokratizatsiya: The Journal of Post-Soviet Democratization* 12, no. 2 (Spring 2004): 169–94, are included in Chapter 5, reprinted with permission of the Helen Dwight Reid Educational Foundation and originally published by Heldref Publications, 1319 18th Street, NW, Washington, DC, 20036-1802, www.heldref.org, copyright © 2004. A large part of "Explaining Machine Politics in Russia's Regions: Economy, Ethnicity, and Legacy" is integrated into Chapter 4, reprinted with permission from *Post-Soviet Affairs* 19, no. 3 (July–September 2003): 228–63 (© V. H. Winston & Son, 360 South Ocean Boulevard, Palm Beach, FL, 33480. All rights reserved). And several adapted paragraphs from "Russia's Presidential Election and the Fate of Democracy: Taking the Cake," *AAASS NewsNet* 44, no. 3 (May 2004): 1–6, appear in Chapter 6. The author also acknowledges the valuable services provided by ISI Emerging Markets and Eastview's Universal Database of Russian Newspapers, from which some of the Russian-language materials cited herein were obtained through institutional subscriptions. David Johnson's Russia List (hereafter JRL in the text) also circulated some valuable material.

NOTE ON TRANSLITERATION

Russian language material is transliterated here using the Library of Congress system with the following exceptions:

General Exceptions:

- Y is used at the beginning of soft vowels (ya, ye, yu) that are the first letters in words.
- Soft signs are omitted at the end of proper names (i.e., Perm, not Perm').
- Common spellings are employed for words or names that widely appear in English-language media (i.e., Chechnya, not Chechnia; Zyuganov, not Ziuganov).

Exceptions Made for People's Names:

- Soft signs are omitted from people's names (i.e., Yeltsin not Yel'tsin) except where used by a person him- or herself in Western publications (i.e., Marat Gelman but Vladimir Gel'man).
- The letter y is used at the end of names that would otherwise end in ii or iy.
- The letters ie are substituted for 'e (i.e., Glaziev, not Glaz'ev or Glazev; Vasiliev, not Vasil'ev or Vasilev; Afanasiev, not Afanas'ev).

1

Electoral Markets and Russia's Political Smorgasbord

When Mikhail Gorbachev first introduced the USSR to competitive nationwide elections in 1989, comparative social scientists looking into a crystal ball would have seen the future they were expecting if their gaze had happened to fall on parliamentary elections in St. Petersburg's Vostochnii District a decade later. There, four major candidates were each appealing to voters on the basis of party platforms covering the most important issues of the day. Irina Khakamada, a telegenic star within the Union of Right Forces, championed radical economic reform. Stepan Shabarov extolled the patriotic socialism of the Communist Party of the Russian Federation. The Yabloko Party's Yury Nesterov advocated a gentler market and emphasized human rights. And Aleksandr Morozov appealed quite specifically to the interests of the older generation as a nominee of the Pensioners' Party. Indeed, while political scientists have disagreed markedly on almost everything else, one thing upon which almost all have concurred is that political parties are inevitable in democracies. Seminal works call democracy without political parties "unimaginable" (Max Weber), "unthinkable" (E.E. Schattschneider), "unworkable" (John Aldrich).[1] The conceptual consensus underlying such statements is that electoral institutions and important social divides combine to force sets of likeminded politicians to work together or to give up their dreams of influence.[2]

If our crystal ball were capable of ranging beyond Russia's "window to the West," past the Urals, and on to the distant Omsk Region's Bol'sherechenskii District, however, these same political scientists would have been quite surprised by another image of the same 1999 parliamentary elections. While the presence of two opposing party nominees would have looked familiar (a Communist Party man, Vladimir Dorokhin, and a Yabloko candidate,

1 Aldrich 1995; Schattschneider 1970; Weber 1990.

2 Aldrich 1995; Cox 1997; Duverger 1954; Kitschelt, Mansfeldova, Markowski, and Toka 1999; Kitschelt 1992; Lipset and Rokkan 1967; Taagepera and Shugart 1989.

Gennady Girich), a third pretender to office (Aleksandr Podgursky) was clearly different. This candidate, general director of the regional firm *Bekon*, represented no political party. What he did represent was the powerful provincial political machine headed by the sitting governor.[3] In fact, the Omsk machine did not back a party nominee in any of the three parliamentary districts falling within its jurisdiction, preferring to remain independent. Nevertheless, it was clearly the region's dominant political force, winning two out of the three parliamentary races in the province, including Podgursky's.

Were the prescient orb to have detected signals from the even more distant Siberian region of Krasnoiarsk, our would-be visionaries of 1989 might have encountered an even more baffling image, this one from the gubernatorial contest of 2002. In this race, hardly a peep was heard from political parties. While the Communist Party fielded one of its best-known backers, Sergei Glaziev, neutral observers never counted him among the real contenders. Neither was there a powerful gubernatorial machine to dominate the campaign. In resource-rich Krasnoiarsk, what mattered most were the province's largest two financial-industrial groups, each of which had advanced its own candidate for the governorship. In one corner stood Aleksandr Uss, the chair of the regional legislature who stood for the huge metallurgical concern Russian Aluminum (RusAl), which controlled a large part of the province's southern economy. The challenge was issued by Aleksandr Khloponin, a former top executive in the gigantic firm Norilsk Nickel, based in the northern Taimyr autonomous district within Krasnoiarsk and owned by the Interros group. Stoutly independent, these candidates did not pay parties so much as lip service. Instead, virtually all observers saw the election as a struggle between "oligarchic" financial-political clans representing very narrow business interests. When Khloponin won, this was interpreted as a victory for nickel and a crushing blow to local aluminum.

Our crystal ball also might have picked up any one of the presidential contests of 1996, 2000, or 2004. While these races consistently featured party candidates, our orb-gazers surely would have found it striking that the incumbent president ran as an independent in each of these contests despite the urgings of many advisors and aspiring party-builders.

Foreign tourists peering at these future images in 1989 might have been tempted to see an analogy with the smorgasbord that structured their gastronomical experiences in the largest Soviet hotels of that era. Political parties were not the only items they would have seen on this organizational *shveskii stol*; in fact, what has made transitional Russia remarkable in comparative perspective is that parties were generally not even the main dish. At times

[3] For simplicity's sake, in this volume the term "governor" is generally used to refer to the heads of the executive branch in Russia's provinces even where they may have other formal titles.

they mounted strong support for their designated candidates and monopolized the choice set presented to voters, as in St. Petersburg, yet in places like Omsk and Krasnoiarsk they also faced stiff competition from candidates backed by governors' political machines, financial-industrial groups, and other nonparty forms of organization.

This represents the great puzzle that Russia's short experience with political parties poses to both interested observers and social science: Why have Russian political parties failed to fully penetrate the polity over 15 years since Gorbachev first instituted competitive nationwide elections? Answering this question is the central task of this volume.

THE PUZZLE OF STALLED PARTY DEVELOPMENT IN RUSSIA

Perhaps because the degree to which parties dominate politics has ranged so widely across transitional Russia's regions and institutions, there has been great variation among scholars as to whether this country's parties are best characterized as "strong" or "weak," "growing" or "stagnant." On one hand, a vast body of research argues or even takes for granted that Russian parties have been nothing if not weak.[4] There is a great deal of evidence for these claims. Most obviously, both of Russia's presidents have eschewed party labels in all four elections to this post, most recently in 2004. Regional governors ran for reelection as major-party nominees only 3 percent of the time from 1995 to 2000. As Kathryn Stoner-Weiss has observed, less than 14 percent of all deputies elected to regional legislatures in 1993–4 carried a party affiliation. For the period 1995–7, she reports, this figure had risen to just 16.8 percent.[5] Political organizations have flashed into the political pan for one election cycle, only to evanesce into the ether the next. Such disappearing acts were performed quite convincingly by the Democratic Party of Russia, the Party of Russian Unity and Accord, and Our Home is Russia.[6] Countless others never managed to generate so much as a spark of public interest in the first place. In 1995 alone, some 43 organizations won places on the party-list ballot for their parliamentary candidates. Only the Communist Party has received more than 6 percent of the vote in all four national party-list parliamentary elections (1993, 1995, 1999, 2003). As if this were not enough to make the point, other researchers have reported sure signs that many of these parties have persistently lacked clear, distinguishing programmatic platforms.[7] Moreover, the high hopes of many Americans and Europeans that Yabloko or the Union of Right Forces would create a

4 McFaul 1999a; Reddaway 1994; Rose 1995, 2000; Rutland 1994; Slider 2001; Stoner-Weiss 2001.

5 Stoner-Weiss 2000.

6 Rose and Munro 2002.

7 Kitschelt and Smyth 2002; McFaul 1999b.

powerful, pro-Western liberal bloc in the parliament were brutally dashed when both parties in 2003 failed even to reach the 5 percent threshold for winning an officially registered parliamentary delegation (called a "fraction") in party-list voting. Equally, however, many Western social democrats and moderate socialists have been disappointed that the Communist Party remained the primary organizational representative of the Russian left as late as 2005.

Experts have advanced numerous explanations for parties' purported weakness, some of which are listed here:

- Voters have been suspicious of the mere idea of "party" after having had a very bad experience with the Communist one under the USSR;[8]
- The Soviet regime destroyed the social cleavages and related social infrastructure that are said, following Seymour Martin Lipset and Stein Rokkan, to give birth to parties. The transition, this argument goes, has failed to create new stable cleavages;[9]
- Russian political institutions have not provided proper incentives for party formation;[10]
- Russian political tradition involves strong executives and weak legislatures, thereby reducing the chances that parties will form in legislatures;[11]
- Few organizational resources have been available in society for leaders to use to build party structure;[12]
- A rise in "post-materialist" values such as environmentalism, the atomizing effects of television, and other factors related to "modern European society" have made parties weaker and more volatile in Russia much as they have in European politics;[13]
- Russia's governors have intentionally kept parties weak in order to bolster their own power and pursue their own economic interests;[14]
- Potential activists have had too little economic opportunity available to them and thus fear losing their jobs if they become politically active and irritate powerful incumbents;[15]
- Leaders' concrete decisions regarding party development, notably Russian President Boris Yeltsin's personal decision to neglect and even subvert party formation, have nipped Russian parties in the bud;[16]

[8] Hough 1998a, pp. 685–8; McFaul 2001b, p. 315; Sakwa 1995, p. 184.

[9] Hough 1998a, pp. 688, 696; Lipset and Rokkan 1967; McFaul 2001b, p. 316; Sakwa 1995, pp. 191–2.

[10] Hough 1998a, p. 691; Ishiyama 1999, p. 200; Ordeshook 1995; Sakwa 1995, p. 169; Smyth 1998.

[11] Hough 1998a, p. 691.

[12] Ishiyama 1999, p. 200.

[13] Sakwa 1995, p. 190.

[14] Stoner-Weiss 2001.

[15] McMann 2002.

[16] Hough 1998a, pp. 699–700; McFaul 2001b, pp. 315–17.

- Russia's particular form of postcommunist transition has produced an "oligarchic capitalism" in which those with resources don't need parties and those without resources are too fragmented and disoriented to organize them effectively.[17]

Despite the seeming weight of all these "pessimistic" accounts, a different set of scholars has come to strikingly rosier conclusions, implying that the St. Petersburg image of Russian politics is more reflective of the whole polity than these other works have supposed.[18] These researchers have begun with the conventional social science expectation that electoral competition provides strong incentives for politicians to band together and that it is only a matter of time before a sturdy party system emerges in Russia. Despite all of the problems parties have faced in Russia's postcommunist environment, they have contended, the bottom line is that party reputation is an efficient way for politicians to communicate policy stands to citizens and to cultivate voter loyalties. Most researchers in this loosely defined camp suggest that a learning process has been taking place whereby parties develop reputation, cultivate nascent loyalties, and build organization. Since many in this school have focused on the usefulness of parties in guiding citizen voting decisions, they have frequently used surveys to ask citizens directly about the importance of political parties in influencing their choices of candidates. They have reached a series of compelling findings.

First, these studies have quite convincingly established that Russia's parties do distinguish themselves clearly in the minds of voters on the basis of issues and that they do so in ways that one would expect given the parties' stated views.[19] Second, these studies have reported not only that voters have tended to correctly identify party stands on key issues, but also that, to a significant degree, voters have been basing their voting decisions on these policy positions.[20] Arthur Miller and his colleagues found that although Russians have selected parties partially because of the personal appeal of party leaders, issue stands have nevertheless been a large part of these decisions.[21] Third, these partisan voting patterns have been rooted in postcommunist social cleavages, as the classic comparative framework[22] would lead us to expect. Geoffrey Evans and Stephen Whitefield, for example, found that Russian partisan voting patterns have been rooted in socioeconomic class cleavages.[23] Thomas Klobucar and Miller likewise detected strong correlations between

[17] McFaul 2001b, pp. 317–19.

[18] Brader and Tucker 2001; Colton 2000; Colton and McFaul 2003; Miller, Erb, Reisinger, and Hesli 2000; Miller and Klobucar 2000; Moser 1999.

[19] Klobucar and Miller 2002; White, Rose, and McAllister 1997.

[20] Miller et al. 2000; Miller and White 1998; White, Rose, and McAllister 1997.

[21] Miller et al. 2000.

[22] Lipset and Rokkan 1967.

[23] Whitefield 2001; Whitefield and Evans 1999.

citizen self-identification with traditional class cleavages (peasant, worker, intellectual, and so on) and party loyalties.[24] Fourth, party loyalties have been emerging among the Russian population.[25] Different scholars, working with different surveys or measures between 1995 and 2000, have concluded that as many as half of Russian voters can reasonably be called something akin to "transitional partisans."[26] Fifth, this "transitional partisanship" has been found to be one of the most important determinants of voting in Russia. In fact, one of the most thorough studies of overall voting behavior in Russia to date finds that as early as 1995 transitional partisanship was more important than attitudes toward individual leaders, evaluations of incumbents, or issue opinions taken alone.[27] Sixth, strong evidence has been presented that party activists have shown signs of being ideological "true believers" rather than mere political opportunists.[28] And finally, parties have been shown to act in a distinctly coherent manner in the lower house of parliament (the Duma), influencing the activities of legislators in important ways. Thomas Remington's research on Russian legislative behavior has found that party discipline in the Duma has been relatively high and that parties have regularly influenced member voting patterns independently of legislators' personal, regional, or institutional interests.[29]

We are left, then, with an intriguing puzzle. Why does the evidence seem to be so strong that parties have been important both in the electorate and in the Duma at the same time that parties have strikingly failed to penetrate the vast bulk of elective state institutions and have not been able to dominate elections?

Several answers suggest themselves. For one, some of the "pessimistic" studies were conducted with the snap 1993 elections (Russia's first multiparty parliamentary elections) in closest view, while many of the "optimistic" works have focused on later elections for which parties had much more time to prepare and learn the rules in advance. This is certainly not the case with all pessimistic studies, however; Michael McFaul and Richard Rose and Neil Munro, for example, base their conclusions on developments throughout the 1990s and into the presidency of Vladimir Putin.[30] A more promising answer is that most of the optimistic analyses have been based on mass surveys of potential Russian voters, whereas most of the pessimists have focused on macropolitical outcomes (such as low party penetration of provincial

24 Klobucar and Miller 2002.

25 Brader and Tucker 2001; Colton 2000, pp. 112–15; Miller et al. 2000; Miller and Klobucar 2000.

26 Brader and Tucker 2001; Colton 2000, pp. 104, 112–15; Colton and McFaul 2003; Miller et al. 2000.

27 Colton 2000.

28 Klobucar and Miller 2002.

29 Remington 1998; Smith and Remington 2001.

30 McFaul 2001b; Rose and Munro 2002.

organs or the frequent appearance and disappearance of parties).[31] This suggests the possibility of another answer, which is that these scholars may be implying different definitions of party "strength" and "weakness." Survey research can tap into mass attitudes about parties but cannot directly assess the relative capacity and longevity of party organizations themselves. Studies of macro-outcomes without micro-level data usually cannot rule out that low party penetration of state organs and high party volatility might result from factors *other* than thin party organization, undeveloped reputation, or even a lack of popular support.

The pattern of evidence cited by the two camps, therefore, suggests that it may be possible that *both* the "pessimistic" and "optimistic" interpretations of Russian party development are at least partially right. Parties may enjoy significant resonance among the population and be coherent organizationally at the same time that factors other than intrinsic "weakness" hinder them from actually dominating the political system. Existing frameworks for considering party development in Russia, therefore, may have led some researchers to imply unwarranted extrapolations about the whole "electoral elephant" based on impressions about the particular part of that elephant that they have happened to be studying. Russia's parties have been a *specific mix* of both strength and weakness.

The possibility that both sides are right actually poses the biggest puzzle. How can we explain this odd pattern of established partisanship among large numbers of voters accompanied by differential party penetration of important state institutions?

POLITICAL SCIENCE AND PARTY SYSTEM DEVELOPMENT

Lest one think that the phenomenon of partial party development is unique to Russia, it is important to note that other societies have passed through analogous periods early in their democratic histories. After the Federalist Party largely disappeared and the Jeffersonian Republican Party crumbled following President James Monroe's retirement, U.S. politics was characterized by state-level political machines that were for the most part independent.[32] Some parts of the country at different times were essentially company towns where electoral politics were under the thumbs of powerful industrial interests.[33] India endured a similar period before Congress transformed itself into a full-fledged party of national scope.[34]

31 An important exception is Rose and Munro 2002, which integrates a careful study of voting behavior with a focus on macro-level "supply side" dynamics that determine the choice set voters face.

32 Aldrich 1995; Hofstadter 1969; McCormick 1966; Remini 1959.

33 Shefter 1977, pp. 403–52, 451. See also Shefter 1994.

34 Weiner 1967.

Even those political scientists who have looked comparatively at such phenomena, however, have tended to assume that parties are an exclusive and natural product of political institutions and societal cleavages given electoral competition. This has led them primarily to investigate differences among systems where parties already predominate. How many parties?[35] What kind of parties?[36] What patterns of interaction among parties?[37] How stable or representative the system of parties?[38] The fundamental question of how a political system becomes a *party* system in the first place remains remarkably underresearched and undertheorized.

The dominant approach to this question proceeds from the belief, noted earlier, that democracy is unworkable without parties.[39] As Aldrich has elegantly argued, parties solve key problems of collective action and social choice for office seekers and holders.[40] It follows that they will emerge naturally. Thus, many outstanding works on the formation of party systems tend to treat the "preparty period" as a shapeless transitional phase.[41] The image is one of parties, like gases, expanding to fill an institutional void due to the benefits they bring politicians and voters. Some have noted the importance of nonparty forms of political organization, not unlike the Russian financial-industrial groups and independent political machines described previously, during the initial stages of democratization. The assumption of party inevitability, however, has led these writers to characterize party formation as a relatively smooth process of "absorbing" or outcompeting alternative forms.[42]

A few have made advances in understanding the dynamics of the absorption process. Myron Weiner showed that the Indian Congress Party used its control over the state to "nationalize" other groups.[43] This finding is in line with Alan Ware's contention that U.S. parties have regularly exploited their control over the state to preserve their own power against antiparty groups and Gary Cox's finding that the electorate became primarily party-oriented

[35] Cox 1997; Downs 1957; Duverger 1954.

[36] Ansell and Fish 1999; Boix 1998; Chhibber 2001; Chhibber and Kollman 2004; Epstein 1967; Katz and Mair 1995; Kirchheimer 1966; Kitschelt 1989; Kitschelt et al. 1999; Michels 1962; Ostrogorski 1964; Panebianco 1988; Rohrschneider 1994; Sartori 1976; Shefter 1977.

[37] Dahl 1966; Sartori 1976.

[38] Bielasiak 2002; Geddes 1995; Lijphart 1994; Mainwaring 1998.

[39] This volume generally follows Huntington's (1991) definition of democracy, a system by which "the most powerful collective decisionmakers are selected through fair, honest, and periodic elections in which candidates freely compete for votes and in which virtually all the adult population is eligible to vote."

[40] Aldrich 1995.

[41] Aldrich 1995; Beer 1982; Cox 1997; Duverger 1954; Shefter 1977, 1994; Snyder and Ting 2002; and Weber 1990.

[42] Duverger 1954; Hofstadter 1969; LaPalombara and Weiner 1966; O'Donnell and Schmitter 1986; Ostrogorski 1964; Panebianco 1988; Sartori 1976; Schattschneider 1970.

[43] Weiner 1967.

in Great Britain after back-benchers were stripped of policy initiative in the House of Commons.[44] James Coleman and Carl Rosberg have argued that colonial-era norms and procedures institutionalized African parties prior to independence.[45] Martin Shefter implies that parties originating in state institutions can outmuscle autonomous organizations at will; variation depends on whether they are forced to choose mass mobilization due to an electoral threat from a powerful rival.[46] In a series of meticulous studies of Norway, Rokkan stresses the role of competitive pressures in driving parties to co-opt or supplant nonparty organizations by aggressively recruiting local nabobs regardless of ideological stripe; he attributes intracountry disparities in the pace of the process to geographical and historical factors.[47] Aldrich presents the most theoretically developed account, demonstrating how Martin Van Buren united key U.S. state-level machines to form America's first modern party (the Democratic Party) for the 1828 elections by providing them with a noncontroversial states' rights platform, a victory-bound presidential candidate (Andrew Jackson), the promise of a share in the "spoils of office," and the prospect of repeating the process over multiple election cycles.[48] Virtually all of these works contain what appears to be an assumption that parties were the inevitable outcome.

In some instances, it may be justifiable to take parties as givens. One such set of cases involves polities that legislate a monopoly for parties in proportional-representation election systems. But such legislation must itself be explained and most major countries do not legislate party monopolies, the United States and India being only two of the best-known examples. The question of how parties come to dominate political systems is thus a very appropriate one to pose. Russian experience drives this point home forcefully. Here we have a case where parties had manifestly failed to monopolize the polity more than 15 years after Gorbachev's initial electoral reforms. Because earlier scholarship has left largely unanswered the question of why this might be, including the literature on Russia itself, we currently have little insight into such phenomena.

ELECTORAL MARKETS: THE POLITICS OF SUPPLY AND DEMAND

The approach developed here begins by understanding political party development as an outcome of a market for electoral goods and services. In this electoral market, would-be candidates are the consumers and parties are suppliers of products, such as reputation, organization, and financing, that

44 Cox 1986; Ware 2000.
45 Coleman and Rosberg 1964, p. 664.
46 Shefter 1977, 1994.
47 Rokkan 1970.
48 Aldrich 1995.

candidates hope will help them get elected. From this perspective, party systems form when candidates decide to "buy" party products, agreeing to run for office on party labels.

The Market Basics of Party Formation

It is reasonable to make several general assumptions about voter and candidate behavior for the purposes of theory-building. Voters cast ballots for candidates who they think will represent their interests (broadly conceived). Candidates, in turn, want to be elected. To win office, therefore, candidates compete to show voters that they can best represent voter interests, whatever they might be.[49] It can also be safely assumed that a relatively plentiful supply of people will decide to run for office for any number of reasons. As one of the foremost theorists of elections notes, this is often the case in new democracies where candidates have little history by which to judge their own and others' electoral prospects.[50] Given an abundance of candidates wanting to win votes, it is natural to assume that these desires will create demand among these politicians for goods and services that will assist them in their electoral endeavors.

Political parties are a particularly important supplier of these goods and services demanded by candidates. Building on the conceptualizations of Giovanni Sartori and E. E. Schattschneider, a party is here defined as an enduring association of people who identify themselves by a public label and who are joined together under this label for the primary purpose of winning control of the government by means of presenting their own candidates in elections for public office on the basis of a common platform.[51] Comparative theory focuses on four major electoral benefits that parties are said to provide candidates.[52] First, parties supply organizational support, something that is almost universally agreed to benefit campaigns. Second, by associating themselves with the stands of a well-known party, candidates can gain an "instant reputation" that better connects them to targeted voters, be it through issues, personalities, or well-known patronage networks. Third, parties can provide material benefits that can be used either to invest in a campaign or to provide a basis for patronage politics, both of which can facilitate electoral success. Fourth, parties can confer "focal" status on a candidate, lending an aura of credibility to the candidacy through the commitment of party supporters to form a core of electoral support.

These dynamics, taken together, constitute a kind of market. The *demand side* of the production equation in the market for electoral goods and services

49 Downs 1957.
50 Cox 1997, pp. 151–2.
51 Sartori 1976, pp. 58–64; Schattschneider 1970, pp. 35–7.
52 Aldrich 1995; Cox 1997; and Kitschelt et al. 1999.

includes those factors affecting the amount of electoral goods and services that candidates (consumers) are willing to buy from parties at a given price. The *supply side*, then, refers to factors that affect the amount of electoral goods and services that producers (in this case, parties) are willing to supply to candidates at a given price.[53]

Parties operating in this market face some important constraints. For one thing, they are restricted in the number of nominations they can meaningfully supply by the number of districts and mandates at stake in the election. Parties' provision of electoral goods and services is also limited by costs associated with building organization, eliciting collective action, and developing reputation, none of which can be taken for granted.[54] Parties thus cannot be expected to nimbly and flexibly expand or adjust to meet every candidate demand. Even once parties are created, they always face real limits in the amount of resources they can mobilize to respond to competition in any one campaign.

Competition is also imperfect because the goods proffered by different political parties are not exactly the same. Some specialize in ideational goods, to which brand-name distinctions are critical, whereas others concentrate more on administrative goods such as campaign services and financing, a difference that will become quite important in the chapters that follow.[55]

This basic market model provides us with some valuable intellectual tools for understanding both the origins of individual parties and the development of whole party systems, the central topic of the present volume. The following subsections describe how.

A Market Explanation for Party Origins and Survival

Aldrich has argued that parties exist because they provide two important sets of goods and services that are useful to politicians in pursuing their own ends. First, in order to win office, candidates need to persuade as many voters as possible to support them and then to mobilize this support. This constitutes a *collective action problem* that parties can help solve by supplying candidates with ready-made organization, an established "brand name," and material resources. Second, candidates face an important *problem of social choice* once they are in office.[56] Since the process of forming coalitions to pass bills can generate great inefficiencies if this negotiation process has to take place from scratch on every issue, parties reduce these transaction costs by including politicians in lasting coalitions that have developed procedures of consensus-building around certain core programmatic principles.[57]

53 Samuelson 1970, p. 59.
54 Aldrich 1995; Cox 1997; Kreps 1990; Olson 1965; and Treisman 1998b.
55 Kitschelt et al. 1999; Hanson 1998, 2003; Smyth 1998.
56 Aldrich 1995, especially pp. 28–60.
57 Aldrich 1995; Kitschelt et al. 1999; Wright and Schaffner 2002.

Full-fledged parties in fact integrate these functions. The same programmatic principles that help legislators resolve the social choice problem can also be part of a party's brand image that helps candidates win election by solving the collective action problem.

Political Capital

Herbert Kitschelt and colleagues advance the useful observation that parties can invest in solving either, both, or neither of these problems that politicians face.[58] Implicit in this argument is a theory of political capital. The term "capital," in this economic sense, refers to a stock of accumulated goods that can be devoted to the production of other goods or income.[59] Winning votes and the exercise of power within state organs (that is, the generation of "political success") can be seen as one category of such "other goods or income" for aspiring or actual state officeholders. We thus define *political capital* as any stock of assets that can be devoted to the generation of political success. To paraphrase Kitschelt and his coauthors, then, parties can invest in different forms of capital that can be devoted to solving either the collective action problem or the social choice problem that Aldrich identifies.

This capital can be seen as falling into two categories, although these categories of capital do not cleanly overlap with the two categories of problems that Aldrich argues parties solve for politicians. On one hand, party entrepreneurs can invest in *ideational capital*. This kind of capital refers to a stock of core principles or ideas that form the basis for two key party functions. First, these principles or ideas help solve the social choice problem legislators face by providing them with ready-made agreements ("permanent package deals") on policy issues that will be decided in state structures.[60] Critically, however, ideational capital also helps solve the collective action problem since politicians can win votes by campaigning on the basis of these principles.[61] By developing brand images in tandem with these principles, parties become able to communicate a vast amount of information about future candidate behavior in a very efficient manner. Within a legislature, ideational capital primarily involves the development of a consensus-building mechanism to agree on specific translations of these core principles into legislator behavior in making specific decisions. Outside the legislature, ideational capital mainly means the cultivation of a *reputation* for standing for the associated principles.[62] Ideational capital, then, works primarily through

58 Kitschelt et al. 1999, pp. 46–9.

59 *Webster's Ninth New Collegiate Dictionary* (Springfield, MA: Merriam-Webster, 1988), p. 204.

60 Kitschelt et al. 1999, p. 46.

61 See Hanson 1998, 2003 on how one form of ideational capital, ideology, may have specially powerful effects on party development and survival.

62 Ideological capital is one very important subcategory of ideational capital, but the latter can also convey ideas that are not systematically interrelated enough to meet the most common definitions of ideology.

indirect exchanges with voters, members, and activists. That is, there is no quid pro quo involved; politicians promise only to pursue certain types of policy packages once elected rather than to provide specific, contingent, and direct benefits to particular voters in exchange for their ballots.[63]

The second category of political capital that is important for party formation is usefully called *administrative capital*. Again following Kitschelt and colleagues, we can define this sort of capital as a stock of assets facilitating the provision of direct selective material or symbolic advantages to those individuals who demonstrably support the party's candidates, be these individuals voters, members, or activists. These advantages "typically take the form of monetary transfers, gifts in kind, jobs in the public sector, preferential treatment in the allocation of social benefits (e.g., housing, welfare payments), regulatory favors, government contracts, and honorary memberships and titles."[64] The capital that produces these "advantages" therefore typically includes such things as financial resources and preexisting organization. Thus, administrative capital can be seen as being the particular kind of resources necessary for a party to undertake a *clientelist* strategy in the very broad sense of the term employed by Kitschelt and his coauthors.[65]

Administrative capital, like ideational capital, can be useful in solving both the social choice and collective action problems identified by Aldrich. In legislatures, party discipline can be assured by the promise of a long-run stream of benefits or the threat of specific punishments made possible by these assets. In elections, this form of capital is of enormous value in overcoming the collective action problems facing a candidate who wants to win office. Indeed, campaign teams can be hired and voters won through promises of direct exchange, for example the delivery of targeted transfers of resources ("pork" in the American political vernacular) in return for ballots.

Since both forms of capital can contribute to the fulfillment of the two major party functions Aldrich identifies (solving both the social choice and the collective action problems), it is theoretically possible to have a party based almost entirely on one or the other form of political capital. In reality, of course, all parties include at least some measure of both ideational and administrative capital. But since parties possess and rely on these different forms of capital in greater and lesser measure, it will prove helpful to develop a typology of four kinds of parties. This typology is not meant to perfectly reflect reality, of course; the goal is to highlight certain differences in party-building strategy that can have important implications. The categories,

63 Kitschelt et al. 1999, p. 48.

64 Ibid., pp. 47–8.

65 Kitschelt et al. (1999, 46–9) use the term clientelism not only to refer to specific patron–client relationships as typically conceived, but to capture any form of exchange based primarily on direct instead of indirect exchange. In this sense, a party that pays off ballot-counters is engaging in clientelistic exchange through this direct and selective exchange.

TABLE 1.1. *Types of Parties*

	Ideational Capital	
Administrative Capital	High	Low
High	Programmatic parties	Clientelistic parties
Low	Ideational parties	Minor parties

then, are ideal types as defined by Weber.[66] To the extent that different parties approximate these ideals, however, we will refer to them by these labels in order to simplify discussion. The ideal types are summarized in Table 1.1.

The types break down as follows. It is helpful to begin by noting those organizations that have relatively low levels of both ideational and administrative capital, or *minor parties*. This term captures those myriad party-building initiatives that vie for power in new democracies but that remain mere footnotes in history texts. Parties that have high levels of ideational capital but low stocks of administrative capital can be called *ideational parties*. In the era of mass communications and widespread media, it is entirely possible for a party to win office almost solely on the basis of ideational capital. Parties that are strongly identified with popular positions on important issues can at least in principle get their messages out through news coverage or the enthusiastic activities of individual supporters. In Western societies, political organizations closest to the ideational party ideal type tend to be single-issue or even protest parties, such as the Antimasonic movement in the early United States or arguably the Greens in some European countries. In contrast, those parties that rely primarily on administrative capital (including money, regional structures, and political networks) as opposed to ideas to connect with voters might be dubbed *clientelistic parties*. This terminology follows the broad usage of the term "clientelistic" employed by Kitschelt, as noted above. Clientelistic parties include a variety of subtypes that are found to be important in different societies, as with "parties of power" in postcommunist contexts or, arguably, the "catch-all" parties described by Otto Kirchheimer.[67]

Those that have achieved high levels of both ideological and administrative capital can be called *programmatic parties*. Programmatic parties represent the theoretical "ideal" held up in most works on political party development, organizations that establish clearly formulated ideational forms of linkage with voters and that are also characterized by strong and ubiquitous local structures, powerful financing, and extensive connections among the political elite. The major parties of Europe have typically fit this mold, such

[66] Weber 1949.
[67] See Kirchheimer 1966 and Smyth 2002.

as the Labour Party in Great Britain or the Christian Democratic Party in Germany. The term *programmatic* is used here since it has already been used by Kitschelt to refer to essentially the same concept developed here. Readers should not be led by this term to confuse programmatic and ideational parties; the concept of programmatic party implies, according to Kitschelt and his coauthors, "considerable administrative-infrastructural investments" as well as a strong ideational component.[68] Importantly, all types of party can coexist in the same polity.

The success of any particular party-building project depends at least in part, then, on what might be called the *starting political capital* of the political entrepreneur who launches it. This notion refers to the personal assets brought by the entrepreneur to a party project that enable the resultant party to begin solving the collective action and social choice problems facing politicians described above. This might include assets as abstract as charisma, a particular kind of ideational capital around which parties can certainly be built.[69] Some entrepreneurs might have longstanding personal reputations for certain kinds of policy stands, reputations with which they then endow their parties during the formation process and which therefore constitute an important form of starting capital. Others are likely to possess assets that fall into the category of administrative capital: connections to powerful state or economic authorities, possession of significant financial resources, or control over large preexisting organizations that could potentially be applied to achieving electoral goals. The shadow of the past, therefore, tends to have a large impact on future political party development since legacies from the old regime and the transition itself largely determine the allocation of starting political capital, with the exception only of a few intangible assets like charisma and innovative ideas.[70]

Strategy and Contingency

Starting political capital alone, of course, does not guarantee success when competition is present. Indeed, it is probably safe to assert that the history

[68] Kitschelt et al. 1999, p. 48.

[69] Personalistic parties, centered purely around some notion of the personality and personal capabilities of the party leader, are thus a certain kind of ideational party. Whereas reliance on personality itself as a mobilizational tool does not bode well for the long-run survival of a party, charisma can serve to attract or create other forms of capital (both administrative and ideational) that can augur well for future party success. Additionally, it is important to note, as Colton (2003) has demonstrated, that what might appear to be the personal appeal of party leaders often reflects much more than the mere force of their personality, including party loyalties and even important ideological components or principles. As Ansell and Fish (1999) have effectively argued, however, it is important not to treat "personalistic parties" as a single, undifferentiated category.

[70] Ekiert and Hanson 2003; Grzymala-Busse 2002; Kitschelt et al. 1999; Kitschelt and Smyth 2002.

of every democracy is littered with examples of smart, rich, or powerful politicians with good ideas who tried but failed to develop strong parties. In some cases, this might still be explained in terms of capital: Smart, rich, and powerful entrepreneurs with good ideas can be driven out of business by people who are smarter, richer, more powerful, or have better ideas.[71] But because entrepreneurs can choose to use their capital in different ways in response to competition, entrepreneurship always involves strategy. The most important kinds of strategic choices are two: those of party-building and the conduct of election campaigns. At this point, one might even venture a hypothesis: Given equal starting political capital, those parties that are most successful in a polity's initial electoral battles will be those that adopt party-building and campaign strategies that best "fit" their particular initial holdings of political capital.[72]

The relevance of *party-building strategies* primarily involves the straightforward fit of capital to strategy. For example, entrepreneurs with strong ideological reputational resources but weak organization are less likely to succeed if they seek more indiscriminately to expand their organization; a willy-nilly joining with candidates who do not share (or who even oppose) the candidate's ideology can undermine this very reputational asset in the eyes of voters. Likewise, leaders emerging with the backing of powerful provincial political machines but without much common ideational ground are more likely to succeed if they focus on integrating these machines into a massive vote-mobilizing organization than if they eschew organization and rely primarily on an ideology that has to be imposed on the organization.[73]

Campaigns represent special opportunities for party-building, hence *campaign strategies* deserve separate treatment here. This is true because the mass public and powerful elites are most directly focused on party activity during campaign periods and are explicitly evaluating parties with an eye to choosing one to support. Campaigns most directly, of course, impact party reputations, stocks of ideational capital. Successful campaigns can strengthen party brand names while unsuccessful ones can fail to make any difference and bad campaigns can undermine a party's reputation. The strategic interaction among parties also cannot be overlooked, as opposing parties seek to alter their rivals' images to gain electoral advantage. The impact of campaigns on reputation can be critically important during a "founding" campaign, where parties as such have had no prior opportunity to build

[71] For example, Golosov (1998), following Panebianco (1988), argues that those parties that possessed the greatest levels of organization were the ones to survive Russia's initial political battles.

[72] As will be illustrated in Chapter 2, it is posited that holdings of political capital can be identified in objective ways that can be employed prior to the point of initial democratization to predict party success and failure with reasonable accuracy.

[73] This is in line with Panebianco's (1988) argument that a party's origins constrain its future development.

reputation as institutions (although their leaders may well have had such opportunities separately). The high levels of public attention to parties during campaigns, of course, can also facilitate the accumulation of certain kinds of administrative capital, such as financial assets through fund-raising drives.

Lasting Effects of Initial Outcomes

The victories of the winners in a country's first multiparty elections can produce a snowballing effect, in which capital coalesces around those parties with proven track records of victory and flees from those suffering initial defeats. As in the world of business, powerful elites tend not to want to risk wasting resources on likely losers.[74] Guillermo O'Donnell and Philippe Schmitter thus refer to the "freezing" of electoral patterns after what they call "founding elections," the first votes in newly democratic systems.[75] Once the initial victories have been won, it becomes increasingly difficult for new players to move in, even with superior starting capital. Others have characterized this as an effect of path dependence; once institutions (such as parties) have begun to function, the costs and risks involved in breaking with the old institutions and creating entirely new institutions can become greater than the costs and risks involved in sticking with older institutions, even when the latter are less efficient or represent people's interests less effectively or reliably.[76]

This process of party development and survival can be termed one of achieving *critical political mass*. Critical political mass is defined as the possession of sufficient strength that the party's nominee, regardless of who the nominee is and solely by virtue of this nomination, always acquires "focal" status as one of the candidates believed by both voters and important political elites to have a good chance to win a seat in a given election.[77] Once a party achieves critical political mass, it starts to attract elite and mass support from those who do not want to waste their votes or resources on losers and who consider the party their best *realistic* chance to have their interests represented. Winning different offices, of course, requires different levels of support. For example, in Russia as of 2003–4, a party needed just

74 For the most elegant and rigorous statement of this well-established assertion, see Cox 1997.

75 O'Donnell and Schmitter 1986, pp. 61–2. See also Lipset and Rokkan 1967 and Panebianco 1988.

76 See the seminal North 1990.

77 To use Cox's (1997) language, a more precise definition is that a party achieves critical political mass when its nomination of a candidate puts this candidate among the M + 1 viable contenders for any elected office when all candidates and elites perfectly understand their candidates' electoral chances. M represents the number of seats to be filled in any given individual race. The strict number M + 1 is derived from the assumption that all candidates and elites perfectly understand candidates' electoral chances; when such information is unclear or otherwise imperfect, somewhat more than M + 1 candidates can become "focal," seen as realistic contenders for office and not "wastes of votes."

5 percent of the vote to win a fraction in the Duma but (effectively) a majority for its candidate to win the presidency. The notion of critical political mass, then, is institution-specific. A party may achieve critical political mass for the parliament but not the presidency. But achieving critical political mass for one office, such as the party-list-elected half of the Duma, certainly enhances a party's prospects of achieving critical political mass for offices with higher hurdles since this achievement guarantees a certain minimum level of resources and the opportunity to develop them further through performance while in office.

The logic of path dependence and critical political mass suggests that over time, those parties that are capable of creating expectations of victory, that are "frozen" into positions of power in founding elections, tend to find it much easier at that point to build up those forms of political capital in which they were previously deficient as elites abandon the initial losers and seek out proven winners. Since programmatic parties, those with high levels of both ideational and administrative capital, are generally seen to be the strongest parties, a party's optimal strategy would seem to be the following: seek first to establish one's party among the set of winners by investing primarily in one's asset strengths; at this point, party leaders will be in a much stronger position to attract or cultivate those forms of capital in which their party is lacking. Clientelistic parties, once they attain seats in parliament, can begin staking out ideational territory through their legislative votes. Ideational parties, once they win legislative or (better) executive office, can then attract financing, build organization, or otherwise accumulate administrative capital through the contributions of those wanting ties to powerful officeholders and willing to pay the price of supporting the party's ideational line. Ideational parties can then also actively work to shape their ideational capital to take on new issue stands or adjust old ones in response to new challenges.[78]

A Market Explanation for Party System Development

It might seem that we have effectively reached the end of our story, that party system development is simply the "frozen" legacies of initial political battles fought by those party entrepreneurs with early access to large holdings of political capital. Which kinds of parties wind up with the strongest starting political capital could be seen as resulting from the kinds of deep social cleavages about which Lipset and Rokkan write as well as from the historical inheritances on which Kitschelt focuses. Political institutions round out the story, setting the rules by which the initial battles are fought, as scholars from Maurice Duverger to Cox have argued.[79] This, indeed, would be a restatement of the dominant perspective in social science thought on party systems.

78 Rohrschneider 1993.

79 Cox 1997; Duverger 1954; Kitschelt et al. 1999; Lipset and Rokkan 1967.

Basic market theory, however, suggests not only that such a story is incomplete, but that it could be a serious mistake as an explanation for the degree to which a polity develops a party system. This is because it purports to predict the size of the "party industry" (that is, the degree to which parties are created and become important suppliers of electoral goods and services) by focusing *exclusively on parties* as the suppliers of electoral goods and services demanded by candidates. The demand side of a market equation does not simply reflect the desire for a good potentially on the market but also the availability and relative price of *substitutes* for these goods.[80] As the price for the good in question rises, more people will turn to available substitutes that can satisfy the same basic demand, albeit imperfectly. If the price of a cappuccino goes up, for example, price-sensitive consumers may decide to settle for a regular coffee rather than absorb the new additional cost of the fancier beverage. In the context of political party development, the clear implication is that we must look not only at factors affecting the supply of and demand for *party-provided* goods and services when estimating levels of party development, but also at the potential availability of *substitutes* for these electoral goods and services.

Party Substitutes and Party Systems

In fact, parties are not the only institutional forms capable of helping candidates win elections by providing them with organizational support, reputation, or material resources. In almost all democracies, there exist other organizational forms that can supply some or all of these same sorts of things to candidates independently of parties, making them what we call here *party substitutes*. In Russia, major party substitutes have included the powerful political machines of provincial governors like the one in Omsk and politicized financial-industrial groups such as RusAl and Interros in Krasnoiarsk. In the United States, party substitutes have historically included everything from immigrant societies and agricultural cooperatives to more modern advocacy groups such as the powerful National Rifle Association and personal vote organizations.[81] These organizational forms are not parties themselves because they do not provide a public label under which their candidates campaign, do not run multiple candidates on the basis of common public platforms, do not aspire to full organizational control of the polity, and/or do not seek to institutionalize the ties beyond a given electoral cycle. These are no mere semantic distinctions. These functions that party substitutes can fail to serve are some of the very ones that lead

[80] Kirzner 1973, pp. 104–7; Samuelson 1970, pp. 58, 409, 415–16.

[81] On such organizations in Western Europe, see Lawson and Merkl 1988, especially the introductory chapter by Lawson, "When Linkage Fails," pp. 13–38. Many of the "alternative organizations" that she mentions, however, would fit the definition of "party" given earlier in this chapter. On personal vote organizations, see the classic Cain, Ferejohn, and Fiorina 1987. For a more recent treatment, see Herrera and Yawn 1999.

scholars to consider parties vital for democratic development and state stability. Explicit labels and public platforms, for example, are critical to efficiently organizing choice for voters. Organizational control of the national polity and institutional endurance over time are vital to providing stability and structure to democratic politics. All of these things are important in facilitating elite accountability before voters.[82]

Candidates decide to join parties, then, not only when parties provide them with useful goods and services, as standard accounts tend to imply, but when parties provide them with useful goods and services better than other available suppliers do. One critical implication is that *parties will close out an electoral market, coming to dominate the political system, only when they establish themselves as the main credible suppliers of electoral goods and services*, when candidates come to believe that they need political party affiliation and support to have a real chance to win. A second important implication is that *parties can fail to close out a country's electoral market even when they are in fact successful and powerful providers of electoral goods and services*. If party substitutes are equally strong, some candidates can be expected to continue to choose them even over political parties that have proven their ability to win votes for their nominees by providing them with large-scale organizational support, material resources, and powerful brand reputation.

The Party-Party Substitute Balance as the Key to Explaining Party System Development

To address the fundamental question of why political systems become *party* systems, therefore, requires explaining why parties gain the advantage over the best available party substitutes. In so doing, it is less appropriate to ask "what benefits do parties provide to candidates or voters?" than "what benefits do parties provide to candidates and voters *better than available party substitutes do*?" Delving deeper, we are also led to ask *why* parties might be capable of providing something (to a degree) that party substitutes do not. The market perspective would lead us to look for answers in either capital or the institutional framework in which the market operates.

CAPITAL. Just as the origins of particular parties can be traced to particular political entrepreneurs who had access to particular forms of political capital, so can the origins of party substitutes. If comparative theory sees successful parties possessing political capital that grounds them firmly in major social cleavages (such as religious, ethnic, or socioeconomic divides), party substitutes can be expected to arise from *meso*-level concentrations of power and resources that are not broad enough to constitute social cleavages but that entrepreneurs might still use for electoral ends. In the Russian case, this

[82] Huntington 1968; Lipset 2000; Mair 1990.

sort of capital has most importantly meant regional administrative hierarchies and firms in control of company towns or broad clientelistic networks. In other countries such capital has involved self-organizing local immigrant networks or particularistic ideas that are shared by significant segments of the population but that do not correspond cleanly with traditional party lines (as with special interest groups[83] or political action committees[84]). This implies a strong role for path-dependent legacies of the past in determining what forms of political capital are available for entrepreneurs in the present; different legacies can be expected to lead to different degrees of advantage of parties over party substitutes (or party substitutes over parties).[85] The focus on capital also suggests a strong role for transition processes themselves; if legacies merely weight the dice in certain directions, then decisions made in transitions from authoritarian regimes or command economies are likely to have independent effects of their own.[86] Indeed, processes of regime change and marketization frequently involve changes in property rights and power relationships; while sometimes these might favor parties, at other times they might advantage party substitutes. More broadly, environmental factors may also affect the relative value of the kind of capital wielded by parties vis-à-vis party substitutes. To the extent that parties base their claims on ideational capital, we would anticipate that higher levels of education would make this sort of capital relatively more attractive than that proffered by party substitutes. Taking a cue from Rokkan, the largest or most populous countries may strengthen the hand of local party substitutes relative to national parties since such parties face greater costs in organizationally penetrating the most remote regions or most densely populated cities.

INSTITUTIONAL FRAMEWORK. Very few markets are fully free, and electoral markets are no exception; they are defined by sets of institutional rules that create the offices that are contested, determine who can contest them, and establish the conditions under which contestants then seek the offices. At the most obvious level, this means that the design of electoral rules will have an impact on the relationship between parties and party substitutes. For example, we would expect party substitutes to be stronger in those many countries that allow candidates to run for office as independents than in those where ballot access requires party nomination. In the latter cases, candidates may still rely on nonparty organization (such as personal vote organizations[87] or political action committees[88]) to win votes

83 Lawson and Merkl 1988.

84 Jacobson 2001.

85 A seminal theoretical work on path dependence is North 1990.

86 On the role of "agency" in transitions from authoritarian rule more generally, see Karl 1990; Karl and Schmitter 1991; McFaul 2001b; O'Donnell and Schmitter 1986; Przeworski 1991; Rustow 1970.

87 Cain et al. 1987.

88 Jacobson 2001.

or gain places on a party list, but these party substitutes are still forced to at least pay lip service to parties.[89] What is of even greater significance, however, is the broader institutional context of a country that defines and enforces political property rights, regulates competition within a given set of institutional rules, and permits certain powerholders to strategically alter the rules.[90] This volume focuses special attention on the institution of the executive branch following a logic laid out by Joel Migdal and Shefter. Executives have strong incentives to weaken the very institutions that would help them govern effectively because these same institutions can potentially come to rival the executive, and this applies even to an executive-oriented party.[91] Where executives are powerful, therefore, the holders of this office have cause to intervene in the market in ways that disrupt party formation, giving party substitutes a decided advantage. At the same time, even the strongest of executives will be willing to risk party formation if an opposition party manages to form and forces the incumbents to counterorganize.[92] The stronger the executive, the less likely the executive is to experience a challenge serious enough to justify the risks involved in forming an executive-based party. We will see that one reason Russia has remained a preserve of nonpartisanship for so long is precisely because its overly strong executive branch persistently tilted the electoral market in favor of party substitutes. Moreover, this volume will present evidence from 25 postcommunist countries revealing a strong correlation between executive branch strength and low party penetration of the polity. Nevertheless, we also find that Russia's executive branch during 2000–5 led a major effort to bring parties to Russia "from above" by consolidating party substitutes after it was forced to do so by a surprising challenge that emerged in 1999.

THE RUSSIAN CASE AND COMPARATIVE THEORY: HOW THE VOLUME UNFOLDS

Chapter 2 begins by examining the nature of political partisan entrepreneurship in Russia's electoral market, exploring the starting political capital available to that country's first party-builders thanks to a legacy of "patrimonial

[89] Even in closed-list proportional-representation systems restricted to parties, party substitutes can lobby to have their preferred candidates named to favorable positions on party lists or can reward and punish various parties for acting in particular ways by lending them or their opponents political resources. Such activity can serve to dilute the issue stands of parties as well as the loyalty of individual candidates to the party that nominates them, potentially having an impact on legislative activity.

[90] Leading studies of such things in the rise of economic markets include North 1990 and North and Thomas 1973.

[91] Migdal 1987, 1988.

[92] This draws from Shefter 1977, 1994.

communism."[93] It finds that those parties that emerged and survived for significant periods of time were those that possessed the largest stocks of starting political capital and then most consistently chose party-building and campaign strategies that fit this capital. This capital, it is shown, came almost exclusively from some connection to the state. Importantly, however, the chapter also finds that Russia's extremely powerful presidency at times actively intervened in this market, using its vast resources to radically alter the stocks of capital available to particular political parties and to restrict how this capital was used. This activity, frequently referred to as attempts to "manage" democracy, had a significant impact on Russia's party system over the years and worked largely to the Kremlin's[94] advantage.

Chapter 3 provides a comprehensive assessment of the strengths and weaknesses of political parties in Russia through 2005. Examining evidence on the presidency, the Duma, governorships, and regional legislatures, it shows that Russia's major political parties were long capable of providing significant support to candidates in elections and had cultivated loyalties among a large share of the population fairly early on. Very interestingly, however, it finds that while the major parties developed quite markedly during the mid-1990s, this development had largely "stalled" by the late 1990s. There were some signs of a possible breakthrough for parties in 2003, but primarily in elections to the Duma and regional legislatures. The realm of federal and regional executives, in contrast, experienced much lower levels of party penetration through 2005. It was regional executives, however, that were explicitly targeted by Russia's president in September 2004 when he called for major political reforms, reforms that seemed designed in part to promote a greater party role in these institutions.

Chapter 4 employs the market logic to explain the central puzzle of Russian politics in comparative perspective, the fact that its political system remained only partially a "party" system. Russia's parties failed to fully penetrate the polity by 2005 not because they lacked organization or positive reputations. Nor was the problem that institutions failed to give parties incentive to build organization. Nor can we accurately say that Russia lacked significant societal cleavages of the kind that could be mobilized by a political party. Rather, Russia's political system remained only a partial party system because candidates running for office had options other than parties to serve their electoral needs. If they disagreed with important planks in party platforms or wanted autonomy from party discipline once they reached office, candidates were often able to balk at parties and run with the direct and powerful backing of major party substitutes like the unaffiliated provincial political machine in Omsk described above, or the politicized

93 Kitschelt et al. 1999.

94 The term "Kremlin" is frequently used in this volume as a shorthand referring to officials of Russia's executive branch as well as those unofficially working for it.

financial-industrial groups identified in Krasnoiarsk. Elections in Russia, therefore, could not adequately be characterized as battles between competing parties. But to speak only of individual candidates and their personal resources does not accurately render the political system either. Instead, in a large number of cases, these contests should be seen as intense struggles pitting parties not only against each other but also against financial-industrial groups, political machines of powerful regional officials, and simple independents with significant personal resources. This is demonstrated through concrete examples and statistical analysis of candidate performance in four sets of elections (presidential, parliamentary, gubernatorial, and regional legislative) from Russia's appearance as a postcommunist state through 2005. Party substitutes are shown to have been in competition with political parties and to have successfully outcompeted them for large parts of the vote. A consideration of cross-regional patterns within Russia identifies some important environmental factors that give relative advantages to parties over party substitutes, including higher education levels, certain electoral institutions, and aspects of political geography.

This chapter also explains the emergence of Russia's major party substitutes and why they became strong enough to challenge political parties in most of Russia's major electoral arenas. It begins with Kitschelt's and his coauthors' notion of a patrimonial communist legacy, which for Russia and other states has involved extremely strong presidencies, widespread single-member-district elections, and extensive patron-client relationships.[95] When this path-dependent inheritance was combined with federalism and President Boris Yeltsin's contingent decision to pursue a particular form of privatization and to cede a great deal of power to provincial leaders, the result was the organizational smorgasbord that has lasted well into the current decade.

Chapter 5 asks the broader question why the balance between parties and party substitutes in Russia has been sustained for so many years in Russia, why Russian parties had still failed to close out the political market by 2004, when Putin announced reforms that appeared to push in a new direction. While the capital distribution explained historically in Chapter 4 accounts for the rise of party substitutes, Chapter 5 addresses what has preserved them and kept them distinct from parties for so long. The chapter does identify a gradual trend whereby party labels have become increasingly valuable and thus more capable of defeating or absorbing party substitutes in electoral battle. But this process is found to have been rather slow, indicating that the most important factors impacting the balance between parties and substitutes in a given polity are not those that hinge on improving the value of party labels and the capacity of parties to communicate with voters. Instead, the

[95] Kitschelt et al. 1999.

balance between parties and substitutes can be most radically changed "from above," when state officials with the authority to regulate or change rules in the market use this capacity strategically to maintain their own positions of power. Thus, from the time the USSR broke up until 1999, we find the Kremlin consistently undermining attempts by its own allies to anchor Russia's party system with a genuine pro-presidential party. As Migdal's logic anticipates, the executive leadership feared creating an institution that could later come to challenge it or discredit it. What changed in 1999 was a major and unexpected challenge to Kremlin insiders' rule, the emergence of the Fatherland–All Russia coalition of governors and other leading politicians that as late as September 1999 was widely considered a favorite to capture the presidency in the 2000 elections. This challenge only barely failed, and Kremlin officials realized that they owed their political survival to both blind luck and, critically, the last-minute creation of a counter-coalition party dubbed Unity. Determined to prevent such future challenges, the Kremlin embarked on a major effort to promote the party penetration of Russia's polity, strongly privileging Unity and its successor, United Russia, in the process. Weakening party substitutes and forcing them into a manageable party framework, Putin announced the coup de grace in September 2004 by announcing major institutional reform.

Chapter 6 concludes the volume by summarizing the argument, presenting supportive comparative evidence from 25 postcommunist countries, and discussing implications of the electoral market model for political science theory more generally. The particular version of the market approach elaborated in this volume, it is ventured, provides a dynamic logic with the potential to generate new findings in globally comparative research on party development, national integration, and transitions from authoritarian rule.

Some of the pages that follow present findings from survey data and/or regression analysis. Supplemental information on such findings, including the English-language translation of survey questions used and technical information on statistical exercises, can be obtained through the Web site www.whynotpartiesinrussia.com or by contacting the author directly.

2

Party Entrepreneurship in Russia's Electoral Market 1989–2005

Entrepreneurship begins with a dream but gets nowhere without capital. Political entrepreneurship is no different. In the land of electoral opportunity that was transitional Russia, there was no shortage of dreams. Political capital, the set of tangible and intangible resources with the potential to translate into electoral success, was another story. The USSR's history of "patrimonial communism" and the particular path that Russia's leaders chose for its transition to markets and electoral democracy had left in place a society in which political capital was highly concentrated in a few pockets, most of which required access to the state to obtain. With few exceptions, then, only a small set of individuals with strong connections to Russian power structures had a realistic chance to launch Russia's initial political parties. But if dreams and political capital were necessary to get a party off the ground, still more depended on how the political entrepreneur chose to use this capital; like financial capital, it could be squandered without the skill and forethought to develop a solid strategy for long-term growth. Party leaders were still not completely in control of their own fates, even given healthy supplies of political capital and favorable institutions; events that are best considered random exogenous shocks periodically rocked the Russian political market in ways nearly impossible for any theory to predict. Russia's presidential administrations also intervened at times to tip the political scales away from certain party-building projects. The party entrepreneurs who emerged and survived as major players during the first 15 years of Russia's electoral markets, then, tended to be those who had acquired large stocks of political capital through prior connections with the state, who had developed party-building and campaign strategies that fit their particular forms of political capital, who had sustained these strategies through the vicissitudes of successive election cycles, and who had experienced at least some good luck in the tumultuous period that was Russia's emergence from Communist rule.

In making this argument, the present study shows how a market approach can answer a question that is rarely addressed in the vast comparative literature on party systems as well as the myriad works specifically devoted to Russia's party system: Why did Russia end up with the *particular* set of parties that it had as of 2005? While countless studies in comparative politics seek to explain why party systems contain certain kinds of parties or fixed numbers of parties, few have carefully examined why some specific party-building projects but not others have succeeded in filling theoretically anticipated niches (i.e., the particular two parties in a two-party system or the particular parties that in fact emerge to represent certain social cleavages like religion or class). To the extent that existing studies do provide accounts of how certain parties emerge to fill these "slots," they almost never carefully consider control cases, that is, rival attempts to fill these same niches or to create entirely different niches that failed.[1] While of great theoretical importance, party losers tend to get short shrift because they no longer impact current events. Without considering the "dogs that did not bark," however, we are left wondering whether the factors that are said to produce success might also have been present among the failures. This chapter thus demonstrates that the market approach outlined in Chapter 1 can explain the successes in light of those party-building projects that failed in Russia.

The chapter begins by briefly characterizing the notion of patrimonial communism and proceeds to show how it shaped both the rules and the resources by which Russia's would-be party-builders struggled for dominance. It then turns to a close analysis of how leadership strategy and contingent events affected the process by which some parties emerged as successful players in the electoral market while others failed.

RUSSIA'S LEGACY OF PATRIMONIAL COMMUNISM

Kitschelt, Zdenka Mansfeldova, Radoslaw Markowski, and Gabor Toka have developed a very helpful typology of communist regimes based on the extent to which each relied on clientelistic as opposed to formal-rational institutional structures and the degree to which each tolerated modest

[1] Perhaps the most clear-cut exceptions are Golosov (1998), who draws on Panebianco 1988 to argue that strong organization is the key to why some parties and not others survive, and Hanson (1998, 2003), who argues that parties with strong ideologies are more likely to thrive. These claims differ from the one advanced here. A partial exception is advanced by Rose and Munro (2002), who adopt a "supply side" focus on the state as a major factor determining which mix of parties is offered to voters. Others stressing the role of (usually state) elites in determining party supply in the Russian context include Colton and McFaul 2003 and McFaul 2001b. Another small but important literature makes the general point that resource sets and legacies in the Russian context typically work against liberal parties and for the Communists and parties of power: Fish 1996, 1997; Kitschelt and Smyth 2002; Kullberg and Zimmerman 1999; Smyth 2002.

levels of civil rights and elite contestation.[2] *Bureaucratic-authoritarian communist* regimes most closely resembled the totalitarian model, featuring highly repressive and highly bureaucratized regimes; examples include Czechoslovakia and East Germany. Countries with a history of *national-accommodative communism*, which involved formal-rational bureaucratic institutions but were not so repressive, include Hungary, Slovenia, and Croatia. Russia, together with other former Soviet countries and states like Bulgaria and Romania, emerged from a legacy of *patrimonial communism*, which featured a highly repressive regime combined with extensive patterns of patronage politics. This characterization fits well with authoritative classic works on Soviet and prerevolutionary Russian politics, which are frequently characterized as featuring not only extreme repression but also extensive networks of patron-client relations and subtle competition among competing Kremlin clans.[3]

Kitschelt and his colleagues argue that each type of communist regime left a distinct legacy that has had identifiable and systematic implications for a whole host of important decisions that had to be made in countries emerging from communist rule. Importantly, the claim is not that the various features of patrimonial communist societies (vertical chains of dependence, extensive patronage and clientelistic networks, personality cults, low rational-bureaucratic institutionalization, and little tolerance for opposition outside of the regime) simply continued on in the postcommunist polity. The argument is more subtle: The previous regime type *weighted the dice* toward the selection of certain new postcommunist institutions over others by producing particular patterns of interests and particular distributions of resources among these interests. As we will see, the patterns of resource distribution left by communist regimes had very important implications for the kinds of parties that would develop in these countries.

Patrimonial communism had several legacies that are of special importance to the present volume. For one thing, since nonstate forces (the liberal conception of civil society) in these regimes tended to be weak due to repression and a dearth of resources unconnected to state patronage networks, those at the helm of countries emerging from patrimonial communist rule tended to be in a strong enough position to adopt or impose political systems that concentrated a great deal of de facto if not de jure power in the hands of a chief executive.[4] In many countries, this took the form of an extremely powerful presidency. Accordingly, with the balance of power favoring those who already wielded state authority, such countries were

[2] Unless otherwise noted, the discussion in this section refers to Kitschelt et al. 1999. See also Kitschelt and Smyth 2002.

[3] Some such classic works include Hough and Fainsod 1979 and Pipes 1974. For a Russian scholarly account that has gained wide currency, see Afanasiev 1997.

[4] See also Easter 1997.

also typically able to enact electoral institutions that were widely believed at the time to favor incumbents. In most cases, this meant single-member-district election systems.

Since authorities were wary of encouraging organized opposition, and since they wanted to maintain their own freedom of maneuver, there was strong incentive not to restrict any of these district elections to parties alone. Moreover, because the patrimonial communist state so thoroughly penetrated the economy and because so much of organized society was already involved in longstanding patronage networks, Russia's first postcommunist party entrepreneurs could be expected to have little political capital to work with other than that connected to the state. The following section describes how Russia's leaders came to set the institutional "rules of the game" by which politicians would play for years to come.

CREATING THE INSTITUTIONAL RULES OF THE GAME IN RUSSIA 1989–2005

Soviet leader Mikhail Gorbachev instituted the Soviet Union's first competitive elections in 1989, but these elections constituted only a national-level parliament. Facing little organized opposition to push for a different system, Gorbachev opted for a parliament that was constituted partly through single-member-district elections and partly through choices made by various organizations that were generally controlled by Communist Party officials. While Gorbachev easily won election as the speaker of this body, a post he combined with General Secretary of the Communist Party, he then pushed through the creation of a separate presidency that, after he assumed the new post in early 1990, soon became his chief power base. This presidency, however, was not directly elected but chosen by the parliament. During the 1989 elections that constituted the Soviet parliament, no party other than the Communist Party had the right to compete.

Competitive elections to a legislature for Russia, which at the time was just one of 15 "union republics" in the USSR, were held in 1990, one year after the first Soviet elections. The 1990 Russian parliamentary elections, then, marked the beginning of what scholars have come to call Russia's "First Republic," which lasted from 1990 until the abrogation of its constitution in late 1993. The period starting in December 1993, when a new constitution was adopted, and continuing through the time of this writing is widely called Russia's "Second Republic."[5]

5 Analyses of the formation of electoral rules and early party system development in both the First and Second Russian Republics include: Colton 1998b; Hough 1998b; McFaul 2001a, 2001b. The following account draws on the information compiled in these works.

Federal Institutions of the First Republic

The institutions of Russia's First Republic were almost entirely products of the Soviet era. The parliament, a giant *Congress of People's Deputies* (which then elected a smaller, working organ, the *Supreme Soviet*), was inaugurated in the first half of 1990. Gorbachev's team, which remained firmly in control of the legislation process, designed a system by which all members competed in single-member districts as in races for the U.S. House of Representatives. Unlike the American system, however, winners had to acquire at least 50 percent of the ballots cast to be elected, with runoffs required if no candidate reached this threshold. Only a plurality was needed to win a runoff.[6] While Gorbachev's team expected this system to produce strong victories for his own allies, the 1990 election actually led to a victory for a rival, Boris Yeltsin, whom the new Congress then elected as its speaker.

With Yeltsin in charge of the Russian Republic and in a heated political battle with Gorbachev in 1991, the new Russian leader organized the creation of a directly elected presidency for Russia and in a June vote won the post for himself. Election to the presidency required a candidate to receive at least 50 percent of the vote, mandating a runoff between the top two vote-getters if necessary. The Congress, which Yeltsin had previously led, granted him extensive powers to rule autonomously for one year starting in late 1991 as the Russian leader sought to launch a reform program while the Soviet Union was disintegrating. After the initial year was up, the Congress had ceased to support Yeltsin's reforms, but Yeltsin refused to give up the "temporary" powers. After months of bitter political struggle between Russia's president and its parliament, Yeltsin made his de facto power de jure in 1993 by unilaterally and illegally dissolving the Congress, enforcing this decree with tankfire that killed scores of people in the parliament building, and then conducting a referendum on a constitution that his own supporters had drafted. Yeltsin justified all this by branding the Congress as an illegitimate organ, portraying it as a pure legacy of the Soviet past and arguing for the superiority of his more recent electoral mandate.[7]

For neither the presidency nor the Congress did the crafters of the First Republic attempt to foster the development of political parties other than the Communist Party of the Soviet Union (CPSU). The parliament, which contained over 1,000 seats, held its first elections at a time when the CPSU was the only party eligible to compete. The Congress, therefore, was designed not for multiparty competition but for contests among individual candidates, all of whom were intended by incumbent authorities to represent

[6] If only one or two candidates ran in the first round and no one received a majority of votes cast (votes "against all" were permitted), then the election was to be held again with new nominations, as Hough 1998b reports, p. 44.

[7] For excellent but contrasting accounts of the breakdown of the First Russian Republic, see McFaul 2001b and Reddaway and Glinski 2001.

different interpretations of Communist Party interests. While "informal" political organizations did engage in some efforts to promote candidacies and manage campaigns, they had no right of nomination and "partisan" affiliations did not appear on the ballots.[8] As a result, the literature on this period concurs that the political organization that began to emerge at the time is better characterized as "movement society" or even lobby or protest groups than political parties.[9] These organizations will be discussed further below.

Federal Institutions of the Second Republic

In a vote marked by allegations of fraud, Russian voters ratified Yeltsin's constitution in a December 1993 referendum, marking the official start of Russia's Second Republic. This constitution featured what analysts have branded a *superpresidential* system, one in which the chief executive wields far more power than any other state official or institution through both formal and informal channels.[10] In clientelistic polities like Russia's, the informal powers can be at least as important as the formal ones. One particularly important formal power, however, was the right to issue unilateral decrees with the force of law. To become the Russian president, a candidate needed to win at least 50 percent of the vote, requiring a runoff between the top two candidates if no contender marshaled the appropriate share of ballots in the first round, as was also the case in the First Russian Republic. Also as in the First Republic, the drafters of the legislation regulating the presidency made no effort to facilitate partisanship vis-à-vis this office. Indeed, Yeltsin, who molded the law to strengthen his own personal position, continued to eschew party membership, declaring himself to be "above" parties as the nation's only directly elected representative of the "whole people."

The first attempt by Russian powerholders in over seven decades to "engineer" an electoral system in a way that would promote any party other than the CPSU took place in 1993 with the design of the Second Russian Republic's parliament. This parliament, named the *Federal Assembly*, consisted of upper and lower chambers.

The upper chamber, the *Federation Council*, was not intended to be organized or elected on a partisan basis. Instead, as Timothy Colton has reported, the Federation Council was meant to represent regional authorities. Since Yeltsin had assumed the legal right to appoint chief executives to most regions in 1993, his team expected this organ to become a bastion of loyalists that would meet only periodically to ratify certain decisions made by the lower

8 See McFaul 2001b for an account of these elections.

9 Evans and Whitefield 1993; Fish 1995; Fleron, Ahl, and Lane 1998; McFaul 1993.

10 On the Russian presidency and superpresidentialism, see Easter 1997; Fish 2000; Huskey 1999.

house of parliament.[11] Thus, while parties did have the right to nominate candidates, they still had to clear all of the hurdles that independents had to overcome to be listed on the ballot, including collecting signatures of either 25,000 voters or 2 percent of the region's electorate. In 1995, however, the rules changed, eliminating elections to this body. Between 1995 and 2001, the heads of the executive and legislative branches of each province automatically gained Federal Council membership. As part of new President Vladimir Putin's effort to curb the autonomy of regional leaders, however, the latter lost their Federation Council posts in 2001 and instead gained only the right to appoint two representatives (one from the legislative branch and the other from the executive). Throughout all these changes, the organ's procedures were not predicated on party organization. While some informal coordination among members did take place, the institution's leaders railed against parties, which they regularly declared would "lead to the ruin of the chamber" if organized there.[12]

The lower house, the Duma, was a different story. Michael McFaul reports that there was great disagreement within the team that Yeltsin had assembled to draft the new legislation. Many Yeltsin loyalists favored electing the Duma entirely through single-member districts (SMDs) because they thought that such a parliament would be easier to influence and that creating it could be justified as a way to minimize the control of Moscow-based elites and to maximize individual deputy accountability to voters.[13] Others, notably Viktor Sheinis, pushed hard for a law that would explicitly promote a multiparty system in Russia. According to this idea, a certain portion of the seats would be elected in a proportional representation (PR) system in which people would vote not for individual candidates, but for party lists of candidates whose places on that list would be fixed ahead of time by party leaderships. This would effectively create a party system by fiat since only parties could compete for these seats. Jerry Hough reports that the drafters considered one important purpose of the PR component to be to protect the "most valuable" members of parties (i.e., ruling parties) against defeat in a district election; this would work since such leaders would automatically be elected if their parties cleared a minimum threshold for parliamentary representation regardless of whether they won in their own district.[14] This almost certainly was one reason why the Yeltsin team acceded to the PR component.

Presidential forces decided on a 50-50 PR-SMD mix for the Duma in 1993. McFaul reports that this decision was made in haste under conditions

[11] Colton 1998b, pp. 15–16.

[12] See, e.g., Federation Council chair Yegor Stroev's warnings: *RFE/RL Newsline*, March 8, 2001. On the Federation Council, see especially Remington 2003 and Slider 2005.

[13] McFaul 2001b, p. 218.

[14] In the end this hurdle was set at 5 percent. See Hough 1998b, p. 54.

of great uncertainty, which precluded too much (accurate) strategic planning. Political actors had little time to gather reliable information about how the new electoral system would influence their own personal political fortunes. The even PR-SMD division, then, had more the quality of a "natural" division (or "focal point" in the language of Thomas Schelling) than of a precisely calibrated strategic calculation.[15] Colton, Hough, and McFaul, however, all concur that a great deal of thought went into the general framework and that the goals of Sheinis and his colleagues were clearly to promote the development of a multiparty system in Russia. Theorists like Maurice Duverger were widely acknowledged among informed Russian thinkers to have established that SMD systems tend to promote two parties since people would not want to waste votes on third candidates and would thus choose between the two most likely to win.[16] But as Hough noted, there was no guarantee that the two "parties" in any given district would be the same as the two parties in any other district. Russia's election-system designers further reasoned that the PR component would, as was well documented in comparative research by Arend Lijphart and others, ensure that a core of nationwide parties would exist.[17] This, in turn, was seen as helping remedy the potentially fragmenting incentives of the SMD system by providing for a national party framework into which district-specific organizations could easily assimilate.[18] The PR threshold was set at 5 percent so as to weed out smaller parties. Candidates were declared winners with a simple plurality (with a minimum 25 percent turnout) in an effort to raise the costs of noncoordination among like-minded candidates; failure to join forces could result in a rival winning the race with a small percentage of the vote.[19] These rules were actually imposed by presidential decree before the new constitution came into effect; indeed, the constitutional referendum and the first Duma elections were held on the same day in December 1993.

While various groups proposed major revisions of the Duma's electoral rules, they remained quite stable from 1993 to 2003. The most significant change implemented during this time occurred for the 1995 elections, when parties' names were for the first time listed on the SMD ballots next to their nominees. This amendment had the potential to greatly enhance the reputational value of parties, reducing the likelihood that voters would not be able accurately to connect parties to SMD candidates. Reforms initiated between 2002 and 2005, however, will have major implications for the 2007–8 election cycle. Discussion of these reforms is deferred to Chapter 5, where they are explained.

[15] McFaul 2001a, 2001b; Schelling 1980.

[16] For example, see Duverger 1954.

[17] See, for example, Lijphart 1990.

[18] Colton 1998b, p. 14; Hough 1998b, pp. 48–52.

[19] Hough 1998b, pp. 48–52.

Regional Electoral Institutions

Russia inherited a federal system that by 1993 consisted of 89 administrative regions with federal status.[20] These were grouped into five categories. One important grouping, labeled *republics,* consisted of 21 regions specially designated as homelands for specific ethnic minority groups, even though the "titular" ethnic groups did not always constitute a plurality in their "own" regions. This inclusion of ethnically defined regions makes Russia what is often called an "ethnofederal" state.[21] Two other sets of regions were also designated for particular ethnic minorities, but had a much more ambiguous status than did republics. These *autonomous oblasts* and *autonomous okrugs* – 11 in all – were simultaneously full-fledged federal units with direct representation in the Federation Council *and* component parts of other regions. The "autonomies" or AOs, as they were often called, were therefore quite frequently the subject of long-running jurisdictional battles, especially over budgetary issues. The remaining three categories of Russian "subjects of the federation" did not have any special ethnic designation, but tended to be overwhelmingly ethnic-Russian in composition. These regions, numbering 57, consisted of *oblasts, krais*, and Russia's two largest *cities*, categories that had become virtually identical in terms of authority granted them. For simplicity's sake, this text will refer to the broad set of all Russian subjects of the federation as *regions* or *provinces*. The leaders of all of these territorial entities will generally be referred to as *governors,* even though many provinces formally bestow different titles (such as "president" or "head of administration") upon their chief executives.

The first nationwide round of provincial elections, under rules set by the USSR under Gorbachev, occurred simultaneously with the 1990 elections to the Russian Congress of People's Deputies. At this time, the highest regional organs of power were the legislatures, called *soviets* ("councils"). Since a large number of provincial legislatures backed the anti-Yeltsin coup-plotters in August 1991, Yeltsin immediately pushed a resolution through the Russian parliament creating the new post of "head of administration" (chief executive) in all of the country's provinces except the republics.[22] The Russian president appointed the first heads of administration (on the recommendation of the soviets) but also announced that regions were soon to elect them directly. Worried that conservative forces might win a large number of governorships, however, Yeltsin banned gubernatorial elections (except in republics) from October 1991 until 1993, when he agreed to renew elections after some local leaderships insisted on holding them. After

[20] On how Leninist theories of federalism were sustained during the Soviet period and wound up producing modern Russian federalism, see Walker 2003.

[21] The term was coined by Roeder 1991.

[22] *Vedomosti RSFSR 1991* 34, pp. 1403–4.

Yeltsin's favorites lost seven of the first eight races held in 1993, he reneged and reinstated the ban on gubernatorial elections. The president allowed 13 more elections to be held in 1995 in provinces where he thought the chances of pro-Yeltsin candidates were good; only after his endorsees won 10 of the 13 did he mandate gubernatorial elections nationwide in the autumn of 1996.[23]

In Russia's (ethnically defined) republics, the situation was slightly different between 1991 and 1995. Yeltsin had not created the post of head of administration in these provinces, leaving this decision up to the soviets there. Several did form their own "presidencies" and initiate their own presidential elections as early as 1991–3. In the wake of Yeltsin's October 1993 decision to violently dissolve the Russian Congress of People's Deputies, some of those that had not previously done so rushed to hold gubernatorial elections for fear that Yeltsin might decide to appoint a governor if one was not already in place.[24] Yet even as of 2003, not all republics had opted to abandon their parliamentary forms of local government. Karachaevo-Cherkessiia and Udmurtiia instituted directly elected chief executives only in 1999 and 2000, respectively, and Dagestan enacted a law in 2003 that would institute a directly elected presidency in 2006.[25] All other regions, however, did hold gubernatorial elections by 1998.

All Russian provinces had the right to decide on their own electoral rules, although important constraints, to be discussed later, were enacted under Putin. In choosing how to elect their chief executives during the 1990s, the regions varied in the minimum turnout requirements they set and whether they required winners to obtain a simple plurality or an outright majority of the vote. The promotion of political parties was almost never a concern in the design of gubernatorial election legislation. No region required candidates to be party-nominated and no region gave candidates special incentives to run as party nominees.

The regions varied more significantly in their choice of election laws governing legislative contests. Elections to regional legislative assemblies have been competitive ever since 1990 but became multiparty only after the first set of elections. While five regions had established bicameral legislatures as of the end of 2000, the vast majority had chosen single-chamber systems. The number of seats in each legislature varied quite widely, with an average of 43 deputies per regional body. The vast majority of regions (60) had adopted straight SMD systems, although a significant number (16) had either combined SMD with at least one multimember district (MMD) or, in seven cases, adopted a purely MMD system. Four regions (Sverdlovsk,

[23] See Stoner-Weiss 1997, chap. 3, pp. 56–89.

[24] For an example, see *Delovoi Ural*, November 17–23, 1993, p. 1.

[25] On Dagestan's reforms, see *Vremia Novostei*, July 11, 2003, p. 2, and *Gazeta*, July 10, 2003, 11:03, www.gzt.ru.

Krasnoiarsk, Kaliningrad, and the Koriak AO) elected their legislatures partially through a proportional representation (PR) system as of the end of 2000, but none had chosen to rely exclusively on this form of election. These electoral rules were remarkably stable during the 1990s, with only four regions altering their systems between 1995 and 2000.

After 2000, however, Putin's team initiated two major reforms of regional elections. The first of these took effect in mid-July 2003 and mandated that every region had to institute a PR system for at least half of one chamber of its legislature. This set off a wide range of regional election system reforms since the regions retained the flexibility to decide their thresholds for obtaining the proportionally allocated mandates and the number of seats and chambers in their legislative systems. By August 2004, just 11 regions had held legislative elections under the new legislation and the Central Election Commission had published information on 10 of them on its Web site.[26] Of these 10 provinces, only 5 had opted for a mixed system modeled on the current Duma, where half of the seats were elected by party-list and the other half in single-member districts. The remaining five either allocated somewhat more seats by PR or balanced a PR half with SMD and multiple-member districts of various magnitudes.[27] Most of these 10 regions opted for a 5 percent threshold in the PR competition, but several set a 7 percent requirement and one (Kalmykiia) put the bar at 10 percent.[28] Putin announced a new wave of regional reforms on September 13, 2004, calling for an end to gubernatorial elections; the president would gain the right to nominate governors, who would then have to be approved by the regional legislature in order to take office. This reform is left for discussion in Chapter 5, where the initiative itself will be explained.

Institutions: Summing Up

Overall, we see how both national and regional leaders in Russia's post-patrimonial-communist context systematically favored those already in charge by privileging single-member-district elections and giving extraordinary powers to the executive branch. The primary exception involved the institution of a party-list system for half of the Duma, a system which was seen in part as a way to ensure that establishment elites would make it into the parliament even if they could not win a district seat. Russia's leaders also

[26] The Web site is http://www.fci.ru, accessed August 25, 2004.

[27] For example, Ingushetiia allocated 17 seats by PR, eight seats by four-member districts, six seats by three-member districts, two seats in one two-member district, and one seat in one single-member district.

[28] In most cases, the law also required that at least two parties clear the barrier; if this failed to happen, at least one party gaining less than the threshold was allowed in or elections had to be held again.

tended to avoid rules of the game that would most directly favor party development, restricting PR to only half of the Duma and allowing candidates to run in single-member districts as independents prior to Putin's reforms.

STARTING POLITICAL CAPITAL AT THE LAUNCH OF RUSSIA'S SECOND REPUBLIC

Russia's legacy of patrimonial communism had major implications not only for the rules of the game in Russia's new democracy, but also for the political capital with which Russian parties came to be built. This section examines the stocks of political capital available to aspiring party-builders at the critical moment of December 1993, when Russia held its first nationwide multiparty elections since the collapse of the USSR. The moment was critical because these elections did much to sort out subsequent winners from losers, rewarding the initial winners with parliamentary delegations and enhanced reputations for success and punishing the losers with the stigma of defeat.

Party entrepreneurs preparing for the December 1993 Duma elections found themselves highly circumscribed in the kinds of political capital available to them by legacies associated with patrimonial communism. Truly nationwide political organization independent of the state was very limited at this point. Indeed, prior to 1991, the Communist Party of the Soviet Union (CPSU) had been the sole party allowed to compete in all Russian elections since Lenin's time and truly independent movements had faced harassment if not outright repression. This left precious little opportunity for noncommunist parties or movements to organize. Furthermore, Russia's hierarchical social structure, deeply penetrated and tightly controlled through patterns of clientelist rule, left very few resources available to independent party-builders and made it quite difficult even to mobilize broad support for ideas that did not meet the approval of incumbent authorities. Thus, while the 1990 races for the Congress of People's Deputies had been quite competitive, they featured little political organization (or even informal coordinated activity of any kind) outside of CPSU structures, and most observers were reluctant even to use the term "political party" to describe those noncommunist associations that did exist between 1990 and 1993.[29]

It would be wrong to totally dismiss those 1990–93 independent organizations, however, since some of them did provide at least some political capital that was potentially valuable once Russia inaugurated its new multiparty era. In 1990 and prior to the breakup of the USSR in December 1991, political competition in Russia tended to revolve around two very

[29] Evans and Whitefield 1993; Fish 1995; Fleron et al. 1998; and McFaul 1993.

loose coalitions of forces. The first of these was the CPSU's Russian subsidiary, the Communist Party of Russia, which controlled a large number of seats in the Russian Congress of People's Deputies. This group contained an extremely wide variety of forces ranging from moderate reformers who soon left the formal organization to hardliners who avidly supported the August 1991 coup attempt. Thus, when Yeltsin banned the Communist Party shortly after the putsch, the leadership broke into a number of different and much smaller associations under different names.[30] A second broad political force in Russia, also with sizeable representation in the Congress, coalesced around the label Democratic Russia. This movement had its roots in the preelection period and tended to unite reformers of a wide variety of stripes, many of whom were themselves Communist Party members at the time of the 1990 election.[31] At different points during 1990 and 1991, Democratic Russia was capable of mobilizing some of Russia's largest street demonstrations to date.[32] As McFaul reports, however, this group lost its unifying issue once the USSR broke up and the Communist Party was banned. Many of its most prominent leaders then went into government at various levels, often following Yeltsin's lead in declaring themselves independent of any party in the process. Still other Democratic Russia associates formed new movements of their own.[33] Accordingly, only a rump group continued to function under the label Democratic Russia in the Congress and in Russia's regions by 1993.

During the final two years before its October 1993 demise, the Russian Congress of People's Deputies institutionalized the role of *fractions* (officially recognized parliamentary delegations) in the legislative process. According to the body's rules, a fraction had to have a minimum of 50 deputies to register as such. Once registered, the fractions controlled access to the floor and were represented equally in the key reconciliation commissions, which, as Hough reports, performed some of the most important work of the Congress. As Hough also observes, these rules had the effect of giving incentive for any politician who could gain 49 allies to form his or her own fraction; as of June 1993, therefore, only one fraction (the Agrarian Union) had more than 16 members over the minimum of 50.[34] These fractions (and less formal "deputy groups") were, in most cases, very much "parties-in-government," having little presence outside of the Congress itself, to the extent they were parties at all.

Between the collapse of the USSR and the Congress's violent dissolution in October 1993, five sets of deputies could be said to have had significant

[30] Urban and Solovei 1997.

[31] Hough 1998b, p. 45.

[32] On Democratic Russia, see especially Fish 1995; McFaul 2001b; and McFaul and Markov 1993.

[33] McFaul 1998.

[34] Hough 1998b, pp. 46–7.

organization outside of parliament, including regional branches. These were the Agrarian Union, the Communist Party, Democratic Russia, the Democratic Party, and a newer grouping called Civic Union. The Agrarian Union focused almost entirely on a select set of rural regions but did have extensive organization there. The Communist fraction, legalized in late 1992 and resurrected in 1993, inherited many CPSU loyalists in regional organizations across the country.[35] But as Hough observes, the Communists in the Congress made little effort to develop ties with provincial Communist organizations; the bulk of this work was done much later by a future leader, Gennady Zyuganov, who was never a Congress deputy.[36] The Democratic Russia fraction in the Congress of 1992 and 1993, as noted above, was merely a remnant of the revolutionary anticommunist movement that had been prominent in 1990 and 1991. As such, it contained at this time a relatively small set of activists without anything close to its pre-1991 mobilizational strength in the regions.[37]

Civic Union was an umbrella organization that brought together several Congress fractions and that enjoyed the support of Arkady Volsky's Union of Industrialists and Entrepreneurs, which counted as members and supporters many of Russia's most powerful industrial managers. Volsky himself became head of Civic Union. In late 1992, Civic Union appeared to be coming together as the primary focal point of opposition to the Yeltsin regime, effectively forcing the president to remove Yegor Gaidar (a fierce opponent of subsidies to large Soviet-era industry) as acting prime minister in December 1992 and to insert Viktor Chernomyrdin, himself an industrialist from the important gas sector. Volsky never moved to build a unified party organization, however, letting Civic Union's many member institutions continue to function more or less independently.

Finally, the Democratic Party, led by Nikolai Travkin, was one of Russia's very first noncommunist parties to officially register with Russian authorities. As of 1993, its leadership claimed to have some 50,000 members and over 600 local organizations in all regions but Omsk. Travkin's party had at first been a member of Democratic Russia, then had defected to Civic Union, and finally, in June 1993, had left Civic Union to pursue future elections on its own. The Democratic Party, however, never formed its own fraction in the Congress and Travkin actually resigned his seat in the body during the spring of 1993.[38]

35 Urban and Solovei 1997.

36 Hough 1998b, p. 47.

37 McFaul 1998.

38 In April 1993, a plurality of voters had supported new parliamentary elections in a referendum, although the required absolute majority among registered voters was not achieved to make this legally binding. Travkin thus resigned in a gesture of support for new elections. Information on the Democratic Party comes in part from Daniel Treisman 1998a, pp. 146–7.

The Congress itself did not appear to lend its fractions much in the way of "brand name" appeal. In one of the few surveys taken on parties during this period, researchers found in February 1993 that a full 64 percent of 400 people questioned in the Russian cities of Vladimir and Yurev-Polsky responded that they had no information about any political party in Russia. While taken in areas known for their lack of political activity and with an unknown methodology, this finding is nonetheless remarkable given that respondents usually exaggerate the degree to which they are aware of parties and that city dwellers are usually more aware than rural residents.[39] Only 9 percent said that they supported any of those that they did know. Accordingly, a poll by the highly respected *VTsIOM* survey agency, conducted just prior to the start of the campaign in October 1993, found that none of the parties having more than 5 percent support in the electorate were running for the Duma under the brand name established by their Congress fraction.[40]

What is even more revealing, a poll commissioned by Western scholars Colton and Hough asked voters at the start of the 1993 Duma campaign (in mid-November) whether they knew of the parties that would be on the December ballot. If we look first only at those parties running for the Duma under a name recognizable as a fraction or deputy group in the old Congress (the Agrarian Party, Civic Union, and the Communist Party), we find that these Congress-era brands did not lend their bearers marked name-recognition advantages over other parties, as is illustrated in Table 2.1. The same table does show, however, that 3 of the 5 most widely recognized parties and 5 out of the top 10 did have an organizational presence in the Congress.[41] Thus, while it seems the Congress itself did not do much to create winning party brand names, organizations with roots in the First Republic did tend to perform rather well in the Duma race if they could get onto the ballot. In fact, all but one of the parties with Congressional roots that managed to get onto the 1993 Duma ballot did in fact clear the 5 percent barrier: the Communist, Agrarian, Democratic, and Russia's Choice parties. A political presence in the First Russian Republic, therefore, does seem to have assisted political entrepreneurs in securing a place in the Second.

[39] *RFE/RL, Inc.* [Newsline], no. 21, 1993.

[40] *Argumenty i Fakty* 44, November 1993, p. 2. But this poll clearly underestimated the support for the Communist Party, as respondents had reason to be wary of declaring their allegiance to a hard-core opposition party the very same month that Yeltsin employed deadly force to crush his parliamentary enemies.

[41] The finding on the importance of organization concurs with Golosov 1998. See also McFaul 1998, pp. 118–19. As Hough (1998, 48) notes, the finding that only 61 percent knew of the Communists reflects the fact that many Communist organizations were competing for the CPSU mantle at the time. While voters were certainly familiar with the CPSU, they did not know much about the various new Communist parties, of which the one led by the then-little-known Gennady Zyuganov was only one.

TABLE 2.1. *Percentage of Russian Citizens Familiar with Political Parties at the Start of the 1993 Duma Campaign, November 18–20, 1993*

Name of Party	Know Party	Have Opinion about It
Russia's Choice	74	61
LDPR	73	60
Democratic Party	63	44
PRES	62	44
Communist Party	61	47
Movement for Democratic Reforms	59	46
Yabloko	57	41
Agrarian Party	47	32
Civic Union	43	28
Women of Russia	47	35
Dignity and Compassion	33	22
Future of Russia–New Names	29	18
KEDR-Ecology	27	16

Italic type = parties with brand names used in the Congress of People's Deputies
Bold type = parties with organizational roots in the Russian Congress of People's Deputies
Gray highlighting = parties that cleared the 5% threshold in the 1993 Duma elections
Source of survey figures: Colton and Hough 1998, p. 49.

The most common form of political capital available to political entrepreneurs in the critical fall of 1993, however, tended to involve either personal reputation or connections to the powerful and pervasive state structures emergent from the patrimonial communist regime. These two factors, reputation and connections, were in fact closely interlinked since nearly all of Russia's most popular politicians had become famous through some kind of employment in leading state organs. Table 2.2 provides some information about the background and success of politicians that were found by the country's most prominent survey agency (VTsIOM) to be the most trusted in Russia just prior to the start of the campaign in mid-October 1993. This table makes several points manifest. For one almost all of the most popular politicians had gained their reputations largely through service in some state organ within the preceding four years: Gaidar and Chernomyrdin as prime ministers, Grigory Yavlinsky and Sergei Shakhrai as deputy prime ministers, Aleksandr Rutskoi as vice president, and Anatoly Sobchak, Travkin, and Ruslan Khasbulatov as parliamentarians, to name a few. Many of these traded on their personal standings to form their own parties, bringing other state-connected politicians into their

TABLE 2.2. *Percentage of Russian Citizens Naming Each Politician as the One They Trust Most, October 9–23, 1993*

Yeltsin	24	*Khasbulatov*	3	**Zhirinovsky**	1
Gaidar	14	*Chubais*	2	*Fedorov (S.)*	1
Yavlinsky	13	*Nemtsov*	2	*Poltoranin*	1
Shakhrai	12	*Gorbachev*	2	*Popov*	1
Chernomyrdin	10	*Fedorov (B.)*	1	**Zyuganov**	0 (0.4)
Rutskoi	6	*Baburin*	1	*Makashov*	0 (0.4)
Sobchak	6	***Volsky***	1	Others	10
Travkin	5	*Kozyrev*	1	None	25
Tuleev	4	Borovoi	1	Hard to say	28
Shumeiko	3	*Burbulis*	1		

Italic type = served in executive branch, parliament, or military command of Russia, USSR, or province prior to October 1993
Bold type = formal leaders of parties that made it onto the ballot in the 1993 Duma elections
Gray highlighting = formal leaders of parties that cleared 5% in the 1993 Duma elections
Source of survey figures: *Argumenty i Fakty* 44, November 1993, p. 2.

teams.[42] Table 2.2 also demonstrates that the most popular of the party-formers did tend to translate their political capital into party seats in the PR half of the Duma, with the exception of Sobchak, whose Russian Movement for Democratic Reforms (RDDR) fell just below the 5 percent mark in the December elections. The leaders of four parties that ultimately cleared the 5 percent hurdle, however, either did not have the trust of as much as even 1 percent of the public (Communist Party, Liberal Democratic Party) or did not make it onto pollsters' "radar screens" at all (Agrarian Party, Women of Russia) as of October 1993.[43]

Of course, access to powerful state institutions in and of itself was also one very important form of administrative capital that could easily be employed for party-building. Thus, although Gaidar had a fair degree of personal

42 Rutskoi had his own party, but it was barred from the competition, as was Sergei Baburin's. Politicians (mostly government and Yeltsin administration figures) joining Gaidar's Russia's Choice party included Anatoly Chubais, Gennady Burbulis, and Mikhail Poltoranin.

43 The "trust" ratings of Vladimir Zhirinovsky, leader of the Liberal Democratic Party of Russia (LDPR), are probably understated here. A wild nationalist, he had been well known since he stunned observers by finishing in third place in the 1991 Russian presidential race with 8 percent of the vote. This result alone demonstrates that he had already cultivated strong personal reputational resources. Accordingly, the Colton-Hough preelection poll found that the LDPR was known by 73 percent of Russians. Nevertheless, this party's extreme nationalist stands and status as public anathema led many of its supporters to keep quiet, explaining why this support did not show up in the VTsIOM survey.

popularity, his status as Yeltsin's favorite and newly appointed first deputy prime minister (having been forced out as acting prime minister in December 1992) made his party, Russia's Choice, the bet of most Russian elites to come away with the largest share of the vote. Surely this widely perceived connection to the Kremlin underlay the Colton-Hough finding that this new party was the best known in Russia at the start of the campaign and the report by VTsIOM that some 41 percent of the electorate planned to support Russia's Choice as of October 23–5, 1993.[44] Shakhrai's party was also widely viewed as having at least some support from the Kremlin, as Shakhrai was recognized as one of Yeltsin's closest and most powerful advisors.

If we turn from organizational to financial forms of administrative capital, we find that monetary resources were also relatively scarce among would-be political entrepreneurs outside of state structures. The Russian privatization program was only partially complete as of late 1993 and the entrepreneurs now called "oligarchs" had not yet amassed their vast riches through the most lucrative privatization schemes like the infamous loans-for-shares arrangement of the mid-1990s. Certain bankers, many of whom had evolved from the Gorbachev-era cooperative banking sector as did Menatep's Mikhail Khodorkovsky, had accumulated significant resources. But they did so mostly through the good graces of state patrons. The banking system, in addition, was quite fragmented at this time, as central banks had not yet made their major push into the vast Russian territory outside of Moscow. Bankers and nonstate economic actors, then, were scarcely poised to launch their own party projects in the fall of 1993, although they certainly mobilized to back those that they supported. As Juliet Johnson reports, however, the bankers primarily channeled funds to parties that were friendly to the Kremlin or, at a minimum, to free-market reforms more generally. In practice, this meant Gaidar's Russia's Choice, Shakhrai's PRES, and Yavlinsky's Yabloko Party.[45]

Table 2.3 sums up our brief survey of political capital on the eve of Russia's first multiparty parliamentary elections. Critically, these assessments were made with data available prior to these elections, not just in hindsight. The table shows that someone who before the voting had measured just two elements of starting political capital, First-Republic organization and personal reputation, would have produced a fairly accurate prediction of which parties would successfully clear the 5 percent barrier in the PR voting in the Duma in 1993.[46] Strikingly, both of these assets largely reflected ties to

44 *Argumenty i Fakty* 44, November 1993, p. 2.

45 Johnson 2000, p. 117. On the state of the banking system at this time, see also Hough 2001.

46 No party won even close to enough district seats (35) to have officially registered a party delegation ("deputy group") in the Duma on its own without also clearing 5 percent in the party-list competition.

TABLE 2.3. *The Distribution of Political Capital at the Start of the 1993 Duma Campaign*

Parties Running 1993	Starting Assets of Party Entrepreneurs: Organization in Congress	Personal Reputation	Kremlin Connection	Bank Backing	Percentage of Vote 1993 PR	Number of Seats 1993 SMD
LDPR	–	+	–	–	23	5
Russia's Choice	+	+	+	+	16	24
Communist Party	+	–	–	–	12	10
Women of Russia	–	–	–	–	8	2
Agrarian Party	+	–	–	–	8	16
Yabloko	–	+	–	+	8	7
PRES	–	+	+	+	7	4
Democratic Party	+	+	–	–	6	0
RDDR (Sobchak)	–	+	–	–	4	5
Civic Union	+	–	–	–	2	10
Future of Russia	–	–	–	–	1	2
KEDR	–	–	–	–	1	1
Dignity & Compassion	–	–	–	–	1	3

Shaded rows identify those parties that either (1) cleared the 5% hurdle without much visible starting political capital or (2) failed to clear the 5% hurdle despite being in possession of at least one form of significant starting political capital.

Source for election results: Grigory Belonuchkin, *Politika*, http://www.cityline.ru:8080/politika/fs/gd1rezv.html, accessed May 28, 2004.

the Russian state. The fit is not perfect, however; shaded rows identify those parties that do not fit the pattern, either clearing the 5 percent hurdle without much visible starting political capital or failing in the PR voting despite being in possession of at least one form of significant starting political capital. These findings, therefore, demonstrate the importance of starting political capital in explaining which particular parties come to form a country's party system but also strongly suggest that we must consider additional, less easily measurable factors. One of the most important of these, it is argued in the pages that follow, is the set of strategies that political entrepreneurs adopt in their pursuit of success.

EXPLAINING INITIAL PARTY SURVIVAL: CAPITAL, STRATEGY, CONTINGENCY

Why have some parties made effective use of their starting political capital while others have not? Similarly, why have some proven able to succeed with what initially appeared to be low stocks of electoral assets? The critical factors are found to be the party-building and campaign strategies of Russia's parties. These factors help us explain not only why some parties and not others made it onto the parliamentary map in the 1993 Duma elections, but also why some subsequently came to anchor the political party system in Russia whereas others did not. Indeed, only two parties (the Communist Party and the LDPR) have remained major, autonomous peddlers of electoral wares through all of Russia's national electoral cycles between 1993 and 2005. While chance certainly played a role, parties were to a significant degree in control of their own fates, albeit in a highly competitive environment subject to occasional Kremlin intervention.

Since campaigning is so critical, representing an arena in which parties can either lose or achieve critical political mass in short order, each successive round of elections acts as something of a sifter. If one refers to the first multiparty elections as founding elections, one might dub the subsequent election or two "weeding elections." Thus, with this in mind, we first turn to blocs that failed to achieve critical mass in Russia's "founding" Duma election. Eight parties, however, survived this first cut. We then turn to those eight and discuss the ones that failed in the second electoral round of 1995–6, explaining what had changed for them between 1993 and 1995. The next section examines the two organizations that survived as major parties for three successive rounds of elections, only to fall short in the most recent one, 2003–4. The chapter then considers parties that might be called quadruple success stories, those veterans that have survived every Russian national election cycle to date, identifying the factors that differentiated them from all of the relative failures. Finally, we examine the many parties that attempted to "crash the party" by breaking through to major-party status after having failed in at least one previous election. While few such efforts succeeded, the ones that have done so are among the most important phenomena in Russian politics.

In the discussion that follows, parties are considered "successes" and "major parties" either if they cleared the 5 percent barrier necessary to form a Duma fraction according to regulations in place from 1993 to 2003 or if their nominees won enough district seats to register a "deputy group," which required a minimum of 35 elected deputies between 1993 and 2003.[47] This operational threshold for defining success and major-party status makes sense because it represents the minimum amount of voter support necessary for a party to fulfill the fundamental goal of winning a significant number of seats in national office. To keep the discussion as succinct as possible, given that many dozens of organizations have appeared on the ballot in Russia's various parliamentary contests, parties are not examined below if they fit the theory in the least interesting way – that is, if they lacked any significant administrative or ideational capital (as measured above) and failed to succeed in at least one Duma election.

First-Round Failures

We open by focusing on two parties that began with considerable starting political capital but then failed to make good with it during the 1993 Duma campaign. These organizations, Civic Union and the Russian Movement for Democratic Reforms, both went into the campaign with assets that Table 2.3 suggests might have led to success. We find that both failed largely due to major problems that arose during the course of the campaign, many of which were of their own leaders' doing.

Civic Union

During the summer of 1992, while the Communist Party was still banned, some of Russia's best-known figures converged in a coalition known as Civic Union that for nearly a year looked to be emerging as the focal opposition to the government that Yeltsin was backing. Key figures included Travkin (who brought in his Democratic Party), Vice President Rutskoi, and Volsky, the head of the Union of Industrialists and Entrepreneurs. The presence of such well-known figures under one coalitional roof, as well as the might of the large state enterprises that supported Volsky's organization, were the bloc's chief starting assets. It was immediately able to gain media attention when it lambasted acting Prime Minister Gaidar and his "shock therapy" reforms and called for a more measured approach to economic reform with an

47 After the 2003 Duma election, the new Duma raised the threshold for forming a deputy group to 55 deputies. See *RFE/RL Newsline*, December 30, 2003.

emphasis on supporting the state and former state enterprises that the Gaidar government hoped to bankrupt.[48]

Things started to fall apart in 1993, however, due to a variety of leadership failures. First Travkin pulled his Democratic Party out, complaining that Rutskoi was taking his oppositionism too far.[49] Rutskoi then sided with the Congress against Yeltsin in the violence of September–October 1993, winding up in Lefortovo prison. This left Volsky the most visible leader, a man who Daniel Treisman describes as "an inveterately careful politician whose reputation had always rested on an aura of behind-the-scenes influence, never on performance in electoral competition."[50] This lack of campaign acumen translated into a disastrous election effort. Whereas parties like Yabloko and PRES ran fast-paced, image-conscious media campaigns, Civic Union used its state-allocated time on national television to hold droning live panel discussions. Against a plain black background, the gray and dilapidated Volsky, frequently betraying a hacking cough, expounded upon the evils of Gaidar's economics and invited party colleagues to chime in.[51] In the end, Civic Union managed a paltry 2 percent in the PR voting and just 10 district victories, not nearly enough to register an independent delegation in the new Duma. This signaled its end as an independent political force.

Russian Movement for Democratic Reforms (RDDR)

Like Civic Union, the RDDR began with a significant stock of starting political capital. As Table 2.2 shows, its leader, Sobchak, was in late 1993 polling at roughly the same level as or higher than other politicians who did later guide their parties into the parliament. Having made his name as one of the most charismatic new deputies in the USSR's first competitively elected Congress, Sobchak had translated this success into election as mayor of Russia's second city, St. Petersburg. His movement was noted for including many other reformers who were not primarily associated with Yeltsin's governments, including Aleksandr Yakovlev, a former top Gorbachev aide widely reputed to be the mastermind of *perestroika*. Since it possessed precious little organization and scarce administrative capital outside of the St. Petersburg mayor's office, then, its chief asset was decidedly ideational, the non-Yeltsinite reformism of its famous leaders.

During the campaign, however, the party opted not to run on its reformism but instead to attempt an "all things to all people" approach. Its professed goal became to serve as a "super-party structure" uniting any democratic

48 McFaul and Markov 1993, p. 20.
49 Treisman 1998a, pp. 146–7.
50 Ibid.
51 For example, the broadcast on First Channel, November 12, 1993, 21:50 Moscow time.

forces who wanted to join.[52] It thus made little effort to build long-lasting regional organization and did not attempt to define a sharp ideological reputation for fear of driving away potential allies. The RDDR's television campaign in 1993 focused largely on the leadership qualities of Sobchak, stressing his avowedly proven ability to get things done, and emphasized the general moral authority of Yakovlev.[53] Sobchak's popularity, however, was based less on any ability to get things done than on his bold early stands in favor of democracy and reforms at the first USSR Congress of People's Deputies. Moreover, the bloc's top leaders were certainly not known at the time as "can-do" politicians, as Yakovlev was widely associated with Gorbachev's failure to keep the USSR together and another prominent leader, Gavriil Popov, had resigned as Moscow mayor in 1992 after proving unable to cope with the responsibility. As a result, the RDDR netted just 4 percent of the party-list vote and only five district seats, whereupon its most prominent leaders and supporters shifted to different parties, formed their own new ones, or left politics altogether.

Second- and Third-Round Failures

A total of eight parties survived where Civic Union and the RDDR failed. Like the latter two parties, the eight began with political capital that the preceding analysis suggests augured well for success in the December 1993 election. These parties either started with significantly greater concentrations of political assets or used what they had more effectively. We now turn to those that survived 1993 but that had subsequently failed by 1995 or 1999, examining what differentiates them from the 1993 failures but also setting the stage for an analysis of the factors that ultimately left them out of the set of longer-term winners in Russian party politics.[54]

Sergei Shakhrai's Party of Russian Unity and Accord (PRES)

The leading political entrepreneur for PRES was Shakhrai, a lawyer by training who possessed a great deal of political capital in 1993 due largely to his close association with the Yeltsin regime.[55] Starting his political career in the Russian Congress of People's Deputies, he held a number of senior state posts

[52] Treisman 1998a, p. 144.

[53] RTR, *Federal'naia Sobraniia*, December 2, 1993, 19:10 Bashkortostan time.

[54] Since the successor organization to Russia's Choice succeeded in 1999 after failing in 1995, this party is discussed below as a "fourth-round failure."

[55] Information in the following paragraph is from Grigory Belonuchkin, "Shakhrai, Sergei Mikhailovich," *Politika*, http://www.cityline.ru/politika/ks/shahrai.html, accessed January 11, 2003; Johnson 2000, p. 117; Treisman 1998a, pp. 145–6; *Nezavisimaia Gazeta*, November 6, 1992, p. 1; and an interview with a senior leader of a regional organization of PRES and a 1993 PRES candidate for the Duma, March 9, 1999.

before becoming the cabinet official in charge of relations with provincial governments, where he gained much influence by distributing subsidies to the republics.[56] Shakhrai's high-profile activities helped make him the fourth most trusted politician in Russia according to one mid-October 1993 survey (see Table 2.2). Shakhrai started building his party as early as June 1993 in anticipation of early elections, recruiting a deputy prime minister (Aleksandr Shokhin) and a prominent Yeltsin advisor (Sergei Stankevich) and securing the tacit support of Prime Minister Chernomyrdin. PRES also won significant business support from such business entities as the gas monopoly Gazprom, the Association of Young Enterprise Leaders, and the Association of Russian Banks.

During the 1993 Duma campaign, Shakhrai openly declared that his party was not based on "ideology" and advocated a pragmatic approach to solving Russia's problems.[57] The PRES platform primarily called for more moderate reforms and promised to listen to the regions without making substantial commitments as to what "moderate" meant or what the outcome of such listening would be. Television advertisements were heavily image-conscious, sometimes presenting only the party's symbol and at other times showing feel-good footage of a great Soviet-era hockey team in by way of stressing that "unity and accord" were necessary for victory.[58] Clips also highlighted Shakhrai's leadership style and personal qualities.[59]

While a similar "catch-all" strategy proved disastrous for Sobchak's RDDR, which lacked significant administrative capital but initially possessed a great deal of ideational capital, it was a good match for the stock of starting political capital that PRES possessed. The combination of Shakhrai's personal popularity as a pragmatic leader and the party's strong ties to the Yeltsin-Chernomyrdin tandem were enough to ensure the support of much big business as well as provincial authorities capable of delivering votes in large numbers. Given this, the party's ideational stands had to be just vague enough not to alienate these groups but just strong enough to convince them that PRES was significantly different from Gaidar's Russia's Choice. Thus, the leader of one of Russia's largest and most autonomy-minded provinces, Bashkortostan, spurned Russia's Choice but was willing to support PRES as the "only" party putting support for the regions at the center of its platform despite the ambiguity of this

[56] Golosov 2003, p. 30.

[57] PRES advertisement, First Channel, November 19, 1993, 21:45 Bashkortostan time.

[58] Author's observations of PRES advertisements, including those aired on: First Channel, November 19, 1993, 21:45 Bashkortostan time; First Channel, November 23, 1993, 21:45 Bashkortostan time; St. Petersburg Television Network, November 28–9, 1993, 0:00 Bashkortostan time; *Radio Maiak*, November 18, 1993, 20:35 Moscow time.

[59] Treisman 1998a, p. 155.

support.[60] Similarly, the party's vague call for moderate reform facilitated support from those governors who wanted to be in the good graces of Russia's all-powerful presidency but who were opposed to Gaidar's brand of reforms. Accordingly, the party tended to do better in those oblasts and krais where support for Yeltsin was strongest and to perform uniformly well in the more autonomy-minded republics.[61] Thus, PRES managed to win 7 percent of the party-list vote, putting it in seventh place among the 13 competing parties, and netted three district seats.

After PRES failed to win him the chairmanship of the Duma that he had openly sought, and after the Kremlin abandoned Russia's Choice as a viable party of power (see below), Shakhrai joined PRES with an effort to build a new party of power that would be openly led by Prime Minister Chernomyrdin in 1995.[62] But when Chernomyrdin denied him the spots on the party list he demanded, Shakhrai formally pulled PRES out.[63] Virtually all of the governors and important candidates who had once backed PRES opted to stick with the prime minister. When election day rolled around in 1995, PRES won only a third of 1 percent of the party-list vote and just one district seat, after which experience it effectively disappeared from the political arena.

The Democratic Party of Russia

The Democratic Party of Russia, founded by Nikolai Travkin as one of Russia's first parties, represents a different path to party failure after an initial success.[64] The party project's starting political capital involved Travkin's own personal reputation as well as a strong ideational component. Travkin, a construction boss, originally made his name by initiating a new form of work organization that boosted production in the early 1980s. This earned him the prestigious title Hero of Socialist Labor. Winning election to the new USSR Congress of People's Deputies in 1989, he gravitated to the reformist deputy coalition co-led by Yeltsin. For the 1990 elections to the Russian Congress of People's Deputies, he joined Democratic Russia and became one of this bloc's three coordinators. Once the USSR legalized alternative political parties, Travkin pushed the movement to turn itself into a full-fledged party in opposition to the Communist Party. When this proposal was rejected, he founded his own party, the Democratic Party of Russia. Staking out a moderate reformist position, he vigorously opposed the Gaidar government,

60 *Sovetskaia Bashkiriia*, December 4, 1993, p. 1; *Vecherniaia Ufa*, December 9, 1993, p. 2.

61 Treisman 1998a, p. 168.

62 Belin and Orttung 1997, p. 34.

63 Ibid., p. 59.

64 Information in this section comes from the following sources unless otherwise indicated: Treisman 1998a; Yabloko party Web site, http://www.yabloko.ru/Persons/Travkin/travkin_bio.html.

joining the Civic Union coalition in the Russian Congress. By October 1993, he had become one of Russia's most trusted politicians and his party was one of the best known in the country, poised in most precampaign polls to clear the 5 percent Duma hurdle with little problem (see Table 2.2).

His party's "founding campaign" was unremarkable either for brilliance or blunders, playing heavily on his personality and leadership style. Travkin urged people to "vote for those you trust" and his campaign manager based the party's election effort on the principle "Centrists are distinguished not so much by what they do as by how they do it." Consistent with its ideational capital as a democratic organization skeptical of Yeltsin's rule, the party placed special emphasis on its opposition to the violent way in which Yeltsin had handled the October 1993 dispute with the Congress. The party's essential task, Travkin's strategists held, was not so much attracting new voters as keeping those that it already had.[65] This indeed translated into his party's receiving a share of the vote quite commensurate with what preelection polls had indicated (see Table 2.3).

Once in the parliament, however, Travkin advocated cooperation with the Yeltsin administration whereas two other prominent Democratic Party leaders, economist Sergei Glaziev and filmmaker Stanislav Govorukhin, pushed for a vote of no confidence in the government. Travkin lost this power struggle and in 1995 left the party to join Our Home is Russia.[66] Bitter, he blamed the presidential ambitions of his rivals for fatally crippling his party-building project.[67] Govorukhin and Glaziev themselves split over alliance partners for the 1995 Duma elections, with Glaziev leading one Democratic faction into the party KRO (see below) and Govorukhin competing in a bloc named after himself that won less than 1 percent of the party-list vote.[68] By the end of 1995, then, the Democratic Party had lost virtually all of its prominent leaders and mass following. For the 1999 election, its remnants became a minor partner in the Fatherland–All Russia coalition (see below). While it did compete on its own in the 2003 Duma contest, it netted less than a quarter of 1 percent of the party-list vote.

The Agrarian Party of Russia

Like the Democratic Party and PRES, the Agrarian Party started out with great promise but was unable to manage initial success. Its most important starting capital was the Agrarian Union, a network of over 8,000 collective farm chairs, 65 large agro-industrial enterprises, and the largest trade union

65 Treisman 1998a, pp. 148, 154.

66 Belin and Orttung 1997, pp. 53, 175 (fn97); Belin and Orttung 1995; and Korguniuk 1999, p. 76.

67 Interview with a person familiar with these developments, September 13, 1999.

68 Korguniuk 1999, p. 76.

in Russia with the largest fraction in the Russian Congress.[69] Some 19 percent of the party's 1993 list of candidates, which also featured First Deputy Prime Minister Aleksandr Zaveriukha, had full-time regional or local state jobs, mostly related to agriculture. The party was also endorsed in rural districts by the Communist Party, which saw the Agrarians as allies.[70] The Agrarian Party was certainly not leader-oriented; Mikhail Lapshin was not considered charismatic and was not even included in VTsIOM surveys on "most trusted" politicians in October 1993 (see Table 2.2).

The party's strategy for the "founding elections" of 1993 was simply to mobilize its very clear-cut base, which critically included collective farm chairs who wielded tremendous power in the farm villages. The party platform advocated protectionism for farmers and other producers, opposition to violence in politics, free land distribution to rural residents to run their own farms but not to sell, and a state-managed transition to a socially oriented market.[71] With this combination of ideational and administrative capital, the party received 8 percent of the PR vote and captured 16 district-elected seats.

Once in the Duma in 1994 and 1995, the Agrarian Party acted very pragmatically to obtain as many state subsidies for the agricultural sector as possible, often tacitly backing the government against Communist challenges in the process. Laura Belin and Robert Orttung cite evidence that this undermined much of the party's ideational capital since its rural constituencies tended to be quite anti-Yeltsin. The party thus came to rely more on administrative capital. Indeed, some 43 percent of Agrarian Party candidates on the 1995 party list were government officials at some level.[72] This lack of fit between party-building strategy and party stocks of capital after the 1993 elections helps explain why Agrarian support dipped to just 4 percent in the 1995 vote despite a campaign highly similar to that of 1993. While the party captured 20 district seats, this was not nearly enough to register a deputy group in the Duma.

Perhaps because the Agrarian Party initially combined significant amounts of both administrative and ideational capital, it has weathered splits and strategic missteps better than parties such as the Democratic Party in 1995 or the RDDR in 1993. Thus, after one-half of the party effectively joined the Communists while the other ran in coalition with the Fatherland–Russia Party in 1999, the latter half reemerged to run independently in 2003. While the fact that it netted just two district seats bespeaks organizational losses due to the party's split, its 4 percent showing in the party-list competition

[69] Belin and Orttung 1997, p. 46; interview with the organizational director of the APR, Bashkortostan branch March 11, 1999.
[70] Davidheiser 1998, p. 194.
[71] *Izvestiia*, November 27, 1993, p. 4.
[72] Belin and Orttung 1997, pp. 47, 118.

reportedly reflected an influx of financing directed by the Kremlin, which hoped that the Agrarians would siphon votes away from the Communists, the chief rivals to the pro-Putin United Russia Party.[73] Thus, while the party remained a failure, netting just 4 percent of the vote, it was still a minor but noticeable player in Russia's electoral market as of 2005.

Women of Russia

The bloc Women of Russia initially traded almost entirely upon its name, bringing what it presented as a "woman's approach" to politics. All party candidates were female. It was formed by political unknowns from a variety of social organizations, most notably a network of "women's councils" that Gorbachev had set up to help mobilize support for his reforms.[74] The bloc's leaders said that their gendered approach meant increased attention to social security, support for education, the development of culture, the provision of health care, and, generally speaking, a more moderate and less extreme form of politics. The bloc also championed the rights of children and opposed discrimination against women. Treisman quotes the bloc's chair, Alevtina Fedulova, as saying that if a woman were to gain some real power, "maybe then our Russian house would stop resembling a cold bachelor's apartment."[75] In the end, Colton's survey research found that not only did many women simply vote for women, but a large part of the electorate liked the party because of its perceived social policies.[76] Thus, the self-proclaimed women's bloc pulled in 8 percent of the vote in the 1993 party-list race, though it garnered only two district seats.

In attempting to navigate a middle road between the Communists and the government while in parliament, however, the bloc frequently got caught up in the logrolling process, changing positions on important issues or appearing to vote in contradictory ways on adjacent issues.[77] While this sacrifice of ideational capital posed one major problem for Women of Russia, in the 1995 election they faced a number of other parties (including the Communists and Yabloko) that had nominated major female figures partly in response to the 1993 success of Women of Russia.[78] Thus, while Women of Russia almost succeeded in 1995, it mustered just 4.6 percent of the vote in the end, short of the all-important 5 percent mark.

This taste of failure provoked a major split in the party. One faction, rather ironically, joined with the "Fatherland" movement in forming the

73 Interview with a participant in spring 2003 campaign planning sessions for United Russia, December 9, 2003.

74 Golosov 2003, p. 33.

75 Treisman 1998a, pp. 147–51.

76 Colton 1998a, p. 100.

77 Belin and Orttung 1997, p. 54.

78 Ibid., p. 83.

Fatherland–All Russia bloc. The other ran on its own in 1999, but then found itself up against another explicitly women's party, the Russian Party for the Defense of Women. In the end, Women of Russia won just 2 percent of the party-list vote in 1999, after which point it effectively departed the political scene and did not contest the 2003 elections.

Fourth-Round Failures

Russia's Choice, Russia's Democratic Choice, and the Union of Right Forces

As previously noted, Russia's Choice started out with tremendous political capital in mid-1993.[79] It was the brainchild of many of Yeltsin's closest advisors, notably Gennady Burbulis, who thought that the rabble-rousing image of the broad Democratic Russia coalition had become inappropriate after self-styled "reformers" led by Yeltsin were in power. Its public leaders were nearly all well known government officials, including former acting Prime Minister Gaidar (the formal party leader), "privatization tsar" Anatoly Chubais, and Foreign Minister Andrei Kozyrev. These leaders, moreover, were publicly associated with specific sets of ideas, notably their opposition to the communist regime and their advocacy of Western-style free-market economics and the radical "shock" method of getting there. Although bitterly opposed by many, such ideas were not unpopular in 1993. The basic economic program later advocated by Russia's Choice had won the approval of 53 percent of all voters in an April 1993 referendum. Additionally, as late as November 1993, the Colton-Hough survey had found that 46 percent of the population believed marketization was a correct course for Russia and that 45 percent backed privatization, whereas only 27 percent and 35 percent, respectively, opposed these policies.

Despite the high degree of ideational capital possessed by its leadership, Russia's Choice adopted party-building and campaign strategies that centered far more on its vast administrative capital than its free-market ideas. The party's chief patron (Yeltsin) scheduled the inaugural Duma elections for less than three months after he had illegally called new elections and shelled those in the opposition Congress who had tried to resist. While Russia's Choice had started party-building long before this, the snap election left potential opponents precious little time to mobilize and coordinate. Key critics of the Yeltsin regime, such as former Vice President Rutskoi's party, were banned from participation. Russia's Choice also had an overwhelming advantage in recruiting regional elites who sought the favor of the newly victorious presidential regime. Indeed, many governors had been appointed

[79] This account draws heavily on McFaul 1998 except where otherwise noted.

by Yeltsin precisely for their loyalty after the August 1991 coup attempt. The party's allies were also in a position to gerrymander so as to maximize the number of pro-Yeltsin districts.[80] Naturally, the Kremlin connection attracted ample financing from key banks.[81] Finally, all of Russia's major television networks at the time were state-owned, resulting in disproportionate coverage for Russia's Choice on news and analytical broadcasts.[82] In this coverage, these media and the party's campaign sought mainly to attract support by stressing its candidates' generic government experience and by communicating to voters and elites that it was a sure winner, placing very little emphasis on the specific reformist ideas that polls showed still commanded a great deal of public support.[83]

There were some major flaws in a strategy that relied so heavily on administrative capital. For one, Russia's Choice was not in a position to make iron-clad promises on behalf of the Kremlin since Yeltsin declined to actually join the party and Prime Minister Chernomyrdin tacitly backed PRES instead. Gaidar was only first deputy prime minister in 1993 and had a reputation as an idea man, not as a powerful administrator. Additionally, Russia's Choice's party-building plan, adopted over the summer of 1993, was essentially to supplant rather than to build on the old Democratic Russia network and ideology, focusing instead on the recruitment of powerful elites such as governors. This not only alienated a large and formerly loyal group of activists and supporters but also helped undermine the party's ideational appeal, since many such regional elites were known more for strong-arm methods of administration than for a commitment to markets or democracy.[84] As a result, two or more candidates nominally from Russia's Choice actually competed against each other in 16 Duma districts in 1993. Moreover, by nearly all accounts, the fact that Yeltsin had won his violent victory so decisively in October and that his administration was working primarily to support Russia's Choice inculcated a sense of overconfidence in the party. Its strategists thus made no effort to craft a campaign message, targeted no social groups, and neglected to define any clear policy stances, instead seeking mainly to remind people that Russia's Choice represented the victors in the recent struggle and to imbue the party with a positive image.[85] When Gaidar appeared on television, he did try to inject ideational content into the campaign but did so in lengthy and turbid discourses on the finer points of economic theory. Thus, although leaders had previously talked of a

[80] *Pravda*, November 5, 1993, p. 1.

[81] Johnson 2000, p. 117.

[82] See Shakhrai's complaints voiced in an interview on the show *Itogi*, St. Petersburg Channel, November 14, 1993, 21:00.

[83] *Argumenty i Fakty* 46, November 1993, p. 2.

[84] See Reddaway and Glinski 2001.

[85] McFaul 1998, p. 129.

large Russia's Choice victory if not an outright majority, the party won just 16 percent of the party-list vote in the 1993 election and only 24 of the 225 district seats.

This unexpectedly poor showing knocked Russia's Choice down but not completely out. Most importantly, Yeltsin abandoned it as a party of power and in its place created new projects led by Chernomyrdin and Duma speaker Ivan Rybkin (see below). While Gaidar stayed on as party leader, other top Russia's Choice members fled to create as many as eight different parties that then appeared on the 1995 Duma ballot; another dozen on the same ballot included leaders who had once been part of Democratic Russia.[86] While the party retained a core organization under a new name, Russia's Democratic Choice, it won only 4 percent of the vote and just nine district seats in 1995.

The core began to regenerate in the run-up to the 1999 election, spurred on by the fact that all of the Russia's Choice successor parties had failed despite collectively receiving far more than 5 percent of the vote. Chubais controlled the party's largest stock of administrative capital; between 1996 and 1999 he had served as Yeltsin's chief of staff, first deputy prime minister, and starting in 1998, chairman of the board of Russia's partially state-owned electricity monopoly, Unified Energy Systems. The party also maintained close relationships with other Kremlin-connected structures having access to significant resources in the regions, including Yeltsin's plenipotentiary representatives to the provinces. Largely on this basis, Chubais was able to bring old Russia's Choice figures like himself and Gaidar together with newer stars in more recent Yeltsin governments, notably former Prime Minister Sergei Kirienko, former First Deputy Prime Minister Boris Nemtsov, and former state committee chair Irina Khakamada. The self-proclaimed "liberals" put market-oriented "rightist" ideology at the center of this coalition, accordingly named the Union of Right Forces and widely known by its Russian acronym, SPS. Chubais became campaign manager and ran a very tight ship, frequently gathering party leaders to work out clear party messages on every developing issue. Perhaps the defining moment of its 1999 campaign came when Putin began a large-scale military incursion into Chechnya after blaming a series of terrorist acts on Chechens; despite major disagreements within the party on how to respond, Chubais got party leaders to publicly support the new war. This enabled it to discredit its chief rightist rival, the Yabloko party, as described below. No less importantly, Chubais also won the approval of SPS to back Prime Minister Vladimir Putin for the presidency in 2000, thereby gaining favorable coverage on Russia's state-owned television networks and benefiting from the popularity that Putin was fast acquiring in the fall of 1999. Effectively combining a strong and credible ideological stand with significant administrative capital, SPS surprised almost all observers by

86 Ibid., p. 135.

surging to a 9 percent showing in the party-list competition and netting five district seats.

If the SPS campaign in 1999 was extraordinarily well run, its 2003 effort was quite different. One bad omen was that Kirienko, who had led the 1999 party list, departed the party in 2000 to become Putin's representative to the Volga Federal Okrug, where one of his main tasks became to secure victory for United Russia in the 2003 Duma race. The organizationally gifted Chubais was no longer campaign chair, entrusting this task to an associate who then made a series of highly questionable decisions. For example, the party's television advertising campaign relied almost exclusively on a clip featuring Nemtsov, Khakamada, and Chubais working with laptop computers on a private luxury jet labeled "Russia" soaring up into the blue sky. Intended to activate the aspirations of an incipient business class, the ad was almost universally criticized for instead suggesting that the party leaders were in fact quite out of touch with regular people's lives. The party also devoted a very large share of its campaign budget to a smear campaign against Yabloko; the goal was to knock Yabloko below the 5 percent mark so that SPS would become the leading "liberal" party. Without Chubais devoted fully to forging and enforcing a party message, SPS also failed to take a clear stand on Putin in 2003; while Chubais remained largely supportive, his colleagues Nemtsov and Khakamada became increasingly critical as election day neared. Moreover, with the Kremlin now deciding to back United Russia wholeheartedly (see Chapter 5), SPS lost the active presidential support from which it had benefited in 1999. The coup de grace for the party was that Putin and his favorite party, United Russia, were now implementing most of the economic reforms that SPS had been advocating. With SPS unwilling to take a clear and strong stand against Putin on the issue of democratization, liberals could be justified in wondering just why they should vote for SPS rather than United Russia. Thus, despite the fact that SPS continued to benefit from support from Unified Energy Systems and other economic forces, a poor campaign dropped it to just 4 percent of the party-list vote and just three district seats in the Duma election of 2003.

The intraparty dispute over Putin then led to a full-fledged split in the run-up to Russia's 2004 presidential election. While Chubais argued that SPS's best hope of revival lay with continuing to back Putin, Khakamada rejoined that this was a recipe for the party to become absorbed by United Russia and to sacrifice its ability to mobilize pro-democracy sentiment in Russia. Accordingly, she made known her own interest in challenging Putin in the presidential race. Chubais, however, had the most control over the party's leadership and ensured that SPS, at a pre-election convention, nominated no one for president and did not even endorse Khakamada. Khakamada ran anyway, and after receiving about 4 percent of the vote and coming in fourth place out of six candidates, she announced that she was leaving SPS to form her own party, first known as the "Free Russia Party" and then as the "Our Choice" party.

Yabloko

Yabloko's most valuable starting political capital consisted of the personal reputation of its leader, Grigory Yavlinsky.[87] Yavlinsky became widely known in 1990 when he was a deputy prime minister in Yeltsin's Russia. A young economist, he was reputed to have been the main author of the famous 500-Day Plan, a package of economic reforms for which Yeltsin lobbied loudly and which Gorbachev at one point advocated before giving in to the opposition of his prime minister, Nikolai Ryzhkov. When Gorbachev effectively torpedoed the plan, Yavlinsky resigned his post in Yeltsin's government. He reappeared immediately after the August 1991 putsch, however, when Gorbachev and Yeltsin confirmed him as the deputy head of the "interim" USSR government, the Committee on the Operational Management of the National Economy. During this time, Yavlinsky consistently spoke out for the economic need to maintain the unity of the USSR and proposed a series of policy documents intended to achieve this. His stands on the economy and the union brought him into opposition with his former patron, Yeltsin, and the latter's new premier, Gaidar, who had embarked on his own economic reform package without paying so much as lip service to Yavlinsky. After the USSR finally collapsed, Yavlinsky achieved a bit of notoriety by sending his team of economists to work on economic reforms in Russia's third-largest city, Nizhnii Novgorod.

These well-known programmatic stands proved to be promising ones in late 1993. Many Russians favored market-oriented reforms and opposed communism but lamented the rise of new borders within the USSR's geographic space and suffered severely during the economic collapse brought on by the Gaidar reforms. At a time when many Russians were disgusted with the Yeltsin administration's tendency to use brute force in matters of politics and economics despite its democratic rhetoric, Yavlinsky presented voters with the notion that reforms could be undertaken more democratically, more honestly, and more effectively, with an emphasis on human rights. At this time, he was also seen as someone with government experience, having served under both Yeltsin and Gorbachev and then having worked with Nizhnii Novgorod's regional government. As a result, Yavlinsky was found to be the third most trusted politician in Russia in mid-October 1993, trailing Gaidar by less than two percentage points (see Table 2.2).

He initially possessed very little administrative capital, however. Since running afoul of Yeltsin and Gaidar in 1991, Yavlinsky had little direct connection to state authorities outside of Nizhnii Novgorod. Likewise, he possessed no nationwide organization of any kind prior to Yeltsin's call for snap elections in September 1993, having not previously been engaged in mass politics.

[87] For more details on the points made here about Yabloko, see Hale 2004d.

Yabloko was thus built in great haste. Yavlinsky's strategy for party-building during this short campaign period was to capitalize on his chief asset, reputation, to cobble together an organization that was little more than the bare minimum needed to field a party list based on strong ideational content. Essentially, this meant rounding up as many advocates of free markets and democracy as possible who had been left out of Russia's Choice or otherwise alienated by the Gaidar and Chernomyrdin reform efforts. Yabloko's core leadership thus came from: a group of economists that he knew personally, a collection of economists and businessmen linked to economist Ivan Grachev, scholars at an institute run by the former dissident Viacheslav Igrunov, the free-market and St. Petersburg-based Regional Party of the Center, a set of leader-oriented micro-parties, and a few other prominent individuals such as former Russian ambassador to the US Vladimir Lukin and corruption-fighter Yury Boldyrev. The name Yabloko, which means "apple" in Russian, was thus originally an acronym for the official label, "Bloc: Yavlinsky-Boldyrev-Lukin." By virtue of his bloc's pro-market stance, Yavlinsky was able to secure backing from some important emerging banks, notably Most Bank (run by Vladimir Gusinsky, with whom Yavlinsky was personally close) and Menatep Bank (which was run by Khodorkovsky and provided Yabloko's offices with copy machines, fax machines, and other supplies).[88]

As befit a party with substantial ideational but little administrative capital, Yabloko's strategy for the fall of 1993 was not to meld these disparate forces into a programmatic political party with nationwide organization but to concentrate heavily on the central media campaign so as to win a large fraction in the party-list voting. Yabloko's 1993 campaign was regarded by observers as being effectively on-message but underorganized.[89] The message was sharply focused: A market economy could be introduced into Russia rapidly without the disastrous short-term results of the Gaidar-Chernomyrdin reforms. In his television spots, Yavlinsky proved to be an effective communicator. For example, in one of these Yavlinsky explained in very simple terms why there was inflation and how one could get rid of it. High prices, he averred, were being instituted by monopolists and the way to reduce prices was to create more competition in the economy, breaking up the giant concerns that Chubais had been planning to privatize intact.[90] Given that Gaidar and his colleagues made little attempt to explain market economics in terms average people could understand, this approach was effective. Yabloko probably undersold itself, however, since it actually avoided many campaign appearances on the theory that, in the words of its campaign manager, "the more rarely we appeared, the less the electorate would get sick of us." Thus, while

88 Johnson 2000, p. 117.

89 Treisman 1998a, pp. 154–5.

90 Yabloko spot broadcast on RTR, December 3, 1993, 19:10 Bashkortostan time.

Yavlinsky performed well when he performed, he actually turned down 87 requests by journalists for interviews and held not a single press conference for a whole month during the height of the campaign.[91] So, although Yabloko was not able to translate Yavlinsky's preelection status as Russia's third most popular politician into a third-place finish, its ability to play to its reputational strengths was sufficient to win 8 percent of the party-list ballots and six district seats.

Between 1993 and 1999, Yabloko prioritized the development of its ideational capital and only secondarily worked to cultivate administrative capital.[92] While the party did start building regional organization in 1994, it aimed not for mass membership but rather for small cadres of committed party loyalists who shared Yabloko ideals. Its priority was strengthening these ideals. Primarily, this meant substantiating its central claim that Yeltsin's path to the market was not the only one available. Yabloko churned out mountains of "alternative" bills and budgets, proposing complete and concrete packages of legislation that stood in contrast to government initiatives. Yavlinsky also demonstratively opposed many Yeltsin economic policies and regularly blasted what his party portrayed as corruption in the government. While such stands appealed strongly to Russian intelligentsia and professionals who had suffered most from Yeltsin's economic reforms, they left the party vulnerable to the critique from Gaidar loyalists that Yabloko was little but a talking shop that lacked the will or capacity to do the dirty work involved in actually trying to get something done in Russia. Yabloko also took a strong stand in 1995 against the Chechen war that Yeltsin had launched in late 1994. The result was something of a "wash" in the 1995 campaign: Yabloko cleared the 5 percent barrier again but did not win substantially more votes in the party-list contest. Although it netted more ballots than in 1993, the fact that more voters participated in the election meant that it got just 7 percent of the party-list vote. Its 14 district seats, however, represented a doubling of its 1993 result.

But while the 7 percent showing in 1995 represented a 1 percent drop from 1993, it was enough to make Yabloko one of only four parties to clear the 5 percent threshold and the only clearly liberal party to do so. Yabloko's stock began to soar as observers regarded it as having attained critical political mass, frequently predicting that it could win between 20 and 30 percent of the vote in future elections and that Yavlinsky might be able to trade in this performance for an appointment as prime minister under Yeltsin's successor.[93] High-level politicians showed unprecedented interest in aligning with the party, culminating in Sergei Stepashin's summer 1999 decision – just

[91] Treisman 1998a, pp. 150, 153–4.

[92] On Yabloko's challenges as a democratic opposition, see Gel'man 1999.

[93] For example, see McFaul 1997b; Sergei Mulin, *Segodnia*, August 30, 1999, p. 1, cited in Colton and McFaul 2003, p. 140; Rutland 1999.

days after the increasingly popular politician had been removed as prime minister by Yeltsin – to run as the number-two candidate on Yabloko's party list, behind Yavlinsky.

Yabloko lost nearly all of this, however, as a result of its disastrous election campaign of 1999.[94] Yabloko made two core mistakes in this contest. First, it treated Stepashin not as a partner but as a way to counter the charge that Yabloko's party list lacked governing experience and thus made little effort to integrate him into any process of crafting a single, coherent party message. This would not have been a likely problem if no extraordinary events had occurred during the campaign, since Stepashin had effectively agreed to back Yabloko's program on the key issues of economics and corruption. But unfortunately for Yabloko, when Putin suddenly launched his major military operation in Chechnya, Stepashin and Yavlinsky found themselves issuing contradictory public statements. Second, Yavlinsky himself failed to take the kind of strong anti-violence stand that would have been most consistent with Yabloko's stock of ideational capital, which involved a tradition of speaking out for civil liberties and human rights and against abuses by the state. Afraid that opposing the surge in nationalist public sentiment accompanying the war would cost him votes, he combined his call for negotiations with an ultimatum: If the weak Chechen government did not fulfill a list of effectively impossible conditions, civilians would be evacuated and Russia would unleash a relentless bombing campaign. As a result, during the fall 1999 campaign, 45 percent of Russian voters reported that they did not know what Yabloko's position on Chechnya was, while 32 percent believed Yabloko had taken a *hard* line. Only 14 percent interpreted Yabloko's autumn statements and actions as indicating a dovish stance.[95] Since no other major party had dared to oppose the war, Yabloko thus sacrificed the possibility of a "peace vote" that by most measures could have been between 15 and 30 percent. Worse for Yabloko was what its indecision said about the party's capacity to govern, points driven home brutally by Chubais against Yavlinsky in perhaps the most dramatic debate of the campaign. Thus, not only did Yabloko fail to stand out on the issue of Chechnya, but only 2 percent of the population believed that Yabloko was the party most competent to handle the problem.[96] Thanks to these and related problems, Yabloko squeaked back into the parliament in 1999 with just 6 percent of the party-list vote and only four district seats, while SPS leapfrogged ahead to become the strongest of the self-proclaimed liberal parties in the Duma.

The repercussions of that campaign were felt far beyond 1999, leading ultimately to Yabloko's failure to clear the 5 percent hurdle in 2003. After

[94] For detailed documentation, see Hale 2004d.

[95] Colton and McFaul 2003, pp. 156, 290.

[96] Ibid., p. 159.

Yabloko had squandered such promise, few analysts between 1999 and 2003 gave it any chance of winning much more than 5 percent of the vote in the 2003 Duma elections. Whereas early 1999 had seen an influx of major independent leaders attempting to get on Yabloko's bandwagon, such instances were few and far between leading up to 2003. With elite funders less confident in a Yabloko victory, the party wound up in significant financial difficulties. These were magnified when Putin's authorities began prosecuting Gusinsky, one of Yabloko's traditional big sponsors. This rendered the party highly dependent on Khodorkovsky, Yabloko's other traditional big sponsor. The newly vulnerable Yabloko eagerly sought a good working relationship with Putin, frequently cooperating with him on certain legislative initiatives. In fact, senior Yabloko officials averred that Putin himself had asked Khodorkovsky's group to continue financing Yabloko.

All this played out in a most unfortunate way for Yabloko in the 2003 Duma campaign. In late October, just before the official television campaign began, state authorities arrested Khodorkovsky. Not only was Yabloko's primary source of funding disrupted, but the arrest also called attention to the fact that the "anti-oligarch" Yabloko had in fact been financed by the largest of oligarchs. Hovering precariously around the 5 percent mark in the polls, Yabloko engaged in a last-ditch effort to salvage the campaign by adopting a strikingly conciliatory stand on the immensely popular Putin. This effort culminated in the final weeks of the campaign, when state-controlled television news aired highly positive prime-time footage of Yavlinsky working with Putin and other Yabloko officials collaborating with Putin associates. This, combined with the public discussions of Yabloko's relationship with Khodorkovsky, seemed to fly in the face of Yabloko's traditional reputation as an uncompromising force for competitive markets, human rights, and democracy. After Yabloko won just 4 percent of the vote and four district seats in 2003, Yavlinsky did return more forcefully to traditional Yabloko values, loudly opposing authoritarian trends under Putin. As part of this rebuilding strategy, and dreading another defeat, the party decided to sit out the 2004 presidential race entirely, explaining the decision as a sign of protest against what its leaders decried as the election's undemocratic nature.

Fourth-Round Successes

The Communist Party of the Russian Federation (KPRF)

Although it might be tempting to dispense with a discussion of the Communist Party of the Russian Federation as uninteresting if we regard its administrative and ideational capital as being simply inherited from the Communist Party of the Soviet Union, it is important to recognize that the KPRF was not the direct or unchallenged heir to the USSR's Communist mantle. Yeltsin had banned the Russian branch of the CPSU and confiscated its property back in 1991 for allegedly participating in the August putsch.[97] The ban splintered Russian communists, with multiple groups of former members founding their own "successor" organizations. In December 1992, Russia's Constitutional Court effectively reinstated the Communist Party, but there was no agreement on which of the self-proclaimed successor organizations should properly inherit this title.

Several claimants would seem to have had particularly strong cases. One was the first secretary of the Communist Party of Russia at the time of the ban, Valentin Kuptsov. Another was the set of nearly 70 deputies in the Russian Congress who had remained loyal to the communist cause, the most prominent leader among them being Ivan Rybkin.[98] As it turned out, however, neither of these men was able to take the lead.

The most powerful claim came to be primarily associated with Gennady Zyuganov. A former teacher, Zyuganov had made his career in the fields of ideology and propaganda within the CPSU, ultimately rising to the rank of Politburo member in the CPSU's Russian branch.[99] An author of the August 1991 coup-plotters' manifesto, he was best known for holding leadership posts in a number of nationalist "patriotic" organizations in 1992–3, most notably serving as cochair of the union of leftists and hard-line nationalists known as the National Salvation Front.[100] This latter movement advocated setting up tribunals for the Yeltsin "occupation government" and using force to bring the former Soviet republics to heel.[101] While Yeltsin outlawed the National Salvation Front in October 1992, citing its call for the removal of the president and parliament and "destabilizing" rhetoric, it was widely perceived as a major political force at the time.[102] One poll reported by the main state-run television network found that 15 percent of the population supported the National Salvation Front, compared with 39 percent for Yeltsin.[103] Even after Yeltsin had banned it, the Front was able to mobilize some 20,000 people in Moscow for a rally.[104] As Veljko Vujacic has documented, Zyuganov complemented these organizational alliances with an effort to craft a public ideology of nationalist socialism, for which he successfully gained great notoriety within leftist and "patriotic" circles.[105] Thus, while others had more direct claim to the CPSU's organizational and leftist ideational legacy, Zyuganov personified an alternative path for the

97 *Vedomosti RSFSR*, 1991, no. 35, pp. 1426–7, 1434–5; *Vedomosti RSFSR*, 1991, no. 45, pp. 1799–1800.
98 Urban and Solovei 1997.
99 Davidheiser 1998.
100 *Izvestiia*, November 19, 1993, p. 4; Urban and Solovei 1997.
101 *Den'*, October 25–31, 1992; *Izvestiia*, October 26, 1992, p. 4.
102 *Nezavisimaia Gazeta*, October 30, 1992, p. 1.
103 *Itogi*, First Channel, October 24, 1992, 22:00 Moscow time.
104 *Nezavisimaia Gazeta*, November 11, 1992, p. 1.
105 Ansell and Fish 1999; Vujacic 1996.

revived communist organization, one aiming to unite both communists and nationalists.[106]

After the court ruling, Kupstov quickly convened an Initiative Committee, which then called a Party Congress for February 1993 to revive the party formally.[107] Over the objections of some, Kuptsov withdrew his own leadership claim in favor of Zyuganov's since the activity of the National Salvation Front had demonstrated that patriotic ideas were capable of mobilizing large segments of the population. Delegates then elected Zyuganov first secretary of the new party, which took on the formal name Communist Party of the Russian Federation. Some radical leftists refused to join, rejecting the nationalist turn. Viktor Tiulkin, for example, formed the Russian Communist Workers' Party and the coup-plotting former KGB chief, Anatoly Kriuchkov, founded the Russian Party of Communists. Ironically, however, Yeltsin himself helped lock in the KPRF's claim to the communist brand by scheduling elections so soon after his surprise September 1993 decree disbanding the Congress; since none of the other communist organizations had the time to meet all the registration requirements, the KPRF became the only communist party on the ballot.

Having sorted out leadership and the direction in which it would develop ideational capital, the party then turned to administrative capital.[108] One of the party's chief starting assets was, of course, what remained of the CPSU's extensive organizational networks. At the very first stage, Kuptsov and his colleagues essentially recognized anyone who could present a party card from the old Communist Party as a "Communist" with the right to join a local initiative group that would then send a delegation to the "re-founding" party congress.[109] In many cases, regional networks had remained effectively in place after the ban, having simply changed their names to avoid prosecution.[110] Since the Yeltsin regime remained virulently anticommunist, the KPRF received little friendly coverage on state-owned television in 1993 and bore the brunt of much critical attention.

The KPRF managed a clearly focused and issue-based "founding campaign" in 1993, getting its message out primarily through a massive grassroots effort and the appearances on television and in newspapers that election law granted to all parties.[111] Zyuganov and his colleagues blasted Yeltsin and his governments, calling for the following: civil accord and legality (a reference to Yeltsin's violent and illegal dissolution of the Congress); rejection

[106] Ansell and Fish 1999.

[107] *RFE/RL, Inc.* [Newsline], no. 13, 1993.

[108] On the organizational and ideological development of the KPRF, see March 2002.

[109] Interview with the first secretary of the Leningrad Oblast Committee of the KPRF, March 23, 1999; Urban and Solovei 1997, p. 49.

[110] Interview with a leading Bashkortostan KPRF official, March 11, 1999.

[111] Davidheiser 1998, pp. 183–4.

of the Gaidar-Chernomyrdin economic reforms; active state intervention in the economy; "extreme" measures to battle crime and corruption; restoring extensive social services to workers; the priority of state over private property; a more nationalist foreign policy; and restoration of some form of union among the former Soviet republics.[112] At the local level, while most party activists were happy with the message, many were so unhappy with Yeltsin's unilateral imposition of political institutions that they chose to boycott the election so as not to confer legitimacy on Yeltsin's actions. Despite this, the Communist Party scored 12 percent of the party-list vote and its nominees won 10 district seats in 1993, making it the third-largest bloc in the Duma.

The KPRF built on this success in 1995 and 1999 largely by doing more of the same. Its 12 percent in the 1993 party-list race demonstrated that it had reached critical political mass. The party thus came to attract new members who had previously doubted its electoral prospects as well as new supporters looking to back a winner, including some big businesses desiring influence in the Duma. In the 1995 parliamentary election, therefore, the party nearly doubled its result, obtaining 22 percent of the party-list vote even though other communist parties (such as Tiulkin's) were also on the ballot. It also gained 58 district seats, almost three times more than any other party. This momentum continued throughout the next four years, during which time the KPRF consistently outpolled every other party by a large margin. After its 1995 success, the party attracted substantial financial support from such major financial-industrial groups as Gazprom, LUKoil, Vladimir Potanin's Interros, and Khodorkovsky's Menatep, all hoping for good relations with what was expected to be the Duma's largest fraction.[113] While a few prominent leaders broke with the KPRF prior to the 1999 election after losing battles for top spots on the party list, the party brought in many others. Its 1999 campaign followed the usual script, relying primarily on a grass-roots effort while making use of the limited free television time that Russian campaign law provided to all parties. Its campaign was familiar and stayed on-message; even on the unexpected issue of Chechnya, the Communists took a stand that resonated with their stock of ideational capital, blaming the whole crisis on the government's failure to provide economic development for the renegade region.[114] The KPRF thus registered its strongest party-list showing ever in 1999, claiming 24 percent of the vote, and won 46 seats in the district competitions. The party continued to poll between 20 and 30 percent through the fall of 2003, when the next campaign began, and was almost universally expected to repeat its performances of 1995 and 1999.

112 *Izvestiia*, November 19, 1993, p. 4; *Sovetskaia Bashkiriia*, December 12, 1993, p. 2.

113 Kolmakov 2003.

114 *Polit.Ru*, October 5, 1999, 17:54; *ITAR-TASS*, November 16, 1999.

The party attempted this same winning formula again in 2003, but one critical set of factors had changed: the Kremlin now had a strong party in the form of United Russia and had decided to pull out all the superpresidential stops so as to ensure it a major victory. This meant, in part, a doublebarreled assault on United Russia's strongest rival, which the Communist Party was. One "barrel" was state-owned television, which directed negative attention to the KPRF as never before in a Duma race. Nightly news programs skewered the self-proclaimed workers' party for hypocrisy and corruption in accepting money from big business and naming several millionaires to top spots on its party list. When prosecutors on the eve of the campaign arrested Khodorkovsky, whose business associates had long helped finance the KPRF, top party leadership was put in the very awkward position of having to defend its acceptance of big-business financing while the government claimed the mantle of the country's chief opponent of oligarchic vice. The second Kremlin barrel was the financing and even creation of a set of leftist "decoy" parties designed to catch the votes that the media attack was designed to shake loose from the KPRF; these parties reportedly included not only the Agrarian Party mentioned above, but the Motherland bloc to be discussed below. Television would thus report on Communist Party corruption and then interview people who identified themselves as communists saying that they were coming to see Motherland as a truer, uncorrupted representative of communist ideals.

Failing to realize the seriousness of the attacks, the KPRF did not mobilize strongly or effectively to counter them; the party even decided not to participate in the highest-profile televised debates (hence ceding the "leftist" corner to Motherland) in response to United Russia's own refusal to debate. The result was crushing for the KPRF, which was reduced to just 13 percent of the party-list vote and a stunningly small set of just 12 district victories for its nominees.

With the initial preelection polls indicating Zyuganov would fare far worse in the March 2004 presidential race than he had in either 2000 or 1996, the Communist leader declined to be his party's standard-bearer in the contest for Russia's top post. Instead, the party nominated someone who even some party insiders characterized as a colorless figure with no chance to compete with Putin, Nikolai Kharitonov. Kharitonov, in fact, was not even a party member although he was the head of the consistently pro-Communist faction in the Agrarian Party and had run regularly on the KPRF list in Duma elections. His primary goal as presidential nominee, most observers agreed, was to reaffirm the party's status as Russia's number-two party (which he did by winning 14 percent of the vote) while sparing Zyuganov the humiliation of a crushing loss to Putin. As a pro-Zyuganov figure, Kharitonov's participation also ensured that Zyuganov's real rivals in the KPRF did not get the nomination and use it to take over the party. These rivals, notably the "red millionaire" Gennady Semigin, attempted a takeover during the party's summer 2004 convention and claimed to be successful, but Russia's Ministry of Justice ruled that Zyuganov's forces had actually won and awarded continued control of the brand to the KPRF's long-time leader. Zyuganov remained at the party's helm through mid-2005.

The Liberal Democratic Party of Russia (LDPR)

The exact nature of Vladimir Wolfovich Zhirinovsky's starting capital remains shrouded in mystery. What is clear is that Zhirinovsky himself proved to be an extraordinarily charismatic politician, known for his "common touch" on the hustings and his ability to capture and manipulate the anger and ennui fermenting within a vast population of male residents in Russia's small, depressed cities. Prior to 1993, he had also cultivated a strong ideational reputation for advocating tough law-and-order policies, territorial expansion, and a pragmatic (noncommunist, non-Gaidar) approach to economic reform.[115] Zhirinovsky first gained visibility in 1991, when he contested the Russian presidency and shocked observers by finishing as high as third place with 8 percent of the vote. Ever since this time, he has been one of the best-known politicians in Russia.

Many observers, however, have suggested that Zhirinovsky owed a greater debt to a different form of starting political capital: ties to hard-line, antidemocratic Soviet structures, if not to the KGB itself.[116] While accounts differ as to whether Zhirinovsky was a career agent or only turned to hard-line state organs in order to obtain the administrative capital necessary to succeed as party-builder, the logic is essentially that conservative Soviet forces sought to use Zhirinovsky covertly as an *agent provocateur* with the aim of discrediting the very idea of multiparty democracy in its early stages.[117] While Zhirinovsky denies these accounts, his career path, including various foreign jobs and mastery of five languages, is consistent with KGB links.[118] As independent pro-democracy organizations began to sprout during Gorbachev's perestroika period, Zhirinovsky was repeatedly forced out of or barred from joining various pro-democracy movements on suspicion of being a KGB agent. He wound up cofounding the Liberal Democratic Party of the Soviet Union (LDPSU) in 1990 and quickly took control after a power struggle with his original partner, Vladimir Bogachev.[119] Interestingly, this party's activity was widely covered by conservative media that did not tend to pay attention to parties other than the CPSU.[120] This party was renamed the Liberal Democratic Party of Russia after the Soviet Union collapsed.

115 On the LDPR's ideology and its role in the party's development, see Hanson 1998, 2003.

116 McFaul and Markov 1993, pp. 243–5; Umland 1997.

117 See Korguniuk 1999, pp. 287–91; McFaul and Markov 1993, p. 243.

118 Belin and Orttung 1997, p. 49.

119 Korguniuk 1999, pp. 287–91; Davidheiser 1998, p. 188.

120 Fish 1995, p. 123.

Wherever he got his starting material resources, Zhirinovsky capitalized on his personal charisma and attention-getting ideas by running a remarkably well organized and tactically savvy 1993 campaign.[121] While all parties were guaranteed a significant amount of television airtime by law, Zhirinovsky bought nearly three additional hours on the two nationwide networks with the largest audiences in an effort to be on the air as much as possible. He seemed to appear every evening in an address to voters, each one beginning with a lucid explication of a topical issue but ending with Zhirinovsky working himself (and many viewers) into what Evelyn Davidheiser called a "righteous rage." While the ads had something of a willy-nilly character and often seemed purely insane to Westerners, many Russians saw a fairly coherent set of themes based on principles of nationalism, authoritarianism, and noncommunist government for the common man. Some appearances sought primarily to grab the attention of this "common man" by providing entertaining viewing. His call for lower vodka prices, for example, certainly had this effect. He surely attracted an even more rapt audience by devoting one of his thematic broadcasts to sexuality. According to his sexual history of Russia, Bolshevism was rape, Stalinism was "man abusing man," Brezhnevism was masturbation, and Gorbachev and Yeltsin were just plain impotence. What was needed, he then rumbled, was Zhirinovsky! Lending his campaign a sense of closeness to the masses, Zhirinovsky presented his contact telephone number during almost every appearance and regularly encouraged voters to come see him personally at Saturday rallies at the Sokolniki subway stop in a working-class sector of Moscow.

Not even included in the questionnaires of many initial polls, the LDPR surged into the lead during the very last week of the 1993 Duma campaign. The Kremlin's last-minute effort to direct the media against the LDPR actually served to establish the LDPR as the party most feared by the Kremlin.[122] This played right into Zhirinovsky's hands since he was aiming to tap a well of deep popular anger that had accumulated at Yeltsin. Zhirinovsky then rode a giant protest vote into first place in the party-list competition on election day, garnering a stunning 23 percent of the ballots cast, far outpacing the second-place Russia's Choice.[123] The Colton-Hough election survey, taken after the voting, found that Zhirinovsky had indeed connected with his target electorates. Colton describes these voters as consisting mostly of "villagers and small town dwellers, blue-collar workers, the poorly educated, ethnic Russians in the oblasts and krais, the Orthodox devout, provincials from

[121] Information on the campaign comes from the author's own observations (including the following political advertisement broadcasts: First Channel, November 26, 1993, 20:15 Bashkortostan time; RTR, November 29, 1993, 23:30 Bashkortostan time; First Channel, November 29, 1993, 21:45 Bashkortostan time; First Channel, December 10, 1993, 22:15 Bashkortostan time) and Davidheiser 1998.

[122] McFaul 1998, p. 131.

[123] Davidheiser 1998.

the European South, the young, males, and persons who had been outside the CPSU under Soviet rule." Its voters were also decidedly anti-Yeltsin.[124] While the party came in first place in only five district contests and thus finished just behind Russia's Choice in the overall tally of Duma seats, the election was widely interpreted as an LDPR landslide.

The Liberal Democrats plowed much of the spoils of their success into organizational investments. Qualifying for large numbers of state-funded regional parliamentary reception offices and staff, the LDPR aggressively used these as local party headquarters throughout Russia. The LDPR also made active use of the opportunity to provide constituent services, holding regular reception hours at local branches during which the public could come by for free legal advice or help in resolving various personal issues. The regional structures it set up were to be tightly disciplined, with the central organization requiring each branch to fill out detailed forms reporting its activities and to implement strictly any decisions made by Zhirinovsky. The party accepted virtually all comers as members.[125] In this early stage, Zhirinovsky engaged in regional party-building personally and energetically; one individual who had signed up for the LDPR in 1993 reported that he originally suspected that his friends were playing a joke on him when his wife answered the phone one day and told him that a "Vladimir Wolfovich" wanted to talk to him. But it turned out to be the party leader himself encouraging him to help lead the new local branch.[126]

When the 1995 Duma elections came around, Zhirinovsky used essentially the same campaign formula, targeted at the same sorts of disgruntled and usually apolitical voters. The personality of Zhirinovsky was front and center, mocking the establishment and aiming for attention by any means possible. At one point he tossed a glassful of orange juice on the reformist Nizhnii Novgorod Governor Boris Nemtsov during a live television debate. In a precampaign Duma session (September 9, 1995), he actually engaged a female Duma deputy in a physical fight caught by television cameras.[127] On the hustings, he gave out samples of new brands of vodka and beer named after himself. While the party could not repeat its first-place finish of 1993, it still came in second with 11 percent of the party-list vote; it won only one district seat, however.

Whereas some observers interpreted Zhirinovsky's 6 percent showing in the 1999 Duma competition as evidence of his party's inexorable decline, in reality the problem was a more contingent one of campaign strategy

[124] Colton 1998a.

[125] Interview with the coordinator of a district LDPR organization in St. Petersburg and a Duma assistant to Zhirinovsky, February 23, 1999.

[126] Interview with a senior official of the Bashkortostan organization of the LDPR, March 11, 1999.

[127] Belin and Orttung 1995, pp. 50–51.

and relations with the Central Election Commission (CEC). First, in what appeared to be a fund-raising move, his party nominated people reputed to be major organized crime figures, including two with underworld nicknames, *Avera* and *Mikhas*, and one for whom an arrest warrant had actually been issued for contract murder.[128] This provoked the CEC to disqualify the party on the grounds that key figures had failed fully to report personal assets as required by law. While Zhirinovsky did regroup by successfully registering a shortened and cleaned-up new list under a new name, the Zhirinovsky Bloc, this cost a significant degree of campaign time and forced him to devote many party advertising spots just to explaining the name change. Additionally, many observers concluded that Vladimir Putin, by sending the military into Chechnya while using gangland language to describe what he would do to the terrorists, stole much of Zhirinovsky's nationalist thunder and transferred it via endorsement to the upstart Unity Bloc.

When it was free to run its usual high-energy campaign in 2003, however, the LDPR surged back into prominence. Wasting no opportunity to appear on television, Zhirinovsky openly called for a "police state," growled that other former Soviet states would "pay" for mistreating ethnic Russians, and advocated the "very harshest treatment" of oligarchs and bureaucrats. He verbally savaged virtually any party representative that opposed him in a debate and provoked a fistfight after one particularly heated encounter on national TV. Rather than oppose Putin, he stated that he considered himself simply a tougher version of the president. Anticipating the Communists' woes, the LDPR targeted their voters, in part by adding "we are for the poor" to its standard slogans and leaning more to the left than in the past.[129] The party received remarkably favorable treatment on state-controlled media, reinforcing the interpretation that the LDPR was at least tacitly state-supported. Indeed, many observers noted that the party had very frequently sided with the Kremlin on important votes during previous Duma sessions. By election day 2003, Zhirinovsky's organization had surged to 11 percent of the party-list vote, although as in 1999 it failed to win any district seats. Sticking with his refusal to compete against Putin, the LDPR's leader declined to throw his own hat into the ring for the presidency in the 2004 elections, instead tossing in the headcovering of his bodyguard, Oleg Malyshkin, who proceeded to come in fifth place out of six candidates with 2 percent of the ballots.

Party Upstarts: Trying to Crash the Party

Numerous parties and proto-parties have attempted to join the club of major parties since the 1993 elections, but they have found it very hard to nudge

[128] *Izvestiia*, October 5, 1999.

[129] Interview with a senior member of the LDPR parliamentary delegation, October 29, 2003.

their way in. As the notions of founding elections and critical political mass imply, once a party system is formed, it becomes very difficult for a party to jump in and establish itself. The vast majority of such efforts have failed, many of which were among the 43 parties that ended up on the 1995 party-list ballot for the Duma. A few, however, have succeeded; the key is that the starting political capital required for success in such efforts is much higher than in founding elections. While campaigns can still break party-building projects, rarely do they make them. The following paragraphs illustrate this briefly by examining six attempts to "crash the party" in 1995. One attempt, Our Home is Russia, was successful that year but petered out by 1999. Two others, the Rybkin Bloc and General Lebed's movement, began with high expectations but stumbled once out of the gate, never reaching critical political mass. The fourth, Motherland, succeeded in the most recent election, 2003. The most important party-crashers of all, however, have been Fatherland–All Russia and Unity, which later merged to become United Russia. Since these represent special cases that are central to the argument of this volume, they are treated only briefly here before being considered in more depth in Chapter 5.

Our Home is Russia and the Rybkin Bloc

After the failure of Russia's Choice and PRES to win a majority in the first Duma, Yeltsin and his team opted for a new "parties of power" strategy in the 1995 elections. As described above, the failure of Russia's Choice to meet initial expectations cost it Yeltsin's confidence. Furthermore, Russia's Choice in late 1994 and early 1995 opposed Yeltsin's decision to launch the first war in Chechnya, further alienating some of the president's most fervent supporters in and around the government. Yeltsin thus opted to hedge his bets in 1995 by sponsoring two parties of power that aimed to become the basis of a two-party system in Russia. Announced by the president on April 25, one bloc would be slightly right-of-center and would back the government, whereas the other would be slightly left-of-center in order to serve as a "loyal opposition."[130]

The left-of-center bloc was a nonstarter.[131] Yeltsin had announced that it would be led by Duma Speaker Ivan Rybkin. Rybkin had been coleader of the Communist fraction in the Russian Congress of People's Deputies and became an early leader of the KPRF but ran for the Duma in 1993 on the Agrarian Party ticket, where he won a parliamentary seat. He then became speaker of the Duma by building a broad coalition of opposition parties, including the Communists, Agrarians, Women of Russia, the Democratic Party, and even the LDPR. The Kremlin quickly managed to lure him out of hard opposition, however, as he declared after becoming speaker

130 Belin and Orttung 1997, p. 32.

131 This paragraph draws heavily on Belin and Orttung 1997, pp. 36–7.

that he would cooperate with the government. Thus, while he was widely known as Duma speaker in 1995, he had sacrificed much of the ideational appeal that he had initially brought to the Duma. He also brought no significant organizational capital to the effort since he had defected from the Communists in 1993, and the Agrarians later expelled him rather than join his bloc. The number-two man on his party list as of August 1995 begged off shortly thereafter. When Yeltsin dubbed Rybkin's new bloc a "loyal" opposition, its credibility as an opposition force was undermined still further. Rybkin himself played right into these difficulties by opting not to develop a clearly expressed ideological line during the campaign, calling only vaguely for slower reforms and more effective welfare programs. Its problems were exemplified by its inability to come up with any name other than the Bloc of Ivan Rybkin, a name which Belin and Orttung wrote "reflected its membership all too accurately."[132] It garnered a pathetic 1 percent of the party-list vote in 1995 and captured just three district seats.

The "right-center" party of power, however, rapidly achieved critical political mass since it was led by Prime Minister Chernomyrdin. Chernomyrdin was not perceived as a radical "shock therapist" but instead as a pragmatic industrialist with a long career in the gas sector, ultimately heading the giant state-run monopoly Gazprom before joining the government. During his time in office between early 1993 and the 1995 elections, certain economic indicators such as inflation had begun to stabilize. While Russia's economy continued its unprecedented decline, Chernomyrdin himself was not blamed nearly so much as were the figures who had started the reforms, notably Gaidar and Yeltsin. The prime minister, then, represented a very impressive starting asset for a party-building project. Joiners could hope to benefit not only from direct access to government, but also from the support of the super-rich Gazprom and even from public association with a moderate, pragmatic approach to reform.

Kremlin insiders quickly went about building the broadest possible organization around the prime minister. They began with a show of government force, mobilizing nearly the entire Russian cabinet.[133] This, together with the prime minister's leadership, made it very easy for the party-builders to line up the support of powerful regional elites. Even where governors themselves declined to formally join, they frequently charged senior deputies in their administrations with building their provinces' party branches. Indeed, in St. Petersburg, the regional Our Home coordinator in 1995 was none other than Mayor Sobchak's second-in-command, one Vladimir Putin.

[132] Belin and Orttung 1997, p. 36.

[133] Exceptions included Russia's Choice loyalists Kozyrev and Chubais and Agrarians Aleksandr Zaveriukha (deputy prime minister) and Aleksandr Nazarchuk (minister of agriculture). See Belin and Orttung 1997, p. 34.

Both Chernomyrdin and Yeltsin set an anti-ideational tone for the campaign in 1995, openly eschewing ideology.[134] In reality, of course, the party was clearly associated in public minds with government performance. This was not a major plus at the time. Yeltsin's own popularity was in the single digits, tainted with blood shed in the Chechen war and the lack of robust improvement in the economy. Accordingly, opposing parties sought to paint Our Home in the most unattractive colors of the Yeltsin administration.[135]

Its 1995 election result was disappointing for those seeking a first-place finish but a success according to the minimal criterion of winning entry into the Duma. Our Home is Russia became the only party in 1995 to break the monopoly on Duma fractions held by parties initially elected in 1993, winning 10 percent of the party-list vote and 10 district seats.

While Our Home's initial strategy of focusing on its administrative assets fit well with its particular stock of starting political capital, it failed to make any investment in building up ideational capital. In fact, it continued even after the Duma elections to denigrate openly any attempt to create an ideational basis for the party. This left Our Home extremely vulnerable to exogenously imposed changes in its own store of administrative assets. Disaster for the party struck when Yeltsin, in a move that surprised most observers, suddenly fired Chernomyrdin as prime minister in March 1998 and replaced him with a political neophyte, Sergei Kirienko. Now the party of power no longer had much real power on which to trade. Our Home's governors found themselves free to seek new alliances, having been bound together by little more than a common desire for access to the prime minister. While the party's young second-in-command, Vladimir Ryzhkov, did proceed to launch an effort to build an ideational foundation for the organization in 1998 and 1999, this proved to be too little, too late. The party thus received only 1 percent of the vote and seven district seats in the 1999 election.

Motherland, the Congress of Russian Communities (KRO), and General Lebed's Parties

In December 2003, the newly created Motherland party surged into the Duma with 9 percent of the party-list vote and victories in eight districts.[136] By the summer of 2004, many pundits were speculating that it could form the basis for a new, moderately leftist party that would supplant the KPRF as Russia's number-two party. To understand this party's starting political capital and just how it was able to pull off the rare accomplishment of

134 The following information on the campaign is taken from Belin and Orttung 1997, pp. 33–6.

135 Belin and Orttung 1997, pp. 34–5.

136 Except where otherwise noted, this section draws on Korguniuk 1999, pp. 273–6, for much of its material prior to the 1999 Duma election.

"crashing the party" in the Duma, we need to go back to 1993 to examine its organizational ancestors. We find that as with almost every other party that has successfully broken into the Duma after 1993, the decisive asset proved to be administrative capital coming from a strong connection to Russia's superpresidency.

Motherland, at least as it existed in 2003–5, is best understood as the political descendant of the Congress of Russian Communities, widely known by its Russian acronym, KRO. Its chief founding entrepreneur was Dmitry Rogozin. He began as a part of what many have called the USSR's "golden youth," the offspring of prominent Soviet officials (in his case, a KGB general according to one source) who inherited insider status and all the accompanying social connections. Starting his career as a foreign correspondent and youth activist, Rogozin had been involved with several Russian proto-parties prior to 1993, but none of these achieved any political success. Astutely recognizing in early 1993 that he possessed neither ideational nor administrative capital in sufficient volume to stand out in a campaign where many others with similar ambitions would be competing, Rogozin launched a movement intended to develop this capital through high-profile work outside of the realm of elections. Trading on one important nationalist issue, his central idea was not simply to lament the poor treatment of ethnic Russians in the "near abroad," but actually to mobilize them to further their own cause, an effort that he hoped would generate attention and cast him as a leading doer of real nationalist deeds. Thus in March 1993, he organized the first Congress of Russian Communities, gathering representatives of ethnic Russian organizations from different former Soviet republics and providing them with a framework for working together to advance their own rights. When Yeltsin called the surprise December 1993 elections, Rogozin attempted to get the Russia-based part of his organization on the ballot under the name "Fatherland," but this effort was premature; he was unable to collect sufficient signatures within Russia proper to register a party list. But "congresses of Russian communities" continued to convene after the 1993 campaign and began to put his organization in the spotlight, especially after Zhirinovsky's surprise victory in the 1993 PR race called attention to nationalist issues.

Pragmatically realizing that he still lacked the personal gravitas for a major political showing, Rogozin traded on his growing reputational and organizational assets in order actively to recruit figures that were more prominent than himself for the 1995 campaign. In 1994, Rogozin succeeded in getting Petr Romanov to accept the leadership of what then became formally known as the organization Congress of Russian Communities. Rogozin retained for himself the chief administrative position in the party. Romanov's accession represented a breakthrough because he was the strong director of the major Yenisei enterprise in Krasnoiarsk and had been touted by some as a potential presidential candidate. Gaining credibility with this acquisition, Rogozin was then able to recruit a bigger prize, former Russian Federation

Security Council chief Yury Skokov. Skokov had been Chernomyrdin's chief rival for prime minister in 1992 and it was widely believed he had the backing of the military-industrial complex in Russia.[137] Skokov replaced Romanov as KRO leader in January 1995.

Most dramatically, this momentum even drew in the biggest hero of those who championed the cause of "Russians in the near abroad," General Aleksandr Lebed. Lebed had led Russia's 14th army in Moldova during that country's civil war in 1992. He stood out for taking it upon himself to fend off Moldovan attempts to reincorporate a Russian-majority splinter of territory known as Transdniestria, whose leaders wanted integration with Russia and feared winding up in a Romanian-dominated country. After resigning from the military, Lebed assumed deputy leadership in KRO in April 1995. Others soon followed him into the movement. One of these was Travkin's successor as leader of the Democratic Party, economist Sergei Glaziev, who brought in a large component of his party's organization to help form KRO's provincial structures. By the time the 1995 campaign started, therefore, KRO possessed not only a clearly expressed nationalist message but significant star power and even some local organization as well. It was widely considered a favorite to hurdle the 5 percent mark in the 1995 party-list contest despite what appeared to be a very crowded field. Observers saw it as a more moderate nationalist alternative to the LDPR, hence capable of stealing away those voters who supported Zhirinovsky in 1993 since his was the only noncommunist nationalist party but who nevertheless did not care for his wild rhetoric and unruly antics.

KRO's campaign strategy, however, largely undermined these aspirations. One blunder involved the choice of figurehead. Instead of putting its most popular figure (Lebed) in the top spot on its party list, the party installed the formal leader, the nondescript Skokov. While Skokov was reasonably well known, his main strength was his authority within the powerful military-industrial sector (and hence an ability to bring in funds for the campaign) and his reputation as a solid manager. He was decidedly uncharismatic as a public figure, portrayed by mass media as a shadowy character who liked to manipulate events behind the scenes. This contrasted sharply with Lebed, whose growling bass and gruff directness had gained him extensive media coverage and popularity during his Moldova activities in 1992. Seen by many as a charismatic no-nonsense outsider capable of cleaning up the mess that Yeltsin's team had made in Russia, Lebed was by the start of the campaign Russia's most popular politician.[138] He was, however, stuck in the party's number-two position during the campaign and accordingly deemphasized. Signaling frustration in this position, Lebed actually launched his own independent political movement, Honor and Motherland, in October 1995, right

[137] Belin and Orttung 1997, p. 51.
[138] Ibid., p. 52.

in the middle of the Duma campaign.[139] Nevertheless, Lebed also remained with KRO through election day.

While it did sound many of the expected themes during the 1995 campaign, KRO (to its credit in moral terms) proved unwilling to play the xenophobic or racist cards very strongly. Thus, at the same time that it called on ethnic Russians to unite in the face of "danger" and appeared with representatives of the Russian Orthodox Church, the party leadership took pains "to define 'Russian' in terms not of race but of acceptance of Russian language, culture, and Orthodoxy."[140] In Bashkortostan, for example, the movement nominated two ethnic Bashkirs to head the local party. This, one republic party leader noted, confused voters who came to vote Russian but then saw Bashkir names on the list.[141] Evidence suggests that this was a widespread phenomenon for KRO.[142]

Belin and Orttung also report that KRO fell victim to what appears to have been a Kremlin "dirty trick" on election day. The microparty Dzhuna, led by faith-healer Yevgeniia Davitashvili, had also included an Aleksandr Ivanovich Lebed (the same full name as the general's) on its party list. The day before the election, this "other Lebed" announced his withdrawal from the race. The Central Election Commission then issued an order to polling places telling them to erase the name "Aleksandr Ivanovich Lebed" from the ballot. KRO candidate Glaziev later complained bitterly that the wrong Lebed was removed in many instances, confusing voters who were primarily drawn to KRO through the retired general.[143]

In the end, however, Belin and Orttung correctly observe that nationalist issues were not the public's chief concern in 1995. This meant that parties campaigning on them had a relatively small pie to divide in their hopes of clearing 5 percent. The major problem for KRO was that the KPRF and the LDPR both had proven records of winning votes on these issues, having back in 1993 achieved critical political mass and sustained it ever since. KRO, then, had very little margin for error. Its poor tactical decision to place Skokov over the popular Lebed, combined with the election-day ballot "mix-up," resulted in a narrow miss for KRO. While its 4.3 percent of the party-list vote and five district victories meant that it was certainly on the verge of breaking into the exclusive club of major Russian parties, it was a failure nevertheless.

As with almost all of the other parties examined above that only barely failed to clear 5 percent, the result for KRO was a split in the organization's leadership that caused long-lasting political damage. Lebed, unhappy even

139 Korguniuk 1999, p. 293.
140 Belin and Orttung 1997, p. 53.
141 Interview with the leader of Honor and Motherland, Bashkortostan branch, April 20, 1999.
142 Belin and Orttung 1997, p. 121.
143 Ibid., p. 135.

before seeing the result, announced his own run for the presidency in the June 1996 election. Skokov initially agreed to back the former general, but Lebed rebuffed him and resigned his official positions within KRO. When Skokov retaliated by ordering the party's local organizations to cease supporting Lebed, Lebed called on them to back him instead and won the endorsement of most. At KRO's May 1996 convention, delegates went further and voted Skokov out of the leadership, bringing Rogozin himself from behind the scenes to serve as formal party leader. Lebed did not return to the fold, however, effectively banishing KRO to a long period in the political wilderness. Other prominent leaders followed; most notably, Glaziev departed KRO to join the party list of the KPRF in the 1999 Duma elections. Rogozin continued his energetic attempts to build alliances with major figures, however, and in early 1999 appeared to have found a place firmly on the political bandwagon of Moscow Mayor Yury Luzhkov in his bid for parliamentary seats and ultimately the presidency. But by mid-1999, Luzhkov expelled KRO from his coalition so as to attract more important allies, the leaders of the ethnic minority republics of Tatarstan and Bashkortostan who considered Rogozin's ethnic-Russian activism anathema. In the end, KRO managed only an alliance with a Yabloko defector, Yury Boldyrev, and won less than 1 percent of the party-list vote and just a single district seat, Rogozin's own.

Meanwhile, Lebed's political star began to rise and he started to trade on his reputation to build party organization independent of KRO. Thus in his 1996 presidential campaign, Lebed proclaimed himself a representative not of KRO but of Honor and Motherland. His fortunes rose dramatically when Kremlin officials, in an initiative spearheaded by influential Yeltsin insider Aleksei Golovkov, decided to support Lebed's campaign financially in order to siphon nationalist votes from Yeltsin's chief rival, Communist leader Zyuganov. That Lebed proceeded to win 15 percent of the ballots in the first round adds credence to the claim that KRO's poor Duma campaign had cost it a leap to major-party status; when Lebed was positioned front-and-center as part of a well-funded campaign, he proved to have the star power to bring in a large share of the vote. After 1996, however, Lebed engaged in a number of questionable party-building moves. For one, in 1997 he created a second organization, the Russian People's Republican Party, which remained separate from Honor and Motherland. For another, while the combination of these two parties won two governorships (Lebed in Krasnoiarsk and Lebed's brother in neighboring Khakasiia) and fractions in several regional legislatures between 1996 and 1998, Lebed declined to run a party list in the 1999 Duma election. Having become mired in his duties as Krasnoiarsk governor, Lebed reportedly feared that a poor showing by his party would damage his own presidential aspirations despite the fact that polls indicated a "Lebed's list" had a good chance of overcoming the 5 percent barrier. When Putin's popularity rose to daunting heights by the end of 1999, Lebed opted not to challenge him in the 2000 presidential race.

Then, in 2002, Lebed perished in a helicopter accident in a remote part of Krasnoiarsk, driving the final nail not only into his own coffin, but also into that of his two parties.

While KRO had widely been considered all but dead by the end of 2002, the core network of leaders upon which it had been based received a new lease on political life as Putin's administration began actively preparing for the 2003 Duma campaign.[144] By the spring of 2003, as previously noted, the Kremlin had decided that one of its chief tactics in the race would be to launch a negative media campaign against the Communists and, critically, to foster a series of decoy parties that could collect those voters who would become newly disenchanted with the KPRF. Putin's chief of staff Aleksandr Voloshin sanctioned a close associate, the campaign strategist Marat Gelman, to begin to organize one of them. Gelman had been a senior campaign strategist for KRO in its 1995 campaign and thus had a history of working with many of the figures in whom the Kremlin was interested.[145] Gelman, through Voloshin, reportedly secured financing from aluminum magnate Oleg Deripaska and the head of the National Reserve Bank, Aleksandr Lebedev.[146] Gelman, who had been deputy general director of the state-owned First Channel television network since 2002, could also offer a party the ability to influence coverage on Russia's most-watched news and analysis programs. According to one insider, the presidential administration originally planned for Gelman's decoy party to attract 3–4 percent of the vote, most of which was intended to come from the KPRF. Extensive public opinion research led the Kremlin by August 2003 to conclude that the prospects were best not for a leftist bloc pure and simple but for a populist party that cast its leftism as a means to regain Russia's greatness in the world economy and the international political arena. This approach, their research showed, appealed to many highly educated voters in big cities, including large numbers employed in Russia's massive military-industrial complex. These voters had regularly cast ballots for the Communists in the past but had done so only because they saw no other strong alternative to the Yeltsin regime (although some had regularly voted for Yabloko).[147]

With massive administrative resources in hand, the Kremlin sought a team of politicians who were in need of administrative capital but whose own ideational capital would mesh well with the Kremlin's effort to woo the aforementioned electorate away from the KPRF. They found their match

[144] The following account is based on interviews in 2003 with several people involved in the United Russia campaign, two analysts in the Motherland campaign who have longstanding close relationships with the principal party leaders, and, where cited, a variety of published sources.

[145] *NovayaGazeta.Ru*, no. 58, August 11, 2003.

[146] See, in part, *RFE/RL Newsline*, August 22, 2003; and *RFE/RL Newsline*, February 3, 2003.

[147] Interview with Leonty Byzov, analyst for Motherland who conducted this research. December 17, 2003.

in the reunion of prominent leaders associated with KRO during its inaugural 1995 campaign. The list's number-one thus became Glaziev who was available after he fell out with the KPRF. Although he had never joined the KPRF, he had been elected to the Duma on its party list in 1999, ran for Kras-noiarsk governor under its banner in 2002, and then attempted to convince the Communists to join a broad coalition of leftist and nationalist forces to run in the 2003 parliamentary contest. During this period of jockeying in 2003, he assumed the leadership of KRO. When the KPRF rebuffed his coalition initiative, Glaziev announced that he would lead his own bloc.[148] As Glaziev personified the sort of national-revival leftism that appealed to the Communist electorate that the Kremlin was targeting, the Putin administration was eager to covertly assist him in this endeavor. While Glaziev cooperated with the Kremlin only because of a contingent confluence of interests, he later reported that Putin personally requested that Rogozin, a more reliably pro-Kremlin figure, be included in the bloc's top leadership.[149] Rogozin, KRO's founding leader, was at the time serving as Russia's envoy to Europe on the status of Kaliningrad and also as chair of the Duma's foreign relations committee with Kremlin support. Skokov and other figures tied closely to KRO were also centrally involved in working out the new bloc's ideology and campaign. This former KRO network thus formed a nucleus towards which other major figures then gravitated. At a founding convention in September 2003, the "Motherland" bloc was thus christened.[150]

Motherland benefited from relatively positive television news coverage while the Communist Party was pilloried daily on the screen, as described earlier. The bloc's ratings began to rise from the 1 percent range after the televised debates began, especially because the KPRF had decided to boycott the most visible debates (those on the NTV network) and thus effectively let Motherland become the only defender of leftist ideas in these forums. Glaziev and especially the razor-tongued Rogozin also proved themselves to be formidable performers. A campaign insider reports that the bloc's breakthrough came in the final few days before the vote, surging above the 5 percent barrier as voters were fleeing the battered KPRF. With Yabloko's campaign also imploding, as described earlier, a top Motherland analyst calculated that a large number of Yavlinsky's traditional voters also switched to Motherland; this helps to explain Yabloko's surprisingly weak performance in major cities, the home of many intelligentsia voters, at the same time that Motherland did very well there, coming in second place to United Russia even in Moscow.[151] In the end, Motherland netted 9 percent of the party-list vote and eight district seats.

[148] *Tovarishch*, August 18, 2003, 17:13.

[149] *Polit.Ru*, February 16, 2004, 14:40; *RFE/RL Newsline*, August 11, 2003.

[150] *Gazeta*, September 15, 2003, p. 4.

[151] Byzov interview 2003.

Following the 2003 Duma election, the party split when Glaziev announced a bid for the presidency. Rogozin opted to back Putin and, with Kremlin support, managed to oust Glaziev as Motherland leader. Glaziev thus came in third in the presidential balloting with about 4 percent of the vote but lost control of his party. While Rogozin was still only beginning the effort to build full-fledged regional party branches as of 2005, some observers were predicting that the Kremlin would continue to sponsor his pliable version of Motherland in an effort to replace the KPRF once and for all as Russia's second-largest party, possibly even grooming Rogozin for the post-Putin presidency.[152]

Fatherland–All Russia, Unity, and United Russia

As will be discussed in more detail in Chapter 5, this set of parties appeared relatively late in Russia's postcommunist history.[153]

Fatherland–All Russia

The first component to emerge was Fatherland, a movement centered primarily around the presidential ambitions of Moscow's Mayor Yury Luzhkov, a figure particularly rich in administrative capital as will be discussed in depth in Chapter 5. Using the bully pulpit provided to him by his mayoral post in Russia's capital city, Luzhkov began also to cultivate some ideational capital, staking out stands on important national issues shortly after Russia's 1996 presidential election. Many of these flirted with ethnic Russian nationalism, asserting a territorial claim on the Russian-populated but Ukrainian city of Sevastopol, threatening to arm Serbia if NATO launched a ground war to protect Kosovo in 1999, and declaring reunification with Russians in neighboring countries to be a national goal. At other times, though, he stressed the need for good relations with the West.[154] He advocated consolidating Russia's 89 regions into 10–13 provinces, implying that there would no longer be federal regions designated as homelands for particular ethnic minorities like the Tatars.[155] He also sought to stake out a "left-center" position between the far-left Communists and the political "right" occupied by the Yeltsin administration and parties like Yabloko and the Union of Right Forces.[156] At one point, he proclaimed British Prime Minister Tony Blair's Labour Party to be a model, advocating "capitalism, but with a very serious system of social support for the people."[157]

152 *RFE/RL Newsline*, May 21, 2004.
153 Parts of this section are drawn from Hale 2004a.
154 *Associated Press*, Moscow, April 17, 1999; *Kommersant*, February 27, 1999, p. 2.
155 *RFE/RL Newsline* 1, no. 147, Part I, October 27, 1997.
156 Luzhkov, Yury. Interview, *Moskovskii Komsomolets*, June 11, 1999; *Itogi*, May 4, 1999.
157 *RFE/RL Newsline* 2, no. 189, Part I, September 30, 1998.

Luzhkov reserved some of his most blistering language for the Yeltsin administration (though usually not the president personally) and the economic policies it had brought to Russia. Pro-Luzhkov media, notably Gusinsky's NTV network, popularized the term "the Family" to refer to Yeltsin's close inner circle, thereby casting them as a mafialike syndicate.[158] In particular, he lambasted economic "shock therapy" and what he said was corrupt privatization that had transferred important state assets to the control of a criminal oligarchy. The state, he declared, should actually renationalize some of these properties, reallocating their shares to those who suffered losses in the process of the original privatization scheme.[159] His opposition to Yeltsin went so far as to lead him to promise that he would eventually take power away from the institution of the presidency, transforming Russia into a parliamentary state.[160]

By the spring of 1999, however, he had largely failed to win the support from other elite groups on which he had been counting and so made a dramatic move. On August 17, 1999, he agreed to subordinate his own presidential ambitions to a more popular leader (Yevgeny Primakov, whom Yeltsin had fired as prime minister as recently as May) and together they consummated an alliance with All Russia, a coalition of governors of some of Russia's most populous and economically powerful regions. The resulting Fatherland–All Russia bloc, which also incorporated parts of the Agrarian Party and Women of Russia along with others, became the early favorite for the December 1999 Duma contest.

Fatherland–All Russia had counted on winning above all by virtue of their leaders' popularity and the ability of prominent coalition members, notably governors, to deliver the vote through their vast stocks of administrative capital (see Chapter 5 for details). Its strategists were largely blindsided, then, when the Kremlin responded to the bloc's anticorruption rhetoric with a blistering media attack on Luzhkov and then, more subtly, on Primakov. As their standing in the polls dropped to less than half their original numbers during the campaign period, the party rather strangely failed to respond in kind. This was not because they had no resources with which to do so. One of Russia's three largest television networks (NTV) was sympathetic to Fatherland–All Russia and Luzhkov's city government actually controlled its own smaller network (TV Center). While the state-owned First Channel and RTR did reach a few regions that NTV and TV Center did not, the decline in support for Luzhkov and Primakov was broadly national in scope, a phenomenon that cannot be explained solely with reference to the geographic reach of these mass media.

158 Mikhail Sokolov, *Izvestiia*, June 9, 1999.

159 *Vremia MN*, June 10, 1999; *Reuters*, October 7, 1998, JRL; *Financial Times*, September 17, 1998.

160 *Novosti*, TV Center, October 30, 1998, 4:45 EDT.

The reasons for the party's nonresponse in the face of attack appear to be twofold. First, the team members were quite overconfident in the sturdiness of their leaders' popularity and did not believe a dip would shake the loyalty of their governors, on whom they were relying to deliver them the vote. As a result, they had not put much thought into developing a plan of counterattack and were caught flat-footed when the media assault against them started to register in the polls and weaken their alliances with governors. Second, Fatherland–All Russia's campaign organization was anything but nimble, consisting of a loose conglomeration of the various organizations that helped to found it. For example, the Primakov and Luzhkov groups in the party never completely merged and often made campaign decisions independently of each other.[161] To make matters worse, campaign chairman Georgy Boos had little campaign experience and had been appointed largely as a compromise figure with ties to both Luzhkov and Primakov. Other key campaign figures also lacked experience and refused to hire outside professionals in order to economize, a decision that looked good when party leaders expected to waltz to an easy victory.[162] In the end, Fatherland–All Russia won just 13 percent of the party-list vote, far below initial expectations, although its nominees did manage to win a respectable 31 district seats.

Unity

Having decided against sanctioning Our Home is Russia as the party of power for a second year in a row, Kremlin officials and their allies spawned a new party, the Unity Bloc, on October 3, 1999. This party had all the administrative capital one would expect from a presidentially sponsored organization, including the direct involvement of the first deputy head of Yeltsin's administration at the time, Igor Shabdurasulov. Various reports indicate that Unity got much of its funding through government structures and even foreign firms connected to "oligarch" Boris Berezovsky, who worked closely with Yeltsin's staff. One magazine reported that Railroads Minister Nikolai Aksenenko was one important source of financing, as was the concern Transneft.[163] Berezovsky, after his postelection falling out with Putin, let slip that Unity had received funding from Swiss firms that had done business with Aeroflot, controlled by Berezovsky.[164] One high-ranking Unity official, however, quickly denied these assertions as politically motivated.[165]

[161] *Moscow News*, October 21, 1999, JRL; *Polit.Ru*, August 6, 1999, 13:58.
[162] *Moscow News*, October 21, 1999, JRL.
[163] *Profil*, October 4, 1999.
[164] *Polit.Ru*, November 15, 2000, 10:08, 20:12.
[165] Ibid., 14:33.

Created less than three months before election day, Unity's organizers had to rush to put together their candidate lists, giving them a rather slapdash character. According to Shabdurasulov, people were considered for inclusion only if they were not professional politicians, had been outside of major past political battles and scandals, and were in positions of high authority.[166] While Putin had not yet formally endorsed the bloc, he nicely summed up this approach to candidate recruitment in an address to regional election commission heads: "We need not professional patriots, but patriotic professionals."[167] They aggressively courted famous personalities, landing on a *troika* (top three) who were almost completely new to electoral politics. Sergei Shoigu, Yeltsin's longest-tenured cabinet member, was the high-profile minister of emergency situations who almost always reached television audiences as a hero working to save people from some sort of natural or human disaster. Second on the list came Aleksandr Karelin, the multiple-gold-medal-winning Greco-Roman wrestler who is something of a cultural icon in Russia. Third was Aleksandr Gurov, famous as a corruption-fighter and battler against mafia structures.[168] Unity's television campaign, then, could pair the following slogans and candidate images to great effect: "Russia must be honest" (Gurov); "Russia must be strong" (Karelin); "Russia must be saved" (Shoigu).[169] This effort to convey strength was reinforced by the coinage of an acronym derived from the bloc's name: "MeDvEd," the Russian word for "bear."[170] The campaign capitalized heavily on ursine symbolism, not only using bears in its ads but sending activists out campaigning in full-body costumes or even with live bears in tow.[171] Given its Kremlin backing, it is hardly surprising that state-owned media gave it a great deal of positive coverage on news and analytical broadcasts.

Unity's campaign themes gave precedence to style but did include some substance to the same extent that Fatherland–All Russia did. As Colton and McFaul observe, "Unity on the stump conveyed an attitude rather than a concrete program," placing no faith in abstract concepts like socialism or capitalism.[172] The party's statements, combined with its support for Russia's government, did connote a slightly right-of-center stand, however. Other concrete positions stressed publicly by Shoigu during the campaign included a hard line on Chechnya, opposition to capital flow restrictions, support for presidentialism, and abolition of party-list voting for the Duma.[173]

166 *Vremia MN*, September 29, 1999.
167 *Polit.Ru*, October 6, 1999, 14:43.
168 *Segodnia*, October 4, 1999.
169 Ad broadcast on First Channel, November 24, 1999, 21:45 Moscow time.
170 Mezhregional'noe Dvizhenie "Edinstvo" (Interregional Movement "Unity").
171 Colton and McFaul 2000, p. 210; *Polit.Ru*, December 8, 1999, 17:22.
172 Colton and McFaul 2000, p. 209.
173 For example, see Sergei Shoigu, interview, *Itogi*, October 5, 1999; *Vremia MN*, December 1, 1999; *Polit.Ru*, November 10, 1999, 08:58.

All this became secondary, however, as the fall of 1999 progressed. In August 1999, Yeltsin named Putin the new prime minister. After a series of terrorist bombings killed nearly 300 people in Moscow in September, Putin responded by sending troops into Chechnya, a move that proved highly popular. As Putin's political star began to soar, the cornerstone of Unity's campaign strategy became its support for the new Russian prime minister. Shoigu stressed in his speeches that a key goal was to win a sizeable Duma fraction to help Putin in the Duma, although he was very careful to stress that Unity was progovernment (implying Putin), not necessarily pro-Kremlin (implying Yeltsin).[174] Putin, whose popularity was far ahead of Unity's in October and November, intentionally distanced himself from the bloc during this time since he had no clear indication that Unity would succeed. Kremlin strategists feared that Putin's putting his own weight behind one party would alienate some of his supporters and that this was only worth doing if the party was a sure bet to succeed.[175] By mid-November, however, polls consistently showed Unity with over 5 percent support, enough to convince Putin strategists that it was not a loser.

The party's decisive moment came when Putin finally endorsed it unambiguously on national television in late November. With Shoigu by his side, Putin declared that "I personally, as a citizen, will vote for Unity."[176] Unity immediately capitalized, putting out a press release declaring that "Unity supports Putin and Putin relies on Unity. And this is a union of victors."[177] Almost instantly, Unity's ratings surged, rising from 9 percent the week before to 18 percent right after the endorsement.[178] When the votes were finally tallied, Unity emerged with 23 percent, putting it in second place and just one percentage point behind the Communists. It won just 9 district seats, however, although it had nominated only 31 due largely to the late date of its formation.

United Russia

For reasons explained in the chapters that follow, the defeated Fatherland–All Russia consummated a deal to merge with Unity, under Kremlin sponsorship, in February 2002. The product was dubbed United Russia, which worked quickly to solidify and deepen its national and regional party structures. By the time of the 2003 Duma campaign, this party enjoyed unprecedented administrative capital. All three major television networks gave it favorable coverage after the partially state-owned Gazprom managed

[174] *Vremia MN*, December 1, 1999; *Polit.Ru*, October 29, 1999, 09:58.
[175] *Vremia MN*, December 1, 1999.
[176] Colton and McFaul 2000, p. 211.
[177] *Polit.Ru*, December 1, 1999, 18:39.
[178] According to VTsIOM's ratings. See Hale 1999d.

to strip the "oligarch" Gusinsky of his ownership of NTV on account of an unpaid debt. Putin's official representatives in the provinces were instructed to help coordinate its district candidacies and to direct financial and other support to it. And regional authorities, wary of drawing the wrath of the ascendant presidential administration, employed their own administrative resources in its favor. Interestingly, as will be demonstrated in Chapter 3, United Russia came to be closely associated with Putin's policies and thereby accumulated a great degree of ideational capital, espousing strong support for market-oriented reforms. Indeed, during the campaign Putin made repeated prominent appearances on television, clearly communicating to voters that he supported United Russia alone and that this party was the basis for his work in the Duma. Since the president's popularity had been riding steady at near 80 percent for much of his first term, this was no small matter for voters. The result for United Russia was a stunningly large victory in the parliamentary balloting, netting 38 percent of the party-list vote and 100 district wins. Many who had run as independents or even nominees of some other parties soon gravitated to United Russia's Duma fraction, which in January 2004 boasted 306 of the 450 Duma seats.

SUMMING UP

It is useful to summarize the detailed accounts above in order better to start to assess why some party-building initiatives succeeded where others failed in Russia's emerging electoral system in light of the theoretical framework elaborated in this volume. We would ideally have enough cases and sufficiently precise measures to perform a multivariate regression analysis, but given the limited nature of available data, any attempt at this is unlikely to be constructive. Table 2.4 thus lays out only a very crude indication of what has been argued in the preceding pages, connecting the descriptive analysis presented above to the conceptual framework advanced in Chapter 1. This table should not be read as a complete or conclusive summary of the argument. The simple pluses and minuses indicate only the relative presence or absence of factors posited above to help a party establish itself in the Russian context without assessing nuances of degree. Furthermore, the way in which parties are characterized as falling into the *clientelistic, ideational,* and *programmatic* categories offers only rough subjective approximations; it must be remembered that we are talking about ideal types that no real party can ever fully become since real parties always involve mixes of administrative and ideational capital. Nevertheless, at the risk of leading readers to interpret the table too literally, it is helpful to highlight certain patterns that emerge from the preceding narrative accounts by presenting them in summary tabular form.

TABLE 2.4. *Patterns of Party Assets, Strategies, and Success in Duma Elections Given Russia's Institutional and Cultural/Historical Setting*

		1993			1995			1999			2003		
Party-Building Initiative	Starting Capital (A,I)	Overall Fit of Strategy with Capital	Kremlin	Party Type 1993–5	Overall Fit of Strategy with Capital	Kremlin	Party Type 1995–9	Overall Fit of Strategy with Capital	Kremlin	Party Type 1999–2003	Overall Fit of Strategy with Capital	Kremlin	Party Type 2003–4
Civic Union	I,A	–		Minor									
RDDR	I	–		Minor									
PRES	A	+	+	Clientelist	–		Minor						
Democratic Party	I	+		Ideational	–		Minor	o		Minor			Minor
Women of Russia	I	+		Ideational	–		Minor	–		Minor	–		Minor
Agrarian Party	I,A	+		Programmatic	–		Minor	–		Minor	+	+	Minor
Yabloko	I	+		Ideational	+		Ideational	–		Ideational	–		Minor
KPRF	I,A	+		Programmatic	+		Programmatic	+		Programmatic	+	–	Programmatic
LDPR	I	+		Ideational	+		Ideational	–	–	Ideational	+		Ideational
Russia's Choice/SPS	I,A	–	+	Programmatic	–		Minor	+	+	Ideational	–		Minor
KRO/ Motherland	I	+	–	Minor	–	–	Minor	o		Minor	+	+	Ideational
Rybkin	I,A				–		Minor						
Our Home is Russia	A				+	+	Clientelist	–		Minor			
Fatherland–All Russia	A							+	–	Clientelist			
Unity/United Russia	A							+	+	Clientelist	+	+	Programmatic

Starting Capital: I = ideational, A = administrative, as of time party first competes in a Duma election
Fit of Strategy with Capital: + = good fit, – = poor fit, o = no significant capital remaining
Kremlin: +/– = national-level state structures targeted the party for strongly positive/negative treatment during a given Duma campaign
Party Type: A party is coded as a minor party if it does not clear the 5% barrier or win at least 35 district seats in a given Duma election. Parties that won at least 35 district seats or 5% of the party-list vote are coded as clientelistic if they did so primarily on the basis of administrative capital, as ideational if they did so primarily on the basis of ideational capital, and programmatic if they did so on the basis of important stocks of both ideational and administrative capital according to analysis of campaigns in Chapter 2.
Shaded text = party is major party

One striking pattern is that the elections of 1993 do appear to have constituted a kind of "founding election" in the sense described by O'Donnell and Schmitter.[179] While subsequent national campaign cycles have certainly served to winnow out initial winners whose foundations were weakest, those parties that made it into the Duma and gained the right to form their own fractions during the initial elections of 1993 had a strong advantage in returning to the Duma in significant numbers the following years. Thus, it might be useful to refer not only to a single "founding election" but also to subsequent *weeding elections* that serve to narrow down the field of competitors as expectations converge around the most promising winners. Four out of the five parties that were weeded out in 1995 (the Agrarian Party, the Democratic Party of Russia, PRES, and Women of Russia) failed to reclaim major party status in either 1999 or 2003. Moreover, 1993 successes constituted three-fourths of the major parties during 1995–9,[180] two-thirds of the major parties for 1999–2003, and one-half of the major parties for the period that started after the Duma elections of 2003. While these figures do reflect a decline in the status of the veteran parties, it is important to note that all but one of the parties successfully entering the Duma after 1993 have been the beneficiaries of strong Kremlin intervention in one form or other. This most obviously refers to Our Home is Russia, Unity, and United Russia, but also includes Motherland, in whose creation, campaign, and victory the Russian presidential administration was heavily involved. The lone exception was Fatherland–All Russia, which in a telling episode merged with Unity to form United Russia soon after the sole Duma election in which it autonomously participated (see Chapter 5). The only parties demonstrating any potential staying power in Russia, it seems, have been those that originally made it into the Duma in 1993 along with a broadly construed Kremlin "party of power." The notion of founding elections, quickly discarded by many after the 1993 elections produced eight seemingly weak winners, is of some value in Russia after all.

What seems to have made the difference for those parties that survived in parliament from 1993 through 2005? The factor that most clearly stands out is the party-building strategy adopted immediately after initial election. One important dimension was the degree to which a party used its representation in the Duma to develop its reputation in the electorate (maintaining and building its stock of ideational capital). The KPRF and the LDPR all used their standings in the parliament to bolster ideational reputations, the KPRF by demonstratively taking principled stands of various kinds and the LDPR by making loud statements on select issues but otherwise simply engaging in outrageous activities so as to bolster its iconoclastic image and to remain in

179 O'Donnell and Schmitter 1986, pp. 61–2.

180 Or all of them if one counts Our Home is Russia as the heir to PRES, as this chapter implies is defensible.

the news. Yabloko also enjoyed success through effective use of its position in the Duma to develop reputation, although poor campaigns in 1999 and 2003 ultimately squandered it. Women of Russia and the Agrarian Party, on the other hand, proved to be more interested in cutting deals with the Kremlin in order pragmatically to advance their agendas. Whereas such tactics may be reasonable for well-established parties with strong cores of party loyalists, these moves served to undermine the ideational distinctiveness of these organizations on key issues, notably the government's economic reforms. They left the voters little with which subsequently to identify. While both parties did score close to the 5 percent threshold in 1995, both failed to meet this mark, which triggered internal conflict within each organization and ultimately spelled electoral misfortune for each again in 1999. PRES and the Democratic Party fell victim to the power machinations of their own leaders who neglected party-building for the sake of negotiating contingent coalitions with Russia's executive branch. The leader of PRES rushed to hitch his wagon to what he thought was a more promising political engine, Our Home is Russia, while the Democratic Party leadership failed to establish a party line on relations with the Yeltsin administration, resulting in a major split. In the end, both parties had effectively disappeared from the political map by the 1999 election. Our Home is Russia also fits this pattern, having spurned the idea of an ideational reputation in the Duma of 1996–9, only to find itself without much significant political capital at all when Yeltsin unexpectedly fired Chernomyrdin as prime minister.

Russia's Choice, in important ways, is a partial exception that proves the rule. It did self-consciously cultivate a reputation as an economically liberal force during its time in the Duma between the 1993 and 1995 elections. The failing element of its party-building strategy in the run-up to the 1995 campaign was that its leaders and previous supporters did not unite, fracturing their potential electorate. As McFaul has cogently argued, the overall vote for economic liberal parties was roughly the same in 1995 as in 1993.[181] In the end, however, its investment in ideology provided a pool of capital that could later be used for Russia's Choice to make a comeback, this time as the core of a bloc of reunited economic liberals under the name Union of Right Forces. A brilliant campaign would enable the party to trade on its ideological reputation to reestablish critical political mass, again surpassing the 5 percent cutoff in 1999. But a poor campaign in 2003 undid almost everything it had fought so hard to achieve in 1999.

One very important implication of this is that highly contingent factors during a time of initial transition can have a long-lasting impact on the development of a given state's party system. In this particular case, we saw that different parties undertook both good and bad campaign and party-building

[181] McFaul 1998.

strategies. None of these were predetermined; some leaders appear simply to have "gotten it" while others did not. Although they did not always override other important factors (such as levels of political capital), these contingent elements resulted in the implosion of some parties and the dynamic rise of others. Zhirinovsky's LDPR also points out the dramatic importance of personality. In a path-dependent manner, initial successes gave the new parties more resources with which to sustain and build on their successes. Other parties found it increasingly difficult to break into the game – only those parties with the very most powerful of patrons (almost exclusively from the Kremlin) have had sufficient political capital to pull it off. Additionally, one has to consider the importance of blind luck. Had terrorists not obliterated two packed apartment buildings in the center of Moscow in September 1999 and thereby put security atop the list of public concerns, the Yabloko–Stepashin alliance would most probably not have unraveled, SPS would not have had an opening to return to the Duma, and Yabloko consequently could have become a liberal pillar in the party system, something that was completely absent as of 2005. Contingent events can have systemic consequences.

In wrapping up this discussion, however, it is crucial to highlight one additional theme that has shown up repeatedly in these accounts of party fortunes: the direct influence of Kremlin attempts to manipulate the party system. This chapter has demonstrated that there is a fine line between critical political mass and the dissolution of a party project. The difference between earning 4 and 5 percent of the party-list Duma vote has frequently been the difference between the long-term relegation to minor-party status (the RDDR in 1993, the Agrarian Party in 1995, and Women of Russia in 1995) and a guaranteed four years of major-party status and a real chance to sustain it over multiple election cycles. The existence of this "tipping point" means that political actors with the power of Russia's superpresidency at their disposal can have major, long-lasting effects by altering party fortunes only slightly, so long as "slightly" means that a party misses or clears 5 percent.

Thus, while it has been obvious to observers that Kremlin forces have played a role in the success and failure of parties of power, their more subtle operations generate less media attention but can have equally long-lasting effects. Rutskoi's party finds itself disqualified in 1993. KRO has its most popular candidate "mistakenly" crossed off the ballot in many precincts in 1995. The KPRF endures relentlessly negative news coverage on state-owned television in 2003 and then sees many of its votes fall to several leftist decoy parties, including Motherland and the Agrarian Party, that were either created or supported by the Kremlin with the express purpose of diluting the Communist vote. Other examples are even more dramatic and will be discussed in Chapter 5. These are summarized in Table 2.4 in the column labeled "Kremlin," indicating whether the Kremlin worked strongly in favor of or against a particular party in a given Duma election. While the logic of party entrepreneurship outlined here characterizes the central dynamics of the process, the formal and informal institutions connected with Russia's superpresidency (and notably its role in determining how the electoral market is regulated) have given the executive branch a great deal of power to determine which parties stay in business in this highly competitive market. Table 2.4 also shows, however, that this influence has not been everywhere decisive. While the Kremlin could tip the scales, party entrepreneurs and their stocks of capital still determined whether they got to the point at which they were vulnerable to such tipping.

3

How Much Party Is in the Party System?

While the preceding chapter showed why some parties survived while others did not as of 2004, it left two key questions unanswered. First, just how strong have these various surviving Russian parties been? That is, does Chapter 2's account of why some parties beat out others merely reflect the weak defeating the weak, or have parties proven to be capable of mobilizing a great deal of electoral support for their candidates? Second, irrespective of whether they have been capable of aiding their candidates in significant measure, to what extent have these parties actually penetrated and structured Russia's political process from the national to the regional? That is, to what degree can we characterize Russia as having had a *party* system at all through 2004? As was discussed in some detail in Chapter 1, observers have advanced very different opinions on these questions, with some arguing Russian parties have been strong and/or growing while others insist that they have been weak and/or in decline.

This chapter makes a systematic endeavor to answer these two central questions for the period from the Soviet breakup to 2004. Successive sections assess the strength of parties in the electorate generally, in the federal executive branch, in the federal legislature, in the regional executive branch, and in regional legislatures. The discussion of parties in the electorate relies primarily on surveys of voters themselves, exploring different measures of voters' relationships to parties in order to determine more precisely the degree to which parties during this period were communicating policy stands to potential voters and were in fact cultivating mass-level attachments and structuring potential voters' political attitudes and activities. The subsequent sections examine actual voting patterns and other data on all four of Russia's first post-independence rounds of national elections (1993, 1995–6, 1999–2000, and 2003–4) as well as regional elections between 1995 and 2004 to assess the degree to which parties in fact *were* communicating programmatic messages to voters and the extent to which parties actually *did* help candidates in their electoral endeavors.

The overall findings of this chapter paint a much more complicated picture than do most studies, which Chapter 1 showed usually fall into "strong party" or "weak party" camps. The real picture has been one of significant but "stalling" party strength combined with major remaining gaps in party penetration of the polity. Explaining this pattern is then the task of subsequent chapters.

PARTIES IN THE ELECTORATE

Without some notion that parties provide at least a modicum of reputational support for candidates, it is quite hard to explain why major-party candidates for office and their teams spend so much effort distributing mountains of party literature. The following paragraphs demonstrate that parties in fact have established reputations for stands on important issues and have cultivated substantial loyalties among core groups of voters that are based to a significant degree on these issue stands. To show this, it is most useful to draw on studies that actually ask (potential) voters what they think on these and related questions. Fortunately, a series of public opinion surveys have done just this for every round of Russian parliamentary and presidential elections since 1995, carried out by the highly reputable Demoscope Group of the Russian Academy of Sciences' Institute of Sociology led by Polina Kozyreva and Mikhail Kosolapov. The first study, hereafter referred to as the "1995–6 survey," was designed by Timothy Colton and William Zimmerman.[1] The second, the "1999–2000 survey," was crafted by Colton and Michael McFaul, who generously incorporated a few questions suggested by the present author.[2] The third, predictably called here the "2003–4 survey," was designed by Colton, McFaul, and the present author. Each of these surveys is a "panel survey," meaning that within each round of elections, the very same people were interviewed multiple times (in multiple "panels" or "waves"). Both the 1995–6 and 1999–2000 surveys had three waves, the first taking place prior to the parliamentary vote (the "preparliamentary wave"), the second just after this election (the "postparliamentary wave"), and the third just after the presidential contest (the "postpresidential wave").[3] The 2003–4 survey contained just two waves, a postparliamentary

[1] Timothy Colton and William Zimmerman, *Russian Election Study, 1995–1996* [computer file], ICPSR version (Moscow: Russian Academy of Sciences, Institute of Sociology, Demoscope Group [producer], 1996). Ann Arbor, MI: Inter-university Consortium for Political and Social Research [distributor], 2002. See Colton 2000 and Zimmerman 2002 for the flagship products of this survey project.

[2] See Colton and McFaul 2003 for more on this survey and for their own analysis of the data.

[3] The preparliamentary wave of the 1995–6 survey questioned 2,841 adult Russian citizens between November 19, 1995, and December 16, 1995, and the postparliamentary wave reinterviewed 2,776 of the original respondents during the period December 18, 1995–January 20, 1996. The preparliamentary wave of the 1999–2000 survey interviewed 1,919 adult

and a postpresidential.[4] All of these surveys covered more than enough respondents to be considered nationally representative of the voting-age population even in Russia's fragmented political context.[5] Since tiny parties are of little interest here, the pages that follow examine only those parties that can be classified as "major parties" for a given round of national elections according to the criteria given in Chapter 1 in at least one Duma election between 1995 and 2003, except where otherwise noted.

Voter Knowledge of Parties and Party Stands

The three surveys show that Russia's major parties were known to almost all potential voters as of 1995 and that they continued to be known through the 2003–4 election cycle. At least three-quarters of the potential electorate reported knowing each of the major parties that won fractions in the Duma in 1995, and by 1999 no major party that had run under the same name in 1995 was unknown by more than 4 percent of respondents.

More importantly, a majority of voters felt competent to identify the stands of these organizations on critical issues and most of these did so with reasonable accuracy. Let us take, for example, the important question of market reform in the run-up to the Duma election of 1999. To be sure, for each party, between 20 and 45 percent of the population could not place the organization's platform into one of the following categories: returning to the socialist economy, retaining elements of socialism, continuing market reforms but less painfully, or deepening and accelerating market reforms. Of course, we must keep in mind that many people are disengaged from politics and do not vote even in developed democracies, so these numbers do not indicate a great deal of party weakness. More importantly, the parties experiencing the greatest popular ignorance of their positions were those (such as Unity) that had only just been created and those (such as the LDPR) that did not make these particular categories the most relevant elements of their platforms. The figures for late 2003 and early 2004 were similar on the issue of the market, although the percentage reporting ignorance of United Russia's stand in 2003–4 (23 percent) was only about half of the share that reported not knowing Unity's in 1999 (41 percent).

Russian citizens between November 13 and December 13, 1999 and the postparliamentary wave took place between December 25, 1999, and January 25, 2000, and interviewed 1,842 of the people who had participated in the first wave. The postpresidential waves from the 1995–6 and 1999–2000 surveys are not used in the present volume.

4 The postparliamentary wave of the 2003–4 survey included 1,648 adult Russian citizens, who were interviewed between December 19, 2003, and February 15, 2004. The postpresidential wave questioned 1,496 of the original respondents between April 4 and May 11, 2004.

5 Descriptive statistics from these surveys (1995–6, 1999–2000, and 2003–4) are calculated using the Kish weighting procedure to avoid bias due to the possible oversampling of people living by themselves in small households.

Furthermore, when people did claim competency in categorizing parties' stands on the issue of the market in 1999, they were generally quite accurate, with deviations usually reflecting reasonable interpretations of the platforms and categories. Thus, for example, over 90 percent of those who claimed to be able to identify the KPRF's position put it in the socialist or partially socialist camp, and 90 percent of those claiming to know the platform of SPS labeled it reformist. For parties taking more moderate stands on the market, the distribution of such respondents' assessments was similarly reasonable. The 2003–4 survey finds that voters were accurate in the same way during that period.[6] By 2004, then, parties had developed a significant degree of ideational capital in the electorate, capital that had the potential to be successfully applied in electoral politics.

Voter Loyalties to Parties

The notion of "party identification" is one of the oldest and most important concepts of modern political science. Developed by a group of scholars widely referred to collectively as the "Michigan school," the concept originally reflected the argument that people choose parties less through detached, rational rumination on important issues than through long-term processes of socialization and deep-rooted sentiments that are often effectively inherited from one's own parents. Scholars in this tradition have argued that people identify with parties much as they identify with social groups, and the associated attachments can be quite strong and enduring.[7] A newer school concurs that deep-seated party loyalties are important but argues that they are more rationally grounded than previously thought, reflecting longstanding "running tallies" that voters keep of party performance over time. Good performance from the point of view of the voter breeds loyalty.[8] The surveys from 1999–2000 and 2003–4 clearly demonstrate that a significant share of the Russian public had come to identify with political parties by that period and that identification with certain parties was growing, although attachments to other major parties show patterns of rise and decline that correlate with the critical campaign periods described in Chapter 2.

Most major studies of emerging Russian voter loyalties to parties have used only one measure of this phenomenon and have defended it as the best one.[9] As Donald Green, Bradley Palmquist, and Eric Schickler have extensively demonstrated, however, to use a single measure to study partisanship

[6] More detailed findings on which these claims are based are available through the web site www.whynotpartiesinrussia.com or directly from the author.

[7] Bartels 2000; Campbell, Converse, Miller, and Stokes 1960; Gerber and Green 1998; Green, Palmquist, and Schickler 1998, 2002.

[8] Erikson, MacKuen, and Stimson 2002; Fiorina 1981.

[9] Brader and Tucker 2001; Colton 2000; Miller et al. 2000; White, Rose, and McAllister 1997.

is to run a significant risk of measurement error.[10] This risk is compounded in the Russian case, where the standard wording used in studies of the United States (a reference point for most major works on party identification) must be translated into a foreign language and political context.

Fortunately, the surveys used here employ multiple measures as applied to the same respondents, enabling us to more confidently separate real party loyalties from measurement problems.[11] The strictest measure, which we here dub *hard-core partisanship*, was developed by Colton, who regularly asks respondents if there is any party that they can name unprompted that they would go so far as to call "my party."[12] This question is meant to capture the deep-rooted psychological attachment to parties found by many Western scholars to be a key feature of American and European politics. Colton argues, however, that it is unreasonable to expect Western-style hard-core partisanship to be very developed in a country that is as new to elections as is Russia. He thus advanced the notion of *transitional partisanship* in order to capture significant but less time-hardened loyalties that voters may reasonably be expected to develop during the early years of a democratizing polity. Specifically, if respondents answer that there is no party that they call "my party," they are then asked if there is nevertheless some party that "more than the others reflects" their "interests, views, and concerns." "Transitional partisans" are those who answer yes to either the first or the second questions and then name a real party. The set of hard-core and transitional partisanship questions were included in each of the surveys considered here (1995–6, 1999–2000, and 2003–4). We also examine a third measure using standard survey questions asked by the cross-national Comparative Study of Electoral Systems (CSES) project to reflect the notion of partisanship in a wide variety of contexts outside of the United States. This measure asks people whether they usually think of themselves as "close to any particular political party" or other organization with the right to compete in a given election, or at least "a little closer" to some party than to others.[13]

Table 3.1 summarizes the responses of Russians to each of these sets of partisanship measures during the three rounds of federal elections between 1995 and 2004. Turning first to 1995–6, we find that the vast majority, some 78 percent of the electorate, did not consider any major party to be "their party" just prior to the 1995 Duma election while only 22 percent did have

10 Green et al. 2002.

11 The exception is the 1995–6 survey, which only employs one measure.

12 Miller et al. (2000) have criticized this measure, suggesting that respondents might get confused by the wording "my party" and think the goal is to guess the interviewer's party. The question, however, was worded in Russian to avoid this problem and no evidence has been found for it in pre-testing conducted in refining and verifying the survey instrument.

13 The precise wording and sequence of the questions used to measure different forms of partisonship in this volume can be found at www.whynotpartiesinrussia.com. For more on CSES, see the Web site www.umich.edu/~cses. For Colton's justification of his own method, see Colton 2000.

TABLE 3.1. *Percentage of Population Displaying Partisanship for Major Parties by Different Measures in 1995, 1999–2000, and 2003–4*

	Hard-Core Partisanship (%)				Transitional Partisanship (%)				Feeling of Closeness (%)	
	1995	1999	2003–4	2004	1995	1999	2003–4	2004	2000	2004
United Russia and Parties Joining It	2.4	5.1	15.9	12.9	4.8	9.9	26.1	25.8	22.3	27.9
Our Home is Russia	2.4	0.7	–	–	4.8	1.1	–	–	0.7	–
Fatherland–All Russia	–	2.5	–	–	–	5.0	–	–	5.8	–
Unity	–	1.9	–	–	–	3.8	–	–	15.8	–
United Russia	–	–	15.9	12.9	–	–	26.1	25.8	–	27.9
Communist Party	9.9	10.9	5.9	5.2	14.1	16.7	8.4	7.6	20.7	9.1
LDPR	2.9	1.4	3.0	1.6	5.1	2.7	4.9	4.7	2.5	4.6
Russia's Democratic Choice/SPS	1.1	1.4	0.7	0.3	2.0	2.1	1.7	1.2	5.6	1.5
Yabloko	2.0	2.7	1.2	0.8	4.6	5.9	3.3	2.1	5.4	2.7
Motherland	–	–	2.9	1.5	–	–	5.2	3.7	–	4.0
Agrarian Party	1.5	–	–	–	2.5	–	–	–	–	–
Women of Russia	1.9	–	–	–	4.1	–	–	–	–	–
PRES	0.1	–	–	–	0.2	–	–	–	–	–
Democratic Party of Russia	0.0	–	–	–	0.1	–	–	–	–	–
Total for Major Parties	21.8	21.5	29.6	22.3	37.5	37.3	49.6	45.1	56.5	49.8

Note: The years listed are the years in which the bulk of the survey questionnaires were administered; see earlier in this chapter for precise dates.
Sources: The 1995–6, 1999–2000, and 2003–4 surveys.

a major party to call their own, with almost half of these (9.9 percent) being Communist Party loyalists; no other party could claim even as much as 3 percent of the population as hard-core loyalists. If we adopt more moderate criteria for assessing attachments, we see that almost 38 percent could be called "transitional partisans." A plurality of transitional partisans were Communists (about 14 percent), but the LDPR, Yabloko, and the new party of power Our Home is Russia could each boast the loyalty of around 5 percent with Women of Russia just behind.

Moving ahead to 1999, a first glance indicates that the overall level of major-party partisanship had stalled at almost exactly its 1995 level. This lack of growth, however, largely reflects the weeding process described in Chapter 2; the Agrarian Party, Women of Russia, PRES, and the Democratic Party all ceased to be major parties and hence are not included in our table for the post-1995 period. The first two of these had previously counted close to 2 percent of the population as hard-core partisans and between 2 and 5 percent as transitional partisans. Most of the veteran parties that survived, however, gained both hard-core and transitional partisans, although incrementally. This included the Communists, the Union of Right Forces (as compared to Russia's Democratic Choice in 1995), and Yabloko, despite the latter's poor campaign. Of the veterans, only the LDPR lost partisans, a phenomenon likely to be connected to all of the legal and other problems suffered by the party in the 1999 campaign as described in Chapter 2. While Our Home is Russia's partisan base largely collapsed between the 1995 election (when it was the undisputed "party of power") and the 1999 election (when it was decidedly not), one can see that the rise of the new progovernment Unity bloc largely offset this. Moreover, the governors' coalition Fatherland–All Russia, which was later to merge with Unity as an integral component of a new party of power, had also appeared since 1998 and claimed 5 percent of the population as its transitional partisans in the weeks before the 1999 Duma election. Thus, the period 1995–9 should be seen as a period of partisanship growth, albeit incremental growth. The losses in the "total partisanship" category reflect exactly what the theory of party development would lead us to expect, a gradual weeding out of parties that proved not to have critical political mass.[14]

The 1999–2000 survey also includes a different measure of partisanship, enabling us to compare the findings with those using the hard-core and

14 Also in accordance with theoretical expectations, loyalists for these failed parties do not simply transfer their loyalties to new entities, even if the leaders of the failed parties joined one of these entities. Indeed, the leaders themselves often struggled mightily over what to do once their own party projects had foundered; in 1999, Women of Russia split between those joining Fatherland–All Russia and those favoring a new, independent bid while the Agrarian Party was torn between one faction that aligned with Fatherland–All Russia and another that hopped on the Communist bandwagon.

transitional partisanship questions. If we treat partisanship as a matter of considering oneself "close" to a party, as does the CSES project, the picture in 1999–2000 improves considerably; by this measure, more than half (56.5 percent) of potential Russian voters were partisan. One reason why this figure is higher than the transitional partisanship measure, however, probably involves timing; the transitional partisanship query was posed to voters just before the 1999 Duma election while the "closeness" measure was taken after the vote, in early 2000. The process of campaigning and voting, independently of the way the questions were worded, would be expected to have pumped up partisanship in the electorate for those parties that campaigned and performed well. Indeed, a closer look at the distribution of partisanship across parties between the "transitional partisanship" and "closeness" measures reveals that most of the aggregate difference comes from three particular parties, the ones that fared best relative to early expectations in the 1999 election. Far more people claimed a closeness with Unity after the election than transitional partisanship before it and similar but smaller effects were true of the Communist Party and the Union of Right Forces. The three major parties that retained major-party status but did not perform well during that election round displayed postelection "closeness partisanship" at roughly the same level as they did preelection transitional partisanship; Yabloko and the LDPR each dipped by less than a percentage point while Fatherland–All Russia registered an under-1-percent rise. Our Home is Russia, which lost major-party status, saw its collection of partisans dwindle from 1.1 to just 0.7 percent en route to disappearing entirely. This alternative plumbing of partisanship, then, confirms what appears to be a slow but regular growth in partisan attachments to Russia's major surviving parties during the 1990s.

During the 2003–4 campaign, however, things became more complicated and demonstrate the risks of relying on a single measure of partisanship at a single point in time. What appears to have happened is that a trend toward increasing overall levels of major-party partisanship in the electorate peaked with the 2003 Duma elections, despite some losses by the defeated parties, but that the defeated parties then drove a small net decline by not running their strongest candidates in the 2004 presidential voting. This move appears to have driven some of their loyalists to cease seeing them as major players on the political scene. The key to understanding the complicated patterns in Table 3.1 is to keep in mind the relative timing of the different surveys. The columns marked "1999" reflect measures taken during the campaign before the December 1999 Duma election; the "2000" survey was conducted after the December 1999 Duma election but prior to the March 2000 presidential contest; the "2003–4" survey was taken after the December 2003 Duma election but before the March 2004 presidential vote; and, finally, the "2004" assessment was made shortly after the end of the March 2004 presidential race. The indicators of hard-core and transitional partisanship were taken the most frequently and thus provide the best grounds for tracking patterns over time. As Table 3.1 shows, net hard-core identification with major parties surged from a total of 21.5 percent just before the 1999 Duma election to 29.6 percent after the 2003 Duma election, but then very rapidly dropped back down to 22.3 percent following the March 2004 presidential election. The pattern is similar for net transitional partisanship: it rose dramatically from 37.3 to 49.6 percent between the 1999 Duma campaign and the aftermath of 2003 Duma voting, only to fall back a bit to 45.1 percent by the postpresidential-election period in 2004. That is, net partisanship was actually higher than in previous election cycles even *after* the December 2003 elections that held such stunning defeat for some of Russia's most important parties. A slight drop, negating some but not all of the gains apparent since the fall of 1999, came during the spring that corresponds to Russia's 2004 presidential campaign. The CSES-based questions that ask about "closeness" to parties are consistent with this interpretation since the low 2004 values were obtained after the presidential election, at the same time that the low values of the hard-core and transitional partisanship figures were received.

This pattern, a rise in net partisanship through the 2003 election followed by a dip during and perhaps just after the 2004 presidential campaign, primarily reflects the rise of United Russia. By 2003, United Russia had more than tripled the 1999 pool of hard-core partisans for the various (former) major parties that merged to form United Russia (Unity, Fatherland–All Russia, and Our Home is Russia). The devastating losses suffered by the KPRF, SPS, and Yabloko were, interestingly enough, substantially offset by the gains of Motherland and the LDPR between 1999 and 2003–4. The fact that none of Russia's major parties nominated the most popular figure associated with these parties, as reported in Chapter 2, appears to have doomed each of them to at least some decline in loyalty. By effectively foregoing the presidential contest, Russia's major parties raised doubts about their own willingness and ability to remain important parts of Russia's political scene, giving Russian citizens less reason to nurture any loyalty to them or to voice such sentiments in a survey on politics. In the case of United Russia, while its chief patron coasted to easy victory in the presidential race, Putin was not a nominee of the party and did not place the party at the center of his campaign.

Overall, then, we see a significant net growth pattern in major-party partisanship that closely corresponds to what comparative theory and the logic of the present volume would expect. The parties suffering declines in 2003–4 were the ones that ran the worst campaigns as described in Chapter 2 (Yabloko and SPS) or that bore the brunt of the most brutal Kremlin assault (the KPRF). The rise in United Russia's numbers also fits this pattern. Indeed, pioneering works on partisanship have long held that one important source of growth in party loyalty is the performance of governments associated with particular parties.[15] Growing attachment to United Russia thus reflects a very common dynamic as voters increasingly identify it with Putin and his performance in office, which United Russia is well known for supporting. Thus, while one party drove much of the increase in aggregate levels of major-party partisanship between the 1999–2000 and 2003–4 rounds of election and while other parties drove a small net decline in the first half of 2004, this is not inconsistent with what comparative theories would expect since this one party represented incumbent authorities at a time when they were generally quite popular.

Bases of Voter Loyalties to Parties

Not only were party loyalties growing in Russia between 1995 and 2004, but these loyalties also appear to have been strongly rooted in social structure and attitudes toward important issues, as comparative theories of partisanship would expect.[16] The 1995–6, 1999–2000, and 2003–4 surveys each questioned potential voters not only about their relationships to parties, but also about their stands on major issues facing Russia at the time (economic reform, political reform, nationalism, and the state of the country in general) and about their own places in Russian society. Table 3.2 reports findings from an analysis of these surveys designed to determine whether partisans of individual parties stood out for particular kinds of answers to these questions. The columns list only those issue positions or socioeconomic characteristics that *strongly* correlate with transitional partisanship for each of the parties listed in the far left-hand column during the year indicated. By "strongly," the table refers to correlations that so blatantly deviate from typical random patterns that the statistical analysis calculates there is less than a 5 percent chance that there is no relationship between the variables and transitional partisanship. The numbers in parentheses are the same statistical analysis's estimations of the magnitude of these correlations. For example, the first cell under the column heading "Economy" indicates the following: a typical person in the 1995–6 survey who was in favor of protectionism was 3 percent more likely to be a transitional partisan for the Communist Party than was a typical person who did not support protectionist policies in the survey; those typical citizens who asserted opposition to the transition to a market economy were 2 percent more likely to be Communist transitional partisans than they otherwise would have been; and those typical potential voters who spoke out in the survey against the privatization process were

[15] Erikson et al. 2002; Fiorina 1981; Green et al. 2002.

[16] Researchers stressing attachments rooted in social structure include Bartels 2000; Campbell et al. 1960; Gerber and Green 1998; and Green et al. 1998, 2002. Accounts emphasizing positions on fundamental issues and the performance of incumbents include Fiorina 1981 and Erikson et al. 2002.

TABLE 3.2. *Bases of Transitional Partisanship for Major Parties 1995–2004**

		Issue Positions				
		Economy	Political System	Nationalism	Social Background	View of Current Conditions
KPRF	1995	Protectionist (3%) Antimarket (2%) Antiprivatization (1%)		US is threat (2%) Dislike Jews (1%)	Older (8%) Was CPSU member (4%) Lives in south Russia (2%) Smaller settlement (2%)	Economy not improving (1%) Dissatisfied with Russian democracy (1%)
	1999	For socialism (6%) Protectionist (3%)	Order over liberty (2%)		Older (13%) Was CPSU member (7%) Smaller settlement (7%) Middle class (2%) Male (2%)	Economic opportunity declining (3%)
	2004	For socialism (6%) Anti-oligarch (1%)			Older (5%)	
Yabloko	1995		Party competition good (2%)		Higher education (5%) Larger cities (2%) Lives in north Russia (1%)	
	1999	Proprivatization (8%)	Electing leaders important (7%)		Larger cities (7%) Higher education (5%) Female (3%)	Economic opportunity improving (8%) Own finances improving (6%)
	2004		Democracy over strong leader (5%)		Higher education (5%) Not in collective farm (3%)	

(continued)

TABLE 3.2 *(continued)*

		Issue Positions				
		Economy	Political System	Nationalism	Social Background	View of Current Conditions
SPS	1995 (RDC)	Antiprotectionist (1%) Proprivatization (1%)	Propresidentialism (2%)		Higher education (2%) Not in collective farm (2%) Lives in east Russia (1%)	Economy improving (4%)
	1999					Own finances improving (2%)
	2004				Not in collective farm (3%)	
LDPR	1995	Antiprivatization (1%)	Order over rights (2%)	U.S. is threat (1%) Approve Chechnya war (1%)	Younger (3%) Male (1%) Lives in west Russia (1%)	Suffered wage arrears (1%)
	1999	Antiprivatization (1%)		Keep Chechnya at all costs (1%)	Younger (2%) Was CPSU member (1%)	Suffered wage arrears (1%) Police can provide security (1%)
	2004				Job in private sector (2%) Lives in west Russia (2%) Male (1%)	Own finances not up (1%)
United Russia (and parties that later merged with it)	1995 (OHR)				Older (6%) Lives in east Russia (2%)	Economy improving (6%) Personal finances up (5%) Economy not way down (2%)

	1999 (OHR)				Job in private sector (3%) Not in collective farm (1%) Smaller settlement (1%)	
	1999 (FAR)	Protectionist (3%)	Against high regional autonomy (2%) Electing leaders important (2%)		Higher education (4%)	Own finances improving (4%)
	1999 (Unity)	Against socialism (1%)	Propresidentialism (2%)	Against Russia–Ukraine union (1%)	From east Russia (2%) Smaller settlement (2%)	
	2004 (UR)	Against socialism (6%)	Propresidentialism (7%)	Pro-West (6%)	Older (13%) Middle Class (9%) Lives in south Russia (9%) Lives in east Russia (8%)	Economy improving (15%) Satisfied with Russian democracy (8%)
Motherland	2004				Higher education (4%)	
Agrarian Party	1995				Smaller settlement (4%) Lives in west Russia (1%) Job not in private sector (0%)	Suffered wage arrears (0%)
Women of Russia	1995				Younger (6%) Not in collective farm (5%) Female (4%)	Economy way down (2%)

* This table reports those issue stands, social background characteristics, and assessments of the situation in Russia that public opinion survey respondents reported and that were calculated with at least 95% confidence to be correlated with transitional partisanship for particular major parties. Technical information about these findings can be obtained through the web site www.whynotpartiesinrussia.com.

1 percent more likely to be Communist loyalists than they would have been had they not been against privatization.[17]

Several important findings emerge from this exercise. Most generally, we see that loyalty for each major party had some grounding in either an issue position or social structure since 1995. The thinnest over this whole period of time was Motherland, created with Kremlin support just months before the 2003 Duma election less to be a viable party than to lure away voters dissatisfied with other parties, notably the Communists. The only distinguishing feature of people who declared themselves to be Motherland loyalists, this study finds, was having higher levels of education. The results for the Agrarian Party and Women of Russia indicate that Motherland has a hard task ahead of it if it is to survive in Russia's party fray, however; neither of the 1993-vintage organizations managed to build a cadre of partisans that stood out on major issues of the day and both had ceased to be major parties after the 1995 elections, failing to make it into the Duma in significant numbers. While each demonstrated some ability to appeal to core constituencies (the rural residents for the Agrarians; youth, nonfarmers, and women for Women of Russia) this proved not to be enough given the parties' failure to carve out distinctive ideational niches as described in Chapter 2.

Of Russia's "veteran" parties, those with their roots in or before the 1993 parliamentary elections, the Communists and Yabloko cultivated loyalties solidly grounded in both issue positions and social structure, indicating that their investments in ideational capital paid off at least to some degree in terms of party attachments. Ever since 1995, the KPRF's transitional partisans consistently distinguished themselves as supporters of socialism and members of the elder generation, although in different rounds of elections they also stood out strongly for being former members of the Communist Party of the Soviet Union and for living in smaller communities. Interestingly, nationalism and authoritarianism did not tend to set Communist loyalists apart from others. While the party's supporters may have espoused such views, they did not appear to be driving KPRF partisanship significantly; nationalist views registered only in the 1995–6 survey and an authoritarian tendency only in 1999–2000. Yabloko's transitional partisans were remarkable throughout the entire 1995–2003 period primarily as ardent proponents of democracy, residents of the most urban communities, and possessors of higher education. It is noteworthy that no position on the economy and no

[17] The statistical model used here is multinomial logit, appropriate when the dependent variable (in this case, choice of party) is categorical and nonordered. The estimated magnitude of the effects and levels of statistical confidence are generated using the software CLARIFY, which operates with the statistical package *Stata 7.0*. The estimates are generated through a stochastic simulation technique based on the results of the multinomial logit regression. For more details on how CLARIFY works, see King, Tomz, and Wittenberg 2000; and Tomz, Wittenberg, and King 2003. See the web site www.whynotpartiesinrussia.com for more details.

attitude toward nationalism was consistently a distinguishing trait of transitional partisanship for Yabloko. While the 2003–4 survey indicates that opposition to the use of violence in Chechnya did make one likely to be among the few who retained loyalty to Yabloko after its 2003 Duma election failure, a finding not reported in Table 3.2 because it falls just outside the required 95 percent confidence level, the party's muddled message in 1999 precluded this from being a significant source of party attachment during that election cycle.

Very striking also is the complete lack of issue-grounding for loyalties to the Union of Right Forces (SPS) and the Liberal Democratic Party of Russia (LDPR). This is least surprising for the LDPR, which most analysts see as being based primarily on the appeal of its charismatic leader, Vladimir Zhirinovsky. While his common oratorical themes of order and nationalism were associated with his devotees in 1995–6 and 1999–2000, the magnitude of the effects was rather small and they did not register as significant in 2003–4, when Table 3.1 shows the party nearly doubled its number of transitional partisans with regard to 1999–2000. Table 3.2 quite clearly confirms, however, that the appeal of Zhirinovsky's party was consistently to males and the economically downtrodden, those reporting that they had either not been paid their due wages or that their own family's economic situation had not been improving. The LDPR also tended to stand out for its strength in western Russia. It is quite surprising, however, that SPS loyalists have not been set apart by any issue stand since 1995 according to these surveys. This is probably because, as Table 3.1 demonstrates, SPS and its predecessors were never found to have more than 2.1 percent of the population as their transitional partisans; this leaves the statistical analysis with very few SPS loyalists to analyze, making it unlikely to find any results with 95 percent confidence. Those few SPS loyalists that existed did tend to stand out somewhat as being among the most prosperous Russian citizens, not living in collective farms, and/or reporting that their own families' economic situations were improving. The connection between SPS partisanship and positive opinions of the economy, however, steadily diminished as the time when SPS's key leaders were actually in charge of the economy became more distant.

Perhaps the most important dynamic revealed in Table 3.2 is the steady "ideationalization" of the party of power. Devotees of Prime Minister Chernomyrdin's Our Home is Russia, essentially uncontested as the party of power in the 1995 Duma race, did not distinguish themselves on any issue position; instead, they tended strongly to be those people who believed that the economy was improving and that tended to be of an older generation, long accustomed to voting for authority figures or Communists (Chernomyrdin, of course, being the former). The brand-new Unity bloc, which the new Putin government backed during the 1999 parliamentary campaign, was associated with an entirely different kind of loyalist; not standing out on any assessment of how the economy or political system was faring, these transitional partisans displayed distinct positions on the economy, the political system, and nationalism. While the magnitude of the relationships was not large, Unity's transitional partisans were against socialism, preferred a strong presidency to a parliament-dominated system, and did not think that Russia should pursue reunification with Ukraine – positions, interestingly, often asssociated with SPS's predecessor (Russia's Democratic Choice) in 1995. By 2003–4, United Russia's pool of partisans, now many times larger than Unity's had been in the fall of 1999, were strongly distinguished by almost identical issue stands but in much larger measure. United Russia devotees stood out from others for being antisocialism, propresidentialism, and antinationalism (believing that Russia should treat the West as an ally or friend rather than as a rival or enemy). Indeed, being against socialism as of 1999–2000 and 2003–4 was a much stronger predictor of loyalty to United Russia or Unity than it ever was of devotion to Yabloko or SPS. Moreover, by 2003–4, United Russia appears to have grounded itself in a broad but distinctive social base, in particular attracting the fondness of people who were older, considered themselves members of the middle class, or lived in southern or eastern Russia. Very importantly, United Russia also strongly appeared as of 2003–4 to be building its cadre of followers on the basis of both economic and political performance, taking aboard those who differed from others in believing that the economy was getting better and that democracy was in good shape in Russia.

Not only was major-party partisanship in Russia steadily growing, then, but it was developing along patterns that were quite in keeping with comparative theoretical expectations. Partisanship for every major party has been found to have had at least some grounding in views on fundamental issues facing Russia or socioeconomic characteristics of the individual. Even more critically, the Kremlin's party of power strongly attracted followers based on the performance of the government and president and was increasingly associated with a socioeconomically broad and ideationally distinct set of transitional partisans. This growing group of citizens is shown to have been robustly bullish on the economy and polity, against a socialist economy, for a strong presidency, and for cooperative relations with the West. The results also indicate that loyalties to other parties tended to crystallize around opposition to the issues with which party-of-power partisans were associated; the KPRF attracted large numbers of those who were the most critical of the market economy and Yabloko gathered many who placed a high priority on democracy in Russia. No party capitalized consistently on a nationalist cleavage to gather partisans in opposition to the pro-Westernism of the United Russia camp. While Zhirinovsky certainly spouted such views regularly, his appeal appears to have been more personalistic and targeted at economically disadvantaged males who did not have markedly more nationalistic views than did devotees of other parties. While SPS leaders publicly stressed an ideology of liberalism, they were not able to attract many loyalists on this basis and remained, if anything, primarily a party of those who had prospered under the reforms since 1992 and, most probably, of residual Yeltsin loyalists who formed their attachments to the Gaidar–Chubais team when they were effectively running the government during the fateful early 1990s. Indeed, United Russia's economic liberalism appears to have stolen much of the ideational thunder of SPS.

Having examined general voter attachments to parties, we now turn to a consideration of the degree to which parties during this same period penetrated the most important elected organs of state power and the contests that filled them in Russia. We begin with the presidency and then proceed to the parliament, governorships, and finally provincial legislatures.

PARTIES AND THE PRESIDENCY

While observers typically think of the Russian presidency as a preserve of nonpartisanship, presidential *elections* do not fit this mold so tightly. To be sure, Russia's only two presidents to date have opted to remain above the partisan fray. Yeltsin, after bolting the Communist Party of the Soviet Union in 1990, stubbornly resisted the advice of some aides who urged him to form and lead his own party. Putin was the St. Petersburg head of Our Home is Russia when he was Mayor Sobchak's first deputy, but this was more of an assignment by his boss than a personal choice and the future president dropped this affiliation long before running for the country's top job in 2000.

When one's attention turns to challengers, however, the picture changes entirely. All challengers receiving more than 1 percent of the vote in any of Russia's three presidential elections have been party members, as indicated in Table 3.3. Thus, while nonpartisan incumbents have had a headlock on Russia's most powerful post, no other candidates have managed to mount anything close to a successful challenge without presenting themselves as the representatives of some kind of party organization. While Russia's presidency has been nonpartisan, presidential elections have actually been relatively partisan affairs. Chapter 5 will discuss further why incumbents, unlike major challengers, have tended to shun party labels.

PARTIES AND THE DUMA

The Proportional-Representation (PR) Half of the Duma Elections

Since the law governing Russia's parliamentary elections between 1993 and 2005 required half of the Duma to be contested by party lists through a proportional-representation system, we naturally expect to find a strong role

TABLE 3.3. *Party Affiliation of Presidential Candidates (First-Round Elections) in Russia 1991–2004*

	Party	Result (%)
1991		
Yeltsin	None	57
Ryzhkov	Communist	17
Zhirinovsky	LDPSU	8
Tuleev	Communist	7
Makashov	Communist	4
Bakatin	Communist	4
1996		
Yeltsin	None	35
Zyuganov	Communist	32
Lebed	Honor and Motherland	15
Yavlinsky	Yabloko	7
Zhirinovsky	LDPR	6
Others	Various	<1
2000		
Putin	None	53
Zyuganov	Communist	29
Yavlinsky	Yabloko	6
Tuleev	Communist	3
Zhirinovsky	LDPR	3
Titov	SPS	1
Pamfilova	For Civic Dignity	1
Others	Various	<1
2004		
Putin	None	71
Kharitonov	Communist	14
Glaziev	Motherland	4
Khakamada	SPS	4
Malyshkin	LDPR	2
Mironov	Party of Life	<1

there for political parties.[18] While party strength can crudely be judged based on how many votes each party list received in a given Duma election, we are also interested in more fine-grained assessments of party strength. In particular, we want to know the degree to which voters are basing their choices of

[18] Russian law generally defines the term "party" more narrowly than does this volume. For our purposes in the Russian context, however, the term "party" is used here to refer to any organization that is officially registered by the Russian Ministry of Justice as eligible to nominate a slate of candidates in the PR voting for the Duma.

parties for the parliament on sophisticated understandings of representation. To tackle this question, we can employ a statistical analysis much like the one reported in Table 3.2 that examines the bases of transitional partisanship.[19] The bases of the vote might be expected to differ somewhat from the bases of partisanship since more people tend to vote for a party than tend to consider themselves party loyalists. Thus, the vote is likely to be more sensitive to tactical moves that parties make during the campaign, such as stressing certain issues over others, trying to stake out a new position on a new issue, or targeting certain social groups more than others in order to reach beyond the party's loyal core of voters. Table 3.4 is thus formatted a lot like Table 3.2 except that instead of reporting the results of a statistical analysis of the correlates of transitional partisanship, it provides the results of a statistical analysis of the correlates of the party-list vote from the 1995 election through the 2003 contest. We find that parties were connecting with their parliamentary voters strongly on the basis of issue positions and socioeconomic factors in much the same way that they had been connecting with their own transitional partisans.

The Communists benefited strongly from the opinion divide on economic reform; an otherwise typical voter who strongly opposed the market economy was 10 percent more likely than those who voiced other or no opinions to vote KPRF in 1995, 20 percent more likely in 1999, and 12 percent more likely in 2003. While they successfully won voters in 1995 and 1999 on the basis of nationalist issues (especially anti-Semitism[20]) and political questions (preferring a strong parliament to a dominant presidency), these issues did not significantly help them in 2003. This is most likely because the Kremlin's hard-hitting negative campaign in 2003 managed to strip away all but the hardest of hard-core KPRF partisans, whose chief issue tended to be opposition to market reform, as Table 3.2 demonstrates. Whereas KPRF partisans did not stand out for any particular assessment of economic trends, KPRF campaigns won votes from those who, more than others, believed that the economy was faring poorly. The party's voters also stood out for being elderly, living in the smaller Russian communities, and formerly belonging to the USSR's Communist Party.

Despite the fact that the Yabloko Party placed a great deal of emphasis on its ideas for economic reform, its strongest suit between 1995 and 2003 was consistently the party's support for democratic values. Indeed, it was the only party to stand out on the pro-democracy side of this issue in all three of the

[19] The statistical technique used is exactly the same; the difference between the exercises is that in Table 3.4 the dependent variable is the party vote instead of transitional partisanship as in Table 3.2.

[20] While the KPRF generally won votes on the nationalist end of the political spectrum, in 1995 it opposed Yeltsin's bungled decision to wage war in Chechnya and attracted ballots on this account.

TABLE 3.4. *Bases of the Vote for Major Parties 1995–2003**

		Issue Positions				
		Economy	Political System	Nationalism	Social Background	View of Current Conditions
KPRF	1995	Antimarket (10%) Protectionist (4%) Antiprivatization (3%)	Order over rights (5%) Antipresidentialism (5%)	Dislike Jews (6%) US is a threat (6%) Oppose Chechnya war (4%)	Older (22%) Smaller settlement (11%) Was CPSU member (9%) Lives in south Russia (9%) Lives in west Russia (4%)	Own finances worsening (6%) Economy not improving (5%) Economy way down (5%)
	1999	For socialism (20%)	Antipresidentialism (7%)	For Russia-Ukraine union (6%) For limiting Jews (5%)	Older (36%) Smaller settlement (12%) Was CPSU member (11%) Lower education (8%) Lives in south Russia (8%) Lives in east Russia (7%)	Dissatisfied with Russian democracy (6%) Economy not improving (5%)
	2003	For socialism (12%) Punish oligarchs (4%)			Older (16%) Smaller settlement (3%)	Economy not improving (2%)
Yabloko	1995	Pro-market (5%) Antiprotectionist (3%)	Party competition good (4%)		Younger (8%) Higher education (7%) Bigger cities (5%) Male (5%) Lives in north Russia (3%)	
	1999		Liberty over order (5%)	Against Russia-Ukraine union (6%) Against limiting Jews (6%)	Not in collective farm (11%) Bigger cities (7%) Lives in north Russia (5%)	
	2003		Democracy over strong leader (12%)		Higher education (7%) Not in collective farm (6%)	

SPS	1995 (RDC)	Antiprotectionist (2%)	Propresidentialism (4%) Party competition good (2%)		Higher education (4%) Bigger cities (4%) Not in collective farm (3%) Home privatized (2%) Lives in east Russia (2%)	Economy improving (3%) Economy not way down (2%)
	1999	Against socialism (7%)	Liberty over order (5%)	Against limiting Jews (4%)	Bigger cities (12%) Younger (11%) Not in collective farm (10%)	Economy improving (5%)
	2003				Bigger cities (4%) Not in collective farm (3%)	Own finances not bad (3%)
LDPR	1995	Protectionist (1%)	Order over rights (4%) Propresidentialism (2%)		Younger (5%) Lives in west Russia (4%) Male (3%) Lower education (1%) Home not privatized (1%)	Economy way down (3%) Dissatisfied with Russian democracy (2%)
	1999				Male (6%) Not in collective farm (4%) Lower education (3%)	
	2003				Younger (11%) Male (7%) Middle class (4%) Lower education (2%)	Own finances not improving (3%)
United Russia (and parties that later merged with it)	1995 (OHR)	Proprivatization (6%)	Party competition bad (7%)	Don't dislike Jews (11%)	Bigger cities (9%)	Economy improving (14%) Economy not way down (8%)
	1999 (OHR)	Against socialism (1%) Revisit privatization (1%)	Electing leaders important (1%)		Job not in private sector (1%) Not in collective farm (1%) Was not CPSU member (1%)	Economy not way down (1%)

(*continued*)

TABLE 3.4 *(continued)*

		Issue Positions				
		Economy	Political System	Nationalism	Social Background	View of Current Conditions
	1999 (FAR)		Against high regional autonomy (8%)		In collective farm (59%) Bigger cities (17%) Higher education (10%) Non-Russian (9%) Lives in west Russia (9%) Lives in north Russia (7%)	Economy not improving (8%) No wage arrears (6%)
	1999 (Unity)		Order over liberty (10%) High regional autonomy (6%)		Smaller settlements (21%) Younger (18%) Not in collective farm (15%)	Economy improving (10%)
	2003 (UR)	Against socialism (17%)	Strong leader over democracy (10%) Propresidentialism (8%)	Pro-West (14%)	Female (15%) Lives in south Russia (12%) Lives in east Russia (11%) Lower education (10%)	Economy improving (10%) Satisfied with Russian democracy (9%)
Motherland	2003				Lives in north Russia (6%)	
Agrarian Party	1995				Small settlements (12%) Lives in west Russia (3%) Older (2%) Job not in private sector (1%) Home not privatized (0%)	
Women of Russia	1995				Younger (12%) Female (9%)	

* This table reports those issue stands, social background characteristics, and assessments of the situation in Russia that public opinion survey respondents reported and that were calculated with at least 95% confidence to be correlated with the vote for a particular major party in a given election (as reported by the respondents). Technical information about these findings can be obtained through the web site www.whynotpartiesinrussia.com.

last parliamentary elections. Yabloko was also consistently favored by voters set apart by higher education and residence in Russia's larger communities. These appeals, however, proved not to be strong enough for the party to win entry into the 2003–7 Duma. This finding does suggest, however, that Yabloko has at least a chance to regain its political standing should its leadership prove able to recapture and develop its status as the primary pro-democracy party in Russia.

The Union of Right Forces in 1995 and 1999 also won votes on the basis of democratic values, but lost this distinction in 2003, evidently because its campaign associated itself too closely with President Putin; self-professed democrats who thought Putin was good for democracy voted for his favorite party, United Russia, whereas other democrats did not appear to see SPS as a credible defender of democracy, preferring Yabloko. A similar dynamic seems to have befallen SPS in 2003 on its other chief issue, economic reform; whereas the party and its chief predecessor successfully wooed pro-market voters in both 1995 and 1999, in 2003 the only party to win votes on the basis of pro-market sentiments was United Russia. The voters that SPS won in 2003, then, stood out mainly as being among those who had benefited either directly or indirectly from the reforms associated with the party's leaders and those who did not live in collective farms but who resided in larger cities. The party in 2003, therefore, indeed appears to have flown too close to Putin's sun, whose energy was almost entirely captured by United Russia.

The findings also reinforce the interpretation of the LDPR as a largely personalistic party capable of mobilizing a very distinct electorate, particularly young, the poorly educated the males, and people not benefiting from the decade's economic reforms. Interestingly, voters do not appear to have been swayed by Zhirinovsky's nationalist rants.

While Table 3.2 reports that transitional partisanship for parties of power became increasingly grounded in issue stands and social structure, the bases of the actual vote for parties of power was remarkably consistent between 1995 and 2003. In both 1995 and 2003, those casting ballots for the party of power had distinctly promarket, nondemocratic, and antinationalist attitudes as well as a decidedly bullish view of the economy. The differences in performance between Our Home is Russia and United Russia appear largely due to United Russia's more effective mobilization of people with these points of view and the greater number of people in 2003 that shared these opinions. For example, if in 1995 only 9 percent believed that the economy had improved over the previous year, by 2003 the analogous figure had risen to 35 percent according to the surveys. Significantly, United Russia also shifted the party of power's demographic appeal, moving from Our Home's vote concentration among urbanites to a strong showing among women, people without higher education, and residents of Russia's South (previously a bastion of Communist support) and East.

The 1999 election represents something of an interlude since there was at the time no proper "party of power," a party openly backed by the Kremlin designed primarily to win a large propresidential representation in the Duma. Our Home is Russia had lost this status when Chernomyrdin was fired as prime minister in 1998, and Fatherland–All Russia, which includes many governors, was in opposition to the Kremlin. Unity has been reasonably dubbed a party of power, but as Chapter 5 will show, it was created virtually from scratch less than three months before the 1999 election and its primary aim was not to win a large Duma delegation for the president, but to draw votes (and gubernatorial patrons) away from Fatherland–All Russia as a means of preventing its leaders from gaining momentum for a presidential bid.[21] Furthermore, with less than a month to go in the campaign, Putin also lent support to SPS as an acceptable alternative progovernment party, further muddying the "party of power" waters. Under these conditions, voters for the various parties that later combined to form United Russia were quite distinct from one another on key dimensions. If Unity's 1999 voters were distinguished for optimism on the state of the economy, Fatherland–All Russia backers were decidedly pessimistic (although they tended to live in some of the most well-run regions, those not experiencing wage arrears). Unity and Fatherland–All Russia also squared off on the issue of regional autonomy; the former proved to be a more credible advocate of significant regional autonomy, whereas the latter's electorate was set apart by a strong stand for balanced relations between center and periphery. A contrast was also found in demographic bases; while Unity found its strongest support in small, nonfarming settlements, Fatherland–All Russia did best at the extremes, in big cities as well as on collective farms. Where Unity's voters were younger, Fatherland–All Russia's were more highly educated, frequently non-Russian, and concentrated in northern and western Russia. Unity differed most dramatically with Our Home is Russia on the issue of democracy, with voters for the new pro-presidential party showing much greater willingness to sacrifice individual rights for the sake of order than voters for the old pro-presidential party. Whereas Unity was not distinguished by particularly pro-market voters, those few who voted for Our Home is Russia that year were against socialism. It is testimony to the power of United Russia's 2003 appeal, grounded in the performance of the presidency with which it was associated, that the merger of these three parties took place so smoothly during the four years following 1999 and produced an ideational mix so consistent as that displayed by United Russia's 2003 electorate.

Overall, then, we find strong evidence that Russia's parties during the first ten years of Duma elections connected with voters not purely on the basis of personalistic sympathies or largely unthinking reflexes, but to a significant

[21] For more details, see Hale 2004a.

TABLE 3.5. *Percentage of People Who Say They Would Have Voted for Same Major Party for Which They Voted in 1999 Duma Elections Had That Party Been Led By a Different Individual*

	Would Not Vote for Party Under a Different Leader (%)	Would Vote for Party Regardless of Leader (%)	Depends on Who the Different Leader Is (%)
Our Home is Russia	0	44	56
KPRF	9	61	24
Yabloko	19	34	36
SPS	25	29	39
Fatherland–All Russia	30	12	49
Unity	31	19	39
LDPR	39	25	28

degree on the basis of viewpoints on important questions of the day and links to key elements of social structure associated with particular interests. We find some additional evidence for this assertion in the 1999–2000 survey, the only one of the set used here to ask voters directly whether they would have voted for the same party had it been headed by a different leader. Over two-thirds of Russian voters said they would have considered supporting the same party under a different leader and 37 percent indicated that they would have voted for the same party regardless of who the leader was. Only 21 percent said that their choice of party in the PR competition in 1999 was wholly due to the particular party leader at the time. There is, of course, variation across parties here. Table 3.5 provides a breakdown by party of the percentage who said that they would not have voted for the party under a different leader. These numbers tell us that the existing leadership was the most important for Zhirinovsky's LDPR, although even there only 39 percent of voters were so loyal to him personally that they declared they would not have voted for the party had he not been in charge of it. Unity and Fatherland–All Russia fairly closely followed the LDPR in the degree of leader-orientation professed by their voters. Far and away, Communist Party voters declared themselves to be the least leader-oriented, with only 9 percent threatening defection were Zyuganov to resign his post as party chief. That a large percentage of Our Home is Russia voters denied leader orientation surely reflects the fact that its few 1999 voters were primarily those who had not abandoned it after its leader, Chernomyrdin, lost his most attractive trait when he was fired as prime minister in 1998. Behind the Communists and Our Home, the most clearly ideational parties (Yabloko and SPS) had the highest percentages of their voters aver that they would have voted for the party regardless of who led these organizations. Thus, while party leaders clearly mattered to voters, this was not the whole story. This adds credence to the preceding findings that voters chose parties in parliamentary elections to a significant degree based upon social structure and views on important issues.

Moreover, as would be expected in a developing party system, the success of parties in connecting with voters was found to depend significantly on developments in the country as a whole and on parties' campaign tactics and strategic interaction. Most dramatically, we see how United Russia was able to deepen and significantly expand the traditional appeal of Russian parties of power thanks to what many saw as positive developments in the country. In terms of the bigger picture, the findings show that United Russia, a party that began as a collection of largely clientelistic parties, steadily accumulated a powerful stock of ideational capital. We also observe how ideational parties, such as SPS, could lose this capital through unwise decisions that diluted this capital in the heat of competition from other parties (in this case, United Russia and Yabloko) for the same ideational niches.

The Single-Member-District (SMD) Half of the Duma Elections

In the SMD half of the Duma elections that were conducted between 1993 and 2003, unlike the PR half, parties were not given a legal monopoly on ballot access. Instead, hundreds of independents ran for the 225 seats elected in this manner alongside major-party nominees. The SMD Duma elections thus afford an important chance to explore party strength by seeing what happened when both candidates and voters had the option of "going nonpartisan."

Unfortunately, no previous survey project has asked potential voters more than a handful of questions regarding their choices in the SMD elections. Even when such "handfuls" of questions are asked in nationwide surveys, however, it is problematic at best to generalize based on them because the set of survey respondents is not representative in any one district. This is important because the sets of choices among which voters must select have been widely different in different districts. In some constituencies, for example, voters would find a Yabloko candidate on the ballot whereas in others they would not. The same could be said for all major parties. These problems, along with several other technical concerns, make impossible a fully satisfactory study of the role of parties in the actual voting decisions of citizens in these contests.[22]

[22] This has been recognized by some of the premier analysts of the PR and presidential votes in Russia, such as Colton and McFaul. The present author, together with these and other scholars, are in the process of addressing this problem as part of a different project. See also Smyth (2006) for an analysis of potential candidates' decisions to compete or not compete in SMD elections.

These methodological challenges have forced the compilation of an original database culled from those partial sources of information that do exist, a project that proved possible to complete with respect to the 1999 elections. This involved using four main sources. First, Russia's Central Election Commission published candidate biographies, candidate vote totals, and a simple statement of how each candidate was nominated.[23] Second, the East-West Institute tracked many single-member district elections in 1999 through its network of about 70 regional correspondents; the summary tables and raw reports from these local experts were generously provided to the author for the purpose of this analysis.[24] Third, the Russian-language *Radio Svoboda* broadcast reports on the 1999 SMD elections from its network of correspondents across Russia.[25] Fourth, the author was given an internal database of a major Russian political party assessing the 1999 SMD contests. Information on each of the district contests in 1999 was cross-checked in these different sources, although in some cases information on a given candidate was available from only one source. Thus, while no single source taken individually was complete in providing all of the needed information, a careful reading of all of them made possible the construction of a comprehensive database on SMD elections in Russia. Some other sources were used in gathering specific pieces of information and in confirming information from the four main sources just described. For example, in identifying the party affiliation of a candidate who happened to be an incumbent, one could consult official Duma publications to find out the deputy group to which the candidate belonged.

Table 3.6 summarizes some of the findings. Most dramatically, it confirms that parties were only part of the story in the SMD races of 1999. Not one of Russia's major parties managed to place a nominee in even two-thirds of the 224 races that were run.[26] Even the mighty Communist Party nominated candidates in just 129 districts, with the Union of Right Forces placing nominees in just 66.

This table also shows, however, that parties participated in the SMD elections in several different capacities. Some party members ran in the elections, but without their party's formal nomination.[27] Sometimes this involved

[23] Central Election Commission of the Russian Federation *Vybory Deputatov Gosudarstvennoi Dumy Federal'nogo Sobraniia Rossiiskoi Federatsii 1999* (Moscow: Ves. Mir, 2000); candidate biographies posted on the CEC's official Web site: http://www.fci.ru/gd99/spiski/ZAR_F213/Main213_int.htm as updated December 9, 1999, accessed February 2001.

[24] Special thanks are due to Robert Orttung.

[25] Broadcasts during fall 1999, transcripts available at http://www.svoboda.org/archive/elections99, accessed September–October 2002.

[26] No SMD Duma election was held in Chechnya that year.

[27] Often this information was provided by candidates themselves in the official biographies published by the CEC. Incumbent deputies belonging to a party's fraction in the Duma at

TABLE 3.6. *Major Party Activity in the 224 SMD Duma Races of 1999*

	KPRF	Yabloko	Union of Right Forces	LDPR	Our Home is Russia	Fatherland–All Russia	Unity
Number of party nominees	129	114	66	89	89	91	31
Winners	46	4	5	0	7	31	9
Avg. vote (%)	22	9	10	3	7	20	17
Number of partisan candidates	171	119	86	111	97	120	33
Winners	62	5	5	3	10	42	10
Avg. vote (%)	21	10	9	5	8	20	17
Number of candidates endorsed	169	143	161	n/a	n/a	122	n/a
Winners	66	11	26	n/a	n/a	46	n/a
Avg. vote (%)	22	11	14	n/a	n/a	21	n/a
Endorsees affiliated with other major parties	None	5 URF 1 FAR 1 OHR	31 Yabloko 7 OHR 4 Unity 1 FAR	n/a	n/a	1 KPRF 1 Yabloko 1 OHR	n/a

n/a = Data not available

tactical considerations. For example, a Communist Party member who had served as a first deputy prime minister in Prime Minister Primakov's government in late 1998 and early 1999 (Yury Masliukov) had secured the backing not only of the KPRF but also of Primakov's Fatherland–All Russia for his run for an SMD Duma seat in Udmurtiia. To avoid unnecessarily alienating Fatherland–All Russia supporters, Masliukov chose not to be formally nominated by the KPRF. In other cases, party members contested districts against the will of their party's leadership. In one instance, the Communist Party's leadership dropped a sitting Duma deputy (Tamara Gudima) from her favorable place on the 1999 party list. Upset at the central organization's

the time of the election were also coded as being party affiliates unless there was evidence that they had informally broken with their party, as happened in a few instances when incumbents were slighted by the central party organization during the process of nomination. Some of this information came from the regional correspondent reports of *Radio Svoboda* and the East-West Institute as well as the internal assessments of one major political party. Importantly, nomination by a party was counted as making a candidate "partisan" for the purposes of constructing Table 3.6.

decision, Gudima sought nomination as an independent in her home region of Arkhangelsk despite the fact that the KPRF had already placed a candidate there. In still other instances, a party organization would "trade off" one district to another entity in return for that entity's support in a different district, and sometimes the "sacrificed" candidate would not go along with the deal. An example in 1999 involved Vladimir Lysenko, one of the initial organizers of the Fatherland movement. When Fatherland moved to cement its alliance with the All Russia coalition of governors and Primakov, it reportedly conceded Lysenko's district in Moscow Oblast in order to make room for a candidate backed by one of these other partners. Lysenko ran anyway, seeking independent nomination, and ultimately won. Just to look at the number of formal party nominees in a Duma race or in the Duma, then, is to underestimate the level of party penetration of this organ. Still, Table 3.6 shows that even counting these "hidden partisans," no party had more members running than the Communists' 171 in 164 of the 224 district races held in 1999.[28]

Parties often publicly endorsed candidates who were neither their own nominees nor members, but with whom these parties enjoyed good relations.[29] Sometimes, these endorsements reflected deals struck between parties trading support in two different districts. Yabloko and the Union of Right Forces, for example, backed a total of 36 of each other's candidates. In different cases, these party endorsements of candidates involved alliances between candidates who either did not care to join the party formally or whom the party rejected but respected. For example, in Bashkortostan, incumbent deputy Aleksandr Arinin approached both Yabloko and the Union of Right Forces for membership. Yabloko, however, did not want to be too closely associated with what some in the party considered to be his reputation as a Russian chauvinist. The Union of Right Forces, on the other hand, thought him to be too radically opposed to the regional power establishment, with which it wanted to forge closer relations. Both parties were willing to lend endorsement but not formal nomination or membership. In other instances, however, these endorsements did not reflect any real candidate

28 That is, in seven districts (numbers 1, 10, 21, 59, 60, 119, and 173), two Communist Party partisans ran against each other in the same district.

29 Parties' public lists of endorsees were obtained directly for two parties, the Union of Right Forces and Yabloko. For Fatherland–All Russia and the Communist Party, their endorsements were determined by reading and cross-checking reports on the different SMD races from sources noted above (notably the CEC, the East-West Institute, and *Radio Svoboda*). For other parties, however, data were not available. In a few cases where two candidates were running from the same party and no other source explicitly stated which one was favored, it was reasonably assumed that the official nominee was the supported candidate, or, where there was no party nomination, that the candidate with senior status in the party was nominated (as was the case in a very few instances where a partisan Duma incumbent faced a more obscure member of this same party in a given district).

tie to the party, just the party's wish that a given candidate be elected. Although, unfortunately, data were not available for the patterns of endorsement of all major parties, the examples of Yabloko and SPS make clear that actual party involvement in district politics was often much greater than it might appear simply by looking at their formal nominees. Nevertheless, none of the parties on which we have information appear even to have actively endorsed candidates in more than three-quarters of Russia's Duma districts. Moreover, we must treat formal nomination itself as the truest indicator of party *strength* since the fact that tactical or other considerations require avoiding party nomination indicates that parties are not as strong as they might be.

Of course, we want to know not only how extensive party *coverage* of these elections was but how effectively they competed when they had horses in the race. Table 3.6 gives us some indication of this. Only the KPRF and Fatherland–All Russia turned more than 10 of their nominees or partisans into winners in the 1999 Duma contest. These two parties and Unity won roughly one-third of the races in which they had candidates. The other parties fared far worse, winning in fewer than 15 percent of their SMD contests, no matter whether one counts nominees or partisans more generally.

If we turn our attention to the average share of the vote won by a given party's SMD candidates in those races where the party did place a nominee, the results are somewhat contrary to what might be expected. Most observers consider Yabloko and the Union of Right Forces to be very top-heavy, Moscow-based parties with little appeal beyond their most famous national leaders. Lower-level representatives of both of these parties, however, gained larger average shares of the vote in their SMD races than did their party in the party-list competition. This is at least partly explained by the fact that these two parties picked and chose where to run their candidates, selecting those districts where they expected to have the best chances. The KPRF, with the most evenly distributed nationwide support and the largest number of nominees, thus garnered roughly the same share of the vote for its SMD candidates (22 percent) as the party earned in the national arena (24 percent). The most genuinely top-heavy parties, however, did do worse than their party-list performances despite being able to pick and choose districts. Unity's district nominees thus gained an average of just 17 percent of the vote and the LDPR's a mere 3 percent. Those clientelistic parties with the most robust but spotty organization, Fatherland–All Russia and Our Home is Russia, earned far larger average shares of the SMD vote in the districts where they ran candidates than these parties received nationwide.

Table 3.7 puts these figures in broader temporal context and shows that 1999 represents something of an interruption in what is otherwise a relatively steady increase in the level of major-party activity in the districts. This pattern can be seen most clearly in two statistics – the total number of candidates whom major parties nominated in the districts and the total number of seats

TABLE 3.7. *Major-Party Activity in the SMD Duma Races 1993–2003*

	Number of Nominees	Average District Vote (%)	Number of Winners
1993			
Russia's Choice	105	19	26
Yabloko	85	11	6
Agrarian Party	67	18	16
PRES	62	11	3
LDPR	59	12	6
Democratic Party	57	10	1
Communist Party	55	14	10
Women of Russia	6	24	2
Total	496		70
1995			
LDPR	187	7	1
Communist Party	129	21	56
Our Home is Russia	104	12	10
Agrarian Party	87	14	20
Russia's Democratic Choice	80	8	9
Yabloko	69	11	14
Women of Russia	20	11	3
Total	676		113
1999			
Communist Party	129	22	46
Yabloko	114	9	4
Fatherland–All Russia	91	20	31
LDPR	89	3	0
Our Home is Russia	89	7	7
Union of Right Forces (SPS)	66	10	5
Unity	31	17	9
Total	609		102
2003			
LDPR	192	4	0
Communist Party	174	14	12
United Russia	147	34	100
Union of Right Forces (SPS)	114	6	3
Yabloko	103	6	4
Motherland	55	12	8
Total	785		127

that major-party nominees actually won, each of which rose between 1993 and 1995, dipped somewhat in 1999, and then rose again strongly to new highs in 2003. Different sets of parties contributed in different ways to this overall pattern. The Western-oriented promarket parties varied within a relatively narrow range and did not demonstrate a steady rise or decline during the decade under examination here, with the low value being SPS's slate of 66 candidates in 1999 and the high value being the 114 mark that Yabloko reached in 1999 and SPS met in 2003. These parties also never translated many of their nominations into seats; the only times that either of these parties won more than 10 district seats were in 1993 when SPS's predecessor (Russia's Choice) enjoyed sustained Kremlin sponsorship and in 1995 when Yabloko pulled out 14 victories. The overall pattern noted at the start of this paragraph was thus driven primarily by the Communist Party and Russia's government-sponsored parties. The Communists covered just 55 districts with their nominees in 1993, raised this number to 129 in 1995, remained at this same number in 1999, and then increased their coverage to 174 in 2003. But while the Communists expanded their platoon of district candidates in 2003, they suffered a dramatic decline in their ability to convert nominations into both votes and seats. Russia's primary progovernment parties did not show significant increased coverage between 1993 and 1995, nominating 105 candidates in 1993 (Russia's Choice) and 104 in 1995 (Our Home is Russia), but demonstrated a dramatic leap from Unity's 31 in 1999 to United Russia's 147 in 2003. What is even more dramatic, however, is the 2003 surge in the progovernment party's ability to win both votes and seats for its nominees, consistently defeating the Communists in dozens of head-to-head contests on the road to winning a stunning 100 district seats.

Stepping back again to the overall patterns, something seems to have stalled party activity in the districts in 1999 and then generated renewed growth in a way that produced disproportionate success for United Russia. We should not lose sight of the bigger picture here, however, which is that major parties have consistently managed to penetrate only part of the district half of the Duma and elections to it. Only in 2003 did the nominees of Russia's major parties fill more than half of the Duma's 225 district-designated seats, but even that year's figure was only 56 percent of the total.

These figures, however, give us only a bare-bones idea of party activity in the districts. In particular, they tell us little about whether parties have actually been helping candidates do better than they otherwise would have in these elections. Thus, while we know that Yabloko candidates earned an average of 9 percent of their districts' vote in 1999, we do not know if this is any more or less than similar candidates were getting who were not nominated by Yabloko. In fact, it could theoretically be the case that Yabloko's nominees would have gotten more of the vote had they foregone party nomination; the figures presented above simply do not tell us.

For these reasons, it is informative to analyze patterns in election outcomes more systematically. Regression analysis is designed to do precisely this, identifying important patterns in complex data. Table 3.8 reports the results of four separate regressions designed to see whether party-nominated candidates performed systematically better than did candidates without party nomination in the SMD Duma elections of 1993, 1995, 1999, and 2003. This table thus also enables us to detect changes in average party-candidate performance over the course of these four rounds of elections. Specifically, the figures in Table 3.8 represent the estimated additional percentage of an average district's vote that a typical nonpartisan candidate would accrue by running as the nominee of the listed party.[30]

The patterns identified are quite striking. To begin, we discover that those who have proclaimed Russian parties' weakness were absolutely right in 1993 as far as the SMD Duma elections are concerned. Not a single party's nomination, not even the Communists', was associated with any electoral advantage for candidates, or no advantage that we can detect with at least 95 percent statistical confidence. Even more dramatic is the finding that any effect parties may have had in 1993 appears to have been *negative*. With over 95 percent confidence, for example, we find that Yabloko nominees won 4 percent fewer votes than did other candidates, PRES nominees 4.6 percent fewer, Democratic Party nominees 5.5 percent fewer, and so on.

30 For many of the regressions reported in this chapter (Tables 3.8, 3.9, 3.13, 3.14), the percentage of the district vote that each candidate won in the given election is the quantity to be explained. Since this quantity is a percentage, it is bounded between zero and 100 and can be interpreted as a *composition* (a particular allocation of a district's total vote between one candidate and the others). Following techniques developed and tested for analyzing compositional data, we transform the bounded dependent variable into an unbounded log ratio, facilitating the method of ordinary least squares (OLS), which assumes no bounds. Specifically, the ratio is the natural logarithm of the following quantity: a candidate's vote divided by the share of the vote not received by the candidate. Since observations are not expected to be completely independent *within* election districts but *are* expected to be independent *across* districts, the Huber-White estimator of variance is used to obtain accurate estimates of our statistical confidence in the results, and a control variable is also included indicating how many candidates were contesting a given district. Since the coefficients produced by this analysis are log ratios, we use the software CLARIFY to provide the values reported in the tables: the estimated change in a candidate's percentage of the district vote associated with a shift from the absence of a factor of interest to its presence when all other variables are held at their mean values. The main independent variables of interest are dummy variables coded as 1 if a candidate is nominated by a given party and 0 otherwise. On compositional analysis, see: Katz and King 1999; and Tomz, Tucker, and Wittenberg 2002. On the Huber-White estimator, in the *Stata.7* software manual, see [U] 23.11, "obtaining robust variance estimates." The command used is *cluster ()*. The cost of this method is a small loss of efficiency, expected to be negligible in this case given the large number of observations examined. All of the independent variables vary at the candidate level, not the district level, except for the "number of rivals" control. On CLARIFY, see King, Tomz, and Wittenberg 2000; and Tomz, Wittenberg, and King 2003. The only independent variable that is not binary is the "number of rivals" control.

TABLE 3.8. *Estimated Percentage Change in SMD Duma Candidates' Vote Associated with Party Nomination in Elections, 1993–2003*

Year	Party	Estimated Difference in Percentage of the Vote Associated with Variable	R^2	N
1993	Women of Russia	5.2	.36	1,519
	Russia's Choice	1.5		
	Communist Party	1.2		
	Agrarian Party	−0.6		
	LDPR	−1.5		
	Dignity and Compassion	−4.2		
	Yabloko	−4.0*		
	PRES	−4.6*		
	Civic Union	−4.8*		
	RDDR	−5.1*		
	Democratic Party	−5.5*		
	KEDR	−6.5*		
	Future of Russia – New Names	−7.4*		
	Control Variable: Number of Rivals	−25.9*		
1995	Communist Party	17.9*	.30	2,628
	Yabloko	8.8*		
	Our Home is Russia	7.8*		
	Women of Russia	6.9*		
	Agrarian Party	6.2*		
	Russia's Democratic Choice	4.1*		
	Communists for the USSR	2.9*		
	LDPR	1.9*		
	KRO	1.8*		
	Rybkin Bloc	0.6		
	Forward Russia!	0.2		
	Control Variable: Number of Rivals	−13.8*		
1999	Communist Party	18.6*	.27	2,226
	Fatherland–All Russia	15.9*		
	Unity	14.8*		
	Women of Russia	7.2*		
	Union of Right Forces	7.1*		
	Yabloko	5.6*		
	Pensioners' Party	2.5*		
	Communists for the USSR	1.5		
	Our Home is Russia	0.6		
	LDPR	−1.8*		
	Control Variable: Number of Rivals	−12.3*		

Year	Party	Estimated Difference in Percentage of the Vote Associated with Variable	R^2	*N*
2003	United Russia	30.5*	.37	1,888
	People's Party	13.9*		
	Communist Party	11.2*		
	Motherland	8.3*		
	Yabloko	2.0*		
	SPS	2.3*		
	Agrarian Party	1.3		
	Pensioners' Party	0.5		
	LDPR	−0.5		
	Rus	−5.6*		
	Control Variable: Number of Rivals	−12.2*		

* 95% confidence level.

By 1995, however, this pattern had changed entirely. We have over 95 percent statistical confidence that no fewer than nine parties' sets of nominees tended to gain more votes than average, including those of the Communist Party (17.9 percent more votes than average), Yabloko (8.8), Our Home is Russia (7.8), Russia's Democratic Choice (4.1), and the LDPR (1.9).

Table 3.8 also reports that this rapid growth in parties' association with electoral success in the districts had leveled off somewhat by 1999. While the Communist Party, Yabloko, and the successor to Russia's Democratic Choice (the Union of Right Forces) were still strongly associated with better-than-average candidate performances in the SMD races, the magnitude of these advantages was not dramatically larger or, in the case of Yabloko, was a bit smaller than in 1995. The LDPR actually became associated with poorer-than-average candidate showings in the districts, and the "effect" of Our Home is Russia collapsed entirely. We do see extraordinarily strong performance from two new entrants to the party scene, however. Fatherland–All Russia nominees tended to win 15.9 percent more of the district vote than did candidates without this status and Unity was not far behind, with its nomination being associated with a 14.8 percent bump in candidate performance.

The 2003 election represents what might appear to be contradictory patterns. On one hand, United Russia soared to what could be interpreted as a 30.5 percent positive effect on its nominees' chances. Interestingly, this figure is almost exactly equal to the combined 1999 "effects" of the two major parties that merged to form United Russia Unity and Fatherland–All Russia. The new Motherland bloc also proved to be associated with strong district performances, as did the People's Party, a pro-Putin party that was formed by a large number of formerly independent SMD incumbents and that effectively melded into United Russia's Duma fraction shortly after the 2003 Duma election. The Communists, Yabloko, and SPS, however, all suffered declines in the degree to which their nominees outperformed otherwise average candidates, although their nominations were still found to benefit candidates. The LDPR ceased to appear as a liability to its nominees but its nomination was found to have no statistically significant relationship to their performance. Certain parties, such as the tiny new organization *Rus*, were associated with unusually weak candidate chances.

These figures still do not tell us for sure whether parties have ever actually had any effect on candidate performance, however; they only report that starting in 1995, many parties' nominees tended to perform better on average than did other candidates in the Duma district elections. While one explanation would be that parties were increasingly providing candidates with important resources that were helping them win votes, another explanation is that parties were simply getting better at attracting candidates who would have done better than average regardless of whether a party nominated them. Either of these interpretations would be evidence for the importance of parties in Russia. Indeed, theorists generally agree that one of parties' central functions is to organize choice for voters and one way of doing so is to recruit strong candidates to contest important offices. Moreover, observers in the West typically hold that strong parties are good *both* at improving their candidates' chances of election and at bringing good people into politics in the first place. Of course, it is also possible that strong candidates come forward on their own and rather passively accept the labels of parties that seek to back them. This latter possibility would mean that parties are little more than window dressing in Russian politics. It would thus be desirable to establish, for at least one round of elections, that what we see in Table 3.8 between 1995 and 2003 is in fact parties actually helping their nominees win votes or successfully attracting promising candidates.

Fortunately, sufficient information is available for the 1999 district contests to establish, with a great degree of confidence, whether parties were having real effects on candidate performance. This can be done by controlling for the electoral strength that a candidate possesses independently of support from a party.[31] This is done here in two ways.

First, we introduce into the equation a series of control variables that indicate whether a given candidate possesses certain traits or personal resources that might be expected to lead to electoral success irrespective of that candidate's party affiliation. These controls capture whether a candidate was an *incumbent* Duma deputy (elected in the SMD or the PR half of the voting);

[31] On the importance of personal candidate resources, see Golosov 2003; Moser 1999; and Smyth 1998.

a *female*; a *state official* (at the federal, regional, or local level); a *regional* or *local legislator*; or primarily employed (according to biographies issued by Russia's Central Election Commission) in the *military*, the *intelligentsia*, *agriculture*, *politics* (as with full-time party leaders), blue-collar (*proletarian*) work, *sports* (sometimes linked to mafia groups), or private *business*.[32] For reasons that will be explicated in Chapter 4, we also introduce variables indicating whether a candidate enjoyed the backing of the regional *governor* or a *politicized financial-industrial group* (*PFIG*).

A second way in which this analysis controls for the personal strength of candidates so as to isolate the effects of parties in the 1999 SMD Duma elections is to include a variable that indicates whether regional experts considered particular candidates to be "key contenders" *prior* to the voting. The East-West Institute's Russian regional correspondents were each specifically asked to identify candidates who were key contenders in nearly every district prior to the election. We augment these predictions with similar assessments made for a large number of districts by *Radio Svoboda*'s regional correspondents and in almost all districts by a major Russian political party. A candidate was thus coded as a *contender* if any one of these three sources named the candidate as a realistically possible winner or a main challenger. These expert assessments should be expected to capture intangible but very important candidate assets like charisma, popularity, and name recognition, as well as tangible traits like personal wealth that might be known locally but may not be evident from a candidate's official biography. To the extent that party nominees perform better than candidates with similar biographies even when local expert predictions are taken into account, we have a great deal of confidence that parties are directly contributing to their candidates' success and are not succeeding only in recruiting or "rubber stamping" likely winners.

It is critical to note, however, that the reports filed by many of these regional correspondents indicated that they judged candidate prospects not solely by their personal assets, but also by whether they were backed by certain major parties. Regressions including the *contender* control variable, therefore, are likely to *understate* the real level of party vote-winning capacity in the SMD elections. These regressions, reported in the even-numbered columns of Table 3.9, are thus best interpreted as establishing a lower bound to the real average degree to which parties were helping candidates win votes in 1999. The regressions reported in the odd-numbered columns of Table 3.9 do not include the *contender* control variable and can thus be seen as estimating an upper bound of the average percentage of the vote that parties tended to win for their candidates.

32 We also include control variables for important party substitutes that will be discussed in Chapter 4, once we have introduced and operationalized the notion of "party substitutes" with reference to the Russian context.

TABLE 3.9. *Estimated Percentage Change in SMD Duma Candidates' Vote Associated with Different Forms of Party Backing and Candidate Characteristics in Elections, 1999*[a]

	1.	2.	3.	4.	5.	6.	7.	8.
Communist Party								
Nomination	10.1*	8.4*					12.2*	10.1*
Affiliation			10.4*	8.5*				
Endorsement					11.3*	9.4*		
Endorsement w/o Nomination							10.5*	8.2*
Yabloko								
Nomination	5.3*	3.7*					4.8*	3.6*
Affiliation			6.0*	4.2*				
Endorsement					4.6*	3.4*		
Endorsement w/o Nomination							6.4*	5.1*
Union of Right Forces								
Nomination	7.0*	5.7*					7.5*	6.1*
Affiliation			6.4*	5.1*				
Endorsement					5.1*	3.8*		
Endorsement w/o Nomination							3.7*	2.3*
Fatherland–All Russia								
Nomination	7.0*	2.7*					8.9*	4.1*
Affiliation			7.8*	3.8*				
Endorsement					7.7*	4.1*		
Endorsement w/o Nomination							5.4*	4.3*
Unity								
Nomination	10.7*	4.6*						
Affiliation			11.1*	5.2*	10.6*	4.9*	10.9*	5.1*
LDPR								
Nomination	−0.5	−0.3						
Affiliation			0.0	0.1	0.1	0.2	0.1	0.2
Our Home is Russia								
Nomination	−0.3	−0.5						
Affiliation			0.4	0.0	0.1	−0.1	0.3	−0.0
Party Substitute Support								
Governor	11.6*	7.2*	10.5*	6.7*	9.3*	5.9*	9.4*	6.0*
PFIG	8.3*	5.2*	8.1*	5.4*	7.4*	5.1*	7.5*	5.0*
Communists for USSR	2.2	2.1	2.6	2.4	2.1	2.1	2.3	2.1
Women of Russia	5.2*	3.7*	5.7*	4.3*	5.1*	3.8*	5.3*	4.0*
Pensioners' Party	3.1*	4.1*	3.6*	4.3*	3.4*	4.2*	3.3*	4.3*
Incumbent (SMD)	10.0*	3.6*	8.8*	3.4*	8.3*	3.1*	8.2*	3.1*

	1.	2.	3.	4.	5.	6.	7.	8.
Incumbent (PR)	4.1*	0.4	4.0*	−0.3	3.7*	−0.3	3.6*	−0.4
Military	1.2	1.2	1.5	1.4	1.3	1.3	1.3	1.3
Intellectual	−0.2	0.1	−0.1	0.2	−0.2	0.1	−0.2	0.0
Agriculture	4.4*	4.7*	4.2*	4.5*	4.3*	4.5*	4.3*	4.6*
Politics	0.3	−0.3	−0.4	−0.4	−0.4	−0.4	−0.5	−0.5
Proletarian	0.3	0.8	0.4	0.8	0.5	0.8	0.3	0.8
Federal Official	0.3	0.4	0.5	0.5	0.6	0.5	0.5	0.5
Regional Official	3.4*	3.0*	3.5*	2.9*	3.2*	2.8*	3.3*	2.9*
Regional Legislator	5.4*	4.1*	5.0*	3.9*	4.7*	3.7*	4.7*	3.8*
Mayor	2.9*	1.9	2.6*	1.6	2.7*	1.8	2.6*	1.8
Local Official	0.6	0.6	0.9	0.7	0.9	0.9	1.0	0.8
Local Legislator	1.8*	1.9*	1.5*	1.6*	1.7*	1.7*	1.6*	1.7*
Sports	−0.8	−0.6	−0.5	−0.3	−0.4	−0.2	−0.4	−0.3
Business	−0.8	−0.5	−0.6	−0.5	−0.5	−0.4	−0.6	−0.5
Female	0.5	0.6	0.6	0.6	0.8	0.8	0.7	0.8
Railroad	4.8*	5.9*	5.4*	6.2*	5.5*	6.0*	5.5*	6.3*
Number of Rivals	−9.6*	−9.0*	−9.6*	−9.0*	−9.2*	−8.7*	−9.2*	−8.7*
Experts See as Contender		6.9*		6.3*		6.2*		6.2*
R^2	.46	.51	.47	.51	.48	.52	.48	.52
$N = 2,207$								

* 95% confidence level.

[a] Additional technical information on this table can be found on the web site www.whynotpartiesinrussia.com.

Since we have shown that parties were often involved in these elections even where they did not formally nominate candidates, we run four pairs of regressions that allow us to examine the impact parties have had when they backed candidates in different ways. The first two columns of Table 3.9, therefore, report the estimated impact of a party's nomination, plain and simple. Columns 3 and 4 indicate the average boost that a party's candidates got regardless of whether they were nominated (that is, we lump nominees together with party affiliates who were not nominated but were still contesting the race). Columns 5 and 6 report the impact of party endorsement, whether or not the endorsees were actual nominees. The final two columns, 7 and 8, distinguish between the impact of nomination and the effects of endorsements on non-nominees. And again, the odd-numbered columns estimate upper bounds of the effect while the even-numbered ones establish a lower bound.

The overall results, reported in Table 3.9, lend a great deal of confidence to the conclusion that Russia's major political parties were not only recruiting candidates that had the independent capacity to do better than average, but were actively *helping* candidates perform significantly better than they otherwise would have. Even controlling for candidates' "personal resources" and expert predictions as to candidate strength, we find that three of Russia's four longest-standing major parties (the KPRF, Yabloko, and the Union of Right Forces) provided a significant electoral boost for their candidates in 1999. That Communist Party backing can give an average candidate an electoral advantage of 8–12 percentage points is perhaps the least surprising finding given the undisputed strength of the party's organization and brand name. More remarkably, we find that support from Yabloko and the Union of Right Forces typically added between a conservative estimate of 3 percent and a more liberal estimate of 8 percent of the vote to their candidates' totals. Given that over two-fifths of the 1999 Duma races were decided by 7 percent of the vote or less and that roughly half of these involved winning margins of 3 percent or less, the electoral advantage associated here with major-party nomination appears quite significant in real-world terms. The figures in Table 3.9 also show that adding important control variables to the bare-bones 1999 equation reported in Table 3.8 does reduce our estimate of the electoral impact of Fatherland–All Russia and Unity. Nevertheless, we still find in Table 3.9 that even with all of the control variables included, these two parties tended to significantly improve the chances of the candidates they nominated in the SMD Duma elections of 1999.

Table 3.9 also reveals that parties were capable of providing candidates with additional votes regardless of whether the affiliation was formal nomination or public endorsement. When one further observes that these "party boosts" are not wildly different from the levels of partisanship in the electorate detected in the 1999–2000 survey discussed earlier, it strongly appears that Russia's major parties did command the loyalty of small but significant shares of the population that could be counted on to vote for these parties' district candidates. Given the narrow margins of victory in many Duma races, the votes of party loyalists are judged to have had the potential to be quite significant.

We do find that two major parties had no significant effect on their nominees' chances in 1999 despite the fact that these parties were found to have commanded some party loyalty by the 1999–2000 survey. These are Zhirinovsky's LDPR and Our Home is Russia. As Chapter 2 described, the former initially went out of its way to include reputed criminals on its party list in what appears to have been a fund-raising tactic, while the latter was the party of former Prime Minister Chernomyrdin, who was widely held responsible for the Russian financial collapse of 1998. It is no stretch to assume that these parties, having "high negatives," drove as many voters away from candidates as they brought to them.

The control variables also present some patterns worthy of note. Perhaps most importantly, we learn that the expert predictors were in fact good ones; they successfully identified candidates that received, on average, between 6 and 7 percent more of the vote than would have been predicted by all of the "objective" factors included in our equation. This lends credence to the argument that this *contender* variable captures candidates' "personal votes" reasonably effectively and thus that the remaining correlation between vote shares and party nomination reflects parties' "making" of vote-winners rather than just "attracting." Adding to the conclusion that parties mattered, we even find that some of Russia's minor parties tended to produce some electoral benefits for their SMD candidates, particularly those whose brand names directly connoted a significant social group (Women of Russia and the Pensioners' Party). Russia also featured a major incumbent advantage, especially for district-elected Duma members who tended to earn 10 percent more of the vote than otherwise similar candidates in 1999. PR incumbency had a weaker but significant advantage of roughly 4 percent, but such incumbents did not on average perform better than expert expectations. Candidates employed in agriculture, in the railroad industry, or as regional officials, regional legislators, or local legislators also clearly performed better than other average candidates who differed only in lacking these jobs.[33]

In interpreting the findings, it is especially important to note that inserting all of the control variables reported in Table 3.9 into the equation reported in Table 3.8 did not alter our assessments of whether particular parties had positive effects on their nominees' vote-winning capacity in the 1999 elections.[34] This gives us confidence that the regressions reported for 1993, 1995, and 2003 in Table 3.8, conducted without control variables, are capturing reasonably accurately the real impact of parties on candidates' chances in these SMD Duma elections. Furthermore, the estimated magnitude of the effect of Yabloko and SPS nomination on candidate vote totals was almost exactly the same in Table 3.8 and the first column of Table 3.9, and declined by less than 2 percentage points once expert preelection predictions were included as a way to estimate a lower bound for party effects. We thus have special confidence that Table 3.8's regressions for 1993, 1995, 1999, and 2003 were rather accurately reflecting these parties' true impact since there is little reason to expect the control variables to have operated differently vis-à-vis these organizations in 1999 relative to 1993, 1995, and 2003.[35]

This allows us to conclude that, overall, the impact of parties in Russia's SMD Duma races grew substantially during the 1990s, stalled somewhat by 1999, and then grew on the whole again in 2003 but with most of this growth attributing to United Russia and coming at the expense of Russia's veteran parties. This, it should be remembered, largely mirrors the trends in patterns

33 The findings in the box labeled "Party Substitute Support" will be discussed in Chapter 4.

34 The LDPR was found to have a small negative effect that disappeared once the controls were introduced.

35 The one exception is likely to involve Russia's Choice in 1993 since it was then a party of power. Nevertheless, as Table 3.8 reports, this party was found to have had no overall effect on district elections at that time.

TABLE 3.10. *Share of Occupied Duma Seats Held by Major-Party Fractions in the 1994–2004 Dumas*

	Party	Percentage of Seats
1994–5[a]	Russia's Choice	16
	LDPR	14
	Agrarian Party	13
	KPRF	10
	PRES	7
	Yabloko	6
	Women of Russia	5
	Democratic Party of Russia	3
	Total	74
1996–9[b]	KPRF	33
	Our Home is Russia	14
	LDPR	11
	Yabloko	10
	Agrarian Party[e]	8
	Total	76
2000–3[c]	KPRF	18
	Unity	18
	Fatherland–All Russia	12
	Agro-Industrial[e]	10
	Union of Right Forces	7
	Yabloko	4
	LDPR	3
	Total	72
2004[d]	United Russia	68
	KPRF	11
	Motherland	9
	LDPR	8
	Total	96

[a] As of April 1994, calculated from Remington 2001.

[b] As of January 1996, calculated from Remington 2001.

[c] As of January 2003, calculated from State Duma of the Russian Federation, official Web site: http://www.duma.gov.ru/deputats/fraction.htm, accessed January 22, 2003.

[d] As of August 2004, calculated from State Duma of the Russian Federation, official Web site: http://www.duma.gov.ru, accessed August 24, 2004.

[e] The Agrarian Party deputy group in 1996–9 and the Agro-Industrial deputy group in 2000–3 are included here despite the fact that the Agrarian Party lost major-party status in 1995. This is because in 1995 the Communist Party lent the Agrarian Party a sufficient number of deputies in 1995 to reach the 35 needed to register a deputy group, which then became essentially a Communist satellite. In 1999, part of the Agrarian Party ran on the KPRF list and, with the help of Communist Party members, formed the Agro-Industrial deputy group that then became a close KPRF ally.

TABLE 3.11. *Major-Party Fraction Members Voting the Party Line in the 4,144 Most Substantial Votes in the Duma, 1996–9*

	KPRF (%)	LDPR (%)	Our Home is Russia (%)	Yabloko (%)
1996	86	80	71	74
1997	86	86	73	79
1998	86	87	73	81
1999	87	85	73	78

Source: Yu. K. Malov, Analytical Administration of the State Duma of the Russian Federation, "Analitika I statistika," *Garant.Ru*, http://www.garant.ru/files/duma_htm/analit/index.htm, accessed October 2, 2002.

of partisanship in the population more generally that were discussed earlier in this chapter.

The Duma As a Whole

As can be inferred from the preceding discussion, the Dumas elected between 1993 and 2003 were composed of two sets of deputies. One half was clearly partisan, having been elected on party lists. The other half was partially partisan. Combining the two, it turns out, did create an organ that was quite party-dominated, especially given that some independents chose to join officially registered major-party fractions after entering the Duma. Table 3.10 reports the percentage of all occupied seats that were filled by members of the major-party factions for each of the four Dumas that existed since the first one, elected in December 1993, convened in January 1994. About three-quarters of Russia's lower house of parliament was effectively partisan as soon as the institution came into being and United Russia's landslide victory in 2003 propelled very nearly all Duma members to join a major-party fraction. Studies have also found that party discipline was reasonably high in Duma voting during this period. While readers are referred to the work of Thomas Remington for the most thorough studies on this subject, Table 3.11 provides some concrete evidence for this claim.[36]

PARTIES AND THE GUBERNATORIAL OFFICE

There are many different ways to measure the degree to which governorships were party-penetrated in Russia and each can in fact lead to radically different conclusions if examined in isolation.[37] If one looks at the public

36 See in particular Remington 1998, 2001; and Smith and Remington 2001.
37 On gubernatorial elections, see Golosov 2003; Hahn 1997; Ross 2002; and Slider 1996.

declarations of governors leading up to a round of national elections, one might conclude that governors were Russia's leading advocates of political parties. The present author compiled three separate studies seeking to identify the "partisan activity" of governors of Russia's regions during 1999 and found that only seven governors failed to be recorded as affiliating with a major Russian party. A closer look, however, revealed that these affiliations did not reflect significant political investments or loyalties of the type typically found in developed Western democracies: Only 40 of Russia's 89 regional leaders were "monogamous" in their stated party preferences in 1999. Of the polygamists, 42 declared some form of belonging to at least two parties during 1999, with 11 being so promiscuous as to affiliate with three or even four parties, often at the same time. Overall, then, nearly half of Russia's governors appear to have been monogamous party associates and all but seven of the others were quite willing to work within major parties but did not develop single-party loyalties.[38]

If one examines how governors have actually behaved during important elections, however, we find a starkly contrasting picture. One set of elections on which we have good data is the 1999 SMD Duma contest, as described above. These data reveal that governors backed major-party candidates only about 44 percent of the time.[39] Moreover, there is evidence that parties factored little into governors' decisions regarding which candidates to support: Only 19 regions' governors (out of 77 on which we have sufficient information to tell for sure) backed candidates from the same party in more than half of their regions' Duma districts. Of these 19, eight regions had only one district, meaning that the true number of partisan governors is probably less than 19. Seven of the partisan governors were Communists and Fatherland–All Russia could claim nine. But the vast majority of governors backed independents or candidates from more than one party, sometimes opposing parties, in the 1999 Duma elections.

Parties look even weaker when we turn to party activity in gubernatorial elections. The Central Election Commission has made available some useful data on both elections and candidates to gubernatorial office between 1995, when elections for these posts became the norm, and 2003. The data, as can be seen in Table 3.12, reveal that governors ran for reelection as major-party nominees only five times between 1995 and 2003, with just two of these attempts ending in victory. Expanding our view to the entire candidate pool, the major parties still appear to have made little headway in penetrating this particular electoral arena. Even the Communist Party, by far Russia's strongest over the duration of this whole period, nominated candidates for

[38] *Polit.Ru*, September 29, 1999; East-West Institute, *Russian Regional Report*, "Political Affiliations of Russian Governors," October 7, 1999, www.iews.org/rrrabout.nsf/pages/governors + party + affiliation, accessed April 21, 2000; "Uchastie Glav Regionov v Politicheskikh Ob'edineniiakh v 1999 g." Appendix 6 in McFaul, Petrov, and Ryabov 1999.

[39] Data are insufficient for this calculation for 12 percent of the overall cases.

TABLE 3.12. *Formal Major-Party Involvement in 180 of the 183 Gubernatorial Races During 1995–2003*[a]

	KPRF	Yabloko	SPS (or predecessor)	LDPR	Our Home is Russia	Fatherland–All Russia	United Russia/ Unity	Motherland	Major Party Total
Number of races for which a party candidate was nominated, registered	36	9	4	28	2	1	5	0	85
Percentage of races	20	5	2	16	1	1	3	0	47
Came 2nd in runoff[b]	1	0	0	0	2	0	0	0	3
Won governorship	4	0	0	1	0	0	1	0	6
Number of races in which a party member ran but without party nomination	15	0	3	5	4	1	4	0	32
Percentage of races	8	0	2	3	2	1	2	0	18
Came 2nd in runoff	4	0	0	1	0	0	2	0	7
Won governorship	3	0	1	0	0	0	0	0	4
Number of incumbents running as party nominees	2	0	0	0	2	0	1	0	5
(of these, winners)	1	0	0	0	0	0	1	0	2
Average share of the vote won when nominee is advanced[c]	20%	5%	5%	5%	34%	4%	17%	n/a	n/a

[a] The three missing races (the Novosibirsk and Vologda contests of December 7, 2003, and the Karachaevo-Cherkessiia race on August 17, 2003) are omitted because Russia's Central Election Commission had not published the necessary information about them as of this writing.
[b] There were a total of 58 runoffs during 1995–2003. Not all regions had instituted the practice of runoffs (see Chapter 2).
[c] Eleven elections were omitted from this calculation because the CEC did not report complete election results.

these highest regional offices in just 36 of 180 races, winning just four and coming close (finishing second in a runoff) in but one instance. Among Russia's other major parties, only the LDPR (in Pskov) and United Russia (in Sverdlovsk) successfully elected a nominee to a governorship.[40] The finding is particularly striking for United Russia, given its dramatic rise culminating in the 2003 Duma elections. Indeed, even some of United Russia's own most prominent leaders, such as Moscow Mayor Luzhkov and Bashkortostan President Rakhimov, opted to run for reelection to their gubernatorial posts as independents in 2003. This trend continued even after United Russia's landslide 2003 Duma election victory, with United Russia failing to nominate a single candidate in the first ten gubernatorial elections of 2004, held in March of that year.[41] If this was the case for United Russia, it is no surprise that Yabloko was hardly a presence at all during 1995–2003, nominating candidates in just nine races. The Union of Right Forces (and its predecessors) proved even more feeble, formally advancing only four. Even Our Home is Russia, aspiring to be a party of power with strong gubernatorial support during the first half of this period, could muster a nominee in just two contests. Table 3.12 also indicates that races did sometimes feature party candidates who did not seek their parties' nominations, but only the Communist Party and Russia's Democratic Choice (predecessor to the Union of Right Forces) appear to have won any governorships this way, and just four combined.

Tables 3.13 and 3.14 report regression analysis indicating the degree to which party nomination and affiliation helped those few partisans who did contest gubernatorial races between 1995 and 2003. These results must be treated with more caution than those for the SMD Duma races, however, because we do not have the ability here to tell whether any detected correlation between party support and candidate vote share reflects parties' "making winners" out of gubernatorial candidates as opposed to simply "recruiting winners." Nevertheless, as noted above, both "making" and "recruiting" are important functions for parties to perform; thus, we can learn a lot by examining patterns in the available data. Since the Central Election Commission published gubernatorial election data in two different ways for the periods 1995–2000 and 2001–3, and since the latter period largely corresponds with the period when we can expect the effects of President Putin's

[40] While General Aleksandr Lebed's Honor and Motherland is not counted in this volume as a "major party" because it never held a Duma fraction, it was engaged to some degree in regional party politics. It nominated candidates in five gubernatorial races, winning one. This victory was in Khakasiia where the General's own brother won. Lebed candidates ran as independents in three races and won one of these bids, that of Lebed himself in Krasnoiarsk in 1998. Lebed nominees won an average of 10 percent of the vote in these races, a figure clearly pulled up by the two Lebed brothers themselves. Lebed died in a helicopter crash in 2002, effectively ending his party's existence.

[41] The KPRF and the LDPR nominated six apiece in these races. See *RFE/RL Newsline*, March 3, 2004.

TABLE 3.13. *Estimated Percentage Change in Gubernatorial Candidates' Vote Associated with Party Backing and Candidate Characteristics in Elections, 1995–2000*[a]

	Full 1995–2000	Short 1995–2000	Short 1995–6	Short 1997–8	Short 1999–2000
Communist Party					
Nomination	9.1*	10.2*	8.3*	7.9	14.5*
Without Nomination	10.1*				
Yabloko					
Nomination	−6.1*	−4.8	−7.9	−8.9*	3.8
Without Nomination	n/a				
Union of Right Forces					
Nomination	−0.0	−0.0	−0.0	−0.0	−0.0
Without Nomination	7.8				
LDPR					
Nomination	−4.2*	−6.3*	−6.9*	−7.1	−7.0*
Without Nomination	−1.8				
Our Home is Russia					
Nomination	−3.7*	21.3*	21.4*	−0.0	0.0
Without Nomination	−5.9				
Lebed (Honor and Motherland)					
Nomination	−3.7	−4.8	0.7	−11.0*	−0.0
Without Nomination	16.5				
Controls					
Incumbent	42.8*				
Duma Deputy	18.4*				
Federal Official	10.0*				
Regional Official	2.5				
Mayor	19.7*				
Local Official	6.0				
Business	20.5*				
Regional Legislature Chair	28.4*				
Federation Council	4.4				
Police/Military/FSB	11.3				
Number of Rivals	−19.8*	−27.7*	−29.2*	−33.4*	−20.5*
N	791	794	311	130	353
R^2	.48	.15	.16	.17	.13

* 95% confidence level.
[a] Additional technical information is available at www.whynotpartiesinrussia.com.

TABLE 3.14. *Estimated Percentage Change in Gubernatorial Candidates' Vote Associated with Party Booking and Candidate Characteristics in Elections 2001–3*[a]

Major-Party Nomination	Percent Change
Communist Party	5.9
Yabloko	10.3*
Union of Right Forces	5.0
LDPR	−1.0
United Russia	−1.6
Major-Party Partisan, No Nomination	
United Russia	27.2*
Controls	
Incumbent	32.6*
Duma Deputy	4.4
Federal Official	21.8*
Regional Official	15.9*
Mayor	11.5
Local Official	16.7*
Business	1.3
Regional Legislature Chair	23.7*
Regional Legislator	−2.4
Local Legislator	−2.6
Number of Rivals	−6.1
N	190
R^2	.57

* 95% confidence level.
[a] Additional technical information is available at www.whynotpartiesinrussia.com.

many federal reforms to have begun to be felt, the two periods are considered separately in the regression analysis that follows.

The full 1995–2000 regression reported in Table 3.13 confirms the argument begun above that parties had much less important effects on candidate prospects in gubernatorial elections than in the SMD Duma elections. In fact, the Communist Party is the only party found to have significantly helped its candidates' chances in these contests from 1995 through the end of the year 2000. While Our Home is Russia nominees tended to do well overall, we find that in fact they tended to finish with 3.7 percent fewer votes than did candidates with similar biographies without a nomination by this party. Our Home, therefore, appears to have damaged its nominees' fortunes. That Our Home took strong candidates and hurt their chances can be seen by comparing the apparently strong positive effect reported in the "Short 1995–2000" column, which does not include any control variables to capture candidates' personal strengths, and the "Full" column, which reports the findings when such controls are introduced. Moreover, not only Our Home, but also the LDPR and Yabloko are found to have had significantly negative net effects (−4.2 percent and −6.1 percent respectively) on their nominees during this period. It was impossible to draw any meaningful conclusions regarding Fatherland–All Russia and Unity since both nominated a candidate in only one race apiece during the period 1995–2000. The Fatherland–All Russia candidate, running in Tver in December 1999, received less than 3 percent of the vote. The Unity nominee, contesting the governorship of Communist-dominated Briansk, netted a paltry half of a percentage point.

Since we expect patterns to vary over time as parties rise or fall in strength and as Russian circumstances change, it is helpful to break the 1995–2000 data into three time periods: 1995–6 (largely coinciding with Russia's second major round of national parliamentary/presidential elections), 1997–8 (between national election rounds), and 1999–2000 (largely coinciding with the third round of national elections). We can then conduct separate regressions on data from the elections falling into these discrete periods.

The comparison of different time periods suggests that only two parties managed to expand their influence in gubernatorial elections between 1995 and 2000. The Communist Party, for one, lent its nominees an average boost of 14.5 percent of the vote in 1999–2000, up from 8.3 percent in 1995–6 and no significant effect in 1997–8. Yabloko also appears to have improved its effectiveness; while its nomination was not correlated with any statistically significant effect in 1999–2000, this was still better than the average 8.9 percent damage it appeared to do to its nominees' fortunes in 1997–8. Our Home is Russia virtually ceased to contest the elections as the 1990s ended. The new parties appearing during that time, Unity and Fatherland–All Russia, did not move in to fill the gap. The LDPR rather consistently cost its candidates votes.

The analysis of the 2001–3 period, reported in Table 3.14, finds that these same basic patterns continued through Putin's first term in office. Continuing a modest upward trend identified in the 1995–2000 data, Yabloko was the only party whose nominees were found with at least 95 percent statistical confidence to win more votes than their other qualifications would have predicted. This 10 percent boost, however, was nowhere close to enough to win a gubernatorial race, and indeed Yabloko captured not a single governor's seat. Among the other major parties, while very few candidates ran as Yabloko nominees in the first place, those who did so during this period performed no better on the whole than non-nominees. This is true even of United Russia.[42] Nomination by this emergent party of power was not significantly associated with any electoral benefit, and the negative sign reported in Table 3.14 suggests that if it did have an effect, it was negative. In fact, there is some

[42] The category of "United Russia" also includes nominees of its organizational predecessor, Unity.

evidence that the best strategy for United Russia was in fact not to nominate its partisans, but simply to channel support to them.[43]

As for other factors influencing candidate chances, for 2001–3 as in 1995–2000 we find that incumbents wielded the single largest advantage in Russian gubernatorial elections, although the magnitude of this advantage dropped from an average of 42.8 percent to 32.6 percent between these two periods. Also consistent between the two periods, candidates tended to do better if their primary occupation was listed as being a federal official (with the impact of this more than doubling as of 2001–3) or the chairman of the region's legislature. Interestingly, business representatives, mayors, and federal State Duma members appeared to lose their advantage in running for top regional office at the same time that both regional and local officials gained an edge.

Overall, then, we see that political parties played a role in gubernatorial politics but that this was still overwhelmingly the preserve of independent political forces. Although governors frequently pledged allegiance to various parties, these pledges were rarely more than attempts to curry favor with the Kremlin or with forces believed to be positioned to take over the Kremlin. Nowhere was this effect more pronounced than with the current juggernaut United Russia, which governors have flocked to support, at least verbally. The Communist Party remained something of an exception, maintaining the loyalties of at least a few governors despite great pressure from the Kremlin during Russian President Vladimir Putin's first term. Nevertheless, governors generally avoided running for reelection as party nominees (even United Russia nominees) and other candidates benefited little from such nomination, except in a few cases where Communist nomination brought some significant support. In fact, most parties appear to have hurt their nominees' chances. While the KPRF and Yabloko did play a more electorally positive role in gubernatorial contests by the end of the 1990s, overall party penetration of this part of the Russian political arena was extremely low throughout the 1990s and well into the following decade.

PARTIES AND REGIONAL LEGISLATURES

While information on elections to Russia's regional legislatures is scant, there is enough to allow us to conclude that parties had penetrated these organs and the politics surrounding them only weakly by 2003.[44] Figure 3.1 illustrates

[43] In the category of "Major-Party Partisan, No Nomination," we include only candidates who were explicitly listed as such by the CEC so as to maintain a consistent coding rule. This meant including only three United Russia candidates and excluding many sitting governors who had publicly associated themselves with United Russia during this period. Including these governors would only have reinforced the conclusion drawn here since virtually all of them won reelection handily.

[44] Comprehensive works on parties in Russia's regions include Golosov 2003; Hutcheson 2003; and Ross 2002.

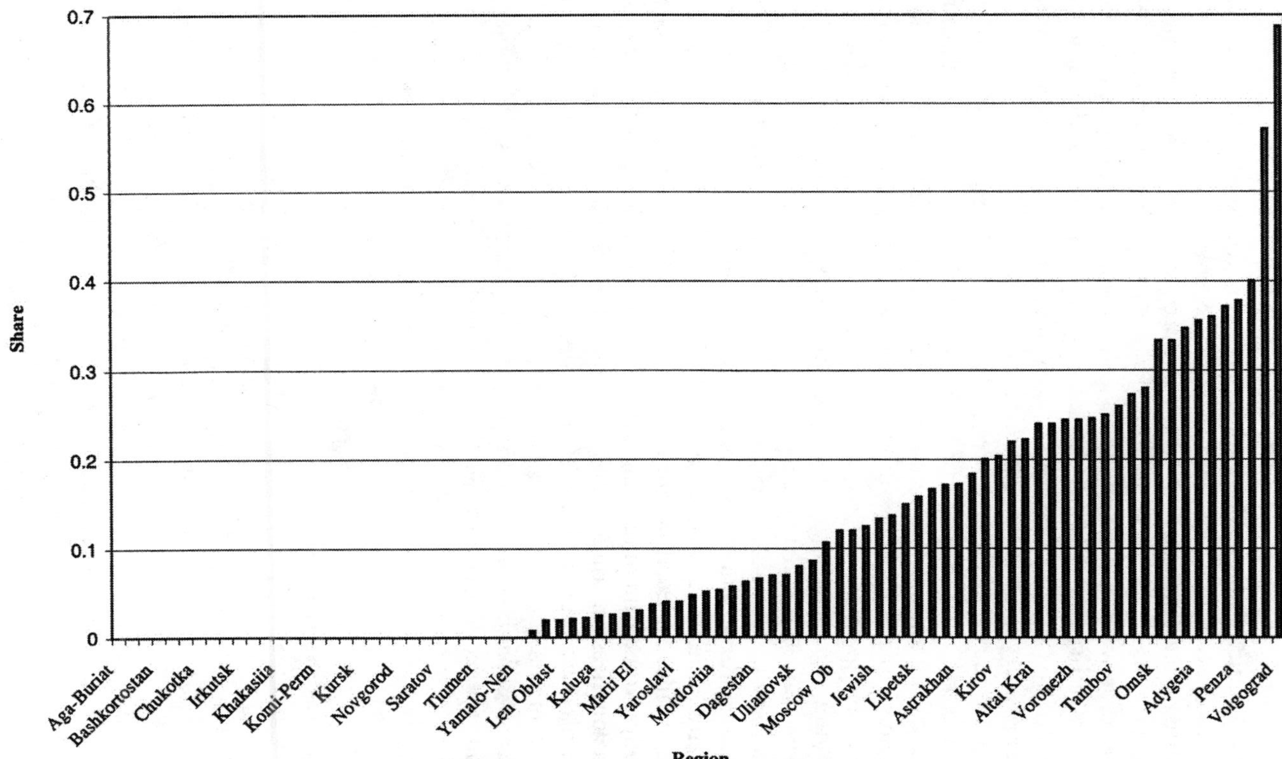

FIGURE 3.1. Share of regional legislative assembly comprised of major-party nominees 1995–2000

the total proportion of seats in regional legislatures won by the nominees of Russia's big seven parties in each of the country's 89 regions except Chechnya in the most recent elections held by the end of the year 2000, the last year for which sufficient data were made available by Russia's Central Election Commission as of this writing. As can be seen, over a third of the legislatures contained no party nominees at all and only 10 regions counted so much as 30 percent of their members as being major-party nominees. Of these 10, only two contained a major-party majority. Figure 3.2 demonstrates that the vast majority of these party legislators were Communists; the presence of any other party, even the former "party of power" Our Home is Russia, was paltry indeed.

We have much less information regarding elections to regional legislatures since Russia's Central Election Commission (CEC) only reports the biographies and vote totals of the winners of these races.[45] Without information on the nonwinners, it is impossible to conduct a comprehensive examination of the degree to which parties penetrated these elections, to say nothing of the kind of regression analysis designed to assess party strength like that conducted on election data for the Duma and gubernatorial elections. The CEC does, however, publish two pieces of information that are illuminating.

First, Figure 3.3 illustrates the average number of candidates formally nominated by any form of officially registered political organization (regional or nationwide) for each provincial legislative seat in the most recent such elections as of the end of the year 2000. Because these figures include major parties as well as all kinds of minor or regional organizations that do not necessarily constitute parties as defined in this text, we do not know the share of these organizations that are in fact real parties. Nevertheless, these figures provide an upper bound to our estimate of the level of party penetration of Russian regional legislatures. We thus learn that robust party competition, where at least two parties have nominated a candidate for every seat on average, took place in no more than 17 of Russia's 89 regions during this period. The average number of party candidates is less than one per seat in 43 regions, of which 11 experienced no formal party involvement in their legislative elections at all.

Since authors in the CEC's main statistical publications evidently had some latitude in what to report in their narrative summaries of legislative election processes, we do have complete breakdowns of party involvement in the legislative races in 30 regions, just over a third of the subjects of the Russian Federation, for the period 1995–7. Since there appears to be no systematic reason why full sets of such statistics were published for some regions and not others, and since these 30 regions include a wide variety of types of province, the figures are likely to be reasonably representative of nationwide patterns. As summarized in Table 3.15, we see that the

[45] Some additional data has been compiled and ably analyzed in Golosov 2003.

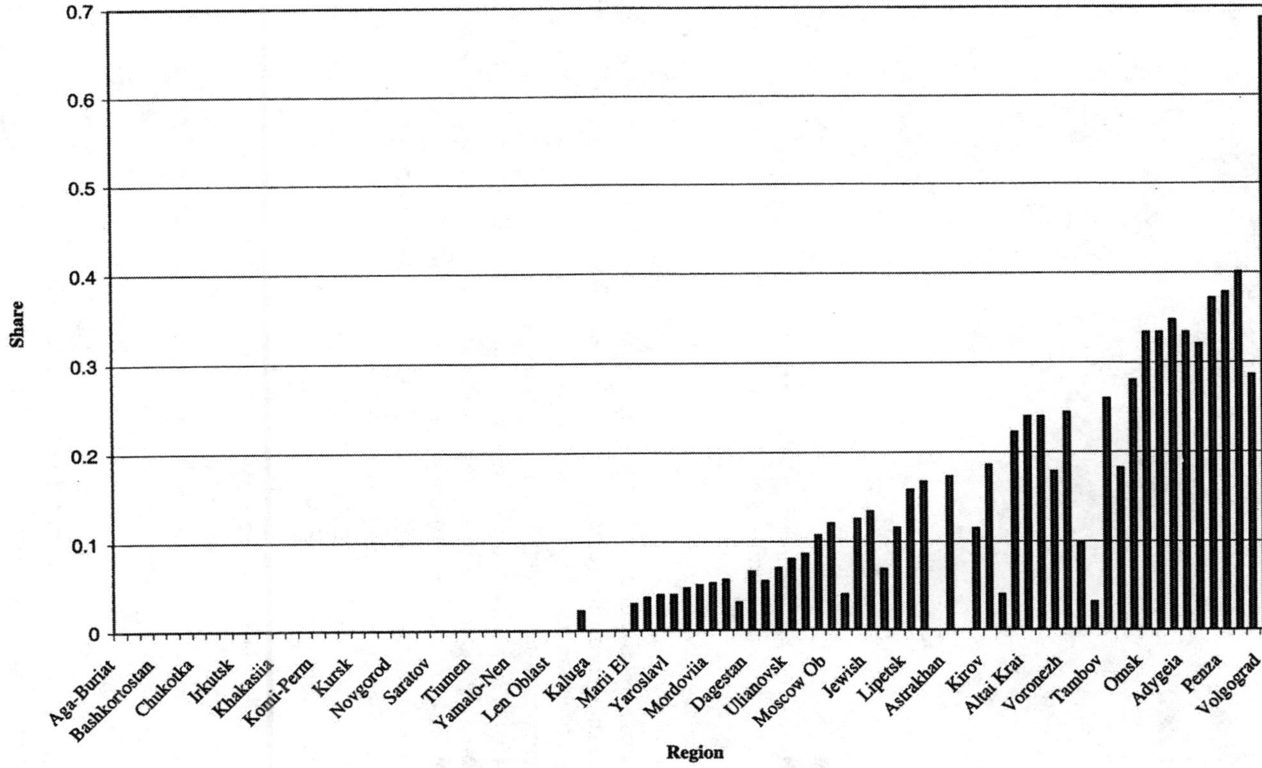

FIGURE 3.2. Share of each region's legislative assembly comprised of KPRF nominees 1995–2000

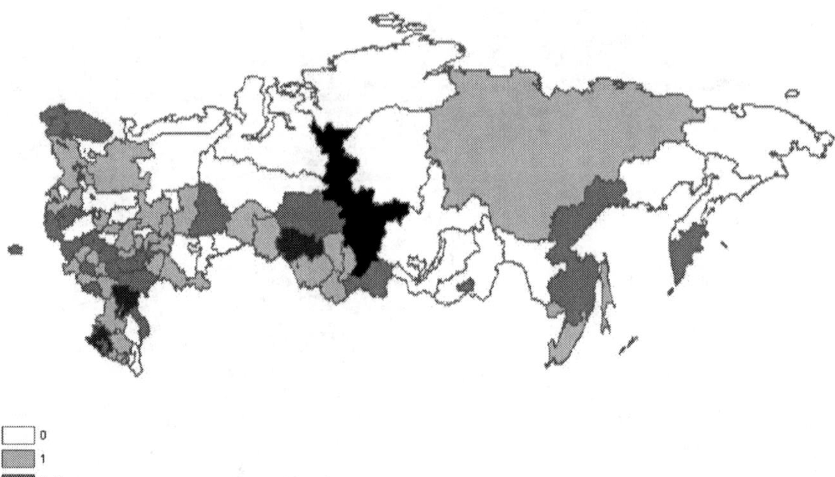

FIGURE 3.3. Average (rounded) number of candidates formally nominated by any regional or national political organization per regional legislative assembly seat 1995–2000 (data for Dagestan not available)

Communist Party and the LDPR were the only parties that can be considered to have been at all active in regional legislative races. While the KPRF was the leader, even this strongest of Russian parties mustered a nominee for only 26 percent of the seats up for election in these regions between 1995 and 1997. The LDPR ran candidates for 12 percent of the available seats, but Yabloko advanced nominees for just 2 percent and all other major parties managed to do so for only 1 percent of the seats or fewer. While Lebed's parties are not counted as major parties for reasons given earlier, it is noteworthy that they contested 5 percent of available seats, more than double the number of seats contested by Yabloko and the Union of Right Forces combined. By comparing the numbers of major-party nominees in this table with the numbers of nominees from all kinds of organizational nominators (Figure 3.3), we can also gain leverage on what share of the numbers from Figure 3.3 reflects the activity of major parties as defined in this volume. Table 3.15 indicates that the major parties on which this volume has focused made up about 60 percent of the political organizations counted in typical CEC statistics for legislative elections. If we expand our list of significant parties to include not only the major parties but also three more that demonstrated at least some noticeably broad activity in regional politics (Lebed's parties, the Agrarian Party, and the radical leftist Russian Communist Workers' Party, or RKRP), then Table 3.15 indicates that parties made up about 70 percent of these figures.

Of course, we must consider that parties may well have fielded candidates while forgoing formal nomination, as was done in many SMD Duma races.

TABLE 3.15. *Party Penetration of Candidate Pool for Legislative Assembly Seats in Regions for Which Full Data Were Presented by the Central Election Commission for 1995–7*

Region	Number of Seats in Legislative Assembly	Total Number of Party Nominees	KPRF	Yabloko	Russia's Choice or Successor	LDPR	Our Home is Russia	Agrarian Party	Lebed parties	Russian Communist Workers' Party
Aga-Buriat AO	15	0	0	0	0	0	0	0	0	0
Amur	30	0	0	0	0	0	0	0	0	0
Chita[a]	39	3	0	0	0	0	0	0	2	0
Chukotka AO	13	0	0	0	0	0	0	0	0	0
Dagestan	121	0	0	0	0	0	0	0	0	0
Evenk AO	23	0	0	0	0	0	0	0	0	0
Jewish AO[a,c]	15	22	11	2	0	4	0	0	0	0
Karachaevo-Cherkessiia	73	49	43	0	0	0	0	6	0	0
Kemerovo[a,f]	21	25	10	3	0	8	0	0	0	0
Khabarovsk	25	51	15	0	1	9	0	5	3	0
Khanty-Mansy AO	23	0	0	0	0	0	0	0	0	0
Komi-Permiak AO	15	0	0	0	0	0	0	0	0	0
Kurgan	33	17	1	2	0	6	0	0	0	0
Magadan	17	7	0	0	0	4	0	0	0	0
Nenets AO	15	0	0	0	0	0	0	0	0	0
Novgorod[a,b]	26	36	9	5	0	12	0	0	4	0
Perm	40	25	11	0	0	2	0	0	9	0
Sakha[a]	70	45	17	0	3	3	0	0	0	0
Sakhalin	27	14	4	0	0	3	1	0	0	0

(*continued*)

TABLE 3.15 *(continued)*

Region	Number of Seats in Legislative Assembly	Total Number of Party Nominees	KPRF	Yabloko	Russia's Choice or Successor	LDPR	Our Home is Russia	Agrarian Party	Lebed parties	Russian Communist Workers' Party
Saratov[a,c]	35	21	4	0	0	11	0	0	0	0
Smolensk[a,d,g]	30	59	23	0	0	4	0	2	11	5
Sverdlovsk[a]	35	51	13	3	0	4	0	0	0	0
Taimyr AO	11	0	0	0	0	0	0	0	0	0
Tomsk	42	73	27	1	0	15	0	0	7	0
Tver	33	8	1	0	0	0	0	0	6	0
Ulianovsk[a]	25	25	9	0	0	8	0	0	0	2
Volgograd[a]	16	42	16	0	1	10	0	0	3	0
Vologda	15	5	1	0	0	0	0	0	0	1
Yamalo-Nenets AO	21	5	0	0	0	4	0	0	0	0
Yaroslavl	50	54	29	0	0	7	0	0	0	1
Totals	954	637	244	16	5	114	1	13	45	9
Maximum share of seats "covered" by party nominees		67%	26%	2%	1%	12%	0%	1%	5%	1%

[a] Totals are based only on the number of candidates who were successfully registered officially.
[b] Eight party candidates were disqualified.
[c] Forty-five party candidates were disqualified.
[d] Nine party candidates were disqualified.
[e] One party candidate was disqualified.
[f] Yabloko reflects bloc including Lebed's Honor and Motherland; KPRF reflects bloc including Agrarian Party and Russian Communist Worker's Party.
[g] Lebed reflects bloc with Yabloko.

There is a great deal of anecdotal evidence that this has been the case. Interviews in Perm in 1999 revealed that as many as 20 candidates from Our Home is Russia made the tactical decision to run for the 40-seat regional legislature as independents since they feared their party label would hurt their chances (a fear that the present study suggests was accurate).[46] Our Home was reported by the CEC to have employed a similar strategy in elections to other regional legislatures, including in the Jewish AO (where endorsees of the party reportedly won all 15 seats up for election) and in Altai Krai.[47] In Volgograd, Yabloko did not formally nominate its candidates but actively backed them in 15 of 16 districts; the CEC reports that they were among the most active and visible in the use of television in their campaigns. In this same race, the CEC noted, the Communist Party nominated 16 candidates but was forced to run four as independents due to unspecified circumstances.[48] The CEC reported similar dynamics even in the remote and impoverished Aga-Buriat and Komi-Permiak AOs.[49] Since nomination is usually a sign of a strong party, however, the figures reported here pertaining to party nominees remain compelling evidence of parties' remarkable feebleness in penetrating regional legislative politics.

While the CEC had not yet published data in systematic fashion for the post-2000 period as of the time of this writing, enough data are available to see that the pattern of extreme party weakness in regional legislatures continued through July 2003, when Putin's reform of regional legislature elections went into effect. In 39 general regional legislative elections held between January 2001 and June 2003, a total of 1,963 seats were contested. According to the published data, the highest overall share of these seats that any single party's nominees won was netted by United Russia, whose candidates obtained a mere 7 percent. The only party that had demonstrated anything even close to national coverage of regional legislative elections prior to 2000, the Communist Party, won just 4 percent of the available seats for its nominees between 2001 and the first half of 2003. SPS, Yabloko, and the LDPR each won only a handful, together less than 1 percent of the total.[50] Other organizations capable of nominating candidates garnered just

[46] Much material on parties and politics in Perm can be obtained from the region's Center for the Development of Political Culture directed by Oleg Podvintsev. See, e.g., Neganov 2003 and Neganov and Podvintsev 2004.

[47] Central Election Commission of the Russian Federation, *Vybory v Zakonotadel'nye (Predstavitel'nye) Organy Gosudarstvennoi Vlasti Sub'ektov Rossiiskoi Federatsii 1995–97* (Moscow: Ves Mir, 1998), pp. 178, 524.

[48] Ibid., p. 258.

[49] Ibid., pp. 529, 534.

[50] Data for this period and for the period beginning July 2003 were obtained from the Central Election Commission of the Russian Federation's official Web site, http://www.fci.ru, accessed June–August 2004. The author thanks Scott Nissen for research assistance in gathering this information.

6 percent of the overall number of seats. While United Russia appeared to be gaining at the expense of the Communists, then, the generally low degree to which parties covered regional legislative elections changed hardly at all between the periods of, January 2001–June 2003, and 1995–2000.

July 14, 2003, however, represents a major breaking point. On that day, as described in Chapter 2, an amendment to Russia's Law on Voter Rights came into effect that was intended by Russian President Putin and his allies to radically boost the level of party organization in regional legislative elections. This amendment required each region to elect at least one half of one legislative chamber by a proportional representation contest in which only registered national parties could compete. While this change had been in effect for only barely over a year as of the time of this writing and the CEC had not yet published complete results of elections held under the new legislation, it is already clear that its effects were substantial in raising the degree of party penetration of regional legislative elections. The main initial benefits, however, accrued to United Russia, which both ran and won seats in the party-list competitions in all 10 regions that held elections between July 2003 and August 2004 and for which the CEC published information. In the seven races for which some voting results were reported, the average vote for United Russia in these regional legislative PR elections was 43 percent. The Communists also appear to have been benefiting, but to a much lesser degree, winning legislative delegations in 8 of the 10 regional PR contests and averaging 12 percent of the vote in these successes. The LDPR cleared the PR threshold in six of the races, averaging 9 percent of the ballots in these cases. Yabloko, however, won a delegation in just one region, as did Motherland, and SPS netted not a single PR victory. One or two minor parties with regional strength did win seats in five of these proportional representation contests, with votes ranging from a low of 6 percent to a high of 19 percent. Just two or three major parties won seats in the regional PR contests in every one of these regions except Yaroslavl, where four made the grade. Overall, then, the new 2003 law was dramatically increasing the degree to which parties were able to penetrate regional legislative elections as of the reform's one-year anniversary, but only United Russia, the Communist Party, and the LDPR appear to have benefited in any significant way.

CONCLUSION

The complex patterns laid out above constitute a major puzzle that defies simple attempts to claim that Russia's parties have been either "weak" or "strong" during the first decade and a half of Russia's post-Soviet existence. On one hand, we find that "parties" taken as a whole grew in aggregate strength between 1993 and 2004 and that they played a significant role in the political life of Russians. By most measures, over a third and nearly half of the population came to identify with a major party, even after the much criticized elections of 2003–4, and there is strong evidence that this partisanship had major effects on voting behavior. Party attachments for the most important parties are also found to have been firmly grounded in issues, ideology, the representation of certain social groups, and assessments of incumbent performance, things that would seem to provide groundwork for democratic accountability. Not only did parties structure voter choices among party lists in the PR competition for the Duma, but they also gave their candidates edges that could be decisive in the SMD Duma contests. Similarly, while incumbents unsurprisingly enjoyed huge advantages in presidential contests, every other major presidential contender was a party representative. Governors themselves frequently found it in their interest at least to pay lip service to the need for party affiliation, especially as the elections of 1999 and 2003 approached. Major parties also appeared to make a significant breakthrough in regional legislative elections with the July 2003 reform.

On the other hand, while parties clearly grew in influence in many ways since 1993, we find that their most robust growth appears to have taken place during the mid-1990s, that development under Putin was largely due to the rise of a single party (United Russia), and that there were still many areas as late as 2004 where parties had made little or no progress at all. While all significant challengers for the presidency were generally partisan, the incumbents consistently refused party affiliation and no challenger had managed to prove this strategy misguided by winning as of 2005. While parties' role in the SMD Duma elections grew dramatically between 1993 and 1995, the estimated effects of party backing for candidates in both 1999 and 2003 showed little improvement except for United Russia, which registered unprecedented levels of party success in the latter elections. Governors' own stated partisanship remained transitory and they hardly ever ran for reelection as major-party nominees. Parties sought to nominate challengers in only a few gubernatorial races, rarely winning when they did. Finally, the involvement of parties in state legislatures was also extremely pathetic until July 2003; not only did major-party nominees rarely win, but parties seldom nominated candidates in the first place. Their progress after July 2003 came only because federal authorities bestowed this gift upon major parties by requiring that regions give them a large share of their legislatures' seats.

The picture that emerges, then, is one of slow, unbalanced, and uneven party development, with major parties failing even to come close to dominating the polity. Russia's major parties did manage to cultivate the capacity to efficiently communicate their positions to voters as well as to mobilize organizational and material resources for their candidates by 2005, but this did not translate into their fully or consistently penetrating the most important elected state organs. Explaining why this was the case – the central task of this volume – is taken up in the following chapter.

4

Electoral Markets and Party Substitutes in Russia

Origins and Impact

How can we explain the puzzling pattern that Chapter 3 found to exist? On one hand, that chapter's exhaustive study of party strength established that parties were in many ways quite strong in Russia as President Vladimir Putin moved into his second term in office. Collectively, they had cultivated distinctive positions on important issues, developed sizable populations of loyalists, and proven capable of significantly enhancing their candidates' chances in parliamentary elections. These findings appear to contradict widespread suppositions that Russian parties were consistently incapable of providing meaningful support for their candidates or were unable to communicate clear policy positions. On the other hand, we also saw that this party development had largely stalled by the late 1990s after progressing markedly in the middle of that decade; while some growth reemerged with the 2003 election, it was unbalanced, with one party (United Russia) accounting for a disproportionate share while some other key parties appeared to be in decline. Moreover, we found that parties had penetrated some organs of power more fully than others. These latter observations seem contrary to the anticipation of many theorists that the incentives provided by electoral competition would inevitably and smoothly lead to the prevalence of party politics in some form.

The logic of electoral markets sketched in Chapter 1 supplies us with some explanatory leverage on this puzzle. If candidates are treated as consumers of goods and services that help them get elected, parties can be seen as suppliers who emerge to meet this candidate demand. Most existing theories typically stop here, looking only at parties as potential suppliers. Basic economic theory, however, tells us that production decisions for any good (an outcome of the dynamics of supply and demand) are not made in a perfectly isolated market involving only that particular good, but in the context of broader markets in which demand for this good can be dampened by competition from "substitute" goods that potentially meet some or most of the same needs, if imperfectly.[1] In the realm of transitional polities, this means that when parties are seemingly stunted in their growth, the reason may lie in the existence of party substitutes that are able to outcompete parties in the provision of electoral goods and services under certain market conditions.

The pages that follow show how the abstract logic outlined in Chapter 1 helps us make sense of the complex and concrete reality of Russian politics in the first decade after the USSR's breakup. The chapter begins by delving into Russian history to document the emergence of important nonparty forms of political organization (party substitutes) that gained the potential to compete effectively with parties on the electoral market. Special attention is given to governors' political machines and politicized financial-industrial groups.[2] A following section discusses imperfections in the electoral market that prevent parties from perfectly responding to competition from party substitutes, thereby resulting in an effect whereby party substitutes can be said to partially "crowd out" parties. The chapter then turns to a rigorous examination of election results for Russia's four most important sets of elective institutions: the Duma, governorships, regional legislatures, and the presidency. This analysis finds strong support for the argument that Russian party development has stalled at least in part because of the rise of party substitutes on Russia's electoral market in the mid to late 1990s.

THE EMERGENCE OF PARTY SUBSTITUTES IN RUSSIA

As described in Chapter 2, Russia's departure from Communist rule left political entrepreneurs with stocks of particular kinds of capital that could be used to build political parties.[3] Russia's transition, however, also left different sets of political entrepreneurs with some of the same stocks of resources as well as other assets that could be applied to influence electoral outcomes, but not necessarily through parties. The pages that follow document two important elements of Russia's transition that facilitated the rise not only of parties, but of party substitutes, most notably provincial political machines and politicized financial-industrial groups. Two particular aspects of the transition proved to be central – one connected with political economy and the other linked to the institutional legacy of Soviet ethnofederalism. The chapter begins with a discussion of the Soviet legacy in each of these areas and then examines the transitional decisions, some of which involved high

1 Kirzner 1973; Samuelson 1970.

2 Other structures could also be seen as party substitutes during this period but are not considered here since financial-industrial groups and governors' machines proved to be the most important. For a consideration of one of these other possible forms of substitute, Russia's federal envoys under Putin, see Hale 2005b.

3 This section and the chapter's concluding section draw heavily from Hale 2003.

degrees of contingency, that translated into the formation of the powerful party substitutes just mentioned.

Soviet Political Ethnicity

Ethnic ties represent a distinct resource in the Soviet context and thus deserve separate treatment. The Soviet state institutionalized ethnicity in ways that have had long-lasting political implications. Most remarkably, the early Bolsheviks, guided in part by nationalities ideologue Joseph Stalin, set out to codify their country's ethnic diversity and to build certain state structures based on these newly codified identifications. They sent teams of ethnographers, many recruited from tsarist Russian academe, into the hinterlands to ask people who they were and where they lived. Soviet authorities then carved out administrative territories to correspond to most of the largest identified groups, taking into account the degree of their geographic concentration, economic considerations, and strategic concerns. The Bolsheviks proceeded to invest these regions with real ethnic content, privileging those groups designated as "native" to the territory, even at the expense of ethnic Russians.[4] Soviet "federal" structure, then, contained 15 *union republics,* each defined by nationality, with the Russian Republic (the Russian Soviet Federated Socialist Republic, or *RSFSR*) being only one of them. The Russian Republic was then subdivided into several categories of regions. The *autonomous republics* (now called simply *republics*) and *autonomous okrugs and oblasts* (here lumped together simply as "*AOs*") were generally designated as ethnic homelands for particular ethnic groups. The other official categories of regions (*oblasts*, *krais*, and the *major cities* of Moscow and Leningrad) had no particular ethnic designation and there was little practical meaning to the distinctions among them in the last decades of Soviet rule.

Perhaps the most striking aspect of these Soviet policies was that many of the ethnic groups that received officially recognized homelands did not previously have a mass group consciousness, meaning that Soviet policies in some real sense actually created many of the nations that it sought to accommodate. As the most widely accepted theories of ethnicity make clear and as studies of human psychology confirm, ethnicity is one of many identifications people have, and the degree to which ethnicity is a dominant "lens" through which people see the world depends very heavily on context. Contexts that accentuate the importance of ethnic distinctions tend to reinforce ethnic identifications.[5] Thus, where there had been no clear-cut ethnic "Uzbek" or "Nenets" identifications rooted in mass consciousness

[4] Major works on these policies include Martin 2001; Pipes 1964; Slezkine 1994.

[5] Classic works on ethnicity include Anderson 1991; Gellner 1983; and Hechter 2000. For a survey of cumulative knowledge and the interpretation of ethnic identity on which this book is based, see Hale 2004b.

prior to Soviet rule, the USSR took certain dialects and dubbed them the "proper" ones, drew up national alphabets, codified these tongues in school textbooks, reinforced these codifications by mass publication of newspapers and other reading material, stamped these national identifications in people's passports, and made people's career prospects heavily dependent on these formal markers of identity, often through "affirmative action" programs.

As the USSR expanded its educational system, it created networks not only of people thinking in terms of these identifications, but of certain kinds of professionals and intelligentsia (including the "half-forgotten poets and lonely philologists" described by David Laitin) who had vested interests in sustaining and strengthening these particular identity networks.[6] Detailed studies by Dmitry Gorenburg have remarkably been able to trace these ethnic networks at a micro-level, establishing their connection to Soviet educational policies and patterns of institutionalization in the ethnically designated autonomous republics of the Russian Republic of the USSR.[7] Even after Stalin cracked down on many of these "nativization" policies, Brezhnev and his next two successors typically left members of the "titular" (native) nationality in the top Communist Party posts of Russia's autonomous republics, although an ethnic Russian was usually kept as the number two authority.

Soviet Political Economy

The Soviet economic system was highly bureaucratized, "USSR Incorporated," as one scholar dubbed it.[8] Virtually all means of production belonged to the state and were administered by various economic ministries, each of which tended to represent a certain branch of the economy.[9] Production decisions were made at the top by the State Planning Agency (*Gosplan*) in conjunction with these ministries. At the regional level, ministerial authority was manifested in executive committees (*ispolkomy*) in most regions (oblasts, krais, AOs, Moscow, and Leningrad) and in provincial ministries in the autonomous republics.[10] Soviet banks were not banks in the Western sense of the term, but primarily served to keep track of and manage the flow of resources in the economy.[11] Each factory or *enterprise* was formally subordinate to the ministry in charge of its sector of production. While enterprises played a role in the development of mandatory production plans, for the most part they were subordinate in much the way that a processing plant might be subordinate to a major Western corporation. Plan quotas were

6 Brubaker 1996; Bunce 1999; Laitin 1998; Suny 1993; Zaslavsky 1982.
7 Gorenburg 2000, 2003.
8 Meyer 1961. See also Rigby 1988.
9 See Kohler 1989; Kornai 1992.
10 Hough and Fainsod 1979.
11 Johnson 2000, p. 27.

mandatory.[12] Beyond this, however, the Soviet system developed many features distinguishing it from a pure Weberian bureaucracy. While a comprehensive description would be an unnecessary digression, two particular innovations are important for the analysis that follows.

For one, due to the impossibility of efficiently and seamlessly administering the entirety of one of the world's largest economies from Moscow, enterprises typically came to take on roles as providers of many social services that are usually provided either privately or by the state itself in many Western societies. A worker in the USSR, therefore, often depended on his or her enterprise not only for a job and a paycheck, but also for housing, health clinics, day care, cinemas, summer camps, cheap vacation resorts, daily high-protein meals, and subsidized food products, all directly provided by the enterprise.[13] Many enterprises owned small farms to provide this food. The largest contained subsidiary factories producing a wide range of goods only indirectly related to the main product that the enterprises were charged with producing for the Soviet economy, all in an effort to achieve what Berliner called "enterprise autarky."[14] The largest of these would sometimes come to resemble "company towns," almost completely dominating the economy where they were located. Mary McAuley, for example, reports that the automobile giant KAMAZ in 1990 employed 150,000 out of the 524,000 people living in the city of Naberezhnye Chelny, which had been home to just 38,000 residents before the USSR ordered that KAMAZ be located there in the 1960s.[15] Kotkin has similarly described how Stalin's USSR built the massive company town of Magnitogorsk out of virtually nothing to become a center of Soviet metals production.[16] The average Soviet citizen's life, therefore, could revolve almost completely around the corporation for which he or she worked. This, needless to say, gave enterprise directors a huge degree of power over people's lives.

Collective and state farms could be seen as extreme (if small) forms of company town. During the process of collectivization under Stalin, private farms were confiscated and incorporated into either state farms (with the status of an enterprise) or collective farms (which were formally not state but "collective" property, although the difference was largely negligible). The geography of these Soviet farms was quite different from typical American farming communities, characterized by vast expanses of land only intermittently dotted with houses. In the USSR, the farmers on one collective farm would typically live together in housing clustered in a single village, with the farmland fanning out radially from this tiny center. Residents, often separated from cities by miles of extremely rough and sometimes impassable

[12] Berliner 1957, p. 1; Hough 2001.
[13] Hough 2001, pp. 24–7; Stoner-Weiss 1997, pp. 39–40.
[14] Berliner 1987, pp. 282–3; Rutland 1993, pp. 160–2.
[15] McAuley 1997, pp. 91–2.
[16] Kotkin 1995. See also Scott 1989.

road, were therefore almost completely dependent on the farm and its director in virtually all aspects of their lives, from the supply of consumer goods in a village store to the provision of health and day care. Soviet farm chairs even conveyed information to their workers directly and personally through gatherings at which officials made announcements regarding events or policies. USSR peasants commonly had very little access even to official printed or broadcast sources of information and were given little encouragement in exercising reading and independent interpretation skills.[17]

A second way in which USSR Incorporated differed from the classic bureaucratic model involves the coordinating role of regional party bosses, dubbed the "Soviet prefects" in Hough's seminal work. If enterprises themselves coped with imperfect coordinating mechanisms by internalizing supply of certain key goods and services, the first secretaries of the regional organizations of the Communist Party of the Soviet Union tended to play a central role in ensuring the overall performance of the provincial economy. Held personally responsible for the output of their regions' collection of enterprises, the first secretaries would organize informal, off-plan exchanges among enterprises within their regions. Even more than this, they would also barter and bargain with first secretaries of other provinces to obtain supplies needed by their own regions' firms. The Soviet prefects, then, played a key role in offsetting some of the distortions that are inevitable in a large bureaucracy.[18]

This, however, put enterprise directors in an odd situation of dual subordination. On one hand, they had to obey the directives and quotas coming down from their branch ministries. On the other hand, the regional party bosses had considerable formal and informal control over personnel in regional enterprises as well as influence on other critical regional conditions on which enterprises depended, making firm directors effectively subordinate to the party secretaries as well.[19] Nevertheless, as Peter Rutland and others have documented much more recently and as Hough has agreed, the party prefects were always less powerful than the branch ministries on key industrial issues (including personnel decisions for the most important enterprises), especially after Soviet leader Nikita Khrushchev's regionalizing "*sovnarkhoz*" reforms were reversed in the 1960s.[20] Importantly, Rutland has also established the critical role of local party leaders in administering agriculture, which tended to be in a state of constant crisis, throughout the Soviet period.[21]

This whole system was held together by a combination of coercion and cooptation. People were given the opportunity for upward mobility and improved standards of living so long as they avoided political troublemaking

[17] Inkeles and Bauer 1961, pp. 171–2.
[18] Hough 1969.
[19] Andrle 1976, pp. 141–2.
[20] Hough 1969, especially chap. 11; Rutland 1993; Stoner-Weiss 1997, pp. 37–9.
[21] Rutland 1993, especially chap. 7.

and were willing to toe the Party line, forging what Victor Zaslavsky called an "organized consensus" on the continuation of this compromise. The state took great pains, however, to ensure that challenges to this compromise did not emerge, brutally punishing dissident voices and restricting citizen mobility across what could be quite elaborate geographic, social, and administrative boundaries.[22]

The Transition

Mikhail Gorbachev initiated a period of change that took a particularly radical turn as the Soviet Union broke apart and Boris Yeltsin seized the helm of an independent Russian Federation. These reforms, as well as the *absence* of radical reforms in a few spheres, had important implications for the development of party substitutes and, hence, parties across the country. The following paragraphs consider changes that were made, as well as some that were not, in industry, banking, and regional politics under Gorbachev and then Yeltsin.

The Gorbachev Reforms

The critical breaking point between the old and new political-economic systems can be marked at 1988, even more so than at 1991.[23] The decisive moment came when the Law on State Enterprises, passed the year before, went into effect, although the important Law on Cooperatives was also launched that year, as was the "parade of sovereignties" that ensured the institutionalization of ethnicity would continue under new circumstances.[24] Gorbachev's Law on State Enterprises radically altered the traditional power relationship between ministries and enterprises, giving the latter the right to make their own production decisions, to retain a share of their income minus expenses, and even to set wages. Strikingly, workers' collectives were at first awarded the power to elect their enterprise directors. This generated a wage explosion as managers sought to please their workers by promising increased incomes, expecting the central government to foot the bill. In 1990, therefore, the government freed the directors from such electoral pressure, leaving them largely autonomous.[25] The enterprise directors had become de facto owners of their enterprises.[26] The Law on State Enterprises also broke up the Soviet Union's "bank" monopoly, dividing Gosbank's mostly bookkeeping functions among a new USSR Central Bank and several "specialized banks"

[22] Zaslavsky 1982.
[23] Coulloudon 2000, pp. 67–87.
[24] Estonia was the first Soviet ethnic region to declare sovereignty, doing so in 1988.
[25] Shleifer and Treisman 2000, pp. 29–30.
[26] Stoner-Weiss 1997, p. 39.

linked to branches of the economy.[27] These specialized banks had evolved into industry-connected commercial banks by 1990. The structure of collective farms and the way they were administered, however, changed relatively little during this time.

The 1988 Law on Cooperatives was noteworthy for legalizing the creation of "cooperative" ventures in both industry and banking, among other things. Roughly 80 percent of these banks were created or sponsored by enterprises to serve their own needs in the transitional economy. Some cooperative banks, however, operated independently of particular enterprises. A number of Russia's largest banks as of the 1990s, including Menatep and Most Bank, in fact got their start in this way.[28] These, however, typically made their fortunes managing money that came from Communist Party structures such as the Communist Youth League (as did Menatep) or state institutions like the City of Moscow. Indeed, entrepreneurial bankers could be quite creative in finding ways to channel official money to their own accounts for use in generating private profit.[29]

Late Soviet politics was largely defined by a multilevel "war of laws" fought between Yeltsin's Russian Republic and Gorbachev's Soviet central government, and regional governments increasingly also joined the fray. Whether the battlefield was the banking system or the distribution of federal powers, the implements of war were ever-escalating promises of autonomy and property to subordinate units in the hopes of securing their loyalty.

In the realm of banking, the Russian government delivered the deadliest blows to Soviet structures in 1990. First, it transformed the Moscow branch of the USSR's State Bank into the Central Bank of Russia. Second, and most devastatingly, it promised individual branches of the specialized banks the right to commercialize themselves as independent entities, essentially letting branch bank managers become bank owners. These banks, in turn, were promised less regulation than the Soviet Union offered. All these bankers had to do was register with the Russian authorities rather than the Soviet ones, which they did. The result was an explosion in the number of banks, including a massive proliferation of regional banks. The enterprise clients of most of these banks got a majority of the shares in these entities.[30] In this environment, the commercial banks (both cooperative and newly commercialized) gained autonomy to engage in a whole series of side activities for private profit, such as the financing of semi-legal trading activities and currency speculation.[31]

[27] Johnson 2000, pp. 4, 29, 30.

[28] Ibid., pp. 33, 37.

[29] For examples, see Remnick 1998, chap. 6; Solnick 1998.

[30] Johnson 2000, pp. 4, 47–50.

[31] Hough 2001, p. 38.

In the realm of center-periphery relations, the union republic of Estonia began the "parade of sovereignties" in 1988 by declaring the supremacy of its law over Soviet law. It was followed by Latvia, Lithuania, Georgia, and Azerbaijan over the next two years. On June 12, 1990, Russia adopted its own sovereignty declaration. This triggered a cascade of sovereignty declarations from virtually all of the autonomous republics within Russia as well as most of its AOs.[32] Yeltsin sought to harness this wave for use in his battle with Gorbachev, famously visiting Bashkortostan, Tatarstan, and other autonomous republics and beckoning them to "take as much sovereignty as you can swallow."[33] Chief among the demands of the autonomous republics (and some AOs) was the promotion of native languages and cultures, including the entrenchment of representatives of these groups in the top positions of political power.[34] This process of competitive bidding for autonomous republics and AO support meant that both the Yeltsin and Gorbachev administrations effectively granted them this power, albeit informally at this point. This ensured the continuation and even the increased politicization of Soviet-institutionalized ethnic networks during the late Soviet period of transition.

The Yeltsin Reforms

In some ways, the reforms Yeltsin implemented after the USSR collapsed in December 1991 ratified, formalized, and accelerated the changes initiated in the Gorbachev era. In the bank sector, state structures increasingly set up cozy relationships with commercial banks that enabled the latter to begin amassing immense sums of money, much of it disposable for private use.[35] The key moment came in 1992 and 1993, when commercial bankers persuaded the Russian central government to grant them the status of "authorized banks" to perform some very important and profitable functions for the state. For example, a pedigreed but little-known foreign trade official, Vladimir Potanin, created the modest Interros foreign trading company in 1990 and then joined with a few other partners to found ONEKSIMbank in 1993. Through his connections in the Russian government, he won the right for this bank to handle all money coming from Russian customs payments. His real breakthrough, however, came when the Ministry of Finance agreed to his proposal that importers be required to pay customs in advance, ostensibly so that there would be no delays in payments. Conveniently, ONEKSIMbank could use this money in the meantime either to serve its own or the government's interests. By the start of 1996, this bank had become the fourth largest in Russia.[36] Analogous processes were evident in Russia's provinces.

[32] Hale 2000; Kahn 2000; Lapidus 1992.

[33] *Izvestiia Bashkortostana*, October 12, 1993, p. 3.

[34] Gorenburg 1999.

[35] Coulloudon 2000, p. 73.

[36] Hough 2001 p. 41; Johnson 2000, p. 121.

Juliet Johnson reports that by 1994, for example, Moscow City had no less than 14 authorized banks, including Gusinsky's Most Bank, which controlled the primary current account of the city's finance department.[37] As the 1990s progressed, however, regional governments tended to focus on fewer banks, often choosing just one with which to work closely and frequently creating an official regional bank.[38]

It is important not to confuse these banks with totally independent entities. For one thing, the biggest banks clearly owed the bulk of their riches to their ties to the state. Furthermore, in return for these opportunities, the banks were expected to continue to be conduits of subsidies to loss-making enterprises, often in the form of "loans" that were never intended to be repaid.[39] The continued granting of such loans by both the major commercial banks and enterprise-connected regional banks is not understandable in terms of a narrow profit motive. Instead, Russian banks were still acting as important agents of the state, leading one analyst to go so far as to characterize this activity as part of a massive, covert scheme to channel financial support to the enterprises on which people continued to depend not only for jobs and income, but also for all of the social services ranging from day care to meals described above.[40] Indeed, the state had no other effective social security program in place during this time. While this provision of subsidies was in general terms an element of continuity, it is vital to recognize that the means for providing these subsidies had altered radically, forcing state officials, bankers, and enterprises to devise ever more complicated schemes for distributing transfers in ways that did not appear to violate International Monetary Fund strictures against such spending and did not involve the formal printing of new money. The complexity grew even more as these processes came to involve the demonetization of the economy.[41]

The privatization process that Yeltsin initiated in 1992 also tended to ratify and accelerate trends of radical change already afoot after 1988. One of the most important such moves was to formalize the de facto ownership that directors had acquired of their firms thanks to the 1988 Law on State Enterprises and its aftermath. Analysts usually parse Russian privatization into three processes: small privatization, voucher privatization, and cash privatization. Small privatization involved the sale of individual shops and other tiny firms, mostly to their management, starting in 1992. Voucher privatization proved to be of much greater political significance, taking place between 1992 and 1994. During this time, Anatoly Chubais' State

37 Johnson 2000, p. 122.
38 Ibid., p. 144.
39 Ibid., p. 106.
40 Hough 2001, pp. 26–41.
41 Ibid.; Woodruff 1999.

Property Committee (*Goskomimushchestvo*, or *GKI*) distributed to virtually the entire population vouchers that were worth a fixed sum in a series of auctions planned for most of Russia's medium- and large-scale enterprises. The government intentionally devised the process so as to give enterprise managers and the work collectives dependent on them an inside track in acquiring controlling ownership stakes in their firms. The government's strategy was to create unambiguous ownership while simultaneously "buying off" an interest group (directors) that was in a position to pose major obstacles to privatization were its members to be shut out of the process.[42] In fact, the edge given to the directors in the privatization process was so great that the banks largely avoided it; indeed, the scheme allowed banks only to procure up to 10–25 percent of an enterprise.[43]

Cash privatization also had lasting implications for Russian political economy in ways that affect political party development. During this phase, launched after voucher privatization was complete in 1994, the government auctioned off some of Russia's most important industrial assets. The emblematic event was the infamous "loans-for-shares" scheme, masterminded by Chubais and his associate Alfred Kokh and implemented during 1995–7. While observers disagree as to the motivation behind this plan, for our purposes it is most important to note only that it gave a small set of Russia's largest banks the right to organize auctions for a collection of the most lucrative ventures in Russia, including some of the world's largest oil and metals companies. Opposition eyebrows were raised but official blind eyes were turned when it emerged that the banks organizing the auctions (or their associates) usually managed to win them.[44] Russia's Audit Chamber later investigated and reported evidence of rigged auctions and strikingly undervalued assets.[45] In separate sales, shares of a few major concerns like the natural gas monopoly Gazprom were transferred to private ownership. Although there are signs that the state did not completely control firms like Gazprom with the shares it retained, it clearly retained veto power over company policy and had a great deal of influence when push came to shove.[46] This was especially true of Gazprom, whose long-time "patron" was the prime minister of Russia during 1993–8.

These events more than any others gave rise to the phenomenon known in popular media as Russia's "oligarchs," a group of several magnates whose financial-industrial groups (FIGs) managed massive flows of economic

[42] Hough 2001, p. 76; Shleifer and Treisman 2000.

[43] Johnson 2000, p. 104.

[44] For different interpretations and descriptions, see Hough 2001; Johnson 2000, pp. 8, 185–7; Reddaway and Glinski 2001; and Shleifer and Treisman 2000.

[45] Reddaway and Glinski 2001, p. 480.

[46] *Polit.Ru*, August 27, 1999, 18:34.

resources. Potanin, the once-obscure foreign trade official described above, now gained control of Norilsk Nickel, holder of 35 percent of the world's known reserves of this metal, as well as an oil company (Sidanko) and other major properties. Menatep, a former Communist Youth League (*Komsomol*) bank owned by Mikhail Khodorkovsky, sunk its teeth into Yukos, Russia's second-largest oil concern. Former car dealer Boris Berezovsky, owner of the FIG LogoVAZ, obtained the oil company Sibneft.[47] While Hough cautions against assuming that these men had too much power of their own since they still depended on the state for much of their profits, they nevertheless went from being "players" to extremely important political forces with a great deal of resources at their disposal to use for both government and themselves.[48] Having become major FIGs between 1995 and 1997, the bank-led conglomerates then won legal sanction to begin aggressively expanding into the regions, opening up branches of their banks in provinces where they had purchased major enterprises.[49] The FIGs also used these resources to acquire important mass media during the 1990s. By 1998, Most Group owned the popular NTV network and Berezovsky effectively controlled the main state television network, First Channel, owning 49 percent outright and possessing the right to manage an additional set of the shares.[50] These oligarchs and others also owned most of the country's major newspapers.

The August 1998 financial crisis, as Russia's default on sovereign debt and its sudden devaluation of the ruble is widely known, produced some redistribution of economic power but left most of the major old players in place. While some FIGs that had been investing heavily in Russian state securities (GKOs) were weakened (notably ONEKSIMbank, Menatep, and Inkombank), only Inkombank actually went completely under.[51] Most major FIGs responded by refocusing their activities to other parts of their empires, notably in their newly acquired industrial holdings. In this way, they remained major players in the political economy of Russia.[52] Not all nationwide FIGs were greatly weakened, moreover. Some, like Alfa Bank and financial institutions controlled by Gazprom, had not been deeply involved in the GKO market and thus came out of the crisis relatively unscathed.[53] Nevertheless, most of these FIGs of national scope did suffer losses during the crisis, which thereby strengthened the relative position of regional FIGs centered around local industries. These regional FIGs, whose banks had not

47 David Hoffman, "Tycoons Take the Reins in Russia," *Washington Post*, August 28, 1998, p. A1.

48 Hough 1999, p. 41; Johnson 2000, p. 187.

49 Johnson 2000, pp. 151–3.

50 Reddaway and Glinski 2001, p. 196.

51 Johnson 2000, p. 201; Reddaway and Glinski 2001, p. 603.

52 Johnson 2000, pp. 201–24.

53 Ibid., pp. 223–4.

invested much in the "GKO pyramid," took the opportunity to expand their holdings in their provinces at the expense of the weakened Moscow-based FIGs.[54]

The political changes in center-periphery relations begun in the Gorbachev era also largely continued and accelerated under Yeltsin. The parade of sovereignties and the legacy of the USSR's institutionalization of ethnicity were effectively ratified first in the 1992 Federation Treaty and then, starting in 1994, with a series of "bilateral treaties" concluded between many of the largest ethnic regions and the Russian central government. The Russian government cracked down only on Chechnya, which had declared independence during the fall of 1991, but the 1994–6 military operation was an abysmal failure. Until Putin came to power, the republics went virtually unchallenged in their drives for sovereignty. As Kathryn Stoner-Weiss has noted, Russia's oblasts and krais also gained a great deal of autonomy over their local affairs during this time, especially when the Kremlin began concluding bilateral treaties with them as well as with republics.[55]

The Impact of Legacy and Transition on Electoral Politics

Both the Soviet institutional "inheritance" and the transition initiated by the Yeltsin administration helped spark the development of what would become Russia's most important party substitutes, politicized financial-industrial groups and regional political machines. They did so not by translating directly into political forces, but by leaving in place certain distributions of administrative capital that, given Russian electoral institutions, proved useful in building party substitutes. It was up to political entrepreneurs to devise ways to invest this capital and to use it in electoral politics, leaving plenty of room for individual skills and contingency to matter.[56] The following sections examine how the legacies and the transition described above, mediated by political actors, led to the creation of strong governors' political machines and financial-industrial groups capable of competing with, and even outcompeting, parties in the Russian electoral arena by the time Putin came to power.[57]

[54] Ibid., p. 223.

[55] There is a vast literature on the development of Russian federalism in the Yeltsin era. Among other works, see the chapters in Alexseev 1999 as well as Hale 2005a; Hale and Taagepera 2002; Herrera 2005; Lapidus 1999; Roeder 1999; Solnick 2000; Stepan 2000; Stoner-Weiss 1997, 1999; Treisman 1997, 1999.

[56] For a parallel argument on the translation of Soviet-era economic skills into postreform success, see Eyal, Szelenyi, and Townsley 1998.

[57] On political legacies of communism more generally, see Anderson et al. 2001; Crawford and Lijphart 1997; Ekiert and Hanson 2003; Fish 1995; Geddes 1995; Grzymala-Busse 2002; Hanson 1995; Jones Luong 2002; Jowitt 1992; Kitschelt et al. 1999.

Politicized Financial-Industrial Groups (PFIGs)

Russia's major financial-industrial groups (FIGs), both nationwide and regional, gained a great deal of power and resources that could be used effectively in the electoral arena during the 1990s. For one thing, FIGs had controlling interests in most major mass media, both print and broadcast. Virtually any Western or Russian campaign manager will affirm that television is an extremely valuable election resource. This was demonstrated vividly in 1996, when the FIG-controlled First Channel (LogoVAZ) and NTV (Most Group) networks lined up with the third major network, RTR (state-owned), to promote President Yeltsin's reelection campaign. According to a study reported by the European Institute for the Media, Yeltsin received 53 percent of the coverage in the run-up to the first round of presidential voting that year, compared to just 18 percent for his chief rival, Communist Party leader Gennady Zyuganov, who had led in the polls for most of the campaign. Of these references, the glowing ones outnumbered the negatives by 247 for Yeltsin, whereas Zyuganov was the subject of 240 more critical reports than positives.[58] This media campaign goes a long way toward helping explain how Yeltsin emerged from the abyss of below-10-percent approval ratings in January 1996 to defeat a Communist challenger whom many noncommunists had expected to win.

Money itself is a major component of administrative capital, and Russia's FIGs began to get involved in electoral politics almost as soon as they gained control of significant flows of resources. In the 1996 presidential election alone, Johnson reports that the major FIGs provided at least $100 million and perhaps as much as $500 million for the Yeltsin campaign, a number especially striking given that the legal campaign spending limit was just $3 million. Aside from backing the country's president directly, the banks-cum-FIGs operated in the electoral arena in 1993 and 1995 primarily by financing the campaigns of major parties in return for their representatives or close allies gaining promising slots on these organizations' party lists. Their aim, which banking representatives claimed was for the most part realized, was to get some of their own people onto key parliamentary committees that oversaw the banking industry and economic policy more generally. The banks primarily backed parties of power, but rarely exclusively since they had an interest in hedging their bets. The other parties that were supported were those considered in favor of the emerging private property rights on which they depended. In 1993, for example, most banks supported Russia's Choice, Yabloko, and/or PRES. In 1995, the focal party was the one led by the prime minister, Our Home is Russia.[59] Candidates for the Duma, governorships,

58 Peter Rutland, *OMRI Presidential Election Report* 15, July 9, 1996, as cited in Johnson 2000, p. 182.

59 Johnson 2000, pp. 116–17, 181–2.

and other offices were also reportedly "bought" by FIGs after they won elections.[60]

By the time the 1999 electoral cycle rolled around, however, several nationwide FIGs were in a position to enter politics on a whole new level, powerfully advancing their own secret slates of *independent* parliamentary candidates running in the single-member-district races as well as putting forth their own people as contenders for key governorships. The analysis above describes what had changed to make this a more promising strategy. For one thing, the nationwide FIGs had gained control of absolutely massive resource flows through attaining authorized bank status and winning other cozy relationships with Russian governments during the mid-1990s. The loans-for-shares program, in particular, catapulted the FIGs into being major political players with national scope by facilitating their direct acquisition of key industrial and natural resource assets in a variety of regions throughout the country. The possession of assets nationwide gave them regional political footholds, local resources, and extra incentive to make sure they were well represented in any state organ that might have some influence over these holdings, including the Duma, provincial legislatures, and, where possible, the local executive branch.

Whereas the old strategy of backing parties and covertly "lobbying" elected deputies had produced some fruit, many FIGs came to decide that they would have more loyal representatives in deputies who were elected on the basis of direct and active FIG support, even campaign management. Those FIGs that were hit least hard by the August 1998 crisis (such as Gazprom, LUKoil, and Alfa Group) and those that had acquired industrial assets making up a sizeable component of regional economies (such as Interros) enjoyed particular power. They would typically not attempt to cover all regions, but just those where they had special interests and capabilities. LUKoil, for example, tended to focus on the largest regions, especially those like Perm where it had significant economic interests.[61] Regional FIGs, boosted by the August 1998 financial crisis and having been winnowed down to only a few powerful players in each region by 1999, were also in a newly strong position to influence regional elections autonomously at the close of the decade by backing their own candidates in SMD races for the Duma, regional legislatures, and governorships.

A good example of this phenomenon is LUKoil-Permneft in Perm Oblast. With the approach of the December 1999 Duma elections, LUKoil made a decision aggressively to politicize its business, aiming to have strong and direct representation in the Duma. LUKoil initially achieved a great deal of sway in the "governors' bloc" All Russia (which soon became part of the Fatherland–All Russia coalition) since it provided much of the bloc's financial

[60] *RFE/RL Newsline*, January 10, 2002.

[61] Ibid.; interview with a regional campaign official for a LUKoil subsidiary, fall 1999.

backing. LUKoil also decided, however, to put forth its own candidates directly as such candidates would be the most reliable in representing the corporation's interests due to their direct dependence on the firm and immunity to interference from party leaderships. LUKoil actually had three separate structures in Perm: LUKoil-Permneft, LUKoil Perm, and Permneftorgsintez, the latter a processing firm. While these three organizations had separate election teams, they worked together in supporting their candidates. LUKoil-Permneft, our case study subject, had its own full-time election "headquarters" consisting of a core of 5 people plus 15 more central support staff. One person involved in the firm's political effort said that this PFIG's regional "army" of deployed activists totaled some thousand people, a figure that could not be confirmed but which there is little reason to doubt. (The other two LUKoil structures were said to have the same.) This kind of powerful structure was stronger than any political party, claimed this official, since it combined generous material support, a strong election campaign team that provided its candidates with top-of-the-line polls and other important information, and large numbers of activists, all coming from the powerful institutional structures of LUKoil that already existed in the region. In return for this support, candidates had to agree to represent the interests of LUKoil in the Duma, although they were said to be free to vote their conscience on issues that did not concern the firm. LUKoil-Permneft did not provide any particular ideology for its candidates, although the campaign official said that most candidates tended to believe even before the agreement of support that what was good for LUKoil was good for their district and for Russia as a whole. The Perm organization very much saw itself as being at the forefront of a major LUKoil move to create a loyal political structure covering its interests in the whole country.[62]

In a few cases, PFIGs took on a very high profile in elections. The example of Krasnoiarsk's 2002 gubernatorial race, described in the opening paragraphs of this book, is perhaps the best known of these cases. Intense media coverage swirled around the battle of metal magnates, the "Man of Nickel" Khloponin versus the "Man of Aluminum" Uss, while treating partisan candidates (even Communist heavyweight Glaziev) as little more than a sideshow. Of course, the Krasnoiarsk image reflects only one pattern in Russian regional politics. What makes Krasnoiarsk stand out in light of the preceding discussion is its high concentration of major FIG-owned assets, key elements of which were obtained during the loans-for-shares auctions (most obviously, Norilsk Nickel). An excellent study by Orttung lends confirmation to this general conclusion, associating PFIG political dominance of a region with the degree to which major FIGs have managed to obtain ownership in key provincial assets.[63]

62 Ibid.
63 Orttung 2004a.

Despite this electoral involvement, PFIGs were not "parties" according to the definition given in Chapter 1 because their primary organizational purpose was economic (not to govern or to win outright control of the polity), because their candidates typically did not publicly run on the basis of the company label, and because they usually did not make known the "platform" that was the company's condition for lending candidates support. These "party qualities" that distinguish parties from PFIGs are very important since they facilitate accountability, stability, and an efficient structuring of the political process in the polity. Operationally, this nonparty status was reflected in the fact that PFIGs lacked the legal right to nominate official candidates for any elective office in the country.

Regional Political Machines

Provincial leaders (sometimes just called "governors" here for simplicity's sake regardless of their formal titles) also emerged from the mid-1990s with effective possession of a great deal of administrative capital, but this capital did not automatically or immediately translate into provincial machine politics. Instead, the old system of authority, which was centered around branch ministries and Communist Party regional first secretaries, had broken down between 1988 with the Law on State Enterprises and 1991 with the banning of the CPSU. Any political machines that governors controlled by the late 1990s, then, had to have been *built* either by them personally or by their predecessors in the period following the start of these reforms.[64] Success in this endeavor depended in part on personal experiences and skills as well as on personal drive and capacities. Governors were in many ways still dependent on the federal center throughout the 1990s. They had no real independent tax base, instead relying on (negotiated) federal allocations, "loans" that were not expected to be repaid, and underpriced energy supplies.[65] Nevertheless, regional leaders were in a position in the 1990s to have a good deal

[64] By "political machine," we follow Banfield and Wilson (1963, p. 115) in referring to an organization that depends crucially upon inducements that are both specific and material for political power. To clarify the concept of political "machine," it is helpful to quote Banfield and Wilson at some length: "[A] specific (as opposed to general) inducement is one that can be offered to one person while being withheld from others. A *material* inducement is money or some other physical 'thing' to which value attaches. *Nonmaterial* inducements include especially the satisfactions of having power or prestige, doing good, the 'fun of the game', the sense of enlarged participation in events and a pleasant environment. A machine, like any formal organization, offers a mixture of these various kinds of inducements in order to get people to do what it requires. But it is distinguished from other types of organization by the very heavy emphasis it places upon specific, material inducements and the consequent completeness and reliability of its control over behavior, which, of course, account for the name 'machine.'" As it operates in an electoral market, then, a political machine wins support almost entirely through the deployment of administrative capital.

[65] Hough 2001, pp. 29, 44.

of influence over just how reforms in their jurisdictions developed as a great deal became open for negotiation.[66]

For one thing, governors typically had the power to push for local institutional reform in ways that could reinforce the advantages or downplay the disadvantages they inherited at the point of transition. Sovereignty declarations, effectively ratified under Yeltsin, gave republics the right to decide such major questions as whether to institute a regional "presidential" or parliamentary system and exactly how to structure and elect their regional assemblies, as described in Chapter 2. Governors also possessed great potential to influence how their economies came to be arranged through the economic reform process. Most directly, the Yeltsin administration intentionally gave them a major role in shaping the privatization process as a way of "buying" their support for this reform, providing them with a stake in carrying it out.[67] For one thing, regional authorities were afforded control over the privatization of small enterprises and were able to keep the proceeds for their own budgets. More importantly, the Chubais reforms awarded provincial organs the right to administer the voucher auctions that took place in 1992–4. Concretely, Chubais' GKI set up a property committee and a property fund in virtually every region, with the property fund actually gaining legal property rights to the assets pending auction. Each region's property committee had to produce its own program for privatization.[68]

The reform also allowed regional authorities to keep a significant share of these properties for the regional government, ostensibly for later privatization. Aslund reports that provincial property committees retained voting stakes averaging 15–20 percent in many enterprises.[69] In practice, the regional government would decide what it wanted to keep and what it would delegate to other levels of government.[70] As a result, some enterprises became long-term regional government assets. In some cases, the property being privatized was a major enterprise of nationwide significance that had accordingly been under the direct administration (and then supervision) not of regional authorities but of federal ministries. In these instances, privatization essentially meant a transfer of responsibility and some real ownership from federal to regional governments.[71] Such ownership stakes gave governors the potential to influence the political lines of their enterprises, lines that could be promoted by everything from direct candidate sponsorship to the denial of enterprise venues to opposition candidates.

66 Ibid., p. 43; McAuley 1997, pp. 40, 99.
67 Aslund 1995, p. 246; Shleifer and Treisman 2000, p. 31.
68 Aslund 1995, pp. 245–53.
69 Ibid., p. 237; Shleifer and Treisman 2000, p. 31.
70 McAuley 1997, p. 197.
71 Aslund 1995, p. 237.

The city of Moscow is a classic example of a constructed political machine and illustrates the importance of leadership skills in applying administrative capital to generate long-run political profit. Despite the fact that Moscow was Russia's most diverse and complex economy, Mayor Yury Luzhkov managed to retain or obtain (directly or indirectly) city government stakes in local firms to such an extent that one recent study categorized the capital city as a "single-company town."[72] The "single company" is the Sistema concern, a holding company that Luzhkov and his city of Moscow founded and which, through the privatization process and market operations, became the economic heart of the mayoral machine. In this way, he almost single-handedly illustrates that governors' political machines are not simply the inheritance of the Soviet era nor a direct result of concentrated economies, but had to be crafted and/or sustained by skilled politicians during the transition. That Luzhkov's own characteristics were important is further illustrated by the failure of his predecessor, Gavriil Popov, who in 1992 wound up resigning in frustration as Moscow mayor. Luzhkov, on the other hand, has since the mid-1990s been able easily to generate votes upward of 70 percent for himself in mayoral elections, even in 1999 when he faced the full force of a massive Kremlin campaign to discredit him.

Alongside the ability to keep and acquire important shares of key enterprises for the state, regional authorities also had considerable say in who could obtain the shares that were in fact sold. Aslund reports that voucher auctions were typically "local affairs," dominated by inside players. In principle, anyone could participate, but regional authorities and enterprises frequently colluded to keep critical information about how and when auctions would take place under wraps. It was not uncommon for regional governments effectively to exclude people from outside their jurisdiction, especially when significant local resources were at stake.[73] In this way, regional governments could influence the degree to which certain networks or holding concerns gained control of their economies and could thereby influence the degree of ownership concentration of the local economy. Governors could also use this influence, naturally, to maximize the degree to which people in their own extended networks gained control of these companies. Nevertheless, this power should not be overstated; as previously described, the cards were largely stacked in favor of enterprise directors even if they were not backed by governors.

Regional leaders could also use their power over banks, subsidies, and regulations to influence local politics, either by directly backing (or opposing) certain candidates or by more indirectly pressuring other local powerholders to toe a certain political line. Banks were an especially powerful tool for controlling the economy and hence the political activities of local firms. The

[72] Orttung 2004a.
[73] Aslund 1995, pp. 237, 254.

banks that provincial authorities themselves set up were one such powerful tool, and as other banks were weakened through economic difficulties, governors could gain control over them through a number of levers, including legal and logistical barriers to their operation. As was described above, this power increased after August 1998, when banks with Moscow power bases were weakened.[74] For example, Bashkortostan's administration set up Bashkreditbank and then required all major firms doing business in the region to hold accounts in it, giving the government there a critical lever to use to monitor, regulate, and punish local businesses. Regional firm owners considering involvement with the opposition to republic leader Rakhimov had good reason to think twice about how such political activity might affect their bottom line.[75] Signals sent by Rakhimov could easily send a wave of "voluntary" contributions to favored candidates and could effectively put a funding freeze on disfavored ones.

Since subsidies continued to be critical to most regional economies, those in control of them wielded significant political influence. The Yeltsin reforms gave provincial authorities power over many of the institutions that channeled these transfers, including regional pension funds and banks. Hough likens this subsidy lever to the sort held by the former CPSU regional first secretaries since governors enjoyed the power to decide whether pensions, for example, could be postponed for a few months to pay workers. Such factors naturally gave regional leaders a powerful stick (as well as a carrot) to employ in convincing various constituencies to vote for preferred candidates, further strengthening the potential for provincial machine politics.[76]

Governors were also well known for having accumulated a vast array of regulatory and administrative powers that were not in theory political, but that certainly could be applied with great effect to electoral politics.[77] Typical governors in the 1990s had at least informal control over critical organs such as like the tax police, the prosecutor's office, the sixth directorate of the police, and even the courts due to the impoverishment of regional judges and legal employees. They often wielded regulatory authority in the spheres of health and sanitation, ecological protection, various forms of licensing and quotas, and fire safety. In many instances, leases or residency permits could be granted or denied to individuals or entities, or rates altered.[78] Enterprises, social organization headquarters, even newspapers or the printing presses

[74] Johnson 2000, pp. 151–3, 223–4.

[75] On Bashkreditbank, see Kh. B. Asylguzhin, "Banki," in R. Z. Shakurov (ed.), *Bashkortostan: Kratkaia Entsiklopediia* (Ufa, Bashkortostan, Russia: Nauchnoe Izdatel'stvo "Bashkirskaia Entsiklopediia," 1996), pp. 145–6.

[76] Hough 2001, pp. 45–6.

[77] On the influence of governors on elections, see Berezkin, Myagkov, and Ordeshook 1999; Brudny 2001; Golosov 1997; Hale 1998, 1999a; Petrov and Titkov 1999; Slider 1996; Solnick 1999; Stoner-Weiss 1999, 2001.

[78] Afanasiev 1997, p. 195.

they relied on could fairly easily be shut down when governors put their minds to it. Often, however, just the threat (frequently in the form of disruptive inspections) was enough to cow some organizations and enterprises from unwanted political activity. When these administrative powers were combined with governors' control over "economic" levers (tax rates, flows of subsidies, price regulations, banking policies, and so on), savvy regional leaders could often mobilize a dazzlingly powerful array of forces against wayward subjects, even those that seemingly had independent sources of influence and resources.

Enterprises were not the only forces engaging in economic activity in a given region; regional authorities themselves frequently participated in what Afanasiev has called "administrative entrepreneurship." Regions and even major cities had the opportunity to set up off-budget financial and commodity funds that could then be managed by special regional corporations or trade houses, opportunities of which many leaders successfully partook. These accounts were typically filled either by requisitioning certain contributions from local enterprises or by some kind of contract of exchange. Afanasiev cites the example of Ul'ianovsk Governor Goriachev requisitioning over 5,000 automobiles from his region's major manufacturer (UAZ).[79] Such off-budget resources could be quite useful in either supporting political activity directly (campaigns, for example) or as a source for transfers that could be used to reward loyal political players. In another example, Kemerovo governor Aman Tuleev, by decision of the regional legislature that he controlled, set up a "risk fund" and asked for monthly "donations" from the oblast's 400 biggest enterprises on the order of 4 percent of the wage fund. The province's largest employer, Western Siberian Metallurgical Kombinat (ZapSib), was requested to donate 24 percent. Most firms, it is reported, agreed to pay. ZapSib, the management of which Tuleev had managed to oust, decided to "overfulfill the plan" and give 48 percent.[80]

The leaders of ethnic minority regions (especially republics) had special opportunities, and perhaps special incentive, to mobilize strong political machines. As noted above, the ethnic minority social networks institutionalized by the Soviet regime not only survived the USSR's demise, but actually gained strength as the republics (typically led by titular-group members) declared sovereignty and sought to reinforce the status of their "native" groups through the implementation of language laws, education policies, and preferential hiring practices in state administration.[81] The ethnic claim often served to legitimate what might otherwise be seen as cronyism or sometimes autocratization, although the desire to protect the interests of one's ethnic group against complete absorption into a predominantly Russian society

[79] Ibid., p. 196.
[80] *Kommersant-Vlast*, June 8, 1999.
[81] Gorenburg 1999.

was arguably at least part of the motivation of minority leaders in undertaking such policies.[82] It also appears that regions designated for a particular minority tended to generate a greater sense of efficacy among native-group members than among other local groups, such as Russians, some of whom tended to accept longstanding Soviet-era teachings that the titular group had some kind of special claim to the land. In Bashkortostan, for example, this was evident in the disproportionately large number of Bashkir candidates for the Duma running in 1993, despite the fact that interviews and the statements of opposition leaders revealed no major charges of coercive ethnic filtration of candidates.[83]

All of this gave a titular leader of an ethnic minority region a ready-made, loyal base upon which to expand if he or she was savvy. Thus, Rakhimov quietly kept his ethnically Bashkir base happy through privileging it in appointments and expanding education in its titular language, but made it a central part of his political strategy also to reach out to ethnic Russians and Tatars, claiming (with some credibility) that his "sovereignty" policy was producing real benefits for the whole republic. In this way, an ethnic base constituting just 22 percent of the population (only 17 percent if the criterion is not self-identification but language ability) helped enable Rakhimov to build up one of the strongest political machines in Russia.[84] Giuliano observed a similar dynamic in Tatarstan, where the skillful leadership of Shaimiev was able to overcome intra-Tatar differences and mobilize a broad-based coalition with Soviet-institutionalized Tatar networks at the core.[85]

The agricultural economy also provided governors with a great deal of administrative capital, sometimes making possible the formation of a core base of support around which a political machine could be forged. Agriculture was one of the few sectors of the Soviet economy whose management structure had changed little from Soviet times well into the Putin era. Farmers thus remained heavily dependent on their farm director not only for their livelihoods but also for the information they got about the outside world, reinforcing docile attitudes to political choices.[86] Since farms were still very dependent on the state during this period, their leaders had great reason not to alienate governors who could determine whether or not they received, say, their next fertilizer shipment on time. Since a Soviet-style farm represents an isolated cluster of residents living in a single village, typically constituting a single electoral precinct, it proved very easy for regional officials to determine which farms were loyal and which were not, making the threat of punishment very credible. In many ethnic republics, the minority groups were

[82] Ibid.; McAuley 1997, p. 87.
[83] Hale 1998, 1999a.
[84] Ibid.
[85] Giuliano 2000, pp. 295–316.
[86] Rutland 1993, Chap. 8.

also clustered in rural areas, magnifying the potential for patron-client relationships in electoral politics. Rural areas in many regions, therefore, were known for generating large votes in directions favored by governors. Since farm directors found it easy to mobilize their subordinates given their institutionally reinforced state of subservience, the pro-machine-politics effect of rural communities was often magnified by very high turnouts.[87]

Finally, the Soviet socioeconomic inheritance and Russia's postcommunist transition left regional authorities in possession of other concentrations of administrative capital, capital that did not inevitably become the basis of machine politics and that thus had to be applied by sufficiently skilled governors for such purposes. During processes of privatization, governors could powerfully influence who gained control of local mass media, keeping some (if not all) under state control. Other media could be regulated via licensing restrictions or different administrative measures. The result was that local mass media expansion often represented the penetration of a governor's propaganda machine rather than increased exposure to competing views. During the late Yeltsin and early Putin eras, Russian law also gave governors the right to appoint half of the members of provincial election commissions, which themselves had the right to rule on issues of candidate disqualification and even the validity of elections themselves.[88] Since law also gave legislatures the right to appoint other members, the governor could usually secure a clear election commission majority through allies in the legislature.

These governors' political machines, despite their involvement in elections, cannot be considered parties according to the definition given in Chapter 1 because they did not express their primary aims in terms of an explicit label encompassing their candidates and did not develop public and coherent platforms on which their candidates ran. Moreover they did not officially pretend to the control of the federal government, limiting their scope to districts in their own regions and so certainly could not be considered *national* parties. This is no mere semantic distinction; these functions that governors' political machines failed to serve are some of the very ones that lead scholars to consider parties vital for democratic development and state stability. Explicit labels and public platforms are critical to efficiently organizing choice for voters. Organizational control of the national polity, as opposed to the frequent constitution and reconstitution of new coalitions on every issue to be decided, is important in providing stability and structure to democratic politics as well as efficiency. All of these things are crucial in facilitating elite accountability before voters.[89] Operationally, the nonparty

87 For an example, see Hale 1998.

88 Central Election Commission of the Russian Federation, *Vybory v Organy Gosudarstvennoi Vlasti sub'ektov Rossiiskoi Federatsii 1997–2000* 1 (Moscow: Ves Mir, 2001), p. 35.

89 Huntington 1968; Lipset 2000; Mair 1990; Wright and Schaffner 2002.

status of gubernatorial machines is indicated by the fact that they lacked permission to officially nominate candidates for any elective office in the country.[90]

PARTIES, PARTY SUBSTITUTES, AND IMPERFECT ELECTORAL MARKETS

When party systems are strong, they effectively force candidates to run for office with a party affiliation or not to run at all. Seeking party nomination can be costly for candidates in terms of time, energy, money, and even principle, but when they have no other option they will be willing to pay a higher price for this nomination. The market model suggests that one reason parties seemed to stall on the path to dominating Russia's electoral arena as of the late 1990s was because they simply were not in a position to command high prices from candidates because candidates often had other, more cost-effective options in the form of party substitutes. The costs that Russian parties often required candidates to bear if they wanted party nomination include, aside from the occasional demand for actual cash, everything from waiting for future election cycles to currying the favor of party leaders to reinventing oneself so as to fit with a party's core set of ideas. Yet supply-side restrictions frequently prevented parties from lowering the price of nomination to the point at which they could effectively outcompete party substitutes and monopolize the candidate market for electoral goods and services. Such supply-side restrictions included hard facts like the number of parliamentary seats available for contestation and parties' prior investments in specific forms of political capital, things quite distinct from intrinsic party weakness. Since parties typically could not lower this price without undermining key determinants of what limited success they already enjoyed, most proved able to attract candidates only from very limited pools at the prices they required in order to stay in business. These features of parties' supply functions resulted in a kind of transitional equilibrium of stalled party development by the 1999 elections.[91]

It is not hard to demonstrate this with regard to the elections to various offices held in Russia in the later 1990s. Despite the fact that 141 political associations were registered with the Ministry of Justice as of December 1998, it was painfully clear to Russian candidates that not everyone who

90 *Coalitions* of governors, of course, can and sometimes have constituted political parties in Russia, a possibility that will be considered in great depth in Chapter 5. Likewise, governors can turn their political machines into what are often called parties vis-à-vis *local* elections, where they have pretended to the complete control of the particular level of government for which that electoral competition was organized. The classic example of this is the Transformation of the Urals Party led by Sverdlovsk Governor Eduard Rossel during the latter 1990s. On this case, see Gel'man and Golosov 1998.

91 The level of party development obtaining in this equilibrium need not be permanent, of course, as certain equilibrium-inducing variables can change in ways explored in Chapter 5.

wanted to be the nominee of a strong party could be one any time he or she chose and without absorbing significant costs of various kinds. One such constraint was the number of nominations that each party had to offer each election cycle for each contested institution, a limit determined by the quantity of seats up for election and the frequency of elections. The fact that there was a maximum number of nominations per party meant that candidates had to invest significant resources into competing with others for what valued party slots were available, and it was clear that this often meant waiting for a future election cycle for a promising nomination to open up. Chapter 3 showed, however, that no major party managed to field a candidate for even close to all of the various seats up for election between 1995 and 2000. This does not mean that parties could not find anyone willing to run under their labels, however. The key is variability in the value of party nomination across districts and institutions.

As is the case even in developed democracies, certain parties have better prospects in some places than in others due to regional variation in preferences and perceptions of party prospects. This variability in the value of different party nominations is magnified to the extent that there are not just two strong parties as in the United State or three as in Great Britain, but as many as six or seven. In fact, the stronger the six or seven parties, the more we should expect to find spotty territorial coverage by parties in single-member district elections, since competition in any one district is likely to revolve around just a few of the strongest candidates and frequently around only two.[92] Accordingly, in Russia during the 1990s we saw that Yabloko nominations were quite valuable in St. Petersburg, where its candidates frequently won, while they were considered little better than the paper on which they were written in the most rural Red Belt districts such as the Pochepsky Duma district in Briansk that did not contain any major city and was long dominated by Communists. Union of Right Forces nominations were highly sought after in Perm, where the politics of economic liberalism were well received, but not in Bashkortostan, where the longstanding preference was for more statist approaches to reform. Candidate demand for party nomination, then, will be great where the nomination means the most and can be almost nonexistent where other parties look to be a lock to win.

Far from seeing parties pleading desperately with candidates to run on their platforms, therefore, one quite often found nearly every major party facing the opposite problem in the 1990s: more demand for party nomination than the party could supply. The precise dynamics, however, tended to be different for clientelistic and ideational parties. For the strongest clientelistic parties, especially parties of power, the problem was usually a relatively direct one of allocating a constrained number of promising nominations

[92] For the most rigorous demonstration of this, see Cox 1997.

(called "passing" or *prokhodnie* slots in the Russian political vernacular) among a large number of pretenders. Fatherland–All Russia in 1999, for example, was the product of many deals among major organizations (including trade unions, several smaller parties, and some governors) and it thus found that it simply did not have enough passing nomination slots to go around for those who wanted to run under its banner. Indeed, the young organization was seriously tested when many candidates were given fewer "safe" districts or places on the party list than they had expected, as the party leadership sought to balance its priorities and to keep all of its various coalition partners happy.[93]

The most significant ideational and programmatic parties faced an additional supply-side constraint: longstanding sunk costs in certain kinds of ideational capital. These restrictions were tightest when this capital involved the most specific variety of ideological reputation. As is quite clear in the survey data discussed extensively in Chapter 3, important organizations such as Yabloko and the KPRF depended to a significant degree on some form of issue reputation for what success they had enjoyed in previous election cycles.[94] Reputation, however, can be risky to change when it is an important part of a party's political capital.[95] Developing and maintaining this reputation requires, among other things, ensuring that a party's candidates meet at least a minimum standard of ideological "fit." This presented the most idea-based Russian political parties with a serious constraint in their competition with party substitutes (as well as with other parties). They could not try to compete with party substitutes or other parties by "lowering the ideological price" of their party's nomination by accepting significant numbers of "bad fit" (but otherwise strong) candidates without potentially undermining the reputation that had brought them success in the past and without alienating the electoral base that they had been carefully nurturing. The Communist Party appears to have proven this point in 2003; after the KPRF included several "dollar millionaires" on its party list, state-controlled media reported this relentlessly in a bid to portray the party as hypocritical and corrupt, producing a major drop in Communist support (even among formerly hard-core loyalists) as described in Chapter 2. Thus, with a few exceptions that led to major electoral problems, Russia's major ideational and programmatic parties were in fact rather choosey when picking their nominees despite reputed "weakness" and despite not even endorsing candidates in all districts. Extensive interviews and regional case studies conducted by the author provide many examples, one of the most dramatic of which is that Yabloko actually disbanded and then reconstituted about a dozen of its regional organizations

93 *Moscow News*, October 21, 1999, JRL; interview with a regional Fatherland–All Russia campaign chief, September 17, 1999; *Nezavisimaia Gazeta*, October 6, 1999.

94 See also Brader and Tucker 2001; Colton 2000; Miller et al. 2000.

95 Kreps 1990.

during 1998 and 1999 in an explicit bid to strengthen ideological consistency, spurning many promising candidates and even certain incumbents in the process.[96] The competition among candidates to gain party nomination was of course most pronounced in 2003 for United Russia, which had been riding high in the polls during the precampaign months and which had the obvious backing of the powerful Kremlin. As will be discussed further in Chapter 5, Russia's executive authorities were also careful to select candidates without the most embarrassing or contradictory forms of political baggage.

This competition for limited sets of promising party nominations meant that the effective price for obtaining party nomination was not at all trivial to candidates. Candidates seeking to join an ideational or programmatic party could face a party demand to adjust one's policy stands; this could be quite costly for candidates with prior personal reputations not in keeping with the party's general line. Candidates seeking the nomination of a clientelistic party might have to pay a price in the most literal sense, contributing large sums of money to party coffers or agreeing to donate personal organization or connections for the party's use. An additional cost that a candidate might have to pay in order to obtain party nomination involves time, the willingness to defer one's ambitions to future election cycles in cases where desired party nominations are already taken but could open up in the future. To be sure, most American candidates who lose in the Democratic or Republican primaries but who retain their desire to compete simply wait for another election cycle to try again rather than risk spoiling relationships with their parties and partisan voters by running as independents.

In democracies where party nomination is the only sure way to win office, candidates are forced to bear such costs if they hope to be elected; what has made Russia critically different is that candidates there have had *other good options*. If a would-be candidate saw the price for obtaining party nomination as being significant, he or she could turn to party substitutes to inquire about a better deal and retain a realistic hope of achieving a strong electoral result. Given the supply-side constraints facing Russian parties that prevented them from lowering prices in order to absorb all candidate demand, and given the strength of the kinds of party substitutes described above, some candidates could be expected to turn to party substitutes. When these party-substitute candidates competed with party candidates, and when these party substitutes were as capable of winning votes for these candidates as were parties, parties could find their collective expansion in the polity "stalled." They could become unable to close out the electoral market.

Critically, these reasons for the failure of parties to penetrate fully the Russian polity have little to do with intrinsic party "weakness" (for example, poor organization or thin reputation). Indeed, Chapter 3 demonstrated that

96 Interviews with Yabloko's campaign chair and other party officials during 1999 and 2000. For details, see Hale 2004d.

a significant set of parties were in fact capable of providing organizational, material, and reputational support to candidates that could be quite meaningful in elections. Instead, the failure of parties to penetrate the Russian polity fully had a great deal to do with the dynamics of the electoral market itself. In fact, ideational and programmatic parties like Yabloko and the KPRF were limited in organizational breadth in part *because* of their long-standing sunk costs in and commitment to issue-based reputational development. One critical factor in Russia's stalled party development is thus that the very nature of party reputation itself and the limited number of party nominations that could meaningfully be made available in a given election cycle placed important supply-side constraints on parties in their efforts to peddle electoral goods and services at prices that candidates were willing to pay *given the presence of alternative suppliers of electoral goods and services* (party substitutes).

PARTIES, PARTY SUBSTITUTES, AND VOTING PATTERNS

While the examples given above are illustrative, the following pages seek to demonstrate more systematically and comprehensively that electoral market dynamics, in particular the activities of the kinds of party substitutes just described, help explain why political party development in Russia stalled toward the end of the 1990s. If the market logic advanced in this volume is correct, we would first of all expect to find that a subset of major parties were in fact capable of providing electoral goods and services to candidates in significant measure. Chapter 3 has already established this quite thoroughly. To have full confidence in the market logic, however, we should find two additional hypotheses to be true.

1. Candidates with the active backing of major party substitutes should tend to get more votes than otherwise similar candidates without this backing.
2. There should be a negative correlation between the electoral performance of candidates backed by major party substitutes and that of candidates backed by political parties across districts.

To test these propositions, we consider all four major sets of elections that took place in Russia according to a single-member-district system during the period in question. Russia's SMD election rules allowed candidates to run either as party nominees or as independents, thereby opening a door through which party substitutes could enter the electoral arena without even paying so much as lip service to parties. Partisan ballots in Russia's SMD races thus reflected a *choice* to "go partisan," whereas this choice was made for voters in the PR half of the Duma elections.[97] Likewise, candidate decisions to run as party nominees represented candidate choices to forgo the option

[97] Moser 1999, p. 148.

of running as independents. Russia's various SMD elections, therefore, are well suited to testing a theory of party development that treats a party vote as something to be explained, not taken for granted. The four sets of SMD elections studied here are the Duma, regional legislative, gubernatorial, and presidential contests. We proceed to each in turn.

SMD Duma Elections

This set of elections held between 1993 and 2003, more than the others examined below, allows us to get the best systematic leverage on the relative importance of and interaction between parties and party substitutes. This is due to the number of seats at stake, the fact that elections took place nationwide on the same day, and the availability of the necessary data.[98] The analysis presented here is of the elections of 1999, by which time the above historical discussion indicates the posited party substitutes had come into their electoral own. The data are those already described in Chapter 3.[99]

[98] Hale 2005c.

[99] A few additional notes are appropriate here. Candidate biographies provided by the CEC were incomplete for 19 deputies, meaning that the reported regressions all included 2,207 observations (candidates). Additionally, conclusive judgments regarding governors' support for candidates could not be reached in 27 of the 224 districts based on the sources described in Chapter 3. In these 27 districts, coding for gubernatorial support was done as follows. Where there was some uncontradicted indication (albeit not conclusive) that a governor supported a candidate, this candidate was coded as having gubernatorial support. In the remaining districts, where none of the three sources of district reporting indicated that the governor supported any of the candidates, all candidates were coded as having no governor support (a reasonable assumption if none out of three organizations studying the elections reported any gubernatorial involvement). To be sure that this coding rule (affecting 27 districts) was not skewing results, some regressions were also conducted excluding these 27 districts (which included 281 candidates). The results were very close to being the same, with only minor changes in the coefficient estimates, strongly suggesting that the coding of these 27 cases was not biasing the results significantly. For a candidate to be coded as being a *PFIG* candidate, there had to be evidence not only of a link between a candidate and a major firm, but of the active support of the leadership of this firm for the candidate's run for office. Unless a candidate were him- or herself the owner or president of a PFIG, as was the case with the example of Boris Berezovsky's run for the Duma in 1999, candidates holding positions in a major firm were not as a rule counted as PFIG candidates (a separate variable was included to represent candidates who were primarily employed in private business). PFIGs could be national (as with Slavneft or Interros) or regional. To be counted as a regional PFIG, however, there had to be evidence that the enterprise was a major part of the regional economy – not a run-of-the-mill factory, for example. The giant automobile manufacturing company KAMAZ is one example of a regional PFIG. While there are most probably PFIG candidates that were missed due to their covert nature, this study's approach to data collection lends confidence that we have recorded candidates of the most important PFIGs sufficiently comprehensively to draw meaningful conclusions.

The first hypothesis has in fact already been borne out in the previous chapter's Table 3.9. Readers are now referred to that table's boxed set of findings labeled "Party Substitute Support." These findings show that candidates supported by either governors or politicized financial-industrial groups tended to perform much better than did other candidates, with governors' candidates winning between 5.9 and 11.6 percent more votes and PFIG candidates netting between 5 and 8.3 percent more. This general finding holds even after one controls for all kinds of factors that should reflect candidates' own strength, including the preelection assessments of experts as to which candidates were generally stronger, as discussed in Chapter 3.

It is worth presenting a pair of examples to illustrate how these dynamics worked in two very different regions in 1999. First, in Bashkortostan's District 4, two well-known, seasoned politicians declared their candidacies, including the district's incumbent, Communist Duma Deputy Valentin Nikitin, and former regional Prime Minister Marat Mirgaziamov, considered one of the strongest rivals to the regional governor, Murtaza Rakhimov. These candidates squared off against a series of relative unknowns. One of these unknowns, however, was the regional leader's favorite, the political novice and head of the provincial Academy of Sciences Robert Nigmatulin. One survey, commissioned for internal use by a major political party,[100] clearly showed what local political observers reported in interviews. Toward the beginning of the campaign, Nigmatulin had little name recognition and a far lower percentage of supporters in the electorate (1.8 percent) than did Nikitin (7.7 percent) and Mirgaziamov (10.6 percent), with 44.2 percent undecided, 15.2 percent not planning to vote, 8.4 percent planning to vote against all, and 2.4 percent refusing to answer. Nigmatulin did not display particular marks of personal charisma that would lead one to believe he would be much more successful than other, similarly unknown candidates. Indeed, in the prediction exercise run by the East-West Institute, the Bashkortostan regional expert did not pick Nigmatulin to win this race, instead staking his reputation on the bet that the Communist Nikitin would be reelected. Nevertheless, with the strong backing of Rakhimov, Nigmatulin won comfortably with 34 percent of the vote, compared to just 18 percent for the incumbent Nikitin and only 16 percent for Mirgaziamov.

One can certainly find cases where governors endorsed independently powerful candidates, as happened in District 140 in Perm. In this instance, the governor backed the long-time incumbent and Union of Right Forces candidate Viktor Pokhmelkin, who had built up a political power base (supported by mighty regional PFIGs such as, reportedly, Uralkalii) even before the governor assumed office. Indeed, among regional politicians, a poll

100 This party is different from the one from whose information the 1999 SMD Duma database draws.

conducted by Perm's Center of Election Technologies at the start of the campaign (September 6–8, 1999) found Pokhmelkin to be the city's second-most widely known politician other than the governor and mayor, with name recognition at 41 percent.[101] This "exception" helps prove the rule. Perm's Governor Gennady Igumnov had a reputation as one of the most liberal governors in Russia, promoting a relatively open political atmosphere and rarely directly throwing his weight around in the way that governors like Rakhimov did.[102] This helps explain why Pokhmelkin won by a margin of just 4 percent against a rival who began with less than half (19 percent) of Pokhmelkin's name recognition.[103] Indeed, this avid competitor, newspaper editor Sergei Levitan, was able to mount a spirited challenge without worrying that his newspaper facilities, which he had regularly used to blacken Pokhmelkin's name, might, for example, suddenly be found "failing to meet electrical safety standards" and forced to shut down.

While Table 3.9 shows that party substitutes were very important suppliers of electoral goods and services, our theory goes further and suggests that the existence of strong party substitutes actually hindered party penetration of the political arena. That is, we still need to show that parties were failing to close out the electoral market at least partly *because* of the competition they faced from party substitutes rather than because of their own incapacity to make inroads into what some have characterized an institutionally open political space.

We can test this theory in the following way. If the "intrinsic weakness" hypothesis is right, we would expect to find *no correlation* between the overall performance of party nominees and that of nonparty gubernatorial political machine and PFIG candidates. To say that the major parties were failing purely due to such qualities as poor organizational capacity, a lack of resources, or the absence of meaningful reputation is to say that the share of the vote that major parties "earned" collectively for their candidates through nomination in an average district was not constrained in any way by that part of the vote earned collectively by the party substitutes studied here. Indeed, all of the variables noted above (including parties and party substitutes as well as the controls) explained only about 50 percent of the variation in SMD candidate vote totals, as indicated by the estimated values of the R^2 quantity reported near the bottom of Table 3.9; this at least suggests that parties had room to expand independently of party substitutes but failed to do so. If, on the other hand, the supply-and-demand theory is correct, we would expect to find a *negative correlation* between the performance of important party substitutes (as reflected in the share of ballots won by the candidates

[101] *Kompan'on* (Perm), no. 32, September 14, 1999, pp. 1, 4.

[102] One reputable study found Perm to be the most democratic region in Russia during this period. See *RFE/RL Newsline*, October 17, 2002.

[103] *Kompan'on* (Perm), no. 32, September 14, 1999, pp. 1, 4.

TABLE 4.1. *Correlation Between the Total Share of the District Vote Won by Party Substitute Candidates and the Total Share of the District Vote Won by Major-Party Nominees in the 1999 SMD Duma Elections*

Governors' political machines	−.33**
PFIGs	−.57**
Railroads	−.03
Pseudo-R^2	.03
Number of observations	120

** 99% confidence level

they backed) and the vote totals of major party nominees. According to this interpretation, many factors always go into voting decisions, including such intangibles as personality and even voter preferences for certain physical types; the 50 percent of the variation found to be "unclaimed" by parties, governors, PFIGs, or other factors listed in Table 3.9 likely reflects such intangibles. Just because parties and party substitutes combined do not explain 100 percent of the variation in voting, therefore, does not mean that they were not in competition for that share of the vote that various political service providers *could* hope to capture for their candidates.

One way to test the market theory against the "intrinsic weakness" rival is to see whether those Duma districts with the strongest party-substitute candidates also tended to feature the weakest performances by major-party nominees.[104] Table 4.1 reports the results of such an investigation.[105] As predicted by the supply-and-demand theory, there was a strongly negative correlation between the performance of governor- and PFIG-backed candidates (as measured by the share of the vote won by each) and the overall performance of candidates nominated by the seven major political parties (as captured by the sum of the vote shares of these candidates in each district) in those 120 districts where no major-party candidate happened to be backed by a governor, a PFIG, or the Railroads Ministry according to available data.[106] The findings for PFIGs and governors are reached with

104 Importantly, we are only interested here in *major parties* as defined in Chapter 2.

105 The tobit technique is used to make use of the information that the cumulative vote percentages won by parties (the dependent variable) is effectively "censored" at the value of zero – that is, party performance could not be counted as less than zero no matter how bad the situation got for parties. The fact that some (11) of the races for which data were available actually produced values at this minimum means that we are likely to get more accurate results by treating the data as censored. See King 1998; Long 1997.

106 Naturally, since governors' candidates *were* party nominees in the other 104 districts, the shares of the vote for "governors' candidates" and for "party nominees" vary together there.

well over 99 percent statistical confidence. The coefficients allow us to get an idea of just how powerfully governors and PFIGs were dampening party performance. When a governor's candidate won an extra 1 percent of a district's vote, the share of this vote garnered by Russia's seven biggest parties is found to have dropped by about one-third of 1 percent. PFIGs appear to have "crowded out" parties even more powerfully. For every 1 percent of the vote won by a PFIG candidate, Russia's major political parties are found to have lost well over half of a percentage point of the district's ballots. The stifling effects of party substitutes on political parties, therefore, appear strong.[107]

While the results are compelling in the case of governors' political machines and PFIGs, we would have even more confidence in them if we could include control variables so as to be sure that the observed correlation between party-substitute strength and party weakness does not simply reflect an omitted underlying variable. For example, it might be reasonable to suspect that parties would tend to be weak and party substitutes strong in those districts with the lowest mass education levels; education levels alone, then, may hold the key to both developments without party substitutes actually having any direct effect on party performance. Unfortunately, the Russian government has not made available the necessary data compiled at the level of its Duma districts. We do have such data at the regional level, however, permitting us to address the following question in a rigorous way: Were those provinces with the strongest party substitutes also those regions with the weakest parties?

To answer these questions, we test for the importance of several factors in accounting for variation in party strength as manifested in the 1999 SMD Duma elections across Russia's regions. We measure party strength here as the average share of the district vote obtained collectively by Russia's major parties' nominees in all of the districts in a given region during the 1999 SMD Duma elections. The most important explanatory variables we include, of course, are those indicating the average percentage of each region's district vote obtained by party-substitute candidates. We must be careful here, however; a minority of governors happened to back party nominees in at least one district and nearly half of these (about a quarter of all Russian governors) behaved in a clearly partisan manner, as described in Chapter 3. Where governors are partisan, we would certainly expect them vastly to improve party performance in their regions by lending their vast administrative resources to the achievement of party ends. Indeed, as will be argued in

[107] Railroad (state-owned) affiliation was included in this regression as a party substitute since the Russian Railroads Ministry was a major source of patronage and reportedly was involved in politics in ways that could make it a party substitute. It was found insignificant and dropped from future regressions. Dropping it from Table 4.1's regression makes no significant difference in the other findings.

Chapter 5, the expansion of this phenomenon represents one path by which Russian parties could come to dominate the political market. In the majority of cases, however, governors did not act like partisans in 1999 and, it is argued here, served to dampen party development. To distinguish between these effects, we divide governors' political machines into two camps, the set of those that backed at least one party nominee in the 1999 SMD Duma race (*Party Governor*) and a remaining set (*Nonparty Governor*), and estimate their effects separately. We perform an analogous separation for PFIGs, which were reported above to have backed party nominees roughly one-third of the time, creating one category of regions (the variable *Party PFIG*) in which a PFIG backed at least one party nominee and a second composed of regions where PFIGs were not found to have backed a single party nominee (*Nonparty PFIG*).

These data also permit us to address a more general question: What factors determine why Russia's major parties had quite effectively penetrated some Russian provinces but not others? Indeed, such factors are the control variables we need to include in the equation to be more confident that our findings regarding party substitutes are not spurious. We thus include some of the factors that Chapter 1 suggested could impact the relative balance between parties and party substitutes over time and space. One such factor is institutional design. While all Duma district elections took place under the same set of rules, we might hypothesize that variation in the rules of competition for seats in regional legislatures might impact overall regional environments in ways that advantage or disadvantage parties in competition for Duma district races. For simplicity's sake, we sometimes refer to all regional legislatures as "legislative assemblies" regardless of their formal titles. Three variables representing cross-regional institutional variation are included in the equation: whether the province's legislative assembly had an SMD system (a dummy variable *LA-SMD*); the share (percentage) of the region's legislature elected via proportional representation (*LA-PR Share*); and the average number of registered voters per legislative assembly district in thousands (*LA-District Size*). We also test whether higher *education* levels (the percentage of the population with higher education as determined by the 1989 census) correlate with stronger party performance vis-à-vis party substitutes. To get a sense as to whether any such correlation might be an effect of education itself and the associated awareness of issues that it might be expected to bring rather than an effect of economic prosperity or "modernization," we include regional per capita *income* levels (average monthly personal income in rubles) in 1998 as a variable. It also would appear prudent to include a variable indicating mass media penetration. While this is sometimes seen at early stages of economic development to facilitate the ability of parties to communicate their messages, newer literatures have come to blame mass media access for rendering parties unnecessary since candidates now can appeal directly to voters without party

TABLE 4.2. *Correlates of Regional Party Strength as Measured by the Average Total Share of the Vote Received by Major-Party Nominees in a Given Province's 1999 SMD Duma elections*[a]

Nonparty Governor	−.35**
Nonparty PFIG	−.51*
Party Governor	.64**
Party PFIG	−.01
Education	2.19**
Income	−.004
TV/Radio	.10
LA-SMD	−7.98*
LA-PR Share	−.60*
LA District Size	.06
Population	−5.46**
Distance	−2.03**
Constant	26.39**

$N = 82$
Pseudo $R^2 = .11$
* 95% confidence level
** 99% confidence level
[a] See web site www.whynotpartiesinrussia.com for more information on the variables used here.

organization.[108] We therefore also include an indicator of the number of *television and radio* outlets that existed per million residents in a given region. Finally, we consider that geography might matter: perhaps it is more costly for parties (relative to party substitutes) to penetrate the most remote parts of Russia or to expand in the most populous Russian regions. The variable *Distance* thus measures the distance (in thousands of kilometers) of a region's capital city from Moscow and *Population* indicates the number of a province's citizens (in millions) as of 1998.

Table 4.2 reports the findings. Most importantly for this volume's argument, we again find robust support for the claim that party substitutes were effectively crowding out parties. When governors were most clearly nonpartisan, a 1 percent increase in governor-machine performance corresponds with a 0.35 percent drop in the average vote totals received by major-party nominees. Likewise, when PFIGs were most clearly nonpartisan, a 1 percent increase in their candidates' performance is associated with a 0.51 percent drop in the strength of major parties as measured here. We have added confidence in these findings since the reported coefficients are nearly identical to those reported using the district-level data in Table 4.1; adding control

[108] For one recent work in this tradition, see Oates 2003.

variables and generalizing the findings from the district to the regional level alters our estimates hardly at all. Moreover, in a finding whose significance will be further discussed in Chapter 5, we see that when governors do align with parties, they substantially enhance the electoral strength of parties in their regions. The set of Russia's seven major parties as of 1999 tended to receive 0.64 percent more of the district vote for every 1 percent rise in the average ballot share of the candidates of those governors who were not averse to lending their support to at least one party nominee. Interestingly, the same is not true for PFIGs; there is no statistically significant relationship between the electoral strength of parties in the 1999 SMD Duma elections and the share of the vote received by PFIG candidates in those regions where at least one PFIG backed a party Nominee. We have over 95 percent confidence in the finding for "Nonparty PFIG" and well over 99 percent confidence for the results concerning governors.

While the effects of party substitutes were quite powerful, Table 4.2 also reports that other factors influenced party strength across Russia's regions as of 1999. For one thing, we find a correlation between high education levels and strong political party development, suggesting that better educated people are more receptive to party candidates than to party-substitute candidates. Each additional percent of a region's population with higher education tends to be associated with a 2.2 percent improvement in the performance of major-party nominees in the 1999 SMD Duma election. We have over 95 percent statistical confidence in this finding. No significant relationship, however, is found between either income per capita or mass media penetration and party strength. Strikingly, we find an important indirect effect for institutions; the way in which a region elects its own legislature appears to have statistically significant effects on parties' abilities to win votes for their regional candidates in *national* parliamentary elections. Major-party Duma nominees tended to perform 8 percent more poorly in those regions that elected their regional legislatures solely in single-member districts than in provinces electing their assemblies in other ways.

Somewhat puzzling is the finding that introducing a 1 percent larger share of proportional representation in provincial legislative elections actually correlates with a 0.6 percent *reduction* in the share of seats that major party nominees tended to receive in the SMD Duma race in 1999. This result is obtained at well above the 95 percent confidence level. While at first this seems to have little bearing on this volume's central hypothesis, it can be seen to confirm the value of the general market approach to political parties developed here. Those regions that had introduced limited forms of PR for their legislative elections as of 1999 had not restricted them to federal parties. Thus, while PR did (as many have correctly anticipated) stimulate the development of political organization, it provided no special incentive for these to be national organizations (the parties of most interest in this volume). PR therefore served as much to stimulate local organizations unconnected to major parties as to promote the local development of national parties themselves. This increased local political organization then gave candidates additional options in the locality's Duma elections, reducing their willingness to pay the price necessary for national-party nomination. The net result is that in a mixed SMD-PR regional election system, the regional PR component can actually work against the development of national political parties in nationwide SMD systems at the same time that it may serve to cultivate increased overall national party representation in the local legislature through the PR component.

Finally, Table 4.2 notes the importance of geography. With more than 99 percent statistical confidence, we see that both a region's remoteness and its population size are negatively correlated with party penetration of its SMD Duma elections. For every one million residents, major-party nominees drop an average of 5 percentage points in the parliamentary voting within a given region. Likewise, for every 1,000 kilometers of distance of a province from Moscow, major party nominees' shares of its Duma SMD ballots decline by about 2 percent.

Overall, patterns in the SMD Duma elections of 1999 strongly confirm the market theory and the specific hypothesis that party substitutes are partially responsible for hindering the degree to which political parties dominate elections in Russia.[109] This is significant because, as described above, the data available for the SMD Duma contests are better for theory-testing than those for any other Russian institution. It is nevertheless important to examine what information we do have about these other institutions, a task to which we now turn.

Legislative Assembly Elections

Since the Central Election Commission has not published data on the performance of all individual candidates in Russian regional legislative elections,

[109] These findings are reasonably robust to other, less sensitive or more distorted, measures of key variables. Thus, we still find a negative correlation between party and gubernatorial machine strength when gubernatorial strength is coded as the governor's margin of victory in the most recent gubernatorial election prior to the Duma voting, although not when we indicate gubernatorial strength as the straight share of the vote received by the governor in these gubernatorial elections. We expect distortion here, however, since some gubernatorial elections took place at different times (and hence are less consistent measures) and often three or more years prior to the Duma race, during which time the strength of the governor could surely have changed. The findings are quite robust to a different measure of party strength in the Duma elections. If we utilize the much less sensitive party-strength indicator of the share of a region's Duma delegation (that is, the percentage of the deputies that were actually elected in 1999) that was nominated by a major party, we still find a crowding effect for governors with more than 99 percent statistical confidence, although the finding for PFIGs (while negative as predicted) is detected at only the 71 percent confidence level.

we cannot directly test Hypothesis 1 in this institutional setting. We can, however, directly test Hypothesis 2, which assumes a positive answer to Hypothesis 1. The best data available on party performance in regional legislative elections (see Chapter 3) are the number of candidates nominated by an *electoral association* (a general category including both major and minor parties) per legislative assembly seat and the number of winning candidates nominated by a major party. We consider, for each region, the most recent legislative assembly election as of the year 2000, the last year for which the necessary data were available at the time of this writing. In the regressions that follow, we remain consistent with the previous section and consider the same set of regional control variables that were included in the analysis of the SMD Duma elections reported in Table 4.2. Since legislative assembly elections took place in different years and at different times of the year, we adopt an indicator of gubernatorial machine strength that corresponds as closely as possible to the date of each region's legislative assembly election: the governor's margin of victory in the most recent gubernatorial elections as of the end of the year 2000. Given the absence of any other reasonable indicator of PFIG activity in a given region, we employ the indicator of PFIG strength used in our analysis of the SMD Duma elections: the percentage of the SMD Duma vote garnered by PFIG-endorsed candidates in 1999. While far from ideal, it should still capture the general propensity of PFIGs to be involved in a given region's electoral politics. Since we cannot know when party substitutes backed party candidates for these elections, we do not distinguish between party and nonparty governors or between party and nonparty PFIGs as we did in the Duma race where we had the necessary information.

Although these indicators are not ideal, their use has two important implications for how we interpret the results. First, since we lack information on which electoral association nominees were *also* backed by party substitutes, any results we obtain are likely to *underestimate* any dampening effect that party substitutes actually had on party development. The following regressions are thus a conservative test of this volume's central hypothesis. Second, because of the large degree of noise introduced by imperfect indicators and the fact that these regional legislative elections were spread out over several years during which much happened in Russia, any findings that nevertheless emerge above the noise at statistical confidence levels of 90 percent or more can be regarded as quite compelling, especially in light of the confirmatory findings from the SMD Duma elections.

We first turn to a study of variation in the degree to which electoral associations cover SMD elections to Russia's regional legislative assemblies with their nominees in the most recent rounds of voting as of the end of the year 2000. As Table 4.3 reports, we find the predicted result: there is a negative and statistically significant relationship (at the 90 percent level

TABLE 4.3. *Correlates of Regional Party Strength as Measured by the Number of Candidates Nominated by an Electoral Association per Seat Up for Election to a Given Region's Legislative Assembly in the Most Recent Elections as of Year-End 2000*[a]

Governor	–.005[t]
PFIG	–.029**
Education	.129**
Income	–.0004
TV/Radio	–.023
LA-SMD	–.110
LA-PR Share	.070**
LA District Size	.008[t]
Population	.020
Distance	.017
Constant	.206

$N = 81$
Pseudo $R^2 = .219$
[t] 90% confidence level
* 95% confidence level
** 99% confidence level
[a] *See* web site www.whynotpartiesinrussia.com for more information on the variables used here.

or greater) between this measure of party strength and both party substitutes investigated here.[110] In terms of the magnitude of these relationships, regions where PFIG candidates got an average of roughly 30 percent of the 1999 SMD Duma vote more than in otherwise identical regions tended to have one more electoral-association-nominated candidate per regional legislative district. The estimated effect for governors appears to be much smaller: Where an incumbent governor lost an election by 50 percent of the vote (indicating great gubernatorial machine weakness), the region tended to have half an electoral-association nominee more (on average) per contested legislative seat than those regions in which the incumbent won by a margin of 50 percent. We must keep in mind that these results are expected to underestimate the real party-dampening effects of party substitutes for reasons stated above.

To further evaluate the market theory, we consider a second indicator of party penetration of regional legislative assemblies: the share of the seats

[110] This finding of statistical significance at least at the 90 percent level holds when we use the straight percentage of the vote received by the incumbent governor in the most recent elections as of the end of 2000 in place of the measure reported in Table 4.3, the governor's margin of victory in these elections.

TABLE 4.4. *Correlates of Regional Party Strength as Measured by the Percentage of a Province's Legislative Assembly Seats Obtained by Major Parties in the Most Recent Such Elections as of Year-End 2000*[a]

Governor	−.09[t]
PFIG	−.57*
Education	1.75*
Income	−.01
TV/Radio	−.29
LA-SMD	−.82
LA-PR Share	.95**
LA District Size	.12
Population	−3.17
Distance	−.72
Constant	.05

N = 81
Pseudo R^2 = .06
[t] 90% confidence level
* 95% confidence level
** 99% confidence level
[a] *See* web site www.whynotpartiesinrussia.com for more information on the variables used here.

in these institutions won by nominees of Russia's major parties. Here, too, we find negative relationships between party substitute strength and party power at confidence levels above 90 percent, as reported in Table 4.4.[111] Regions where PFIGs were strong enough in 1999 to win 10 percent more of the vote than average tended to have nearly 6 percent less representation by major parties in their regional legislatures. Regions where incumbents lost their most recent elections as of the end of the year 2000 by a margin of 50 percent tended to have about 9 percent more major-party nominees in their legislative assemblies than did regions where governors won with such large margins. These results, again, are likely to be underestimates.

Tables 4.3 and 4.4 also present some very interesting findings regarding other factors that affect regional party development. First, we again find that regional education levels correspond quite significantly with party penetration of legislative assembly elections. A 10 percent rise in the share of the population holding an advanced degree is associated with an over-1

111 The statistical significance of gubernatorial power drops to the 78 percent level when we use the straight percentage of the vote received by the incumbent governor in the most recent elections as of the end of the year 2000 in place of the measure reported in Table 4.4, the governor's margin of victory in these elections. The estimated relationship remains negative, as predicted.

percent increase in the average number of electoral-association nominees contesting legislative seats and with a nearly 18 percent increase in the share of legislative seats won by major-party nominees. Electoral institutions are also again found to be important. Particularly interesting are the findings regarding the introduction of proportional representation (PR) for regional assemblies. The finding in Table 4.4 reports that major parties were the main beneficiaries of regional PR; expanding PR to cover more of a legislature's seats augments the presence of major parties (as distinct from regional electoral associations or minor parties) in this body by nearly a 1:1 ratio. Even more interesting is the result presented in Table 4.3: PR has not only a direct effect in expanding party representation (through allocating seats to party lists) but also an *indirect* effect that spills over into the SMD elections in regions with mixed electoral systems. Calculating on the basis of the reported results, introducing a PR system to elect 50 percent of an otherwise typical region's legislature (where no PR component existed before) would encourage an average of over three additional electoral-association nominees to run *in the SMD contests*. Thus, while regional PR effectively hurts national parties in national SMD elections by promoting regional parties that compete with the national ones for candidate "customers," it does help national parties in SMD races for regional legislatures by providing them with visibility and regional resources for these particular elections that they would not otherwise have had. Geography does not appear to play a significant role in influencing the party penetration of regional assembly elections.

Gubernatorial Elections

The available evidence on Russia's gubernatorial elections initially appears to present much less convincing findings regarding the importance of party substitutes. In part, we run into some of the same data problems that we encountered regarding legislative elections. Gubernatorial contests took place in different regions in different years at different times of the year, making it quite difficult to detect systematic patterns across large numbers of these races since the influence of highly contingent time-dependent variables can be expected to produce a great deal of statistical noise. Nevertheless, we do have some information about the gubernatorial contests that we lack for the legislative races. Most importantly, the CEC has published brief biographies and the election results for each competing candidate in the races from 1995 to 2000. Since governors themselves are regarded as a party substitute in this volume, the vote for the incumbent effectively indicates the strength of this particular party substitute. Unfortunately, we do not have systematic information on which gubernatorial candidates were backed by PFIGs, leaving us to resort to the same tactic used for the regional legislative races: using each region's 1999 SMD Duma vote for PFIG candidates to measure the level of overall PFIG electoral power there. Thus, while the data

TABLE 4.5. *Correlates of Regional Party Strength as Measured by the Total Share of the Vote Received by Major-Party Nominees in a Region's Most Recent Gubernatorial Race as of Year-End 2000*[ab]

Governor	−.13
PFIG	.03
Education	2.10*
Income	−.003
TV/Radio	−1.24
LA-SMD	−4.80
LA-PR Share	.55
LA District Size	−.09
Population	−2.62
Distance	−.67
Constant	−5.07

$N = 80$
Pseudo $R^2 = .06$
* 95-percent confidence level
a The two instances where incumbent governors ran as party nominees during these elections (in Altai Krai and Tambov) are not included in this analysis.
b See web site www.whynotpartiesinrussia.com for more information on the variables used here.

do not present the methodological advantages that the SMD Duma data do, we have more to work with than for the regional legislatures.

We begin with a test of Hypothesis 1, the prediction that candidates backed by party substitutes will perform better than otherwise identical candidates. Since we do not know which candidates were supported by PFIGs, we cannot test this claim here. Turning to governors, Table 3.13 has already presented the results of a statistical analysis designed to identify those candidate characteristics associated with the best vote-getting potential. While the attention there was on the impact of parties, we now direct readers' attention to the finding that incumbent governors enjoyed a gargantuan advantage when up for reelection; incumbent status correlates with a 42.8 percent better showing for candidates than what an otherwise identical candidate could expect. This incumbent advantage is far greater than that reported for Duma elections, where officeholders previously elected in an SMD Duma district could expect only between 3.1 and 10 percent more of the district vote than candidates with similar biographies.

When we turn to Hypothesis 2, however, we find no significant relationship between a governor's margin of victory (or for that matter his straight share of the vote) and the total percentage of ballots netted by major-party nominees. This is reported in Table 4.5. Nor does this analysis find any statistically significant relationship between PFIG strength as indicated in the 1999 SMD Duma elections and party nominee performance in the gubernatorial elections. In fact, of all of the variables representing different theories that we have tested throughout this chapter in different institutional settings, the only one that turns out to be related to party performance in gubernatorial elections is education, with a 1 percent increase in the share of the regional population possessing a higher education corresponding to a 2 percent stronger showing by party nominees. Thus, although governors' machines have an enormous advantage when they themselves are running for reelection, they and PFIGs appear not to explain any of the variation across Russia in the strength of major political parties. We have evidence for Hypothesis 1 but not 2.

These findings, however, are also consistent with another interpretation: Incumbents and other party substitutes dominated these races to such an extreme that there was very little variation in party performance left to explore. As a result, we simply may not have enough variation across Russia in the degree of party penetration of these races to allow us to learn anything from what little variation does exist. This interpretation finds some confirmation when one notices that party candidates received *zero* votes in a full 60 of the 85 regional elections considered here; in only 10 instances did party candidates get more than 10 percent of the vote and only twice did the sum of party-candidate ballots constitute more than 30 percent of the total. These figures are much smaller than the analogous ones for regional legislatures, not to mention the Duma district races. It is helpful to view this in light of the results reported in Table 3.13, where incumbency was found to give candidates an average boost of 42.8 percent of the vote and other qualities, such as experience as the chair of a regional legislature, were found to improve candidate chances by well over 20 percent. Furthermore, there is strong anecdotal evidence that PFIGs can play a very powerful role in many of these elections. One of the electoral portraits with which this volume opened, for example, demonstrated how the Krasnoiarsk gubernatorial elections of 2002 were almost entirely dominated by PFIG candidates, with parties and even the acting governor himself being largely relegated to the sidelines. Nevertheless, there is also evidence that PFIGs quite often backed incumbent governors in these races so as to stay in the good graces of patrons; this would explain why the PFIG variable does not show up as significant on its own. This, in turn, is quite consistent with the theory advanced in this volume.

Overall, then, there is good reason to believe that we have so little leverage on the determinants of party strength in gubernatorial elections precisely *because* party substitutes were so strong as to have almost entirely crowded out political parties. This, of course, begs the question of why incumbent governors and PFIGs did not choose to work *through* parties. Chapter 5 takes up this issue directly.

PRESIDENTIAL ELECTIONS

The presidential elections provide us with the least information by which to test the market logic elaborated in this volume. Critically, we have only four contests to examine, one of which took place before the USSR collapsed. Moreover, all significant candidates but the incumbents were party affiliates, as noted in Chapter 3.

One thing we can tell, however, is that the Kremlin itself behaved in these elections as what might be called Russia's ultimate party substitute. The Kremlin has long held vast resources at its disposal that have been capable of influencing electoral outcomes. For one, the Russian state since the USSR collapsed has owned majority stakes in two of Russia's biggest three media outlets (First Channel[112] and RTR). Since early in Putin's first term the state has also had a powerful lever to influence the third, NTV, via shares held by the state-controlled firm Gazprom.[113] Through its control over subsidies, the Kremlin could also hope to influence governors, potentially winning the use of their political machines for its presidential candidates. In 2000, Putin also instituted a new system of presidential representatives that helped him regain presidential control over local policy and other important organs, all of which could potentially be applied to win presidential elections.[114]

The party substitutes on which we have focused in this chapter, however, were not well suited to independently contest the presidency. Governors, most obviously, were each limited to one of Russia's 89 regions, none of which alone could even come close to producing a presidential victory. Unlike elections for lower-level institutions of government, at the presidential level PFIGs had a difficult time operating independently of state authorities. For one thing, as was described above, PFIGs often had their origins in collaboration with the national government. Thus, the range of available party substitutes in presidential races was substantially narrowed since PFIGs tended very strongly to back the incumbent. In addition, PFIGs rarely actually had comprehensive coverage of the whole federation when it came to anything beyond the ability to transfer money or, in the case of media-owning PFIGs, to communicate information. Most did not own hard assets in a majority of regions, but instead concentrated their interests in a few provinces. For example, LUKoil was very strong in Perm in the year 2000 but had virtually no presence in Briansk. Likewise, the Interros group was extremely powerful in Taimyr but almost completely absent in Bashkortostan. Indeed, some of the most interesting electoral contests took place when one PFIG was trying to move into a new region.[115] Certain partially state-owned concerns, such

[112] Also known as ORT or Channel 1.

[113] As of 1997, the state owned 40 percent of Gazprom's shares (*RFE/RL Newsline* 1, no. 146, Part I, October 24, 1997).

[114] See Reddaway and Orttung 2003.

[115] Orttung 2004a.

as the electricity monopoly Unified Energy Systems and the gas monopoly Gazprom did have critical strangleholds on regions across the whole country, but these were economic entities on which the Russian executive branch refused to release its grip. The best known instance of a PFIG that showed signs of taking on a Russian president in a contest for the country's chief executive office is the Yukos affair, which involved a political challenge by Yukos CEO Mikhail Khodorkovsky to Putin in 2003. Despite the fact that Yukos was Russia's richest company at the time, Putin's government had little trouble jailing its top executives (including Khodorkovsky) and effectively stripping them of much of their asset holdings.[116] Putin's prosecutors dispatched of other potentially troublesome PFIGs in similar ways during his first term, bringing charges that led PFIG owners Boris Berezovsky and Vladimir Gusinsky to flee the country and take up residence in Europe.

When the Kremlin has mobilized its nationwide machine for an election, the results have been dramatic. In 1996, Yeltsin began his reelection campaign with approval ratings under 5 percent. Deciding against calls from close aides to cancel the elections, Yeltsin, through campaign manager Anatoly Chubais, mobilized all major financial-industrial groups in support of the president through promises of lucrative contracts and undervalued privatized assets.[117] In this way, he was able to secure not only generous financing, but also strikingly biased media coverage in his favor and against his rival, Communist Party leader Gennady Zyuganov. All of this helped Yeltsin eke out a runoff victory. In 2000, Russian PFIGs were somewhat divided, resulting in glowing pro-Putin coverage on two of the country's three leading television networks (First Channel and RTR) and subtly critical portrayals of him on the third, NTV. Through its clever use of the media and the "bully pulpit" of the presidency, the Kremlin effectively managed to end the contest before it began. Once the pro-Kremlin party (Unity) had performed far above expectations and Putin's main presidential rivals' party (Fatherland–All Russia) had performed far below expectations, these contenders bowed out and left Zyuganov as Putin's only serious challenger. Russia's PFIGs, naturally, preferred Putin to the Communist leader, especially once it became clear that Putin would win, as will be discussed in Chapter 5. With his popular approval ratings far above 50 percent throughout his first term, Putin sailed to easy reelection in 2004 with the backing of almost every elite group, including virtually every governor and PFIG.

In the absence of Kremlin-challenging PFIGs and given governors' inherently limited geographic scope, it is not surprising that we would find in presidential contests quite high levels of party penetration outside the set of Kremlin candidates. Indeed, as noted in Chapter 3, all significant candidates other than the incumbents were party affiliates (and, in most cases, party

[116] Woodruff 2003.
[117] McFaul 2001b.

leaders) between 1991 and 2004. Thus, although presidents were not partisan, presidential elections were actually quite partisan in relative terms, with one party substitute (the Kremlin) working against party rivals.

Overall, given that we have only three post-Soviet Russian presidential elections to consider, the only thing we can say for sure is that parties played strong roles in these contests but that the Kremlin itself proved to be a much more powerful "party substitute," one available only to the occupant of the presidential office or, when necessary, an anointed successor. With a nonparty candidate virtually guaranteed to be one of the top two contenders, there was little room left for political parties to operate. This leads us back to a question analogous to the one just posed vis-à-vis governors: Why did Russian presidents choose to work without parties rather than either joining or starting one of their own? This question, too, is addressed explicitly in Chapter 5.

CONCLUSION

This chapter has demonstrated that a market logic can help explain why Russia's parties grew in both organization and reputation but were simultaneously unable to fully penetrate Russia's political market. Parties were not the only forms of political organization capable of providing electoral goods and services to candidates; in Russia as elsewhere, potential candidates could also turn to certain forms of party substitutes that proffered these wares without many of the strings and costs that parties could seek to attach. Thus, where in most developed democracies candidates are forced to pay the price demanded by major political parties if they hope to have a real chance of winning office, in Russia candidates have had other options. In the case of Russia, the main such "other options" have been the political machines of powerful governors and politicized financial-industrial groups. Statistical evidence and field research have found that the presence of party substitutes did in fact partially crowd parties out of Russia's electoral market. Parties were partially crowded out in Russia's parliamentary and presidential elections and were largely decimated in elections for governorships and provincial legislatures.

These party substitutes are found to have originally arisen from particular distributions of administrative capital, meso-level concentrations of resources that were fungible vis-à-vis electoral politics and could thus be mobilized by political entrepreneurs. These assets were in part legacies of the pre-transition *ancien regime*, but some were also generated or powerfully influenced by modes of transition themselves.[118] Transition paths, even in the seemingly unrelated sphere of economics, can have a momentous impact on

[118] For a supporting quantitative analysis as well as some additional detail, see Hale 2003.

political party development if Russia is any guide. This conclusion fits nicely with the literature on transitions from authoritarian rule that gives a large role to elites in contingent decision making that can have long-term effects through processes of path dependence.[119] It also falls in the broad tradition of those scholars who have emphasized the importance of leadership in determining political outcomes.[120]

Does the existence of party substitutes doom a country to weak party development forever? The comparative evidence suggests that this is not the case. The United States, for example, once featured very robust party substitutes much like the kind found in Russia. The next chapter, drawing on comparative experience, considers how parties might ultimately overcome party substitutes, closing out the electoral market, and why this did not happen in Russia prior to 2005. It also, however, explains major Russian reforms under Putin directed at dramatically increasing the role of parties and decreasing the role of party substitutes.

119 For example, Gel'man, Ryzhenkov, and Brie 2003; McFaul 2001b; O'Donnell and Schmitter 1986.

120 Breslauer 2002; Brown 1996.

5

Parties and Party Substitutes

Determining the Balance

Whether a political system becomes fully a party system depends upon factors that give parties a competitive edge over party substitutes in a given country's electoral markets. Chapter 4 has already shown how Russia's patrimonial communist legacy combined with its transition path to produce party substitutes that were capable of withstanding or even eliminating competition from parties in struggles for Russia's most important electoral offices. As Chapters 1 and 2 made clear, however, the answer does not end with initial capital allocations, since these can be expected to grow or shrink depending on how they are used and to be used differently as new technologies or opportunities develop. How, then, can we explain the persistence of party substitutes as major players and the consequent inability of parties to close out the electoral market over time? Can the same answer also make sense of the indications in 2005 that parties were in fact gaining some ground? And can this explanation further account for the major reforms announced during the Putin era that appeared aimed at ending Russia's partial party system and establishing party dominance?

The answers to all of these questions, it is argued, can be found in the broad institutional context that defines both the market itself and the abilities of different actors to intervene in and regulate the market.[1] While election rules are found to matter, what is more fundamentally important is the executive branch in Russia, which has the formal or informal power to alter election rules, regulate the market, and intervene selectively in it to shape outcomes strategically. Drawing on seminal insights from Migdal and Shefter, it is argued that incumbent executives in new states have an incentive to weaken important institutions such as executive-led political parties since these run the risk of restricting executive autonomy or even issuing outright

[1] In Russia's case, these institutions can largely be traced to its patrimonial communist legacy as described in Chapter 2. Since similar institutions have arisen from other circumstances, however, the following discussion still has broad application outside of Russia.

challenges to executive authority. Executives are more likely to form parties, however, when they face major challenges that parties prove useful in defeating. Thus, while Shefter observes that incumbent parties in Europe did not tend to mobilize the masses until forced to do so by new competition from the socialists, so one finds in Russia that its superpresidential regime consistently avoided and even undermined the most promising avenues for party-building until it faced a challenge that required a party of its own to defeat. This helps us explain why parties only partially penetrated the Russian polity prior to 2005 but why Putin launched a series of major reforms starting in 2000 designed explicitly to limit the electoral role of Russia's major party substitutes and to gradually give the decisive edge to parties, albeit parties backed by the Kremlin.

PATHS TO A FULLY PARTY SYSTEM: THE IDEATIONAL-CAPITAL-DRIVEN PATH

How might parties overcome party substitutes in a given political system once these substitutes have established themselves? One possibility is that major-party labels might take on greater value, increasingly giving party nominees a competitive edge with which party substitutes cannot ultimately compete. That is, parties may prove to have superior ideational capital, which in developed democracies has usually involved the rise of deep-seated party loyalties (partisanship) that command large shares of the potential vote. There are at least two major ways in which party labels could become more able to win votes than they previously had been: The appeal of party ideas could increase or parties could become associated with positive on-the-job performance by their leaders or patrons.

Party labels could give parties a new edge over party substitutes if the ideas they connote become more popular amongst potential voters and hence more attractive to candidates. One might suppose, for example, that the liberal values espoused by Yabloko and/or the socialist ones advanced by the Communist Party might gain more support in the population than they previously enjoyed. This might happen through a path of direct persuasion, by which parties themselves learn to campaign more effectively, or through some other process of learning or value acquisition. The problem, however, is that most Russians even as of the late 1990s had already adopted positions on the main parties' values. On one issue that Chapters 2 and 3 found to be prominent in party campaigns and in voting behavior, for example, the 1999–2000 survey found that well under 10 percent of the population had no position on whether to return to socialism or deepen the marketization process. It does not appear, therefore, that the persistence of party substitutes was due to any widespread lack of important policy views on the part of the electorate. While the relative share of leftist and rightist views may vary over time, there have been parties representing both views ever since Russia legalized parties, so such shifts should not impact the overall role of parties as opposed to party substitutes in the system.

A more sophisticated argument, however, would look not so much at the distribution of views associated with party labels as at the *salience* of these party-associated views *relative to the other views that may be associated with voting for party-substitute candidates*. Such an approach might begin with a concept that specialists on American politics have called "issue ownership." Quite reasonably taking parties for granted in the U.S. context, these scholars have sought to explain why the very same individuals will often vote for one party's candidate in, say, congressional elections and for another party's nominee in presidential balloting. One important answer has been the idea that different parties are known for being better at different things (that is, each party may "own" a different issue) and that people prefer different candidate or party qualities for different offices.[2] This logic can be extended both to Russia and to the realm of party substitutes. In particular, as races involve more and more locally specific issues, it becomes more difficult for ideational or programmatic parties based on nationally relevant ideas to communicate to voters the information that will be most meaningful to them in making voting decisions. The reputational advantage from which such nationwide parties profit in attracting candidates, therefore, tends to decline as election issues become more local, especially if the particular local issues that are salient vary widely across localities. Many of the party substitutes that we have examined in this volume, notably governors' political machines and regional financial-industrial groups, have specialized precisely in local issues.

Parties can, of course, develop national-level reputations for qualities that are broadly important to people for dealing with local problems. For example, the Yabloko Party, illustrated by its innovating Perm organization led by Liubov Zotina in the late 1990s, enjoyed some local success by applying nationwide Yabloko principles (such as the push for transparency in government and the concern for human rights) on a regional level, engaging in a series of local initiatives and public "good deeds" to improve community life.[3] Kurilla writes that the Communist Party has effectively made itself a substitute for civil society in the town of Uriupinsk.[4] It is less clear, however, that a national party has a competitive *advantage* over local party substitutes in credibility for dealing with local problems. Consequently, we would expect parties' advantages over party substitutes to be lower both for more local elected offices and for smaller constituencies since the national issues on which parties are likely to have the most credibility are less likely to be salient.

[2] Jacobson 1990; Petrocik 1991.

[3] Neganov 2003; Interview with Liubov Zotina 1999.

[4] Kurilla 2002.

This logic finds strong confirmation in the patterns identified in preceding chapters as well as in comparative experience. Chapter 3 showed quite clearly that the institutions with the least party penetration in Russia tended to be those where nationwide party reputations were posited to be the least advantageous, notably elections for regional governorships and regional legislatures. On the other hand, national parties were able to use a reputational advantage to compete more effectively in the Duma and even presidential races. Moreover, the statistical analysis reported in the previous chapter's Table 4.3 found that within the set of Russian legislative races, those regions with the smallest constituencies featured the weakest level of participation by electoral associations. In comparative perspective, this argument is in keeping with broad patterns in contemporary American politics. While presidential and congressional elections are party-dominated, 75 percent of all U.S. municipal elections are nonpartisan and one U.S. state legislature is even elected and functions on a nonpartisan basis.[5] Moreover, it is widely agreed by American politics specialists that partisanship matters more in voting for presidential candidates (where nationwide issues are most salient) than in, for example, senatorial elections.[6] Reinforcing this effect is the fact that more party substitutes are likely to be viable as constituency sizes decrease since fewer resources are required to reach enough voters to win.

While the preceding analysis nicely accounts for much of the cross-institutional and even cross-regional variation found in the balance of strength between parties and their substitutes, it would seem to go too far in predicting no change in this balance within the same institutional setting. Comparative experience does provide examples of such change. As was described in Chapter 1, both India and the United States began with very weak parties that did not fully penetrate even national elections, but they relatively quickly came virtually to close out these political markets.

The work of Pradeep Chhibber and Ken Kollman, when combined with the logic of issue ownership just discussed, points in a very helpful direction. They show that in Canada, Great Britain, India, and the United States parties became more focused on national issues and were more successful in competing with regional parties when these national governments gained more economic and political power relative to regional governments.[7] One might extend this argument to explain not only why national parties might come to defeat regional parties, but why national parties might come to defeat important party substitutes, thereby accounting for how political systems become *party* systems in the first place. When the federal government that parties compete to control gains more power than governors or financial-industrial groups to influence local economies, we might expect the national issues

[5] Wright and Schaffner 2002; Schaffner and Wright, personal communication.

[6] Highton 2000.

[7] Chhibber and Kollman 1998, 2004.

"owned" by parties to become more salient to voters than the local issues "owned" by individual candidates of nonpartisan gubernatorial machines or financial-industrial groups. The particular pattern of institutional party penetration in Russia, then, can be seen as a function of the degree to which Russia's political system has allocated real decision-making authority across different levels of government. Accordingly, we would expect Russian parties to make headway against party substitutes when the Russian polity undergoes periods of centralization.

During the 1990s, Russia was quite well known for its "wayward regions," provincial governments that had either arrogated or been granted a great deal of de facto decision-making autonomy on all kinds of economic and political questions. This went even beyond the officially sanctioned opportunities to shape privatization and local political systems discussed in Chapter 4 and involved a great deal of outright insubordination.[8] One might thus reasonably suppose that this situation of de facto decentralization was one reason why Russian parties remained weak during the Yeltsin era.

But Russia underwent a very important period of centralization after Putin came into office.[9] Most dramatically, almost immediately after his inauguration in May 2000, Putin divided the country into seven federal macro-regions ("federal okrugs") and installed an official "envoy" as the head of each.[10] Putin did not give the envoys a great deal of formal power, but the direct relationship with him that they enjoyed gave them a large amount of leverage to bring regions into compliance with federal law and, as it turned out, to secure the annulment of a host of center-region "bilateral treaties" that had bestowed special autonomy to many Russian provinces. They were, however, given some formal powers where they mattered most, such as the right to sanction appointments to more than 370,000 civil service posts in the provinces, formerly controlled by governors. Over the following four years, the federal government reasserted control over regional police, courts, and, very importantly, the prosecutor general's offices in the provinces. The prosecutors, newly resubordinated to federal authorities, began aggressively forcing regional law into compliance with federal legislation. Putin also claimed control of more of each region's income, weakening provincial leaders' ability to utilize these resources as they saw fit.[11] Putin also stripped governors of their direct representation in the upper house of parliament. By 2003, then, almost all observers agreed that authority in Russia had been significantly centralized.

[8] The literature on this subject is voluminous. See, e.g., Hale 2005a; Herrera 2005; Solnick 2000; Stoner-Weiss 1999; and Treisman 1999.

[9] On Putin's centralizing policies, see in particular the following article and edited volumes: Bahry 2005; Petrov 2003; Reddaway and Orttung 2003; and Reddaway and Orttung 2005.

[10] This paragraph draws on Hale 2005b.

[11] Orttung 2004b.

Despite this major centralization, there was no correspondingly large increase in the overall role of national parties in Russia's various electoral arenas. One might be tempted to point to Table 3.8 to show that the United Russia candidates performed nearly twice as well in 2003 as did Unity nominees in 1999 in the single-member-district Duma races. Yet United Russia was the product of a merger between Unity and Fatherland–All Russia and it turns out that the performance "boost" associated with United Russia in 2003 was almost exactly equal to the sum of the boosts given by Unity and Fatherland–All Russia in 1999, suggesting little net gain in party impact. Moreover, Table 3.8 also shows that the performance of Communist Party candidates dropped by well over a third. The most compelling evidence, however, comes from the provinces. Tables 3.12, 3.13, and 3.14 show that formal party activity and the impact of parties on their nominees' chances remained very near zero, on the whole. Chapter 3 also established that parties did not make significant inroads into regional legislatures until the reform of July 2003, which mandated that part of each legislative assembly be elected in a proportional-representation competition among lists of national parties. The breakthrough in the provincial legislatures, then, came from direct state intervention rather than from any increase in the salience of national party issues induced by Russia's centralization process under Putin. Thus, while centralization might have the anticipated effect in the long run, as of now Russia remains a puzzle to the body of theory that points primarily to this factor in determining the rise of national parties.

If a lack of centralization is not behind parties' inability to squeeze out party substitutes by means of ideational capital, perhaps institutional design is the answer. Chapter 4's analysis of legislative assembly elections showed that parties fared better where regions had adopted proportional representation systems in the voting for larger shares of their seats. We can similarly expect that the nationwide PR competition taking place at the same time as the SMD Duma campaigning has enhanced public awareness of parties' reputations and thus augmented the impact of this reputation on the SMD Duma races. For most gubernatorial elections, however, party candidates receive no such boost. The same could also be said of most legislative assembly races prior to July 2003. While the absence of PR contests may go part of the way in explaining why parties have not closed out Russia's political market, this is hardly a satisfactory answer. For one thing, many countries (including the United States and India) have experienced party dominance without a significant PR component in their election systems. Moreover, we find that PR's effect is far from decisive in a mixed electoral system; indeed, it has certainly not produced complete party dominance even in Duma elections, for which the PR component has had a very high profile. Thus, although we see evidence that the July 2003 introduction of PR into all regional legislative elections has started to lead to a greater role for parties, there is little cause to expect it to lead to a party monopoly in the SMD contests that remain.

In any case, the absence of PR does not explain why Russia has failed to follow other countries, like India and the United State, where SMD systems are associated with strong party systems.

If neither centralization nor institutional design appears to be the main factor maintaining the standoff between parties and party substitutes in Russia, the comparative literature also suggests that the degree to which parties become associated with the state of affairs in the country might be what matters. When times are seen to be good, parties associated with the goodness will make major inroads in the electorate as people vote to reward the incumbents. When times are bad, however, the blamed parties may in fact lose ground in the population. This logic lies at the core of widespread research on "retrospective voting," the idea that people frequently vote based on assessments of how the incumbent party has performed in the economy (as in the "economic voting" literature) or in other important spheres.[12] Some leading works posit that voters do not look solely at the immediately preceding period, but that they keep long-term "running tallies" of party performance in office and that these tallies eventually form the basis for enduring party loyalties.[13] Such a process implies that the "particization" of the polity may be driven primarily by incumbent parties until such time as opposition parties gain positive track records of their own to which they can point.

This logic does appear to take us part of the way in understanding Russia's struggles with party system emergence. Russia's incumbents spawned and primarily backed a different party in each of the first three Duma elections (1993, 1995, and 1999), making it difficult for any of these parties' labels to absorb the glow of any economic or political successes people might have perceived. Of course, part of the problem was also that there were so few perceived economic or political successes in which a progovernment party could bask. Surely the economic decline and political turmoil of the 1990s were one reason why the Yeltsin team kept switching party horses, hoping that voters would blame the problems on the old one and see hope in the new one. These facts, then, could help explain why Russia's parties were unable to outcompete party substitutes during this period; they simply did not look very good because they could not point to major positive economic or political achievement with which they were associated.

The 2003 election, however, represented a major change in that for the first time, the Kremlin backed the same party (or a direct successor) in two

12 On retrospective voting, see in particular Erikson, MacKuen, and Stimson 2002; Fiorina 1981. Some leading works in the voluminous comparative or Americanist economic voting literature include Anderson 1995; Colton 1996; Duch 2001; Kinder and Kiewiet 1981; Lewis-Beck 1988; and Norpoth, Lewis-Beck, and Lafay 1991. For a survey of the literature on voting (economic and otherwise) in the postcommunist region, see Tucker 2002.

13 Fiorina 1981; Erikson et al. 2002.

successive elections. The analysis presented in Chapter 3, and in particular Table 3.4, indicates that Russia's parties of power have in fact received important boosts from being associated with both economic and political improvements when people perceived such improvements. A major difference between 2003 and 1995, then, is that in 2003 far more people believed the Russian economy was improving. A separate study by the present author and Colton employs a much more extensive analysis of the 2003–4 survey data than could be done in Chapter 3 and finds that United Russia was in fact being increasingly rewarded not only when people thought the economy as a whole was improving, but also when they believed that their own family's economic situation had improved; Unity had not benefited from such an effect in 1999. But while these findings indicate United Russia was indeed benefiting as expected from perceived positive performance, this was only one of many factors associated with voting for United Russia and was not even the most important one.[14] Moreover, the evidence given above shows that United Russia continued to be unable to convince gubernatorial candidates to seek its nomination, even when the candidates were prominent leaders of the party, as was the case with Moscow Mayor Yury Luzhkov, who ran for reelection as an independent in December 2003. Thus, while economic growth and its association with United Russia did appear to give a modest boost to United Russia, this was clearly not enough to drive party substitutes out of business, at least not in the short run.

Overall, the preceding analysis has demonstrated that parties were making modest progress in the party system by 2005 after having stalled in the late 1990s, and were doing so in ways predicted by important existing theories of party-system development. We cannot explain the continued strength of party substitutes, therefore, by the absence of the factors these theories posit to be important. Factors influencing the ideational appeal of parties, then, do not appear to be behind Russian parties' failure to close out the political market as of 2005.

PATHS TO A FULLY PARTY SYSTEM: THE ADMINISTRATIVE-CAPITAL-DRIVEN PATH

As it turns out, the failure of the ideational-capital-driven path in Russia so far is quite in line with the experience of other large federal countries. Indeed, Russia has not been alone in enduring a period characterized by strong party substitutes and only a partial party system. For example, America's national parties prior to the 1820s were top-heavy, consisting primarily of sharply polarized national congressional coalitions, and had penetrated state and local offices only thinly. Some states, such as Virginia, had

[14] Colton and Hale 2004.

longstanding nonparty traditions, whereas others were the preserve of localized political organizations. In fact, the U.S. "founding fathers" actually regarded parties as an evil to be avoided, and the Federalists did not believe in mass politics at all, holding that propertied elites were better equipped to run the government.[15] As suffrage expanded, powerful political machines came to dominate state politics, often having little connection to each other across jurisdictional lines and hence effectively constituting party substitutes. Parties overcame these party substitutes not because they outcompeted them with ideational capital, but because *party substitutes effectively became the parties* that formed the enduring party system. That is, parties acquired an edge not so much in ideational capital but in administrative capital and did so by a process of "acquisition" or "merger." This was the historic achievement of Martin Van Buren in the late 1820s, to unite America's state-level political machines into the new Democratic Party, which to this day is one of the country's two system-defining parties.[16] This, combined with the above analysis of the importance of Russia's superpresidential system, strongly suggests that the explanation for developments in the balance between parties and substitutes in Russia is likely to lie at the nexus of the superpresidency and the country's major party substitutes.

The Russian Presidency and Parties

Many observers, both Russian and Western, have called on Russian presidents to promote the development of parties by adding their own imprimatur to one such organization. If Yeltsin had only had the political will to found his own party, writes McFaul, he might have had a much easier time implementing his reforms and Russia would have become a much more stable place as a result.[17] Indeed, the Yeltsin presidency expended much of its energy on clashes with elected parliaments, including a very violent one in October 1993. Given his demonstrated power to win both elections and referenda, why would he not have wanted to lend his political strength to a political party that might have been the base for a close working relationship in parliament? Likewise, ever since Unity's founding in October 1999, its leaders have called on Putin to join the party and become its leader, arguing that it could become a more effective instrument for Putin to stabilize Russia and pass his agenda in the Duma.[18] Why, then, have Russia's presidents refused to become "party men" nearly a decade and a half since the USSR collapsed?

15 Schlesinger 1945, pp. 12–15; Tocqueville 1988, pp. 174–9.

16 Classic accounts of these developments include Aldrich 1995; Hofstadter 1969; and Remini 1959. An outstanding new study is Silbey 2002.

17 McFaul 2001b.

18 For example, see Boris Gryzlov, leader of the Unity Duma fraction, *Kremlin Package*, April 26, 2000; and *Reuters* (Moscow), April 22, 2000, JRL.

Part of the answer must have to do with the nature of presidential incumbency, not the nature of the major pretenders to this office. This follows from an examination of the main challengers to both Yeltsin and Putin in elections for Russia's top job since the Soviet breakup. As was demonstrated in Chapter 3, *all* of those candidates that received at least 1 percent of the vote in one of these elections were the representatives of parties or political movements.

A superficial answer might be that Russian law as of mid-2004 banned sitting presidents, unlike challengers, from being official party members. This answer is superficial because a powerful president can certainly get this law changed, as many presidential officials have suggested will eventually happen.[19]

A more compelling answer begins with an observation by Shefter, who writes that incumbents typically transform elite parliamentary clublike parties into mass organizations only when they are forced to by a challenge from strong mass opposition parties. Thus, Europe's conservative parties tended to reach to the masses and to actively pursue organization only when confronted with the rise of mass socialist parties.[20] These European incumbents simply did not need strong organization until the socialist opposition gained enough mobilizational power to make them think otherwise.

Shefter's logic combines with the argument laid out in this volume to help us understand Russian dynamics. If the Kremlin is the ultimate party substitute, as Chapter 4 observed, then incumbents always have at their disposal tremendous political capital, usually both administrative and ideational. For one thing, presidents can count on great media exposure, facilitating the development of some form of ideational capital. The administrative capital of the Kremlin throughout the Yeltsin and early Putin eras included everything from the outright ownership of two of the country's "big three" television networks (First Channel and RTR) to indirect influence over other media or potential candidate sponsors through extensive state involvement in the economy. Presidents, then, have had cause to see little need for the kinds of support that a party might be able to add in competition with the opposition.

Just because a president does not see the need for a party to win an election does not fully explain why he or she would not create one, however. If a party could help a president win *more*, would this president not still have an incentive to build it? Are not such incentives even stronger given that a president might be able to use a party to stabilize the country's political system, providing the presidency with loyal agents in every region of Russia and a reliable coalition in legislative organs, as Aldrich suggests is the case?[21]

[19] For example, see *RFE/RL Newsline*, February 20, 2002.

[20] Shefter 1977, 1994.

[21] Aldrich 1995.

In short, even if presidents do not need parties for electoral purposes, would not a truly presidential party still make it easier for the president to govern effectively, building a strong and reliable coalition in the Duma as well as in localities?

Even if the answer to the latter question is affirmative, Migdal tells us why presidents might have incentive actually to undermine the very institutions that might make them more effective, a logic particularly compelling in new states with clientelistic social structures like Russia's. The underlying problem is a *principal-agent problem*, which Migdal calls the "dilemma of state leaders."[22] This logic applies to the possible creation of a presidential party in the following way. While a party might help a president rule more authoritatively, the authority that the party itself would accrue through this process could make it a threat to the president's personal power since it is likely to develop interests of its own that might one day contradict those of the president. Building a party that is based on anything more than pure loyalty to the president starts to create a reputation that benefits the party both in elections and in legislative bargains and that therefore becomes costly to contradict.[23] There is also the risk that the party might groom leaders, perhaps a speaker of the parliament or the governor of a prominent region, who could come to rival the president through access to this nationwide organization, perhaps being able to turn the party into an opposition political force. Indeed, Russia had witnessed a vice president leading an armed rebellion against presidential policies in the 1990s, so the idea that a presidential party leader might also mount a challenge was certainly not far-fetched. Comparative research provides additional empirical grounds for such fears: Even ideologically based religious and left-libertarian movements have frequently had trouble controlling their own political progeny once the latter have gained a measure of political power.[24] Migdal reports that such fears often drive state leaders to shake up and weaken their own state institutions intentionally so as to preserve their own power. So might we expect presidents to resist the creation of a presidential party that they believe might come to have authority that might exist independently of the president him- or herself.

The key to presidential party formation, then, is the perceived relative strength of president and opposition. When incumbent presidents feel they do not need parties to win election for themselves or a successor, they are more likely to see dangers than benefits in forming a presidential party. Presidential parties, therefore, tend to appear in one of two ways. First, where an opposition party mobilizes with such elite and mass strength that the incumbent believes his own power may be insufficient to win in the future, a president can feel compelled to countermobilize by forming his or

22 Migdal 1987, 1988.

23 Kreps 1990.

24 Kalyvas 1996, 2000; Kitschelt 1989.

her own party. In such a case, the immediate need to hold on to the presidency outweighs the risks of principal-agent problems. Second, an opposition party might actually win such a contest, bringing partisanship to the presidency from outside the office.

The American case is again illustrative because we see this very logic at work even in a time and place that is highly remote from today's Russia. George Washington, America's first president, considered political parties a social evil and refused to form a party himself, preferring to see himself as a representative of the whole nation. It was only with the rise of the hated Jeffersonian opposition in the early Congress that Washington's Federalist allies, who in principle rejected the idea of party government, effectively turned to party formation themselves in order to win this struggle.[25] Lest we lend early American history too much of a rosy gloss, it is important to note that the Federalists under President John Adams turned to some very repressive measures (such as the Alien and Sedition Act of 1798) to subvert this opposition. Even after the Jeffersonian Republicans eventually won the struggle in the 1800 presidential election, they too continued to adhere to the notion of party-free government as good government. They saw little need to build party organization once the expansion of suffrage led to the Federalists' disappearance and the ensuing "Era of Good Feelings."[26]

In Russia, we see that the superpresidency has endowed the Kremlin with such great power that its occupants for a long time did not see the need for a party (or even the use of one) in securing continued control over the highest office in the land. The office's occupants were thus more likely to perceive dangers than benefits when considering the possibility of creating a truly presidential party. This logic helps us understand why Yeltsin consistently disrupted Russia's developing party system throughout the 1990s, ironically by consistently orphaning parties that he himself helped spawn and that quite loyally supported him. In 1993, most of Yeltsin's government ran for the Duma on the ticket of Russia's Choice, but Yeltsin himself refused to join. After this party fared poorly in the election, reports almost immediately surfaced that Yeltsin was planning a new "presidential party," implying that Russia's Choice was being abandoned.[27] Moreover, in 1994–5, justifying the fear of principal-agent problems like those identified by Migdal, Russia's Choice did in fact come to oppose Yeltsin on one of his most important moves, the decision to send the military into Chechnya and to pummel the renegade republic mercilessly when victory was not achieved in the anticipated two days. As party leader and acting prime minister, Gaidar had achieved some political weight of his own. Moreover, Russia's Choice was based in part on liberal ideology and included a strong pro-human-rights

[25] It is important to remember that the parties of this initial period were primarily coalitions of legislators in the U.S. Congress with little mass organization.

[26] Hofstadter 1969.

[27] *RFE/RL* [Daily Reports], Inc., no. 22, February 2, 1994.

grouping (led by Sergei Kovalev). This party, created to be loyal to Yeltsin, thus wound up working against rather than for the president in this crucial instance. Accordingly, in the run-up to the 1995 Duma campaign, Yeltsin abandoned Russia's Choice (by then calling itself Russia's Democratic Choice) and sanctioned a new party, Our Home is Russia, to be created and led not by himself, but by the post-Gaidar prime minister, Viktor Chernomyrdin. By the spring of 1998, however, Yeltsin had fired Chernomyrdin as prime minister, by all accounts worried that the latter was increasingly being seen as presidential material and a potential threat to Yeltsin's own status and power. This effectively signed the death warrant of Our Home is Russia.

That this principal-agent logic underlay the president's behavior is confirmed in interviews with key Yeltsin advisors who took different positions on this issue. Both Hough and McFaul, for example, report that Yeltsin's closest advisor early in his presidency, State Secretary Gennady Burbulis, said in personal interviews that he had frequently urged the Russian leader to form a true presidential party but that Yeltsin had always resisted, citing his concern that this would commit him to taking particular policy decisions that he might want the flexibility to avoid.[28] Another advisor, a member of Yeltsin's advisory Presidential Council, volunteered in an interview with the present author that he personally had counseled Yeltsin that Gaidar and others in Russia's Choice were party-building in part to become independent of Yeltsin and that the creation of a large, powerful party would result in their becoming obligated to the party itself at the expense of their loyalty to Yeltsin personally. Yeltsin, he reported, therefore sought to hinder this process, not seeing the emergence of a strong party as being in his interests.[29] McFaul reports that highly similar forms of antiparty reasoning were also used by other close Yeltsin associates.[30] Subverting even propresidential parties and refusing to lend all of his authority to a single party, Yeltsin preserved his autonomy to play supporters off of one another and thereby to bolster his own power.[31] Leading into 1999, then, the occupant of Russia's supreme office not only had incentive to undermine opposition party-building efforts but also demonstrated remarkable opposition to constructing a party that would have supported his own presidential policies and initiatives. What happened under Putin will be discussed later in this chapter.

Politicized Financial-Industrial Groups and Parties

Russia's superpresidential institutions combined with the profit motive in keeping Russia's politicized financial-industrial groups from effectively

[28] Hough 1998b, p. 52; McFaul 2001b, p. 155.
[29] Interview with a member of Yeltsin's advisory Presidential Council, February 17, 1999.
[30] McFaul 2001b, p. 155.
[31] On Yeltsin's style of rule, see Breslauer 2002 and Colton 1995a.

"joining" or creating parties and from working exclusively through parties to achieve their political ends through 2005. PFIG leaders were often quite frank in admitting that the desire for profit was their prime motive in becoming involved in elections and government, as reported in an interview project designed to discern the forces driving the activity of business in Russian politics.[32] Since PFIGs generally had a narrow set of business interests growing out of the economic sectors in which they were engaged, their preferences tended to be very strong on a few critical issues but quite weak on others on which parliamentarians or presidents might make decisions. Their chief object, then, was not to be burdened with all realms of state decision making, but to ensure that they got the decisions they wanted on those issues that cut closest to their financial hearts. Operationally, this required both supporting politicians who would support corporate interests and avoiding the alienation of forces that could negatively affect business.

For PFIGs of national scope, Russia's superpresidency was enormously important during this period given the vast powers of this office to affect their businesses either through policy decisions or special treatment from state agencies. Indeed, as was described in Chapter 4, many of Russia's most powerful PFIGs quite directly owed their fortunes to such Kremlin actions. PFIGs thus have had tremendous incentives to fall into line behind the incumbent (or other most likely winner) in any presidential election. And since the president remained nonpartisan through 2005, PFIGs thereby reinforced presidential nonpartisanship by backing the incumbents. As Johnson reports, PFIGs were very reliable donors to parties of power such as Our Home is Russia and Russia's Choice.[33] PFIGs also had incentive, however, to hedge their bets, making at least some donation to any contender seen to have a chance of winning or influencing corporate fortunes in other political arenas. Some PFIG representatives were widely reported to donate funds even to the Communist Party in 1999 and 2003, for example.

While PFIG executives have certainly wanted to have some influence in any party capable of influencing their fortunes, they have had special incentive to maintain some representatives in state organs who were beholden directly and primarily to the PFIG itself. One way to do this was essentially to "buy" votes after the decision-making politicians were elected. As Treisman points out, this highly concrete, immediate form of exchange minimized the risk that the politician, having taken the money and obtained office, would not follow through with the agreement to vote a certain way, a serious danger given what he calls the "undeveloped" nature of Russia's political market.[34] This method, however, could involve costs since the PFIG could not count

[32] Lapina and Chirikova 2002.

[33] Johnson 2000; Lapina and Chirikova 2002.

[34] Treisman 1998b; Interview with a member of Yeltsin's Presidential Council, February 17, 1999.

on any one member being willing to take a bribe on any one issue since that representative might be beholden to other interests for election to office and might have other bidders for his or her vote. Thus, when some PFIGs in the later 1990s gained the capacity, they began directly to put up their own people for elections in certain single-member districts under the agreement that these candidates would vote in prescribed ways on select sets of issues. This kind of candidate support, not complicated by association with a party that might have different goals, provided a more reliable way to further PFIG interests than did backing parties more generally.

PFIGs were most strongly positioned to pursue corporate interests, then, when they had representatives in many parties as well as large collections of candidates beholden exclusively to them for their political careers in a given legislature. They thus tended both to contribute to parties and to advance their own nonpartisan slates of candidates as opportunities arose. Given the power of the superpresidency, PFIGs were highly likely to support presidential incumbents, thereby reinforcing the latter's perceived lack of a need for a full-fledged presidential party. Since governors also had a great deal of influence over local economies, as was demonstrated in Chapter 4, PFIGs were also highly likely to make contributions to gubernatorial candidates no matter whether they were partisan or nonpartisan.

The end result is that PFIGs tended to follow or accelerate trends in the party system rather than to *drive* any such developments. PFIGs could be expected to cease backing independents and turn exclusively to partisan candidates only if they thought that party candidates had insurmountable advantages in the electoral process or if parties were seen as being dominant in the policy process. Whether either of these conditions obtained was thus more likely to depend on governors or presidents than on PFIGs.

Governors and Parties

American mass party development took off when Van Buren managed to cobble together a coalition of regional political machines. What kept Russia's highly inventive political entrepreneurs from following the same path during the 1990s? The truth is that many Russian political innovators saw the potential in this kind of move and some attempted to put it into practice.[35] The problem was that one of the political actors having this dream considered it a nightmare. This was Russia's presidential administration. Indeed, if the president had reason to fear rivalry from among his own allies, the development of strong parties by clearly oppositionist forces was even more frightful.

35 For various interpretations of "governors' parties," see Lussier 2002; Smyth 2002; Solnick 2000; and Stoner-Weiss 2001.

These presidential fears mattered because the Kremlin was able to exploit three major barriers to collective action that were faced by governors intending to form a national party, each springing in part from the form of federalism that existed in Russia between 1993 and 2005. The first such barrier was a *coordination problem*. If we assume that each governor agreed that joining a coalition to capture the parliament and presidency would benefit him or her individually by enabling him or her to gain access to the spoils of presidential and parliamentary office, each was likely to have a preference for being a leader of that coalition. Progress in building the alliance, then, could be slowed or even stalled as different sides held out for what they hoped would be a better deal for themselves. This could be exploited by a presidential apparatus with great powers at its disposal, encouraging different regional leaders at different times, making and revoking promises of tacit support, and even buying off those governors who the Kremlin feared would be focal points or key partners in such a party project.

The second major barrier to collective action that governors faced was a *social choice problem*.[36] For the sake of illustration, let us assume that a majority of governors is necessary to build a party that could win the presidency. Let us also assume that once a sufficient majority is formed, the included governors have incentive to exclude the rest so as to keep more of the spoils of presidential office for themselves. Which governors should be part of this majority and which should be left out? Supposing that governors' economic interests are not in perfect harmony (certainly an accurate supposition in Russia in the 1990s), whose interests should make up the basis for the gubernatorial coalition? The problem is that there are many different conglomerations of regional interests that could achieve the end of creating such a governors' party. In its pure form, the social choice problem can lead to endless "cycling" in the negotiation process, with each governor being able to propose a coalition that could win the support of a somewhat different majority of regional leaders. This, then, can also be exploited by a resource-powerful and energetic Kremlin. One important way in which the Kremlin can do this is by proposing its own rival coalitions to a sufficiently large set of governors and backing these proposals with the resources at its disposal.[37] This, as will be shown below, closely resembled the situation in Russia for most of the Yeltsin era as well as the first years under Putin.

Finally, Russia's regional leaders could foresee their own *principal-agent problem* coming to the fore after agreement was reached, a problem not unlike that faced by the president and his administration in deciding whether

[36] Aldrich (1995) studies the social choice problem involved in party-building at the level of legislators. The social choice problem involved in uniting regional political machines can be seen as largely the same.

[37] For an excellent analysis of the problem of cycling in the Russian Congress of People's Deputies 1990–93, see Andrews 2002.

or not to create their own party. Once provincial bosses successfully agreed on a set of interests to represent and a leader, how could they be sure that the person who would lead this party, having captured the powers of the presidency, would not abandon his or her agreed "platform" and pursue either the narrow interests of the Kremlin or those of his or her home region? It could be difficult to find a person who had the density of strong ties to multiple regional machines and/or the personal reputation such that provincial bosses felt he or she could be trusted as the new party's boss. Committing oneself to a national party was thus risky for governors much as it was for Russian presidents according to Migdal's logic.[38]

Turning again to the American example because of its illustrative value, Van Buren faced highly similar problems when forging the Democratic Party and tackled them in a variety of clever ways by the 1828 presidential election. He solved the coordination problem by finding a popular leader that everyone could agree stood the best possible chance of winning the presidency, the war hero Andrew Jackson. Indeed, Jackson had garnered a clear plurality of the presidential vote in 1824, losing only in the electoral college in a "backroom deal" that hurt the legitimacy of the winner and 1828 incumbent, John Quincy Adams. Van Buren solved the social choice problem in two ways. In deciding on a particular policy stand, he essentially avoided choice altogether, building the party upon the noncontroversial (at least among state-level machines) call for state autonomy, leaving the rest essentially to be decided locally by the state-level machines themselves. The new party did not even attempt to draft a platform prior to the election.[39] In choosing a distribution of the spoils, he used his own influence over the largest state in the union, New York, to get Jackson's backing and thereby to effectively ensure his electoral college victory. Other state leaders could not bring such a valuable asset to the table. This in effect enabled Van Buren to dictate the terms for what emerged as the most promising coalitional deal; no one else was in a position to credibly offer a better deal. Finally, Van Buren solved the principal-agent problem through his backing of Jackson. By initially forgoing a leadership bid of his own, "unselfishly" touting Jackson as

38 Migdal 1987, 1988.

39 Aldrich 1995, p. 110. Silbey (2002), correctly stresses that states' rights was a powerful "party idea" in its own right, rooted in longstanding ideological conflicts between the Jeffersonian Republican Party (which had effectively disintegrated by 1824) and the Hamiltonian Federalist Party (which had virtually ceased to exist by 1824). Gerring (1998, pp. 161–86) attributes some other coherent views to the Democratic Party's first presidential campaign, including the liberties of white people and advocacy of a pre-industrial economic order. Thus, it is incorrect to view the early Democratic Party as devoid of all ideational content, particularly during its campaigns. The important point here is that ideational commonalities were not what primarily drove Van Buren's coalition of political machines to initially come together and not what distinguished Van Buren's machines from those left outside the coalition.

the candidate, Van Buren assured other state leaders in the coalition that this was not merely a move by which New York would take over the country for its own benefit. Importantly, Jackson was also one of those rare individuals who had high national standing without any significant reputation that would suggest to coalition members he would betray their particular interests. Aldrich also stresses the importance of long time-horizons. All of these regional machine leaders and Jackson himself wanted to win access to presidential spoils not only for the period 1828–32, but repeatedly. Since they would depend on each other for these future victories, each had an interest in adhering to commitments made.[40]

This American example is especially interesting since we see a strikingly similar effort undertaken in Russia in 1998–9. While several political entrepreneurs initiated efforts to build "governors' parties" during this time, Moscow Mayor Luzhkov very much appeared to be following the Van Buren path. He forged an "ideology" of can-do pragmatism and no-nonsense professionalism that resonated well with the approach of most governors and, critically, adopted a platform of regional autonomy in deciding how to manage their economies and polities. He used his base in Russia's most powerful region (much as Van Buren used his base in New York) to reach out to other provinces, striking deals to help win their loyalty on terms that were not easily "outbid" by other governors. The coup-de-grace was also a move highly reminiscent of Van Buren: He agreed to play second fiddle in order to get Russia's most popular politician of the time, Yevgeny Primakov, to lead the alliance and thereby to cement it. Like Jackson, Primakov was seen by many as being "above ordinary politics," a consensus figure not associated with major political battles of the past and highly respected as someone who could guide the ship of state strongly in times of trouble. Most analysts over the summer of 1999 fully expected Primakov to be the next Russian president and his Fatherland–All Russia coalition to become the new governing party, as was indicated very strongly by the mad scramble of various politicians to join it.

Why did Fatherland–All Russia crash so thunderously in 1999, leaving Primakov and Luzhkov so demoralized that neither dared even to seek nomination for the presidential election of March 2000? The following pages address this question, taking us back to the collective action problems discussed above. Most importantly, we see that Russia's superpresidency, unlike the weak John Quincy Adams presidency of the United States, was both willing and able to do everything necessary to exploit the collective action problems faced by the opposition coalition of regional political machines. Most critically, the incumbent Russian forces struck at the focal points of gubernatorial coordination, Luzhkov and Primakov, making governors once again vulnerable to coalitional cycling. The Kremlin then exacerbated this

[40] Aldrich 1995.

problem by initiating or covertly encouraging a whole series of alternative "governors' party" projects, of which the Unity bloc was only the most successful. While Unity did not win over all or even a majority of governors, it did manage to break the alliance that Luzhkov had so promisingly forged. A share of the responsibility for Fatherland–All Russia's failure, however, has to go to this party's leaders themselves. These politicians failed to develop a strategy for responding to others' attacks and therefore did not use their immense stocks of administrative capital effectively to counter the Kremlin's negative barrage, as was shown in Chapter 2.

The big Russian picture painted here is thus one of governors who *did* demonstrate an interest in being part of a nationwide party to protect their interests. But it is also one of governors who faced tremendous collective action problems that were ruthlessly exploited by a powerful presidential administration, to the detriment of party formation in Russia. As the latter part of this chapter will show, however, the Fatherland–All Russia attempt provided a key impetus to Russia's executive branch to sponsor the creation of something that as of 2005 increasingly resembled a true presidential party and to enact a series of other reforms that expanded the role of parties in the state at the expense of party substitutes.

FATHERLAND–ALL RUSSIA'S CHALLENGE AND THE KREMLIN'S RESPONSE OF UNITY

Russia's political entrepreneurs had long seen the electoral benefits of having governors on one's side, and the period just prior to the 1999 Duma elections saw a flurry of efforts designed to cobble together coalitions frequently called "governors' parties."[41] All of these initiatives foundered on a series of important collective action problems rooted in Russia's federal structure and its superpresidency. Indeed, the Kremlin is shown to have played a major role in exploiting these collective action difficulties, ultimately subverting the party-building efforts. Strikingly, virtually all of these governors' initiatives began independently of Russia's longstanding major parties: the Communists, Yabloko, the Union of Right Forces, and the LDPR. The next few sections examine the most important such efforts and show how the logic outlined in this volume accounts for their appearances and ultimately their failures. The concluding section, however, shows how the most successful such attempt, that of Fatherland–All Russia, may nevertheless have sown the seeds for longer-term party system development in Russia by providing the challenge that convinced Russia's presidential officeholders that a progovernment party was necessary for their long-run political survival.

[41] This section draws heavily on Hale 2004a.

Fatherland: Initial Failures

Once Our Home is Russia leader Viktor Chernomyrdin was fired as prime minister in early 1998, Moscow Mayor Yury Luzhkov seized the initiative to try building an opposition governors' party on Our Home's ruins. Among provincial leaders, Luzhkov was extraordinarily well positioned to initiate such an effort, possessing unparalleled stocks of administrative capital. Naturally, these began with his job as the leader of Russia's political and economic capital, Moscow, a post that brought high visibility and national power to its occupant even in Soviet times.[42]

Upon becoming mayor in 1992, he wasted no time consolidating a wrestler's grip on the city's enormous economy. As was noted in the previous chapter, Luzhkov proved to be a master of managing the post-Soviet transition, effectively turning Russia's most diverse, complex economy into what Orttung has categorized as a "single-company town" dominated by the Sistema Group that his city of Moscow founded.[43] Through the privatization process and other maneuvers, Sistema acquired over 100 companies during the 1990s, including several banks, electronics firms, media outlets, the Moscow city telephone system, the Rosno insurance group, and ventures like Intourist and the glistening underground Manezh Mall geared largely to Moscow's tourism industry. Its affiliated banks included none other than the Bank of Moscow, the official municipal institution that processed some 30–40 percent of the city's resources and conducted extensive business with other key banks handling city business.[44]

Luzhkov creatively used his control over the capital's economy to build ties and influence with the leaders of a large number of Russian provinces. Since the USSR had run the country almost entirely out of Moscow, virtually all communications, transportation, and other economic infrastructure tended to radiate out from Moscow to each of Russia's other regions. One of Luzhkov's most powerful levers was his cozy relationship with many of the country's most powerful banks, virtually all of which were headquartered in Moscow and most of which had important relationships (directly or indirectly) with other Russian regions. The Sistema banks led the way, having gained rapidly in national standing after the August 1998 financial crisis. Whereas some banks like Menatep and Inkombank were hit hard by these events, Sistema's Guta bank, the Moscow Bank for Reconstruction and Development, Promradtechbank, and Sverdlovskii Gubernskii Bank had not been heavily invested in the GKO (state security) pyramid at the center of that crisis.[45]

[42] Colton 1995b.

[43] Orttung 2004a.

[44] Johnson 2000, pp. 190–93; *Moscow Times*, September 5, 1998.

[45] *Moscow Times*, September 5, 1998.

These resources enabled Luzhkov to become an important source of patronage for poorer Russian regions. In one example, in the first part of 1999, Luzhkov ordered a $5.2 million credit for the region of Yaroslavl to finance the completion of a hockey rink in preparation for that city's hosting of the World Ice Hockey Championships in the year 2000. In another, the mayor approved a transfer of roughly $833,000 to Riazan Oblast to support spring 1999 agricultural projects.[46] In still another, Luzhkov visited the impoverished republic of Kabardino-Balkariia and said he was ready to invest vast sums to transform the region into a vacation site.[47] *The Moscow Times* thus reported that most of the 800 delegates to the April 1999 congress of Luzhkov's new party were directly seeking financial support of some kind.[48] The Moscow mayor had also cultivated close ties with several major non-Sistema banks headquartered in the city, such as the Most Bank that was part of Gusinsky's Most Group, and utilized their regional networks to help develop political relationships.[49]

Luzhkov's post as the capital city's mayor endowed him with certain advantages in the sphere of mass media, as well. For one thing, his alliance with Most Group had the benefit of extending positive news coverage of the Mayor across many of Russia's regions through Most's NTV television network (Russia's third-largest) and publications like the daily newspaper *Segodnia*.[50] Taking to heart the immense power of nationwide television in getting Yeltsin reelected in 1996, Luzhkov sponsored the creation of a new TV network in June 1997 under the control of the Moscow city government. This network, known as TV Center, reached many major cities in Russia by the time of the 1999 election. The city also had influence in a number of major national newspapers, most of which were headquartered in Moscow.[51]

Aiming to make himself a "focal" candidate for partisan and presidential coalition-building, Luzhkov also used his high-profile status as Moscow mayor in the late 1990s to stake out a series of high-profile positions on national issues designed to build ideational capital, as described in Chapter 2. It is important here to recall the special emphasis he put on his opposition to the Yeltsin government, in particular the corruption that he said permeated the government and many of its policies, such as privatization.

Luzhkov set about in mid-1998 to launch a party project built upon this coalition-crafting and reputation-building, institutionalizing and arming the new party to do political battle in the 1999 Duma race and then, he hoped,

46 *Moscow Times*, April 27, 1999; *RFE/RL Newsline*, June 15, 1999.

47 *Novosti*, TV Center, June 25, 1999, 16:30 EDT.

48 *Moscow Times*, April 27, 1999.

49 See Johnson 2000, p. 122, and *RFE/RL Newsline* 2, no. 183, Part I, September 22, 1998.

50 *Argumenty i Fakty*, no. 18, April 1999, p. 15.

51 *Kommersant*, June 26, 1999; Leonid Bershidsky, "Media Watch: Luzhkov's Agitprop Empire," *Moscow Times*, August 14, 1998, JRL.

the presidential contest. In an irony that would be evident 18 months later, the initial reports on these initiatives stated that this movement would be called "Unity."[52] After travels to various regions during the fall of 1998, Luzhkov's team claimed promises of support from 20 regional leaders and now called the movement "Fatherland."[53]

Despite all of these efforts and resources, however, Luzhkov's claims of gubernatorial support turned out to be greatly exaggerated. Not a single governor actually lent his name to the organization's top organs, the political council and the central council, either at the party's founding congress in December 1998 or the party's second congress in April 1999.[54] Even the Luzhkov-oriented newspaper *Moskovskii Komsomolets* reported that Luzhkov looked "gloomy" at the April event because only four governors even bothered to show up.[55]

Why did Luzhkov, in some ways the most natural leader among governors and with plenty of economic and political leverage over the others, initially fail to build and lead a major coalition of provincial bosses? The answer takes us directly back to the collective action problems facing governors discussed above. Here we find the social choice and coordination problems to be particularly stark. As one anonymous governor put it, "No one wants to be a rank-and-file member of a Greek chorus, singing the praises of a candidate for the presidency. All the more so, if there are no kind of guarantees that this will be understood correctly."[56] The principal-agent problem was also clearly in evidence, as the bosses of other regions did not trust Luzhkov in his promises to represent their interests should he become their leader. This fear was exacerbated by a widespread belief that the economic "Moscow miracle" on which Luzhkov campaigned had come at their expense, with the capital's mayor taking advantage of his position at the center of the national economy to suck in resources that rightly should have gone to other provinces.[57] One representative of a provincial Fatherland branch told a reporter that local residents tended to react in the following way when asked about Luzhkov, known for his trademark headpiece: "Aaaa – that's the one in the cap who holds all the money in Moscow."[58]

While these collective action problems alone posed challenges for Luzhkov, it is not clear that they would have proven insurmountable had the Kremlin not been actively intervening to exploit them. Luzhkov's sizzling attacks on corruption and crime in the Yeltsin "Family's" inner

[52] *RFE/RL Newsline* 2, no. 143, Part I, July 28, 1998.

[53] *RFE/RL Newsline* 2, no. 237, Part I, December 10, 1998.

[54] *Uchreditel'nyi S'ezd Obshcherossiiskoi politicheskoi obshchestvennoi organizatsii "Otechestro"* (*Materialy*) (Moscow: Galeriia, 1998), pp. 71–9.

[55] *Moskovskii Komsomolets*, April 27, 1999, JRL.

[56] *Vremia MN*, February 23, 1999, p. 2.

[57] Colton 1999.

[58] *Nezavisimaia Gazeta*, April 27, 1999, pp. 1–3.

circle certainly gave reason for presidential insiders to fear the rise of the Moscow mayor. The vision of his gaining the support of a large number of governors in a bid for parliamentary and then presidential power was therefore a terrifying nightmare scenario for this group, one that they sought wholeheartedly to avoid.

One favorite tactic was for the Kremlin to support rival bids to form winning gubernatorial coalitions, coalitions that would cut Luzhkov and his allies out. Such efforts, supported either directly by the Kremlin or by financial-industrial groups closely associated with the it, included an effort to revive Our Home is Russia (seeking to shift its organizational base from the prime ministerial office that it had lost, with Chernomyrdin's firing, to governors' political machines) as well as such projects as the Russian People's Republican Party of Krasnoiarsk Governor and retired General Aleksandr Lebed,[59] the "My Fatherland" organization of Saratov Governor Dmitry Aiatskov,[60] the Voice of Russia movement of Samara Governor Konstantin Titov,[61] the Revival and Unity bloc of Kemerovo Governor Aman Tuleev,[62] and a project called "Rossiia" undertaken by the prime minister who served between May and August 1999 (Sergei Stepashin).[63] The latter attempt, which might seem to have been quite promising given its leadership by a sitting prime minister, was ultimately undercut by the Kremlin itself. Stepashin thus claimed to have won the support of some 48 governors, but averred that presidential administration chief Aleksandr Voloshin refused to give regional leaders his word that Stepashin would keep his job (and indeed Stepashin was replaced by Putin in early August 1999).[64]

Fatherland's Breakthrough: All Russia and the Primakov Factor

Amidst all this competition to unite governors and the Kremlin's attempts to subvert these efforts through countercoalitions, another governors' bloc emerged in the spring of 1999 that looked quite different from the others. This alliance, in which Tatarstan President Mintimer Shaimiev emerged as

59 *Komsomolskaia Pravda*, May 26, 1998, JRL; *Interfax*, May 25, 1998, JRL; *Jamestown Foundation Monitor*, July 29, 1998, JRL; *Boston Globe*, May 14, 1998, JRL; *Sovetskaia Rossiia*, June 16, 1998, JRL; *EWI Russian Regional Report* 4, no. 20, May 27, 1999.

60 *RFE/RL Newsline* 2, no. 227, Part I, November 24, 1998; *EWI Russian Regional Report* 4, no. 23, June 17, 1999.

61 *EWI Russian Regional Report* 4, no. 22, June 10, 1999; *Izvestiia*, April 30, 1999.

62 Circumstantial evidence of a Tuleev bloc–Kremlin tie can be found in *RFE/RL Newsline* 1, no. 127, Part I, September 29, 1997; *Kommersant-Vlast*, 1, June 8, 1999; and *RFE/RL Newsline*, February 16, 2000. See also *Nezavisimaia Gazeta*, June 8, 1999; *Vremia MN*, June 7, 1999. At times Tuleev denied that his bloc was created by governors, preferring to call it a movement "from below." See *Moskovskii Komsomolets*, June 7, 1999.

63 *Nezavisimaia Gazeta*, June 18, 1999; *Kommersant*, June 23, 1999.

64 Sergei Stepashin Interview, *Nezavisimaia Gazeta*, January 14, 2000.

the most prominent spokesman, included the leaders of such powerhouse regions as St. Petersburg, Tatarstan, and Bashkortostan under the title "All Russia." In some ways, All Russia resembled the Kremlin-backed countercoalitions noted above. For one thing, powerful economic structures partially owned by the Russian state played prominent roles in the bloc's formation, most prominently the oil giant LUKoil and the gas monopoly Gazprom.[65] Moreover, nearly all of the most visible All Russia governors had ties to these concerns.[66] But unlike the Kremlin countercoalitions, All Russia's leaders quickly took up anticorruption themes and raised other issues that resembled Luzhkov's rhetoric and were sure to worry Yeltsin and his inner circle of advisors.[67] Perhaps most intriguingly, as early as February 1999, just as the bloc was first emerging, Shaimiev had called for Primakov to lead it.[68] Since Primakov was prime minister at the time, it is at least possible that he was the "Kremlin" figure mobilizing the oil industry behind All Russia, as a newspaper controlled by one of Primakov's key enemies did speculate.[69] Primakov's tenure was notable in part for prosecutions of major Yeltsin business allies, notably Boris Berezovsky, whom the popular prime minister reportedly brought to "the verge of annihilation" before Primakov was unceremoniously fired by Yeltsin.[70] In fact, a key figure in the bloc's leadership, the head of the Duma deputy group Russia's Regions, Oleg Morozov, voted to impeach Yeltsin in May 1999 after Primakov was removed.[71] All Russia thus appears to have owed its existence far more to forces outside of Yeltsin's inner circle than inside it.

Whereas Luzhkov courted this group from the beginning, he wound up succeeding only when he had borrowed a page from Martin Van Buren's political history. All Russia's governors were initially reluctant to join with Luzhkov's Fatherland since, as Shaimiev reported, they feared the dominance of Moscow in any coalition.[72] Luzhkov achieved his breakthrough by recruiting Primakov, who alone among Russian politicians prior to September 1999 had the combination of administrative and ideational capital necessary to become Russia's Andrew Jackson.

Primakov owed this status first of all to a carefully crafted image as an intelligent, pragmatic, cautious leader, seasoned in years of service in Russia's

[65] *RFE/RL Newsline* 2, no. 228, Part I, November 25, 1998; *Kommersant*, May 25, 1999; *RFE/RL* [*Newsline*], no. 20, January 31, 1994.

[66] *EWI Russian Regional Report* 4, no. 22, June 10, 1999; *Izvestiia*, May 29, 1998, in *Turkistan Newsletter*, BUSINESS: v. 98: 083-02-June-1998.

[67] *EWI Russian Regional Report* 4, no. 20, May 27, 1999.

[68] *Vremia MN*, February 23, 1999, p. 2.

[69] *Nezavisimaia Gazeta*, February 17, 1999 pp. 1, 3. This paper was controlled by Boris Berezovsky.

[70] Andrei Kolesnikov, "Change of Elites," *New Times*, November 1, 1999.

[71] *EWI Russian Regional Report* 4, no. 21, June 3, 1999.

[72] *EWI Russian Regional Report* 4, no. 26, July 8, 1999.

most prestigious foreign-policy institutes (IMEMO and the Institute for Oriental Studies) and then as chief of Russia's counterintelligence agencies and ultimately foreign minister in the late 1990s. His professionalism and avoidance of electoral politics in the post-Soviet era meant that he had alienated neither left nor right even though he was widely viewed as a moderate leftist. This style of leadership, combined with his reputation as a "clean" politician, led none other than the liberal Yabloko leader Yavlinsky to propose Primakov as the "only" possible prime minister capable of holding the country's political forces together in the wake of the August 1998 financial crisis.[73] Primakov, upon being confirmed to this post, proceeded to offer important ministerial posts to members of all major political parties in the Duma at the time.[74] While in government, his central achievement was avoiding the further collapse of the economy after August 1998, an extremely popular feat at the time.[75] When the ruble devaluation of August 1998 began actually to benefit some Russian producers in early 1999, his political star began to rise significantly. As this happened, he started issuing statements challenging the authority of the Yeltsin administration, including calls for the president to cede some powers to the government.[76] By March 1999, Russia's leading polling agency (VTsIOM) found that a potential "Primakov Bloc" would have gained 19 percent of the Duma vote had an election been held at that time, putting this hypothetical party second only to the Communists.[77] His popularity continued to grow after Yeltsin fired him, for (reportedly) fear of his presidential ambitions.[78] By July 1999, the highly respected Public Opinion Foundation found that Primakov was leading the presidential polls and was the politician whom Russians most trusted politically.[79]

Luzhkov's master stroke was to accept the role of second fiddle and aggressively recruit Primakov as a way of cementing the alliance with All Russia.[80] Primakov was acceptable to the All Russia governors both because he was seen as highly capable of winning the presidential race and because he did not personally represent a region to which he might give favorable treatment. The deal was consummated on August 17, 1999, when Primakov made his dramatic announcement that he would lead a united Fatherland–All Russia bloc for the December Duma elections. This bloc then became a center of gravity attracting all manner of small organizations, a few of

73 *RFE/RL Newsline* 2, no. 173, Part I, September 8, 1998.

74 Yevgeny Primakov, *Vosem' Mesiatsev Plius*... (Moscow: Mysl 2001) pp. 14–23; *RFE/RL Newsline* 2, no. 190, Part I, October 1, 1998.

75 *Ekho Moskvy*, radio, October 28, 1998, 18:15; *Washington Post*, September 14, 1998; *RFE/RL Newsline* 2, no. 184, Part I, September 23, 1998.

76 *RFE/RL Newsline*, July 14, 1999.

77 Maksim Sokolov, *Izvestiia*, May 20, 1999.

78 *Kommersant*, June 15, 1999.

79 First Channel (Moscow), July 31, 1999.

80 *Moskovskii Komsomolets*, April 27, 1999, JRL.

which Luzhkov and Primakov took on board. With Yeltsin in ill health and experiencing very low approval ratings, and with no other propresidential candidate polling even close to 10 percent in the polls, most observers in August 1999 saw Fatherland–All Russia as the favorite in the Duma race of December 1999 and Primakov as the man to beat for the presidential election scheduled for mid-2000.

The Kremlin Strikes Back: The Rise of Unity

The fact that these disparate, ambitious, and powerful politicians had actually managed to come together against the Yeltsin team, and so forcefully, sounded alarms throughout the Kremlin. Despite the Communist Party's failure to bring Primakov into their fold, even its leadership began suggesting that it could back Primakov in the presidential race should he perform sufficiently well in the Duma contest and promise to give more power to the parliament.[81] Most worrisome to Yeltsin's coterie, however, were suggestions and even outright declarations that even the president himself could be prosecuted for wrongdoings committed during his tenure.[82] The extended Yeltsin "Family" was usually said to include powerful insiders who had effectively run the country during Yeltsin's long bouts with debilitating illness, alcoholism, and depression. Chief among them were Yeltsin's daughter, Tatiana Diachenko; oil magnate Roman Abramovich; "oligarch" and PFIG owner Boris Berezovsky; presidential administration chief Aleksandr Voloshin; powerful Railroads Minister and erstwhile First Deputy Prime Minister Nikolai Aksenenko; and other senior administration officials, including Igor Shabdurasulov and Valentin Yumashev.[83] Each of these figures owed their massive opportunities for wealth and/or power largely to Yeltsin and stood to lose everything and to face possible criminal prosecution should the Primakov–Luzhkov team capture power.

Luzhkov sensed the danger in pushing the Kremlin to desperation, but also saw the electoral benefit to be gained from continuing to attack its corruption. Thus, while roundly criticizing the administration generally, he proposed various ways of providing Yeltsin (although Yeltsin alone) future security. For example, in June 1999 he suggested that all retiring presidents should become members for life of the Federation Council, a status that would grant them immunity from criminal prosecution.[84] Themselves unprotected, many of Yeltsin's closest advisors and officials began devising ways to bring down the Fatherland–All Russia juggernaut. Their first set of

[81] *Kommersant*, July 9, 1999.

[82] For example, see: Yevgeny Primakov, interview, *Ekho Moskvy* (radio) 15:35, October 1, 1999, in Kremlin Package.

[83] *Kommersant*, June 8, 1999.

[84] *RFE/RL Newsline*, June 10, 1999.

attempts, trying to undermine gubernatorial cooperation by proposing multiple counter-coalitions for governors, had failed as of August 1999. Their more aggressive efforts in the fall of 1999 proved much more effective and included new ways of exploiting governors' collective action problems. They involved several distinct but interdependent tactics, outlined below.[85]

De-Focalization: The Mass Media Assault

During the summer of 1999, Kremlin officials began a series of moves to prepare for a media war. The aim was not simply a negative campaign to reduce the popularity of Fatherland–All Russia in the electorate, but, critically, to destroy the focal point that had allowed Russia's powerful governors to agree on a coalition to capture the Kremlin. The ultimate target was Primakov, but the Kremlin's strategy was first to blast Luzhkov so as to turn him into a burdensome, malodorous albatross around the former prime minister's neck.

The centerpiece of the Kremlin assault proved to be the creation of what could be loosely translated as the "Sergei Dorenko Show" on the state-controlled First Channel network and the decision to pit it directly against the NTV network's famous news analysis program, *Itogi* ("Final Analyses"), seen to be sympathetic to Fatherland–All Russia. Despite the fact that Itogi had long dominated this Sunday evening news analysis niche, the Dorenko Show immediately made waves with its blistering attacks on Luzhkov. On the basis of this political spectacle, it soon actually began to win the ratings battle when Itogi did not respond with equally riveting material. During the weeks of the campaign, Dorenko, in his trademark smirking baritone, lambasted Luzhkov for alleged misdeeds ranging from the plausible (that there is corruption in Luzhkov's Moscow bureaucracy), to the outrageous (that Luzhkov was accomplice to the murder of U.S. businessman Paul Tatum), to the just plain ridiculous (that he had ties to the deadly Japanese Aum Shrinrikyo cult). Nightly news programs on the state-owned First Channel and RTR echoed these themes, only slightly toning down the vitriol.[86] While Primakov was a more difficult target, his association with Luzhkov came to damage his standing and then the direct assaults on him began, depicting him as a relic of the past and a clandestine and ruthless spymaster. In one of the most notorious attacks, one First Channel report claimed that Primakov was terminally ill.[87]

This media assault was devastatingly successful. The reputable VTsIOM polling agency found that the percentage of people planning to vote for Fatherland–All Russia dropped from 22 percent in September to just 12 percent in November. During the same period, Primakov's support in the

[85] For more detail on each, see Hale 2004a.
[86] For one description, see the report in *Moscow Times*, December 11, 1999.
[87] *Moscow Times*, December 11, 1999.

presidential contest plummeted from 19 to 9 percent and Luzhkov's crashed from 10 to just 2 percent.[88]

Counter-Focalization: The Grooming of Mr. Putin

To take full advantage of the renewed collective action problems facing Russian governors who might want to band together to capture Kremlin spoils, Yeltsin loyalists concentrated on finding a new political figure who could potentially serve as a "counter focal point" to Primakov and Luzhkov. While Yeltsin had replaced Primakov with Stepashin as prime minister in May 1999, he makes clear in his memoirs that he never saw Stepashin as more than a transition figure while the real heir (Vladimir Putin) was being groomed.[89] On August 9, Yeltsin fired Stepashin and put Putin in his place. At the time, the vast majority of observers saw Putin as a sure loser.[90] Few people even knew who he was, and his presidential ratings were at a paltry 2 percent shortly after his appointment.[91] Kremlin officials nevertheless believed in his promise, having come to see him as loyal and tough through his service as the Federal Security Service (former KGB) chief and the holder of other executive offices since 1996.[92] More specifically, Putin's experience as the first deputy head of the Yeltsin administration in charge of dealing with the provinces gave him a chance to demonstrate his willingness to put pressure on Russian governors disliked by the Kremlin, something Yeltsin hints Stepashin was too soft to do.[93] As of the summer of 1999, one of his greatest assets, however, was not having any significant negative baggage due to his being a virtual political unknown. But even after he was installed as prime minister and anointed Yeltsin's "heir" by the president himself, Kremlin insiders were still hedging their bets when speaking to outsiders. As late as October 13, 1999, Shabdurasulov, first deputy head of the presidential administration, publicly stated that the administration was not ready to back Putin or any other candidate at that time.[94] It took a crisis in Chechnya and Putin's decisive reaction to turn most Russians and Kremlin cadres into true believers.

[88] Hale 1999c.

[89] Yeltsin 2000, pp. 311–12.

[90] For example, the leading Russian political experts who wrote predictive columns in Hale 1999b did not even see fit to mention Putin as someone who might influence the Duma race. Even in the October 1999 issue (no. 3), commentators did not give him much chance in a presidential bid unless he aligned himself with other political forces.

[91] Hale 1999b.

[92] For example, see Yeltsin's (2000) remarks and Berezovsky's interview in *Vedomosti*, March 24, 2000.

[93] *Komsomolskaia Pravda*, May 26, 1998, JRL; *RFE/RL Newsline* 2, no. 142, Part I, July 27, 1998; *RFE/RL Newsline* 2, no. 99, Part I, May 26, 1998; Yeltsin 2000.

[94] *Segodnia*, October 13, 1999.

The Apartment Bombings of September 1999 and the New Invasion of Chechnya

In August 1999, an absolutely wild set of events started to unfold that soon transformed an apparent Yeltsinite nebbish into a presidential juggernaut. First, in early August, rogue Chechen warlords invaded the neighboring Russian province of Dagestan, declaring their aim to carve out an "Islamic state" in the region. After Russian forces repelled this incursion, on September 9 and then again on September 13, terrorist bombs decimated two large, working-class apartment buildings in Moscow in the middle of the night, timing clearly intended to maximize casualties. Two other apartment bombs were detonated in smaller Russian cities, leaving a total of over 300 innocent residents dead. The terror that then engulfed Russian society was not unlike that which seized the United States after the attacks of September 11, 2001. Putin responded by publicly blaming the secessionist republic of Chechnya for the bombings and ordering a large-scale military operation gradually to seize control of Chechen territory. Average Russian citizens, tired of inaction in the face of seemingly relentless national decline, rallied enthusiastically around their new and decisive leader. When Putin invoked Russian gangland slang to aver that he would "whack" Chechen terrorists "in the john" if he found them there, much of the public took comfort in someone they saw as finally taking action to restore security and order. Indeed, VTsIOM's surveys found that in late November 1999, at the same time people supported the military action by a ratio of over 2:1, more people than not would also have supported a *halt* to the war *if Putin had proposed it* (48 percent to 42 percent).[95] In fact, surveys consistently found throughout the fall of 1999 that only a minority of the population supported preventing Chechen secession at any cost and that a larger share would have either been happy with or at least tolerated independence for Chechnya.[96] What people liked in Putin, then, was not so much the war itself as the fact that he proved to be someone willing to do something dramatic in response to the September terrorist tragedies. Thus, by December his support in the presidential race had skyrocketed to 51 percent (see Figure 5.1) and his approval ratings were some 80 percent as early as November.

95 VTsIOM, "Press-Vypusk 6 Dekabria 1999 goda," www.wciom.ru/EDITION/press15.htm, accessed December 8, 1999. In keeping with VTsIOM's standard methodology, the poll included 1,600 adult respondents in 83 population points in 31 regions of the country. The margin of error is estimated to be 3.8 percent. The survey was taken November 26–9, 1999.

96 In the December poll, 11 percent supported a new option that was presented to respondents: "the independence of Chechnya has already come about," which also implies acquiescence, putting the overall "acquiescence" figure at 59 percent. See VTsIOM, *VTsIOM na Polit.ru*, January 10, 2000, 12:42, www.polit.ru/documents/160134.html, accessed January 10, 2000.

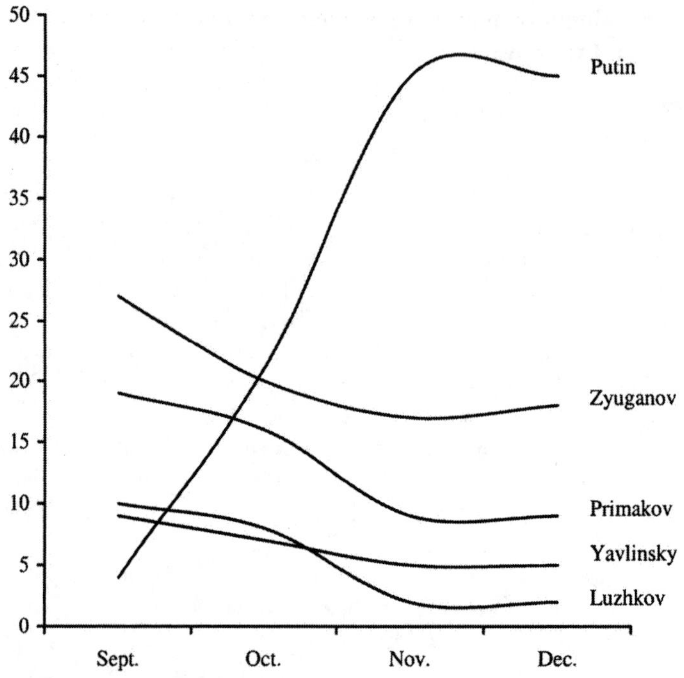

FIGURE 5.1. Presidential ratings September–December 1999 (VTsIOM surveys)

A Decoy Party: The Founding of the Unity Bloc

The coup de grace in this struggle proved to be the last-minute, October 1999 creation of Unity, which was intended primarily as a decoy party designed to help divert governors who were being convinced or cajoled or coerced to abandon Fatherland–All Russia in the December 1999 Duma race. With Putin firmly in place as a "counter focal point" and with the enemy's focal points disintegrating under Dorenko's heat, Unity was important as an electoral counter-coalition of governors that could "outbid" Fatherland–All Russia for the support of enough governors to keep the latter from finishing strongly in the Duma race. A poor Duma showing by Luzhkov and Primakov, it was believed, would weaken their presidential bids. Any Unity success beyond this "anti-party" task would be but icing on the electoral cake.

Indeed, the Kremlin initially had little reason to believe that Unity could be anything more useful than a weapon in an electoral struggle. Past Kremlin efforts to create true parties of power had failed miserably, with former Prime Minister Yegor Gaidar's Russia's Choice garnering a crushingly disappointing 16 percent in 1993 and Prime Minister Chernomyrdin's Our Home is Russia netting a humiliating 10 percent in 1995. With Yeltsin's popularity at a longstanding low, and with Putin remaining a political unknown in late September, there was little reason for the Kremlin to suspect while Unity was being created that a new attempt at a party of power would fare much better.

Spearheaded by first deputy presidential chief of staff Shabdurasulov and "oligarch" Berezovsky, Unity's founding idea was to create a new kind of bloc that not only mimicked Fatherland–All Russia's "can-do" campaign but even outdid it in providing politics without politicians, professionalism without ideological baggage. In the words of Primorskii Krai governor Yevgeny Nazdratenko, an original Unity supporter, "The ideology of Unity is the lack of any kind of ideology."[97] Despite this bravado, Unity's leaders did stress some important issues on the campaign trail, but these were often those emphasized by Fatherland–All Russia. Most critically, this meant Fatherland–All Russia's emphasis on regional autonomy, a key element holding together the Luzhkov-Primakov coalition of governors.[98] The secretary of Fatherland–All Russia's coordination council, clearly vexed by Unity's strategy, called its regional policies the "purest plagiarism" and decried its effort to "confuse" voters and draw votes away from his party.[99] Among unity's issue positions, however, a slight emphasis on free-market economics owing to its support for the government contrasted significantly with Fatherland–All Russia, which put a statist industrial policy strategy at the center of its public effort.

In an attempt to appeal directly to governors' machines themselves, the bloc's top candidate, Emergencies Minister Sergei Shoigu, visited many provinces run by core All Russia governors, including those of Ingushetiia, Tatarstan, Bashkortostan, and St. Petersburg.[100] He even presented Tatarstan's Shaimiev with an award of distinction from his ministry.[101] Shoigu also made special efforts to win over those governors who had been part of the Our Home is Russia party through both a travel itinerary and a phone campaign.[102]

That the party was not expected actually to win many votes is reflected in how governors initially treated it. While the project team early on boasted signatures of support from 39 governors, only one governor (and from a relatively minor region at that) proved willing to place his name on the Unity party list at Unity's October 3 founding congress. This stood in stark contrast to Fatherland–All Russia, which featured major regional figures such as Luzhkov and Shaimiev.[103] Moreover, governors generally did not

97 *Nezavisimaia Gazeta*, October 2, 1999.
98 *Vremia MN*, October 4, 1999.
99 Oleg Morozov, *Segodnia*, October 4, 1999.
100 *Izvestiia*, December 1, 1999.
101 *Polit.Ru*, November 29, 1999, 18:08.
102 Vladimir Ryzhkov, interview, *Moskovskii Komsomolets*, October 8, 1999, pp. 1, 3.
103 Colton and McFaul 2000, p. 205.

even delegate senior associates for the party list, instead tapping minor functionaries at the subregional *raion* or even village level along with other little-known supporters.[104] The other type of Unity candidate might be categorized as the "random celebrity," ranging from an astronaut to a television host.[105] As the effects of Dorenko, the apartment bombings, and Putin's endorsement were increasingly felt, however, Unity's fortunes rose and governors began backing away from Fatherland–All Russia and either hedging their bets or supporting Unity. In the end, only a handful of governors remained true to Fatherland–All Russia, as can be seen from the facts that it received over 30 percent of the vote in just seven regions (mostly where its original backers were governors) but averaged under 8 percent in the rest of the country. Unity on the otherhand, won at least 30 percent (suggesting significant gubernatorial support) in 29 different regions and won under 8 percent (indicating an absence of gubernatorial support) in only two.

Unity's stunning success, which an openly gleeful Shabdurasulov declared a "revolution" and a "colossal breakthrough" after seeing the results, delivered a crushing blow to Fatherland–All Russia, left with just 13 percent of the ballots cast after having projected a strong plurality if not an outright majority just months before.[106] While Luzhkov had given up his own presidential ambitions earlier in the fall, Primakov saw the writing on the wall after the election and agreed to serve quietly in the Duma rather than seek higher political office. With Unity did in fact come victory.

SCARED STRAIGHT: THE RISE OF UNITED RUSSIA AND PUTIN'S PARTY REFORMS

While in retrospect it is easy to see an "inevitable" pattern of the incumbent winning the presidency and his party succeeding in the Duma, Putin and Unity were in fact quite lucky to have won in 1999. Both Putin and Unity were far behind in the polls at the outset of the 1999–2000 campaign season and few elites took them seriously. But they overcame the challenge thanks in large part to a cataclysmic chance event and opponents' strategic blunders. The cataclysmic chance event was the bombing of Moscow apartment buildings that rallied the population around their little-known, novice prime minister after he launched his major military operation in Chechnya. It was Putin's endorsement, after all, that sent Unity's rating skyward. The strategic blunders were those of Fatherland–All Russia, which due to overconfidence and poor organization failed to use its own massive resources to respond adequately to opponents' attacks, as described in Chapter 2. This allowed Putin's and Unity's popularity to soar unchecked despite obvious

[104] *Segodnia*, October 5, 1999; *Izvestiia*, October 16, 1999; *Vremia MN*, October 15, 1999.

[105] *Segodnia*, October 5, 1999; Andrei Stepanov, *Izvestiia*, October 5, 1999; *St. Petersburg Times*, December 21, 1999.

[106] *Moscow Times*, December 21, 1999.

ties to such unpopular figures as Berezovsky and indeed the Kremlin, which was widely seen as corrupt at the time. Had the election occurred in a more normal environment and had Fatherland–All Russia hired more ruthless and savvy campaign managers, observers might have been hailing Russia's first turnover of presidential power from an incumbent group to an opposition group. Moreover, the Kremlin discovered, perhaps to its own chagrin, that *a progovernment political party had proven essential to pulling off this victory.*

All of this strongly recalls Shefter's argument, discussed earlier, that conservative parties sought to mobilize the masses only once they were forced to do so by the rise of strong, mass-organized socialist opposition parties. During the mid-1990s and especially during the 1996 presidential contest, the Russian incumbents' chief opposition was the Communist Party, but this party was saddled with so much ideological baggage from the Soviet period that it was highly vulnerable to attack.[107] As McFaul has argued, Yeltsin's Chubais-led campaign team recognized that they could defeat the Communists by framing the choice as one between an unpleasant past and the chance of a brighter future, by mobilizing the vast resources of the superpresidency to deliver the vote, and, indeed, by making sure its framing of the choice predominated in the media.[108] The party of power at that time, Our Home is Russia, played almost no role in this incumbent victory and executive-branch authorities thus felt little need to bolster it. Indeed, after Yeltsin's 1996 victory, Kremlin insiders sometimes boasted that with their financial resources and control of TV, they could elect "anybody" president of Russia.[109]

But by 1999, the Kremlin found itself up against a surprise opponent that it needed a party to beat. In haste, it created this party, but the blind luck that had made it all work was surely not lost on Kremlin strategists. Indeed, as Shefter's logic would lead us to expect, Putin's new team began to act much more aggressively than the Kremlin had ever done before to accomplish two things. First, it moved forcefully to build a propresidential party with (it hoped) sufficient administrative and even ideational capital to head off or at least resist any future such challenge. This involved turning Unity into United Russia. Having a strong party already in place to rally party substitutes and popular support around an anointed successor would greatly increase the chances that the presidential administration could get its chosen one elected whenever Putin decided to leave office.[110] Second, Russia's leadership enacted a series of reforms that sought increasingly to squeeze out party substitutes and give political parties an advantage in the electoral market. Naturally, United Russia was set to become the prime beneficiary.

107 Hanson 2003.

108 McFaul 1997a.

109 *Los Angeles Times*, January 4, 2000, JRL.

110 After his inauguration in 2000, he repeatedly promised to serve only two four-year terms, the maximum allowed by Russian law at the time.

From Unity to United Russia

The very decision to back the same party in more than one Duma election was itself a landmark move by the Russian executive branch. As described earlier, Russian presidents had opted to trade in their old models for new ones in both previous rounds of elections, those in 1995 and 1999. This new stability between 1999 and 2003 clearly facilitated the increase in the degree to which people identified the party with the incumbent president. As argued above, this helped produce a significant increase in the extent to which voters attributed strong issues stands (those of the president) to Russia's party of power and credited it with responsibility for the state of affairs in Russia, both economically and politically.[111]

Unity's sponsors wasted no time beginning the work of turning it into a robust party for the next election cycle. Its legal existence was initially as a bloc formally constituted by a set of tiny preexisting organizations, a tactic that allowed it to be registered for the 1999 election despite having been created less than three months before the voting. After achieving its successful election result, party leaders met on December 27, 1999, and agreed that they would soon establish Unity formally as a "movement," a legal category giving it certain organizational rights. During January and February, organizers sanctioned provincial party conferences to elect delegates to a national party congress, which took place on February 27, 2000. This party congress officially founded the "movement" Unity, which Russian authorities quickly registered.

Far more aggressively than either Our Home is Russia or Russia's Choice before it, Unity's leaders sought to build a party of power with highly developed local party infrastructure. This was made clear by the movement's early decision to turn into a full-fledged "party" as defined formally by Russian law. Speaking at a party congress in October 2000, Shoigu claimed his organization had already signed up 200,000 members and had created hundreds of local organizations.[112] Trading on Putin's popularity and the vast administrative capital of the presidency, Shoigu was able to assert in December 2000 that Unity had cobbled together enough deputies in regional legislatures to form deputy groups or fractions in 47 of them.[113] The party even began to craft a program in late 2000 based on ideas of economic reform being pursued by Putin. That this was not purely window-dressing is indicated by some low-level conflict that leftist delegates from various regions of Russia initiated in response.[114]

In 2001, the party's main task became absorbing what remained of Fatherland–All Russia. As an appetizer, Unity swallowed Our Home is

[111] See also Colton and Hale 2004.

[112] Misha Fishman, *Polit.Ru*, October 31, 2000, 10:27.

[113] *Kommersant*, December 1, 2000, p. 2.

[114] Misha Fishman, *Polit.Ru*, October 31, 2000, 10:27.

Russia when Chernomyrdin officially dissolved that party in February 2001.[115] In the spring of that same year, Unity's Duma fraction joined with those of Fatherland–All Russia and two registered groups of independent deputies (People's Deputy and Russia's Regions) to create a "group of four" coalition in the parliament.[116] The process was consummated in February 2002, when Fatherland–All Russia, subdued and docile ever since its 1999 defeat, formally dissolved itself to merge with Unity (which also dissolved itself) in forming the United Russia Party.[117]

Showing its great concern to maintain electoral control over the governors in federal elections, the Kremlin used the new authority over governors gained in Putin's above-mentioned centralizing federal reforms to ensure that they backed United Russia and United Russia alone. The envoys that Putin had installed atop the new federal okrugs were charged with coordinating much of this process, helping to recruit candidates, convincing them to run on United Russia's label or not at all, ensuring that propresidential candidates did not compete against each other in the same districts, and channeling resources to the preferred candidates.[118]

These efforts were, on the whole, extremely successful in keeping governors generally on board with United Russia. Perhaps the most widely reported evidence is that its 2003 party list contained 29 of the most powerful governors in Russia, far more than any party had claimed in previous Duma elections.[119] Even more dramatic evidence of United Russia's command over governors' machines in the 2003 Duma elections comes from the 2003–4 survey: Forty-six percent of all respondents believed their governor backed a party in the election and of these, a stunning 83 percent reported that this party was United Russia. Thus, although the Kremlin did not make major efforts to force governors to run as United Russia nominees in gubernatorial elections, it was quite determined to get them to back United Russia nominees for the Duma and enjoyed a great deal of success in this regard.

Putin's Party System Reforms

Almost immediately after Unity's 1999 Duma election success, the Kremlin began preparing a series of reforms that would dramatically increase the role of parties in virtually all major sets of elections and favor the largest parties, of which United Russia was obviously intended to be one. One

115 *RFE/RL Newsline*, February 28, 2001. While Chernomyrdin joined Unity, Vladimir Ryzhkov did not.

116 *Polit.Ru*, April 17, 2001, 13:50.

117 *RFE/RL Newsline*, February 11, 2002.

118 Interview with Volga Federal Okrug official in charge of relations with social groups and parties, April 22, 2003; Hale 2005b; *Kommersant-Vlast*, May 12–18, 2003, p. 15.

119 Governors typically decline their Duma seats after winning them so that they retain their gubernatorial posts; their Duma seats go to the next in line from their party.

such reform was to weaken governors, a major party substitute, through the aforementioned centralizing reforms and the May 2000 creation of seven federal okrugs led by envoys that Putin appointed. These envoys were soon assigned to encourage and pressure elites of all kinds, including governors and business barons, to work through United Russia for the 2003 Duma race.[120] In July 2001, Putin signed the law "On Political Parties," which imposed stricter conditions (such as membership requirements) for parties to meet before being eligible to compete in elections. This law had small practical effect, however, as all major parties had little trouble fulfilling the new legalistic demands.[121] More significantly, though, the law provided for public financing of parties depending upon how well they performed in Duma elections; this was clearly intended to bolster the position of Russia's biggest parties. In mid-2005, the scale of this public financing was raised.

In the first central move to enhance the prospects of national parties in the provinces, the Duma in June 2002 approved amendments to what is usually called the Law on Voter Rights that worked to parties' advantage. The most important change was to require, starting in July 2003, that at least half of one house of regional legislatures be elected in proportional representation (PR) contests among party lists and that only registered national parties would be allowed to compete. Since only a handful of provinces had previously instituted PR systems, and since none of these restricted competition to national parties, this was a major reform that guaranteed Russia's major parties greater representation in these regional organs. As was reported earlier, United Russia was by far the biggest beneficiary in the first set of regional legislative elections to take place under the new law, although the Communists also gained significant representation in multiple regions. A change in the Law on the Election of Deputies to the State Duma instituted a change designed to weed out weaker parties, raising the threshold for winning a Duma fraction in the party-list competition from 5 percent of the vote to 7 percent, effective in 2007. This law, however, included a provision that the four top parties would automatically win Duma seats even if they did not make 7 percent of the vote.

Putin called for another wave of reforms in September 2004, characterizing the long-discussed moves as a response to the horrific Beslan school hostage tragedy and other terrorist acts in which some 400 people perished. One of these changes, which went into effect as of 2005, eliminated the set of elections that had been least penetrated by major parties, gubernatorial elections. Instead, as of 2005, the Russian president now nominates gubernatorial candidates for approval or rejection by provincial legislatures. Since the provincial legislatures are to be significantly penetrated by national parties according to the amended Law on Voter Rights, the post-Beslan reforms

[120] For more on the federal reforms and parties, see Hale 2005b.
[121] Ibid.

are likely to give these parties a more significant role in choosing governors than they had enjoyed in the past.[122] This reform would also have the obvious effect of giving the president greater influence over governors, thereby making it less likely that a governor would operate independently of any future parties of power, or at least that such independent activity would be in opposition to such a party.

The second major change Putin requested in September 2004 (and signed into law in May 2005) would also work to strengthen national parties' advantage over party substitutes. This change eliminates the district half of Russia's Duma elections altogether, making the Duma an organ entirely chosen in PR competition among party lists as of 2007. Interestingly, this reform in some ways can be seen as working against United Russia's own narrow interests and putting other parties in a stronger position. As discussed in Chapters 2 and 3, the bulk of United Russia's supermajority in the Duma elected in 2003 came from district elections; had Putin's proposed changes been in effect for the 2003 voting, United Russia would have claimed only a bare majority of seats and not the constitutional supermajority it actually commanded. Nevertheless, the reform was clearly intended to increase the control of the central party leadership over its own Duma members, none of whom will now have a district base of support to rely on (or be influenced by) in breaking with the party line. Party substitutes will thus be denied the ability to peddle ballot access directly and will have to support individual candidates in more subtle and less reliable ways, such as lobbying party leaders to include candidates on a party list or withholding support from a party in order to affect electoral outcomes.

CONCLUSION

Thus, while Putin continued to resist calls to join United Russia himself as of summer 2005,[123] he endorsed it in 2003 more unequivocally than any president had ever before endorsed a party of power during a Duma Campaign. More importantly, his actions in office have consistently worked to tilt Russia's electoral market in favor of parties over party substitutes. All this is quite consistent with the logic outlined in this volume. Prior to 1999, the Kremlin acted upon the strong incentives it faced to avoid creating a presidential party, thereby ensuring that a major gap existed in Russia's party system. It was the Kremlin's close call in 1999 with Fatherland–All Russia, which it needed a party of its own to defeat, that spurred it to take party-building seriously. While there was some evidence that an increase

122 See Golosov 2003 for a uniquely insightful discussion of governor–legislature relations prior to this reform.

123 At Unity's founding congress, for example, Shoigu called on Putin to lead the party. See *Polit.Ru*, February 28, 2000, 09:35.

in the value of parties' ideational capital was driving a rise in the status of parties relative to party substitutes in the electorate, this rise was quite modest and was not reflected in most major sets of elections in Russia during the Putin era. Instead, Russia strongly appeared as of 2005 to be getting its party system from above, with United Russia in good position to be a highly dominant party.

6

Conclusion

The Market Model and Theories of Parties, National Integration, and Transitions from Authoritarian Rule

The model of electoral markets introduced in Chapter 1 has thus provided us with the intellectual tools to solve the puzzle Russia has posed to comparative theories of party system development. In post-Soviet Russia, parties have stubbornly failed to dominate the political system for nearly a decade and a half, although the state has more recently pushed through a set of reforms that enhance the role of parties in Russian politics. The key has been to think of parties as one kind of producer of goods and services that can help candidates win votes in elections and to think of candidates as the consumers of these goods. Market theory shows that the degree to which one supplier dominates the market is not purely a function of the supply and demand for that supplier's particular products, but that its market share also depends on the availability of substitutes for these goods. This volume has identified multiple kinds of political organization that can function as party substitutes, ranging from the nonpartisan governors' political machines in Russia to political action committees in the twentieth-century United States. Whether parties successfully dominate a political system, closing out the country's electoral market, thus hinges critically on factors that affect the balance between parties and party substitutes in a country. Some important such factors are found to be historical legacies and transition paths that influence the relative quality and volume of political capital available to parties and substitutes. They are also found to be broad institutional contexts that set rules of competition and, even more importantly, that define major actors with the power to alter election rules and otherwise strategically intervene in electoral markets. This logic not only helps us explain the Russian puzzle, but guides us to advances in comparative social science theories of party system development, national integration in federal systems, and transitions from authoritarian rule. The pages that remain address these contributions.

THE PUZZLE OF RUSSIA IN COMPARATIVE PERSPECTIVE

The model of electoral markets provides an explanation for why the hypothetical crystal ball with which this book began found such strange patterns in Russia. Russia's major parties were found to have developed extensive organization, significant loyalties among the citizenry, and the capacity to mobilize critical electoral support for their candidates by at least the late 1990s. At the same time, however, the only elections that these parties dominated consistently as late as 2005 were those for the national parliament, and even there non-major-party candidates won majorities of the district seats until 2003. In almost every electoral arena outside the Duma, the party-free images of Krasnoiarsk and Omsk looked as familiar as the St. Petersburg image of robust party competition that comparative theories of party development tended to expect. Most scholars have focused on only a subset of these phenomena and as a result many have taken stands that Russia either had "strong and growing" or "weak and stagnating" parties during this period. But both arguments can be true in an important sense because parties were not faced with a political vacuum into which they could automatically expand as they gained organizational capacity, financial resources, and a positive reputation on important issues. Instead, Russian parties by the late 1990s confronted a crowded electoral field in which a motley mix of organizational forms competed for candidate affiliation. To expand its representation in a regional legislature, for example, a party often not only had to outcompete other parties but also needed to best slates of corporate agents or candidates backed by the powerful machines of provincial governors.

Just as new institutionalist approaches have looked to path-dependent legacies of the past to explain the emergence of markets in world history, so this volume was led to Russia's particular legacy of communism and its ensuing path of postcommunist transition to understand how this market came to be structured.[1] In particular, the preceding pages found that Russia's institutional structure of strong executive power at both the regional and provincial levels, a legacy of its patrimonial communist past, helped stack the deck in favor of party substitutes over parties in many organs of power. So powerful that they saw little need to take on the political risk involved in building even a true presidential party, Russia's chief executives also frequently destroyed opposition efforts to convert major party substitutes into parties capable of being dominant players in the market for electoral goods and services. The most noteworthy of the latter kind of efforts, Fatherland–All Russia, nevertheless surprised executive authorities and came very close to succeeding. It was defeated only when the Kremlin experienced a good deal of luck and, in a last-ditch effort, created a rival party (Unity) explicitly designed to deflate its opponent. Spooked by this

[1] North 1990; North and Thomas 1973.

near-defeat, Kremlin incumbents then turned avidly to building a fully party system in Russia and ensuring a prominent place in it for a beefed up version of Unity: United Russia. This, we recall, fits well with comparative experience as identified by Shefter: Europe's conservative parties tended to mobilize for mass party-building only after they began to face serious challenges from opposition parties. While Russia's superpresidency insulated its chief officeholders from such pressures through several national elections, or so these officeholders thought, in the end they too succumbed to this logic.

In the most general terms, though, the argument has been that superpresidential systems combined with resource-allocation legacies typical of postcommunist regimes tend to militate against party development because executive officeholders are less likely to believe they need to create parties for their own political survival. Moreover, this volume has found cause to believe that the creation of superpresidential systems and the most party-detrimental allocations of resources are strongly promoted (though not determined) by legacies of patrimonial communism. While a more rigorous cross-national test of these hypotheses and the more nuanced arguments of this volume will have to await further work, the more simple claims about superpresidentialism and communist legacies can be tested here in a preliminary way.

If this logic is correct, looking at the whole set of such cases, we should generally find that the degree to which parties dominate different countries' political systems is correlated with patrimonial communist legacies. Even more directly, we should find that those formerly patrimonial-communist countries that did in fact opt for presidential regimes were characterized by the lowest levels of party penetration. Table 6.1 reports the percentage of seats in parliament (or lower house thereof) won by independent (non-party-nominated) candidates in every Central-East European and former Soviet postcommunist country for which appropriate data were available and juxtaposes this information with each country's type of communist legacy and political regime. We clearly find the expected patterns. Overwhelmingly, the parliaments of post-patrimonial-communist countries with presidential systems (and almost all of these featured superpresidencies[2]) were the least penetrated by political parties. As expected, we also see that while patrimonial communist legacies are strongly correlated with low party penetration, the correlation is even stronger where presidential regimes resulted. Patrimonial communism, then, appears to have weighted the dice in favor of presidential regimes, which in turn tended to weaken party penetration of the polity.[3] Of course, there is a lot of variation left unexplained, including that within the patrimonial-presidential category. The present work hypothesizes that much of this variation is due to particular patterns of resource

[2] Fish 2001.

[3] These simple patterns also hold up to testing through regression analysis, but since the correlation is so obvious these results are not reported here.

TABLE 6.1. *Percentage of Seats in National Parliaments of Central-East European and Post-Soviet Countries Won by Independent Candidates Juxtaposed with Type of Communist Legacy and Regime Type*

Country	Type of Communist Legacy	Regime Type	Year of Election	Percentage of Parliamentary Seats Won by Independents
Belarus	Patrimonial	Presidential	2000	73.6
Kyrgyzstan	Patrimonial	Presidential	2000	69.5
Uzbekistan	Patrimonial	Presidential	1999	50.4
Kazakhstan	Patrimonial	Presidential	1999	44.2
Armenia	Patrimonial	Presidential	2003	28.2
Azerbaijan	Patrimonial	Presidential	2000	20.8
Ukraine	Patrimonial	Presidential	2002	20.7
Tajikistan	Patrimonial	Presidential	2000	15.9
Russia	Patrimonial	Presidential	2003	14.9
Georgia*	Patrimonial	Presidential	2004	9.3
Lithuania	National–Accommodative/Patrimonial	Semipresidential	2000	2.1
Albania	Patrimonial	Parliamentary	2001	1.4
Bulgaria	Patrimonial	Parliamentary	2001	0
Croatia	National–Accommodative	Semipresidential	2003	0
Czech Rep.	Bureaucratic–Authoritarian	Parliamentary	2002	0
Estonia	National–Accommodative/Patrimonial	Parliamentary	2003	0
Hungary	National–Accommodative	Parliamentary	2002	0
Latvia	National–Accommodative/Patrimonial	Parliamentary	2002	0
Macedonia	Patrimonial	Parliamentary	2002	0
Moldova	Patrimonial	Parliamentary	2001	0
Poland	Bureaucratic–Auth./National–Accomm.	Semipresidential	2001	0
Romania	Patrimonial	Semipresidential	2000	0
Slovakia	National–Accommodative/Patrimonial	Parliamentary	2002	0
Slovenia	National–Accommodative	Parliamentary	2000	0
Turkmenistan	Patrimonial	Presidential	1999	0

* Excludes 11 district seats reserved for MPs elected in Abkhazia in 1992 and who are allowed to keep their seats in the new parliament while Georgian elections cannot be held there.

Sources: Fish 2001; Kitschelt et al. 1999; CIA World Factbook 2004, updated September 14, 2004, http://www.cia.gov/cia/publications/factbook/fields/2101.html; Marina Popescu and Martin Hannavy, "Project on Political Transformation and the Electoral Process in Post-Communist Europe," University of Essex, http://www.essex.ac.uk/elections; OSCE Election Reports, Office for Democratic Institutions and Human Rights, http://www.osce.org/odihr/?page=elections&div=reports.

allocation resulting from different transition paths or to more contingent factors like the rise of Fatherland–All Russia and the Kremlin's reaction in Russia. But this hypothesis is advanced here only to suggest an agenda for future research.

THE MARKET MODEL AND THEORIES OF PARTY SYSTEM DEVELOPMENT

The more general electoral markets perspective from which the above argument springs can facilitate theory-building progress on other aspects of party system development applicable well beyond the postcommunist cases. For one thing, it provides a productive framework that unifies and helps us understand older theories but that allows for a broader range of theoretical advancements. Many existing approaches tend to focus on one piece of the puzzle and do not present an underlying logic that can theoretically encompass the other major pieces.[4] Some of the most important works have thus identified important factors that influence how party systems develop, most notably societal cleavages, electoral institutions, elite decisions on what options to give voters, the character of associational life, degrees of regime centralization, and historical legacies.[5] To think of party formation as the product of a market in which parties are suppliers and candidates (not voters) are consumers directs our attention to all of the aforementioned points as factors shaping the contours of a given electoral market. We are led to look at how these factors interrelate to influence the supply and demand for parties and, critically, party substitutes. For example, instead of assuming that cleavages naturally tend to become represented in parties and that the relative size of these cleavages interacts with institutions to determine which are represented, we are encouraged to think of a market by which candidates seek goods and services that help them connect with voters. Parties can be expected to form on the basis of cleavages when appeal to these cleavages is seen by party-building entrepreneurs and candidates to have the potential to win them valuable votes (factoring in institutions) and when particular entrepreneurs have the necessary starting political capital to launch such endeavors.

This focus on entrepreneurship and capital gives us new theoretical insight into precisely how particular cleavages translate into particular parties without resorting to functionalism or determinism. Very importantly, this

4 An important partial exception is the historical institutionalist literature on party systems addressed below.

5 Some important works include the following. Cleavages: Lipset and Rokkan 1967. Institutions: Cox 1997; Rae 1967; Taagepera and Shugart 1989. Elite supply: Rose and Munro 2002. Associational life: Chhibber 2001. Centralization: Chhibber and Kollman 2004. Legacies: Kitschelt et al. 1999.

approach allows us to capture how certain contingencies (such as poor party strategy by those happening to possess the best stocks of capital to mobilize a given cleavage) can in some cases thwart the electoral mobilization of what may otherwise have become a major system-defining social cleavage. The disappearance of pro-democracy liberal parties from Russia's political arena despite widespread support for democracy indicates this is possible.[6] The market logic's emphasis on notions of starting capital and sunk costs also dovetails with the historical institutionalist perspective and thus gives us new insight into the phenomenon of party system "freezing" that major studies have found tends to occur as time passes.[7] Uniting these insights in a market model provides us with a progressive intellectual framework and a dynamic logic that makes unified sense of such contingencies together with the various important regularities identified in other works. It is progressive because it shifts the focus of research from identifying factors to understanding dynamics; understanding dynamics will give us greater ability to identify the most important factors and perhaps to uncover new ones in more than an arbitrary way.

The present study's employment of this model does in fact identify at least one new factor that has largely been neglected in previous work on party system development: meso-level concentrations of resources that are not broad enough to constitute social cleavages but that are of greater general significance than the personal resources of individual candidates.[8] These are such things as the corporate infrastructure on which politicized financial-industrial groups are founded or the administrative structures on which governors' political machines are based. That is, these are the resource concentrations with which party substitutes can be built. Moreover, these resource concentrations can be highly influenced both by legacies of the old regime *and* by contingent decisions of the most powerful elites during initial transitions from authoritarian rule and/or command economies. One conclusion to be drawn from Chapter 4, for example, is that Russia's parties would propably have penetrated its election system more extensively had the postcommunist transition not generated such strong gubernatorial political machines or left such large concentrations of wealth and power in the hands of just a few major state-dependent corporations. One promising avenue for research in transitional countries, therefore, might be to consider how transition- and legacy-dependent distributions of important forms of political capital impact parties' ability to fully capture the electoral arena.

[6] See also Hale 2004d.

[7] On freezing, see in particular Lipset and Rokkan 1967; O'Donnell and Schmitter 1986; Panebianco 1988. Outstanding historical institutionalist works that are highly compatible with the market logic outlined here include Kitschelt et al. 1999 and Grzymala-Busse 2002.

[8] On the personal vote, see Cain, Ferejohn, and Fiorina 1984 and 1987. On the Russian case, see Golosov 2003.

Perhaps the biggest advantage of the market model is that it gives us unique leverage on what may be the biggest question of party system development: Why do we have *party* systems *at all?* While there is a host of research on the rise of particular parties or sets of parties, most work in fact takes largely for granted that electoral competition will come to involve party competition – the questions are primarily ones of kind. The few works that proffer explanations for the phenomenon of party competition generally point to benefits that parties provide politicians or voters.[9] Yet, although this is an important part of the story, it remains only part of the story. The market logic outlined in this volume suggests that the key questions are not about what parties supply and why this benefits candidates or voters, but about what parties supply that benefits candidates or voters *more than what is proffered by alternative available suppliers*. Indeed, the Russian case shows that parties can be quite effective in communicating views to voters and providing organization to politicians (solving the collective action and social choice problems that Aldrich identifies) but that this is not enough to produce party domination of the political system because other, nonparty forms of organization exist that can provide adequate substitutes for these goods and services.

Parties will only close out the electoral market when something about the political system tips the scales in their favor. The Russian case and the comparison with U.S. history suggest that increasing the value of party labels can certainly help parties make some headway, but that the most decisive factors may in fact be broadly institutional and historical. Indeed, the path to party dominance in the United States can be seen as a process whereby, essentially, party substitutes banded together to become parties while in opposition, a process facilitated by the country's relatively weak presidency. We find that Russia's superpresidential system bestowed incentives on elites of various levels that tended to militate against this process, thwarting the most important opposition attempts by governors to become the bases for major parties for years. Table 6.1, above, showed that there is strong reason to suspect related dynamics help us understand variation in parties' penetration of the whole set of postcommunist countries. Russia appeared to move decisively toward more complete party penetration of the polity only when the executive branch itself aggressively sought to promote it. And this happened only after its incumbent officeholders were nearly ousted in 1999–2000, when a particularly resource-rich and skilled political entrepreneur seized a favorable moment to overcome party-substitutes' collective action problems and mounted a surprisingly powerful challenge.

The market approach also provides a new way of understanding how the relative importance of parties, generally speaking, might change over time,

9 Seminal works include Aldrich 1995; Duverger 1954; Hofstadter 1970.

even in developed party-dominated democracies. Indeed, a large comparative literature exists that identifies a "decline of parties" throughout the Western world over the past few decades.[10] A common interpretation of this decline has been that new technologies, such as media of mass communication, have in fact weakened parties by diluting attachments or disengaging the public from partisan affairs. This is puzzling, however, because breakthroughs in communication technology and the proliferation of television should actually be improving the ability of parties to communicate with voters. The market approach might advance another hypothesis: New media may in fact be strengthening parties' abilities to provide electoral goods and services *in absolute terms* by enhancing their communication capacity, but these same media are also strengthening the ability of party substitutes to reach the masses at an even greater rate, producing a *relative* decline in the "production capacity" of parties vis-à-vis party substitutes. With television sets in every home, for example, a political entrepreneur no longer needs a mass organization of the kind traditionally wielded by parties to reach large numbers of voters. Instead, one simply needs enough money to purchase advertising time or a flair for obtaining coverage on television news. In the West, this has meant a sharp rise in power for special interest organizations that can communicate with voters independently of parties and influence elections accordingly.[11] Parties' role in determining electoral outcomes is thus reduced, even where all candidates are nominally party affiliates.

THE MARKET MODEL AND THEORIES OF NATIONAL INTEGRATION

Theorists have frequently cited a strong national party system as an important factor producing integration and coherence in the most successful states, particularly federations.[12] Federations without unified party systems are often said to experience major crises of governance and even of unity, with wayward regions disregarding federal law and falling victim to a host of collective action problems. Authors have recognized, however, that the causal arrow also points in the opposite direction, with federalism often providing advantages to parties with local as opposed to national orientation.[13] Exactly how and when federalism has this effect, however, remains underresearched.

The logic of electoral markets gives us some useful tools to understand federalism's impact on the development of a national party system and hence on

[10] This is a vast literature. For summary discussions of it and important insights, see Bartels 2000; Dalton 2002; Dalton and Wattenberg 2000; Green, Palmquist, and Schickler 2002; Mair 1990.

[11] Jacobson 2001; Lawson and Merkl 1988.

[12] Gibson 2004; Huntington 1968; Ordeshook and Shvetsova 1997; Riker 1964; Slider 2001; Stepan 2004; Stoner-Weiss 1999, 2001.

[13] Chhibber and Kollman 2004; Gibson 2004; Mainwaring 1999; Stepan 2004.

state unity. By these lights, federalism provides more starting political capital for entrepreneurs forming regional parties or regionally based party substitutes than would be the case in unitary states. The preceding chapters strongly suggest that this has been the case in Russia, since the governors to whom federalism devolved a great deal of authority became arguably the most powerful set of party substitutes in Russia, posing major obstacles to national parties attempting to win legislative seats in their districts, not to mention the governorships themselves. This effect depended, however, on the particular way Russian federalism was formed, producing strong regional political machines. Had power in Russian's regions been more dispersed, federalism would probably not have disadvantage parties to such a great degree.

Ironically, the present volume also suggests that one force for national disunity in federal states is actually the combination of federalism with a very powerful central presidency, the very institution often seen as the greatest bulwark of national unity.[14] As Chapter 5 demonstrated, the presidency systematically intervened in the electoral market, notably undermining the Fatherland–All Russia coalition of governors in 1999. This coalition was an effort to tie provincially based political organizations together in a national organization, one that could have constituted a unifying force in the Russian Federation and that could conceivably have lasted much as the American Democratic Party's motley coalition of regional machines did after 1828. Moreover, Russia's "superpresidents" have been, as Migdal's logic fully expects, highly reluctant to form a true presidential party for fear that it could take on a life of its own and ultimately limit or even challenge presidential authority.[15] Chapter 5 documented how President Yeltsin intentionally thwarted such efforts on the part of some aides. After finding that he needed a progovernment party to defeat Fatherland–All Russia in the 1999–2000 election cycle, Putin did move strongly to forge a more complete party system, but it was the superpresidency that had staved off this impulse for several years. And significantly, once the move to a more complete party system was made, it was made largely at the expense of opposition parties with the propresidential United Russia reaping almost all of the rewards.

This suggests that "superpresidential federalism" is likely to be associated with significant instability. Such systems might be expected to vacillate between periods of true federalism (involving significant real local autonomy) in which incumbent presidents actually exacerbate interregional differences in order to stay in power and periods in which central authorities seek to eliminate the resulting political incoherence and embark on programs of recentralization. Part of the recentralization effort can involve attempts

[14] This confirms a conclusion also reached by Mainwaring 1999 and Stepan 2004, although Stepan reasonably specifies that the territorial unity of the state is only actually threatened for multi-ethnic countries.

[15] Migdal 1987.

to strengthen national parties, but usually giving undue advantage to those backed by the central government. If the interests of the proincumbent party and incumbent happen to diverge, however, then Migdal's logic leads us to expect that the president may have incentive to weaken the party, perhaps by exploiting differences among regional authorities. In neither the periods of decentralization nor the times of recentralization is one likely to see a vibrant, nationally integrated democracy with healthy and stable opposition parties.

THE MARKET MODEL, DEMOCRACY, AND AUTOCRACY

The study of electoral markets will also give us better insight into how incumbent authorities might manipulate them. Nearly all markets are regulated in some way, and states frequently alter their institutions or intervene selectively so as to favor preferred national suppliers. Electoral markets, it will come as little surprise, are no exception.

Theorists often seem compelled to brand political systems with labels such as "democracy" or "dictatorship" so as to connote important value judgments. Nowhere does this appear more the case than in Russia, where some specialists have dubbed it reasonably democratic,[16] others have branded it a dictatorship stealthily masquerading as a democracy,[17] and some have simply placed it somewhere in between.[18] Without denying the need to make such value-laden judgments, it is also important for the analyst to develop a set of intellectual tools to make sense of the nuances independently of these contentious labels.[19] The notion of electoral markets helps us move in this direction. When one talks about "market economies," one rarely ever means a completely free market; instead, markets can experience a wide range of degrees and forms of regulation and still be markets and thus still be studied as such. Successful scholarship, then, focuses on how the various forms of regulation have an impact on the functioning of the market.

Electoral markets should be considered in the same way, and the Russian case provides an example of how such an approach can lead to some important insights. The preceding chapters have made abundantly clear that Russia's superpresidential regime and its "supergovernors" in the regions wielded a great deal of power to structure and influence electoral competition in Russia through 2005. Under Putin during this time, executive structures were particularly successful in "managing" elections.[20] Rather than stop here, one must recognize that it makes a great deal of difference

16 Nichols 2002; Shleifer and Treisman 2004.

17 Brovkin 1996; Hahn 2004; Jowitt 1996; Rutland 2004.

18 Colton and McFaul 2003; McFaul, Petrov, and Ryabov 2004.

19 Hanson 2001.

20 Colton and McFaul 2003.

precisely how and why this success has been achieved. Many of Putin's most vociferous critics see autocratic methods based on autocratic traditions and thus expect a continued slide into deeper autocracy so long as Putin and his team are in power.[21] Others see methods that, in comparative perspective, are not fundamentally out of line with the experiences of other developing democracies and thus expect deeper democratization eventually to ensue.[22]

The market approach advanced in the present volume calls attention to the competition between parties and party substitutes, seeing the latter as an important potential source of political contestation along with parties. These party substitutes can potentially compete directly with progovernment authorities (as the PFIG Yukos appeared ready to do in 2003), turn themselves into opposition parties (as the Fatherland–All Russia governors did in 1999), or join with or support opposition parties (as Berezovsky attempted to pull off after his falling-out with Putin). One important question, then, is the impact of the structure of Russia's electoral market on these possibilities.

This volume's account finds strong reason to doubt both the most "optimistic" and "pessimistic" scenarios for Russia, instead calling attention to aspects of superpresidentialism and patrimonial communism that have helped generate a certain *cyclical* pattern of political contestation on Russia's electoral market.[23] Russia's superpresidential system and patrimonial communist legacy have rendered both of Russia's major-party substitutes, regional governors and financial-industrial groups, highly dependent on the presidency. By implication, whenever there has been a presidential election, such elites have had enormous incentive to end up on the winning side lest their future access to resources be jeopardized. This sort of dynamic was seen in the presidential elections of 2000 and 2004 as well as in the parliamentary contest of 2003; in each case, Putin's immense popularity and firm control over the presidency made him the overwhelming favorite. As a result, in each case, these regional and economic elites virtually all clambered for a place on his political bandwagon long before the campaign had even begun, helping to produce magnificently large victories for the party of power and its chief patron. Importantly, this was also essentially the case in 1996, when Russia's emergent business elite converged mightily around Yeltsin against a resource-poor challenger, Zyuganov. While some regional elites initially backed Zyuganov, the majority appear to have been pro-Yeltsin and some who initially backed Zyuganov were induced by the Kremlin to switch sides or at least observe neutrality, resulting in Yeltsin's ultimate victory despite a near-zero popularity rating at the beginning of the election year. Putin, with his strong appeal among the masses, was simply more efficient in using the

[21] Hahn 2004; Pipes 2004.
[22] Shleifer and Treisman 2004.
[23] Much of the following paragraphs draw from Hale 2004c.

powers of the superpresidency to rally the elite in 2000 and 2004, but the dynamic was essentially the same in 1996.

At times of leadership transition, however, when the power of the superpresidency is expected to change hands, one can anticipate a very different dynamic. For one thing, the stakes at such times are extremely high since an outcome of "winner take all" is a strikingly real possibility. While the incumbent can try to engineer a succession, as did Yeltsin in 1999, even a little uncertainty can encourage elites who fear that they might be left out of the new winning coalition to mobilize a countercoalition in a bid to gain or retain access to the "spoils" of superpresidential office and to keep them out of the hands of their opponents. Thus, while the outcome of the 2000 presidential election was essentially determined before the campaign had begun the 1999 Duma contest featured a heated political battle between a challenging coalition of elites (Fatherland–All Russia) and a bloc built by incumbent insider Yeltsinites. As Chapter 5 demonstrated, the Kremlin won only with good fortune, smart strategy, and opposition mistakes.[24]

If Putin does indeed forgo the temptation to revise the law so that he can seek a third term as president, there is at least a chance that the parliamentary elections of 2007 could look more like 1999 than 2003. And if the 2007 elections do not produce a clear resolution, as is possible, then the 2008 presidential race could wind up being quite competitive, with the prospect for post–Soviet Russia's first turnover of power to an opposition. Of course, the competition would not much resemble the ideal of democracy, instead involving a contest of political machines and administrative resources as much as voter sentiments. But at least voters would be given some role to play. And if the many theorists are correct who argue that divisions within the elite are generally the driving forces behind the ultimate adoption of democracy, then even a highly elite-centered contest could provide at least some hope for a democratic future, at least before the next "authoritarian" superpresidential cycle kicks in.[25] Indeed, it is at least possible that incumbent elites fearing loss of control over the superpresidency may initiate a process of dispersing power in order to secure themselves a place in their country's political future.[26] Remarkably, something quite similar was initiated by the occupants of Ukraine's superpresidential office in anticipation of a possible electoral loss in the 2004 elections; ironically, however, this initiative, which was intended to shift more power to the parliament, was initially defeated by the "democratic" opposition, which either saw the chance to take

[24] See Boxer and Hale 2000; Colton and McFaul 2003; Hale 2004c. In a similar vein, Shvetsova (2003) has characterized the 1999 Duma election as an "elite primary."

[25] See, e.g., Bratton and Van de Walle 1997; Gel'man, Ryzhenkov, and Brie 2003; Przeworski 1991; Rustow 1970.

[26] Frye 1997.

control of the superpresidency for themselves or hoped to deny the incumbents any new lease on political life.[27] Ultimately, however, the opposition was compelled to accept such an arrangement in December 2004 as a condition for the incumbents' acceptance of repeat voting after a fraud-filled presidential runoff.

Of course, whether or not such reforms are ever actually carried out in Russia will also depend on the contingent actions of different groups with vested interests in promoting or halting such developments. Putin, who has repeatedly stated his intention to find a suitable successor, has an interest in breaking the cyclical pattern in order to guide his chosen one into the office. Indeed, this volume has suggested that Putin has invested so much effort in building the United Russia Party and tilting the electoral market in favor of parties largely so that United Russia could serve as a vehicle to manage the next transfer of power. If Putin follows through on his stated desire to require presidential candidates to run as party nominees, this mechanism will be all the more effective.[28] But this could wind up creating battles *within* United Russia, which could open up another avenue for political competition and, potentially, the influence of the masses in tipping the balance one way or the other.

At the same time, opposition parties can be expected to struggle to find ways of attracting elites to their own labels in order to contest the 2007 "primary" (the Duma election) and then, especially if they do not win, to make these elite divisions stick. The process of regional elite recruitment began as early as 2003, when the new federal law requiring party-list competition for many regional legislative seats went into effect. Indeed, this law granted parties a critical advantage over party substitutes: a monopoly on nomination to these seats. Regional elites, therefore, found they had to affiliate with federally registered parties in order to compete for these seats, and since United Russia could not accept all elites, some groups were bound to find other party labels appealing. Indeed, strategists even for parties such as Yabloko and the KPRF, which suffered major defeats in 2003, said in interviews with the present author in early 2004 that they were somewhat optimistic about the future. They saw the possibility that Putin's popularity may not last and found the new party-list competition in the provinces to be a potential shot in the political arm, albeit at a local level. But to take advantage of a cyclical upturn in political competition in 2007, opposition parties would also have to cultivate the value of their brands, making them attractive to different elite groups, and avoid major campaign mistakes like those that cost some of them dearly in 1999 and 2003. Political competition in Russia might not be dead just yet, although it may still lie dormant for some time to come.

[27] Christensen, Rakhimkulov, and Wise 2005.

[28] *RFE/RL Newsline*, August 24, 2001.

The market approach, therefore, has the benefit of calling attention to dynamics in the relationship among parties, party substitutes, and the executive branch that in countries like Russia may produce not so much a linear path to autocracy or democracy as a somewhat cyclical pattern of liberalization and concentration of power. Future research, therefore, will do well to consider more precisely how electoral markets function in other countries.

Index

References

Afanasiev, M. N. 1997. *Klientelizm i Rossiiskaia Gosudarstvennost'* (Moscow: Moscow Public Science Foundation).

Aldrich, John H. 1995. *Why Parties?* (Chicago: University of Chicago Press).

Alexseev, Mikhail A. (ed.). 1999. *Center-Periphery Conflict in Post-Soviet Russia* (New York: St. Martin's Press).

Anderson, Benedict. 1991. *Imagined Communities: Reflections on the Origin and Spread of Nationalism*, rev. ed. (New York: Verso).

Anderson, Christopher. 1995. *Blaming the Government: Citizens and the Economy in Five European Democracies* (Armonk, NY: M.E. Sharpe).

Anderson, Richard D., Jr., M. Steven Fish, Stephen E. Hanson, and Philip G. Roeder. 2001. *Postcommunism and the Theory of Democracy* (Princeton, NJ: Princeton University Press).

Andrews, Josephine T. 2002. *When Majorities Fail* (New York: Cambridge University Press).

Andrle, Vladimir. 1976. *Managerial Power in the Soviet Union* (Lexington, MA: Lexington Books).

Ansell, Christopher K. and M. Steven Fish. 1999. "The Art of Being Indispensable: Noncharismatic Personalism in Contemporary Political Parties." *Comparative Political Studies* 32, no. 3 (May): 283–312.

Aslund, Anders. 1995. *How Russia Became a Market Economy* (Washington, DC: Brookings).

Bahry, Donna. 2005. "The New Federalism and the Paradoxes of Regional Sovereignty in Russia." *Comparative Politics* 37, no. 2 (January), pp. 127–46.

Banfield, Edward C. and James Q. Wilson. 1963. *City Politics* (Cambridge, MA: Harvard University Press).

Bartels, Larry M. 2000. "Partisanship and Voting Behavior, 1952–96." *American Journal of Political Science* 44, no. 1 (January): 35–50.

Beer, Samuel H. 1982. *Modern British Politics: Parties and Pressure Groups in the Collectivist Age* [1965] (New York: Norton).

Belin, Laura and Robert Orttung. 1995. "Parties Proliferate on Eve of Elections." *Transition* 17: 42–50.

1997. *The Russian Parliamentary Elections of 1995: The Battle for the Duma* (Armonk, NY: M.E. Sharpe).

Berezkin, Andrei, Mikhail Myagkov, and Peter C. Ordeshook. 1999. "The Urban-Rural Divide in the Russian Electorate and the Effect of Distance from Urban Centers." *Post-Soviet Geography and Economics* 40, no. 6: 395–406.

Berliner, Joseph S. 1957. *Factory and Manager in the USSR* (Cambridge, MA: Harvard University Press).

1987. *Soviet Industry* (Ithaca, NY: Cornell University Press).

Bielasiak, Jack. 2002. "The Institutionalization of Electoral and Party Systems in Postcommunist States." *Comparative Politics* 34, no. 2 (January): 189–210.

Boix, Carles. 1998. *Political Parties, Growth and Equality: Conservative and Social Democratic Economic Strategies in the World Economy* (Cambridge: Cambridge University Press).

Boxer, Vladimir and Henry E. Hale. 2000. "Putin's Anti-Campaign Campaign: Presidential Election Tactics in Today's Russia." *AAASS NewsNet* 40, no. 3 (May): 9–10.

Brader, Ted and Joshua A. Tucker. 2001. "The Emergence of Mass Partisanship in Russia, 1993–1996." *American Journal of Political Science* 45, no. 1 (January): 69–83.

Bratton, Michael and Nicolas van de Walle. 1997. *Democratic Experiments in Africa* (New York: Cambridge University Press).

Breslauer, George W. 2002. *Gorbachev and Yeltsin as Leaders* (New York: Cambridge University Press).

Brovkin, Vladimir. 1996. "The Emperor's New Clothes: Continuity of Soviet Political Culture in Contemporary Russia." *Problems of Post-Communism* 43, no. 2 (March–April): 21–8.

Brown, Archie. 1996. *The Gorbachev Factor* (New York: Oxford University Press).

Brubaker, Rogers. 1996. *Nationalism Reframed* (New York: Cambridge University Press).

Brudny, Yitzhak. 2001. "Continuity or Change in Russian Electoral Patterns?" In *Contemporary Russian Politics*, Archie Brown (ed.), 154–78 (New York: Oxford University Press).

Bunce, Valerie. 1999. *Subversive Institutions* (New York: Cambridge University Press).

Cain, Bruce, John Ferejohn, and Morris Fiorina. 1984. "The Constituency Service Basis of the Personal Vote for U.S. Representatives and British Members of Parliament." *American Political Science Review* 78, no. 1 (March): 110–25.

1987. *The Personal Vote* (Cambridge, MA: Harvard University Press).

Campbell, Angus, Philip E. Converse, Warren E. Miller, and Donald E. Stokes. 1960. *The American Voter* (New York: Wiley).

Chhibber, Pradeep. 2001. *Democracy Without Associations* (Ann Arbor: University of Michigan Press).

Chhibber, Pradeep and Ken W. Kollman. 1998. "Party Aggregation and the Number of Parties in India and the United States." *American Political Science Review* 92, no. 2 (June): 329–42.

Chhibber, Pradeep and Ken W. Kollman. 2004. *The Formation of National Party Systems: Federalism and Party Competition in Canada, Great Britain, India, and the United States* (Princeton, NJ: Princeton University Press).

Christensen, Robert K., Edward R. Rakhimkulov, and Charles R. Wise. 2005. "The Ukrainian Orange Revolution Brought More Than a New President: What Kind of Democracy Will the Institutional Changes Bring?" Draft paper (February).

Coleman, James S. and Carl G. Rosberg, Jr. (eds.). 1964. *Political Parties and National Integration in Tropical Africa* (Berkeley: University of California Press).

Colton, Timothy J. 1995a. "Boris Yeltsin, Russia's All-Thumbs Democrat." In *Patterns in Post-Soviet Leadership*, Colton and Robert C. Tucker (eds.), 49–74 (Boulder: Westview Press).

1995b. *Moscow: Governing the Socialist Metropolis* (Cambridge, MA: Harvard University Press).

1996. "Economics and Voting in Russia." *Post-Soviet Affairs* 12, no. 4 (October–December): 289–318.

1998a. "Determinants of the Party Vote." In *Growing Pains*, Colton and Jerry F. Hough (eds.), 75–114 (Washington, DC: Brookings).

1998b. "Introduction." In *Growing Pains*, Colton and Jerry F. Hough (eds.), 1–36 (Washington, DC: Brookings).

1999. "Understanding Iurii Luzhkov." *Problems of Post-Communism* 46, no. 5 (September/October): 14–26.

2000. *Transitional Citizens* (Cambridge, MA: Harvard University Press).

2003. "Parties, Leaders, and Voters in the Parliamentary Election." In *The 1999–2000 Elections in Russia: Their Impact and Legacy*, Vicki L. Hesli and William M. Reisinger (eds.), 90–120 (New York: Cambridge University Press).

Colton, Timothy J. and Henry E. Hale. 2004. "Context and Party System Development: Voting in Russian Parliamentary Elections 1995–2004 in Comparative Perspective." Paper prepared for presentation at the Annual Meeting of the American Political Science Association, Chicago, September 3.

Colton, Timothy J. and Michael McFaul. 2000. "Reinventing Russia's Party of Power: 'Unity' and the 1999 Duma Election." *Post-Soviet Affairs* 16, no. 3 (July–September): 201–24.

2003. *Popular Choice and Managed Democracy* (Washington, DC: Brookings).

Coulloudon, Virginie. 2000. "The Divided Russian Elite: How Russia's Transition Produced a Counter-Elite." In *Building the Russian State*, Valerie Sperling (ed.), 67–87 (Boulder: Westview Press).

Cox, Gary W. 1986. "The Development of a Party-Orientated Electorate in England, 1832–1918." *British Journal of Political Science* 16, no. 2 (April): 187–216.

1997. *Making Votes Count* (New York: Cambridge University Press).

Crawford, Beverly and Arend Lijphart. 1997. *Liberalization and Leninist Legacies* (Berkeley: University of California Press).

Dahl, Robert A. (ed.). 1966. *Political Oppositions in Western Democracies* (New Haven, CT: Yale University Press).

Dalton, Russell J. 2002. "Political Cleavages, Issues, and Electoral Change." In *Comparing Democracies* 2, Lawrence LeDuc, Richard Niemi, and Pippa Norris (eds.), 189–209 (London: Sage).

Dalton, Russell J. and Martin Wattenberg (eds.). 2000. *Parties Without Partisans* (Oxford: Oxford University Press).

Davidheiser, Evelyn. 1998. "Right and Left in the Hard Opposition." In *Growing Pains*, Timothy J. Colton and Hough (eds.), 177–210 (Washington, DC: Brookings).

Downs, Anthony. 1957. *An Economic Theory of Democracy* (New York: Harper & Row).

Duch, Raymond. 2001. "A Developmental Model of Heterogeneous Economic Voting in New Democracies." *American Political Science Review* 95, no. 4 (December): 895–910.

Duverger, Maurice. 1954. *Political Parties* (New York: Wiley).

Easter, Gerald M. 1997. "Preference for Presidentialism: Postcommunist Regime Change in Russia and the NIS." *World Politics* 49, no. 2 (January): 184–211.

Ekiert, Grzegorz and Stephen E. Hanson (eds.). 2003. *Capitalism and Democracy in Central and Eastern Europe: Assessing the Legacy of Communist Rule* (New York: Cambridge University Press).

Epstein, Leon. 1967. *Political Parties in Western Democracies* (New York: Praeger).

Erikson, Robert S., Michael MacKuen, and James A. Stimson. 2002. *The Macro Polity* (New York: Cambridge University Press).

Evans, Geoffrey and Stephen Whitefield. 1993. "Identifying the Bases of Party Competition in Eastern Europe." *British Journal of Political Science* 23, no. 4 (October): 521–48.

Eyal, Gil, Ivan Szelenyi, and Eleanor Townsley. 1998. *Making Capitalism Without Capitalists* (New York: Verso).

Fiorina, Morris. 1981. *Retrospective Voting in American National Elections* (New Haven, CT: Yale University Press).

Fish, M. Steven. 1995. *Democracy from Scratch* (Princeton, NJ: Princeton University Press).

1996. "The Travails of Liberalism." *Journal of Democracy* 7, no. 2 (April): 106–17.

1997. "The Predicament of Russian Liberalism: Evidence from the December 1995 Parliamentary Elections." *Europe-Asia Studies* 49, no. 2 (March): 191–220.

2000. "The Executive Deception: Superpresidentialism and the Degradation of Russian Politics." In *Building the Russian State*, Valerie Sperling (ed.), 177–91 (Boulder: Westview Press).

2001. "The Dynamics of Democratic Erosion." In *Postcommunism and the Theory of Democracy*, Richard D. Anderson, Jr., M. Steven Fish, Stephen E. Hanson, and Philip G. Roeder, 54–95 (Princeton, NJ: Princeton University Press).

Fleron, Frederic J., Jr., Richard Ahl, and Finbarr Lane. 1998. "Where Now in the Study of Russian Political Parties?" *Journal of Communist Studies and Transition Politics* 14, nos. 1–2 (March/June): 224–52.

Frye, Timothy. 1997. "A Politics of Institutional Choice: Post-Communist Presidencies." *Comparative Political Studies* 30, no. 5: 523–52.

Geddes, Barbara. 1995. "A Comparative Perspective on the Leninist Legacy in Eastern Europe." *Comparative Political Studies* 28, no. 2 (July): 239–74.

Gellner, Ernest. 1983. *Nations and Nationalism* (Ithaca, NY: Cornell University Press) .

Gel'man, Vladimir. 1999. *Transformatsiia v Rossii* (Moscow: Moskovskii Obshchestvennyi Nauchnyi Fond).

Gel'man, Vladimir and Grigorii Golosov. 1998. "Regional Party System Formation in Russia." *Journal of Communist Studies and Transition Politics* 14, nos. 1–2 (March/June): 31–53.

Gel'man, Vladimir, Sergei Ryzhenkov, and Michael Brie, with Vladimir Avdonin, Boris Ovchinnikov, and Igor' Semenov. 2003. *Making and Breaking Democratic*

Transitions: The Comparative Politics of Russia's Regions (Lanham, MD: Rowman & Littlefield).
Gerber, Alan and Donald P. Green. 1998. "Rational Learning and Partisan Attitudes." *American Journal of Political Science* 42, no. 3 (July): 794–818.
Gerring, John. 1998. *Party Ideologies in America, 1828–1996* (New York: Cambridge University Press).
Gibson, Edward L. 2004. "Federalism and Democracy: Theoretical Connections and Cautionary Insights." In *Federalism and Democracy in Latin America*, Gibson (ed.), 1–28 (Baltimore: Johns Hopkins University Press).
Giuliano, Elise. 2000. "Who Determines the Self in the Politics of Self-Determination? Identity and Preference Formation in Tatarstan's Nationalist Mobilization." *Comparative Politics* 32, no. 3 (April): 295–316.
Golosov, Grigorii V. 1997. "Russian Political Parties and the 'Bosses.'" *Party Politics* 3, no. 1: 5–21.
1998. "Who Survives? Political Party Origins, Organizational Development, and Electoral Performance in Postcommunist Russia." *Political Studies* 46, no. 3 (September): 511–43.
2003. *Political Parties in the Regions of Russia: Democracy Unclaimed* (Boulder: Lynne Rienner).
Gorenburg, Dmitry. 1999. "Regional Separatism in Russia: Ethnic Mobilisation or Power Grab?" *Europe-Asia Studies* 51, no. 2 (March): 245–74.
Gorenburg, Dmitry P. 2000. "Not With One Voice." *World Politics* 53, no. 1 (October): 115–42.
2003. *Minority Ethnic Mobilization in the Russian Federation* (New York: Cambridge University Press).
Green, Donald, Bradley Palmquist, and Eric Schickler.1998. "Macropartisanship: A Replication and Critique." *American Political Science Review* 92, no. 4 (December) 883–99.
2002. *Partisan Hearts and Minds* (New Haven, CT: Yale University Press).
Grzymala-Busse, Anna. 2002. *Redeeming the Communist Past* (New York: Cambridge University Press).
Hahn, Gordon. 2004. "Managed Democracy? Building Stealth Authoritarianism in St. Petersburg." *Demokratizatsiya* 12, no. 2 (Spring): 195–231.
Hahn, Jeffrey W. 1997. "Regional Elections and Political Stability in Russia." *Post-Soviet Geography and Economics* 38, no. 5: 251–63.
Hale, Henry E. 1998. "Bashkortostan: The Logic of Ethnic Machine Politics and the Consolidation of Democracy." In *Growing Pains*, Timothy J. Colton and Jerry F. Hough (eds.), 599–636 (Washington, DC: Brookings).
1999a. "Machine Politics and Institutionalized Electorates." *Journal of Communist Studies and Transition Politics* 15, no. 4 (December): 70–110.
1999b. *Russian Election Watch* 2, no. 2 September.
1999c. "On November's Campaign Trail." *Russian Election Watch* 2, no. 5, December.
1999d. *Russian Election Watch* 2, no. 5, December.
2000. "The Parade of Sovereignties: Testing Theories of Secession in the Soviet Setting." *British Journal of Political Science* 30, no. 1 (January): 31–56.
2003. "Explaining Machine Politics in Russia's Regions: Economy, Ethnicity, and Legacy." *Post-Soviet Affairs* 19, no. 3 (July–September): 228–63.

2004a. "The Origins of United Russia and the Putin Presidency: The Role of Contingency in Party-System Development." *Demokratizatsiya* 12, no. 2 (Spring): 169–94.

2004b. "Explaining Ethnicity." *Comparative Political Studies* 37, no. 4 (May): 458–85.

2004c. "Russia's Presidential Election and the Fate of Democracy: Taking the Cake." *AAASS NewsNet* 44, no. 3 (May): 1–6.

2004d. "Yabloko and the Challenge of Building a Liberal Party in Russia." *Europe-Asia Studies* 56, no. 7 (November): 993–1020.

2005a. "The Makeup and Breakup of Ethnofederal States: Why Russia Survives Where the USSR Fell." *Perspectives on Politics* 3, no. 1 (March): 55–70.

2005b. "Party Development in a Federal System: The Impact of Putin's Reforms." In *The Dynamics of Russian Politics: Putin's Reform of Federal-Regional Relations* 2, Peter Reddaway and Robert Orttung (eds.), 179–211 (Boulder: Rowman & Littlefield).

2005c. "Why Not Parties? Supply and Demand on Russia's Electoral Market." *Comparative Politics* 37, no. 2 (January): 147–66.

Hale, Henry E. and Rein Taagepera.2002. "Russia: Consolidation or Collapse?" *Europe-Asia Studies* 54, no. 7 (November): 1101–25.

Hall, Peter and R. Taylor. 1996. "Political Science and the Three New Institutionalisms." *Political Studies* 44, no. 4 (December): 936–57.

Hanson, Stephen E.1995. "The Leninist Legacy and Institutional Change." *Comparative Political Studies* 28, no. 2 (July): 306–14.

1998. "Ideology, Uncertainty, and the Rise of Anti-System Parties in Post-Communist Russia." *Journal of Communist Studies and Transition Politics* 14, nos. 1–2 (March/June): 98–127.

2001. "Defining Democratic Consolidation." In *Postcommunism and the Theory of Democracy*, Richard D. Anderson, Jr., M. Steven Fish, Stephen E. Hanson, and Philip G. Roeder (Princeton, NJ: Princeton University Press).

2003. "Instrumental Democracy: The End of Ideology and the Decline of Russian Political Parties." In *The 1999–2000 Elections in Russia: Their Impact and Legacy*, Vicki L. Hesli and William M. Reisinger (eds.), 163–85 (New York: Cambridge University Press).

Hechter, Michael. 2000. *Containing Nationalism* (New York: Oxford University Press).

Herrera, Richard and Michael Yawn. 1999. "The Emergence of the Personal Vote." *Journal of Politics* 61, no. 1 (February): 136–150.

Herrera, Yoshiko. 2005. *Imagined Economies* (New York: Cambridge University Press).

Highton, Benjamin. 2000. "Senate Elections in the United States, 1920–94." *British Journal of Political Science* 30, no. 3 (July): 483–506.

Hofstadter, Richard. 1969. *The Idea of a Party System* (Berkeley: University of California Press).

Hough, Jerry F. 1969. *The Soviet Prefects* (Cambridge, MA: Harvard University Press).

1998a. "The Failure of Party Formation and the Future of Russian Democracy." In *Growing Pains*, Timothy J. Colton and Hough (eds.), 669–711 (Washington, DC: Brookings).

1998b. "Institutional Rules and Party Formation." In *Growing Pains*, Timothy J. Colton and Hough (eds.), 37–73 (Washington, DC: Brookings).

2001. *The Logic of Economic Reform in Russia* (Washington, DC: Brookings).

Hough, Jerry F. and Merle Fainsod. 1979. *How the Soviet Union Is Governed* (Cambridge, MA: Harvard University Press).

Huntington, Samuel P. 1968. *Political Order in Changing Societies* (New Haven, CT: Yale University Press).

1991. *The Third Wave* (Norman: University of Oklahoma Press).

Huskey, Eugene. 1999. *Presidential Power in Russia* (Armonk, NY: M.E. Sharpe).

Hutcheson, Derek. 2003. *Political Parties in the Russian Regions* (NY: Routledge/Curzon).

Inkeles, Alex and Raymond A. Bauer. 1961. *The Soviet Citizen* (Cambridge, MA: Harvard University Press).

Ishiyama, John T. 1999. "Political Integration and Political Parties in Post-Soviet Russian Politics." *Demokratizatsiya* 7, no. 2 (Spring): 188–203.

Jacobson, Gary. 1990. *The Electoral Origins of Divided Government: Competition in US House Elections,* 1946–1988 (Boulder: Westview).

2001. *The Politics of Congressional Elections* (New York: Longman).

Johnson, Juliet. 2000. *A Fistful of Rubles* (Ithaca, NY: Cornell University Press).

Jones Luong, Pauline. 2002. *Institutional Change and Political Continuity in Post-Soviet Central Asia* (New York: Cambridge University Press).

Jowitt, Ken. 1992. *New World Disorder: The Leninist Extinction* (Berkeley: University of California Press).

1996. "Dizzy with Democracy." *Problems of Post-Communism* 43, no. 1 (January–February): 3–8.

Kahn, Jeff. 2000. "The Parade of Sovereignties." *Post-Soviet Affairs* 16, no. 1: 58–89.

Kalyvas, Stathis. 1996. *The Rise of Christian Democracy in Europe* (Ithaca, NY: Cornell University Press).

2000. "Commitment Problems in Emerging Democracies." *Comparative Politics* 32, no. 4 (July): 379–98.

Karl, Terry Lynn. 1990. "Dilemmas of Democratization in Latin America." *Comparative Politics* 23, no. 1 (October): 1–21.

Karl, Terry Lynn and Philippe C. Schmitter. 1991. "Modes of Transition in Latin America, Southern and Eastern Europe." *International Social Science Journal* 43, no. 2 (May): 269–84.

Katz, Jonathan N. and Gary King. 1999. "A Statistical Model for Multiparty Electoral Data." *American Political Science Review* 93, no. 1 (March): 15–32.

Katz, Richard S. and Peter Mair (eds.). 1995. "Changing Models of Party Organization and Party Democracy: The Emergence of the Cartel Party." *Party Politics* 1, no. 1 (January): 5–28.

Kinder, Donald R. and D. Roderick Kiewiet. 1981. "Sociotropic Politics: The American Case." *British Journal of Political Science* 11, no. 2 (April): 129–61.

King, Gary. 1998. *Unifying Political Methodology* (Ann Arbor: University of Michigan Press).

King, Gary, Michael Tomz, and Jason Wittenberg. 2000. "Making the Most of Statistical Analyses: Improving Interpretation and Presentation." *American Journal of Political Science* 44, no. 2 (April): 347–61.

Kirchheimer, Otto. 1966. "The Transformation of the Western European Party Systems." In *Political Parties and Political Development*, Joseph LaPalombara and Myron Weiner (eds.), 177–200 (Princeton, NJ: Princeton University Press).

Kirzner, Israel M. 1973. *Competition and Entrepreneurship* (Chicago: University of Chicago Press).

Kitschelt, Herbert. 1989. *The Logics of Party Formation* (Ithaca, NY: Cornell University Press).

1992. "The Formation of Party Systems in East Central Europe." *Politics & Society* 20, no. 1 (March): 7–50.

Kitschelt, Herbert, Zdenka Mansfeldova, Radoslaw Markowski, and Gabor Toka. 1999. *Post-Communist Party Systems* (New York: Cambridge University Press).

Kitschelt, Herbert and Regina Smyth. 2002. "Programmatic Party Cohesion in Emerging Postcommunist Democracies: Russia in Comparative Context." *Comparative Political Studies* 35, no. 10 (December): 1228–56.

Klobucar, Thomas F. and Arthur H. Miller. 2002. "Party Activists and Party Development in Post Soviet Democracies." Paper presented at the annual meeting of the American Political Science Association, Boston, MA, August 28–September 1.

Kohler, Heinz. 1989. *Comparative Economic Systems* (Glenview, IL: Scott, Foresman).

Kolmakov, Sergei. 2003. "The Role of Financial Industrial Conglomerates in Russian Political Parties." *Russia Watch* no. 9 (January): 16. Available online at http://bcsia.ksg.harvard.edu/publication.cfm? program=CORE&ctype=paper&item_id=367.

Korguniuk, Yuri. 1999. *Sovremennaia Rossiiskaia Mnogopartiinost'* (Moscow: INDEM).

Kornai, Janos. 1992. *The Socialist System* (Princeton, NJ: Princeton University Press).

Kotkin, Stephen. 1995. *Magnetic Mountain* (Berkeley: University of California Press).

Kreps, David M. 1990. "Corporate Culture and Economic Theory." In *Perspectives in Political Economy*, James Alt and Kenneth Shepsle (eds.), 90–143 (New York: Cambridge University Press).

Kullberg, Judith S. and William Zimmerman. 1999. "Liberal Elites, Socialist Masses, and Problems of Russian Democracy." *World Politics* 51, no. 3 (April): 323–58.

Kurilla, Ivan. 2002. "Civil Activism Without NGOs: The Communist Party as a Civil Society Substitute." *Demokratizatsiya* 10, no. 3 (Summer): 392–400.

Laitin, David D. 1998. *Identity in Formation* (Ithaca, NY: Cornell University Press).

LaPalombara, Joseph and Myron Weiner. 1966. "The Origin and Development of Political Parties." In *Political Parties and Political Development*, LaPalombara and Weiner (eds.), 3–42 (Princeton, NJ: Princeton University Press).

Lapidus, Gail W. 1992. "From Democratization to Disintegration." In *From Union to Commonwealth*, Lapidus and Victor Zaslavsky, with Philip Goldman (eds.), 45–70 (New York: Cambridge University Press).

1999. "Asymmetrical Federalism and State Breakdown in Russia." *Post-Soviet Affairs* 15, no. 1 (January–March): 74–82.

Lapina, Natalya and Alla Chirikova. 2002. "Pragmatism Determines Business Elite's Party Choices." *EWI Russian Regional Report* 7, no. 23 (July 22).

Lawson, Kay and Peter H. Merkl (eds.). 1988. *When Parties Fail: Emerging Alternative Organizations* (Princeton, NJ: Princeton University Press).

Lewis-Beck, Michael S. 1988. *Economics and Elections: The Major Western Democracies* (Ann Arbor: University of Michigan Press).

Lijphart, Arend.1990. "The Political Consequences of Electoral Laws, 1945–85." *American Political Science Review* 84, no. 2 (June): 481–96.

1994. *Electoral Systems and Party Systems: A Study of Twenty-Seven Democracies, 1945–1990* (Oxford: Oxford University Press).

Lipset, Seymour Martin. 2000. "The Indispensability of Political Parties." *Journal of Democracy* 11, no. 1 (January): 48–55.

Lipset, Seymour Martin and Stein Rokkan (eds.). 1967. *Party Systems and Voter Alignments* (New York: Free Press).

Long, J. Scott. 1997. *Regression Models for Categorical and Limited Dependent Variables* (Thousand Oaks, CA: Sage).

Lussier, Danielle N. 2002. "The Role of Russia's Governors in the 1999–2000 Federal Elections." In *Regional Politics in Russia*, Cameron Ross (ed.), 57–76 (Manchester: Manchester University Press).

Mainwaring, Scott. 1998. "Party Systems in the Third Wave." *Journal of Democracy* 9, no. 3 (July): 67–81.

1999. *Rethinking Party Sytems in the Third Wave of Democratization: The Case of Brazil* (Stanford: Stanford University Press).

Mair, Peter (ed.). 1990. *The West European Party System* (Oxford: Oxford University Press).

March, Luke. 2002. *The Communist Party in Post-Soviet Russia* (Manchester: Manchester University Press).

Martin, Terry. 2001. *The Affirmative Action Empire* (Ithaca, NY: Cornell University Press).

McAuley, Mary. 1997. *Russia's Politics of Uncertainty* (New York: Cambridge University Press).

McCormick, Richard P. 1966. *The Second American Party System* (Chapel Hill: University of North Carolina Press).

McFaul, Michael. 1993. "Party Formation after Revolutionary Transitions." In *Political Parties in Russia*, Alexander Dallin (ed.), 7–28 (Berkeley: International and Area Studies, University of California Press).

1997a. *Russia's 1996 Presidential Election: The End of Polarized Politics* (Stanford: Hoover Institution Press).

1997b. "Time Ripe for Yabloko." *The Moscow Times,* September 18, p. 8.

1998. "Russia's Choice." In *Growing Pains*, Timothy J. Colton and Jerry F. Hough (eds.), 115–39 (Washington, DC: Brookings).

1999a. "The Perils of a Protracted Transition?" *Journal of Democracy* 10, no. 2 (April): 4–18.

1999b. "Preface." *Pre-Election Bulletin No.1*, (Washington: Carnegie Endowment, December 2).

2001a. "Explaining Party Formation and Nonformation in Russia." *Comparative Political Studies* 34, no. 10 (December): 1159–87.

2001b. *Russia's Unfinished Revolution* (Ithaca, NY: Cornell University Press).

McFaul, Michael and Sergei Markov (eds.). 1993. *The Troubled Birth of Russian Democracy: Parties, Personalities, and Programs* (Stanford: Hoover Institution Press).

McFaul, Michael, Nikolai Petrov, and Andrei Ryabov (eds.). 1999. *Rossiia Nakanune Dumskikh Vyborov 1999 goda* (Moscow: Moscow Carnegie Center).

2004. *Between Dictatorship and Democracy* (Washington, DC: Carnegie Endowment for International Peace).

McMann, Kelly M. 2002. "The Personal Risks of Party Development." In *Dilemmas of Transition in Post-Soviet Countries*, Joel C. Moses (ed.), 163–86 (Chicago: Burnham).

Mendras, Marie. 1999. "How Regional Elites Preserve Their Power." *Post-Soviet Affairs* 15, no. 4 (October–December): 295–311.

Meyer, Alfred G. 1961. "USSR Incorporated." *Slavic Review* 20, no. 3 (October): 369–76.

Michels, Robert. 1962. *Political Parties* [1911] (New York: Collier).

Migdal, Joel S. 1987. "Strong States, Weak States." In *Understanding Political Development*, Myron Weiner and Samuel P. Huntington (eds.), 391–434 (Boston: Little, Brown).

1988. *Strong Societies and Weak States* (Princeton, NJ: Princeton University Press).

Miller, Arthur H., Gwyn Erb, William M. Reisinger, and Vicki L. Hesli. 2000. "Emerging Party Systems in Post-Soviet Societies." *Journal of Politics* 62, no. 2 (May): 455–90.

Miller, Arthur H. and Thomas F. Klobucar. 2000. "The Development of Party Identification in Post-Soviet Societies." *American Journal of Political Science* 44, no. 4 (October): 667–86.

Miller, William L. and Stephen White. 1998. "Political Values Underlying Partisan Cleavages in Former Communist Countries." *Electoral Studies* 17, no. 2 (June): 197–216.

Moser, Robert G. 1999. "Independents and Party Formation." *Comparative Politics* 31, no. 2 (January): 147–66.

1999. "Electoral Systems and the Number of Parties in Post-Communist States." *World Politics* 51, no. 3 (April): 359–84.

2001. *Unexpected Outcomes: Electoral Systems, Political Parties, and Representation in Russia* (Pittsburgh: University of Pittsburgh Press).

Neganov, Sergei V. 2003. *Regional'nye Otdeleniia Politicheskikh Partii v Permskoi Oblasti* (Perm, Russia: Perm Oblast Administration).

Neganov, Sergei V. and Oleg B. Podvintsev. 2004. *Panorama Issledovanyi Politiki Prikam'ia*, no.2 (Perm: Permskoe Knizhnoe Izdatel'stvo).

Nichols, Thomas M. 2002. "Putin's First Two Years: Democracy or Authoritarianism?" *Current History* 101 (October): 307–12.

Norpoth, Helmut, Michael S. Lewis-Beck, and Jean-Dominique Lafay (eds.). 1991. *Economics and Politics: The Calculus of Support* (Ann Arbor: University of Michigan Press).

North, Douglass C. 1990. *Institutions, Institutional Change and Economic Performance* (New York: Cambridge University Press).

North, Douglass C. and Robert Paul Thomas. 1973. *The Rise of the Western World: A New Economic History* (New York: Cambridge University Press).

Oates, Sarah. 2003. "Television, Voters, and the Development of the 'Broadcast Party.'" In *The 1999–2000 Elections in Russia: Their Impact and Legacy*, Vicki L. Hesli and William M. Reisinger (eds.), 29–50 (New York: Cambridge University Press).

O'Donnell, Guillermo and Philippe Schmitter. 1986. *Transitions from Authoritarian Rule: Tentative Conclusions About Uncertain Democracies* (Baltimore: Johns Hopkins University Press).

Olson, Mancur. 1965. *The Logic of Collective Action* (Cambridge, MA: Harvard University Press).

Ordeshook, Peter C. 1995. "Incentives and Institutions." *Journal of Democracy* 6, no. 2 (April): 46–60.

Ordeshook, Peter C. and Olga Shvetsova. 1997. "Federalism and Constitutional Design." *Journal of Democracy* 8, no. 1 (January): 27–42.

Orttung, Robert W. 2004a. "Business and Politics in the Russian Regions." *Problems of Post-Communism* 51, no. 2 (March–April): 48–60.

2004b. "Key Issues in the Evolution of the Federal Okrugs and Center-Region Relations under Putin." In *The Dynamics of Russian Politics: Putin's Reform of Federal-Regional Relations*, 1 Peter Reddaway and Orttung (eds.), 19–52 (Lanham, MD: Rowman & Littlefield).

Ostrogorski, Moisei. 1964. *Democracy and the Organization of Political Parties* [1902], edited and abridged by Seymour Martin Lipset (Garden City, NY: Doubleday & Company).

Panebianco, Angelo. 1988. *Political Parties: Organization and Power* (New York: Cambridge University Press).

Petrocik, John. 1991. "Divided Government: Is It All in the Campaigns?" In *The Politics of Divided Government*, Gary Cox and Samuel Kernell (eds.), 13–38 (Boulder: Westview).

Petrov, Nikolai (ed.). 2003. *Federal'naia Reforma 2000–2003* (Moscow: Moskovskii Obshchestvennyi Nauchnyi Fond).

Petrov, Nikolai and Aleksei Titkov. 1999. "Regional'noe Izmerenie Vyborov." In *Rossiia Nakanune Dumskikh Vyborov 1999 goda*, Michael McFaul, Nikolai Petrov, and Andrei Ryabov (eds.), (Moscow: Carnegie Moscow Center).

Pipes, Richard. 1964. *The Formation of The Soviet Union: Communism and Nationalism 1917–1923*, rev. ed. (Cambridge, MA: Harvard University Press).

1974. *Russia Under the Old Regime* (New York: Scribner).

2004. "Flight From Freedom." *Foreign Affairs* 83, no. 3 (May/June): 9–15.

Przeworski, Adam. 1991. *Democracy and the Market* (New York: Cambridge University Press).

Rae, Douglas. 1967. *The Political Consequences of Electoral Laws*, rev. ed. (New Haven, CT: Yale University Press).

Reddaway, Peter. 1994. "Instability and Fragmentation." *Journal of Democracy* 5, no. 2 (April): 13–19.

Reddaway, Peter and Dmitri Glinski. 2001. *The Tragedy of Russia's Reforms* (Washington, DC: U.S. Institute of Peace).

Reddaway, Peter and Robert Orttung (eds.). 2003. *The Dynamics of Russian Politics: Putin's Reform of Federal-Regional Relations*, 1 (Lanham, MD: Rowman & Littlefield).

2005. *The Dynamics of Russian Politics*, 2 (Lanham, MD: Rowman & Littlefield).

Remington, Thomas F. 1998. "Political Conflict and Institutional Design." *Journal of Communist Studies and Transition Politics* 14, nos. 1–2 (March/June): 201–23.

Remington, Thomas F. 2001. *The Russian Parliament: Institutional Evolution in a Transitional Regime* (New Haven, CT: Yale University Press).

Remington, Thomas F. 2003. "Majorities Without Mandates: The Russian Federation Council Since 2000." *Europe-Asia Studies* 55, no. 5 (July): 667–92.

Remini, Robert V. 1959. *Martin Van Buren and the Making of the Democratic Party* (New York: Columbia University Press).

Remnick, David. 1998. *Resurrection* (New York: Vintage).
Rigby, T. H. 1988. "Staffing USSR Incorporated." *Soviet Studies* 40, no. 4 (October): 523–37.
Riker, William H. 1964. *Federalism: Origin, Operation, Significance* (Boston: Little, Brown).
Roeder, Philip G. 1991. "Soviet Federalism and Ethnic Mobilization." *World Politics* 43, no. 2 (January): 196–232.
1999. "Peoples and States After 1989." *Slavic Review* 58, no. 4 (Winter): 854–82.
Rohrschneider, Robert. 1993. "New Party versus Old Left Realignments." *Journal of Politics* 55, no. 3 (August): 682–701.
1994. "How Iron Is the Iron Law of Oligarchy?" *European Journal of Political Research* 25, no. 2 (February): 207–38.
Rokkan, Stein. 1970. *Citizens, Elections, Parties* (New York: David McKay).
Rose, Richard. 1995. "Mobilizing Demobilized Voters in Post-Communist Society." *Party Politics* 1, no. 4 (October): 549–63.
2000. "A Supply Side View of Russia's Elections." *East European Constitutional Review* 9, nos.1–2 (Winter–Spring): 53–9.
Rose, Richard and Neil Munro. 2002. *Elections without Order* (New York: Cambridge University Press).
Rose, Richard and Evgeny Tikhomirov. 1996. "Russia's Forced-Choice Presidential Election." *Post-Soviet Affairs* 12, no. 4 (October–December): 351–79.
Ross, Cameron. 2002. *Federalism and Democratization in Russia* (Manchester: Manchester University Press).
Rustow, Dankwart. 1970. "Transitions to Democracy." *Comparative Politics* 2, no. 3 (April): 337–63.
Rutland, Peter. 1993. *The Politics of Stagnation in the Soviet Union* (New York: Cambridge University Press).
1994. "Has Democracy Failed in Russia?" *The National Interest* 38 (December): 3–12.
1999. "Grigorii Yavlinskii." *Problems of Post-Communism* 46, no. 5 (September/October): 48–54.
2004. "Putin Rules." *Transitions Online*, March 15.
Sakwa, Richard. 1995. "The Development of the Russian Party System." In *Elections and Political Order in Russia*, Peter Lentini (ed.), 169–201 (New York: Central European University).
Samuelson, Paul A. 1970. *Economics*, 8th ed. (New York: McGraw-Hill).
Sartori, Giovanni. 1976. *Parties and Party Systems*, 1 (New York: Cambridge University Press).
Schattschneider, E. E. 1970. *Party Government* (Westport, CT: Greenwood Press [1942]).
Schelling, Thomas C. 1980. *The Strategy of Conflict* (Cambridge, MA: Harvard University Press).
Schlesinger, Arthur M., Jr., 1945. *The Age of Jackson* (Boston: Little, Brown).
Scott, John. 1989. *Behind the Urals* [1942] (Bloomington: Indiana University).
Shefter, Martin. 1977. "Party and Patronage." *Politics & Society* 7, no. 4 (December): 403–52.
1994. *Political Parties and the State* (Princeton, NJ: Princeton University Press).
Shleifer, Andrei and Daniel Treisman. 2000. *Without a Map* (Cambridge, MA: MIT).

2004. "A Normal Country." *Foreign Affairs* 83, no. 2 (March/April): 20–38.
Shvetsova, Olga. 2003. "Resolving the Problem of Pre-Election Coordination: The 1999 Parliamentary Election as Elite Presidential 'Primary.'" In *Elections, Parties and the Future of Russia*, Vicki Hesli and William Reisinger (eds.), (New York: Cambridge University Press).
Silbey, Joel H. 2002. *Martin Van Buren and the Emergence of American Popular Politics* (New York: Rowman & Littlefield).
Slezkine, Yuri. 1994. "How a Socialist State Promoted Ethnic Particularism." *Slavic Review* 53, no. 2 (Summer): 414–52.
Slider, Darrell. 1996. "Elections to Russia's Regional Assemblies." *Post-Soviet Affairs* 12, no. 3 (July–September): 243–64.
2001. "Russia's Governors and Party Formation." In *Contemporary Russian Politics*, Archie Brown (ed.), 224–34 (New York: Oxford University Press).
2005. "The Regions' Impact on Federal Policy." In Peter Reddaway and Robert Orttung (eds.), *The Dynamics of Russian Politics: Putin's Reform of Federal-Regional Relations*, 2 (Boulder: Rowman & Littlefield).
Smith, Steven S. and Thomas F. Remington. 2001. *The Politics of Institutional Choice* (Princeton, NJ: Princeton University Press).
Smyth, Regina. 1998. "The Political Implications of Mixed Electoral Systems." Unpublished manuscript.
2002. "Building State Capacity from the Inside Out." *Politics & Society* 30, no. 4 (December): 555–78.
2006. *Candidate Strategies and Electoral Competition in the Russian Federation: Democracy Without Foundation* (New York: Cambridge University Press).
Snyder, James M. and Michael M. Ting. 2002. "An Informational Rationale for Political Parties." *American Journal of Political Science* 46, no. 1 (January): 90–110.
Solnick, Steven L. 1998. *Stealing the State: Control and Collapse in Soviet Institutions* (Cambridge, MA: Harvard University Press).
1999. "Russia's 'Transition.'" *Social Research* 66, no. 3 (Fall): 789–824.
2000. "Is the Center Too Weak or Too Strong in the Russian Federation?" In *Building the Russian State*, Valerie Sperling (ed.), 137–56 (Boulder: Westview).
Stepan, Alfred. 2000. "Russian Federalism in Comparative Perspective." *Post-Soviet Affairs* 16, no. 2 (April–June): 133–76.
2004. "Toward a New Comparative Politics of Federalism, Multinationalism, and Democracy: Beyond Rikerian Federalism." In *Federalism and Democracy in Latin America*, Edward L. Gibson (ed.), 29–84 (Baltimore: Johns Hopkins University Press).
Stoner-Weiss, Kathryn. 1997. *Local Heroes* (Princeton, NJ: Princeton University Press).
1999. "Central Weakness and Provincial Autonomy." *Post-Soviet Affairs* 15, no. 1 (January–March): 87–106.
2000. "The Limited Reach of Russia's Party System." PONARS policy memo no. 123. Available online at http://www.csis.org/ruseura/ponars/policymemos/pm_0122.pdf.
2001. "The Limited Reach of Russia's Party System." *Politics & Society* 29, no. 3 (September): 385–414.
Suny, Ronald Grigor. 1993. *The Revenge of the Past* (Stanford: Stanford University Press).

Taagepera, Rein and Matthew Soberg Shugart. 1989. *Seats and Votes* (New Haven, CT: Yale University Press).

Thelen, Kathleen and Sven Steinmo. 1992. "Historical Institutionalism in Comparative Politics." In *Structuring Politics*, Steinmo, Thelen and Frank Longstreth (eds.), 1–32 (New York: Cambridge University Press).

Tocqueville, Alexis de. 1988. *Democracy in America* [1848], translated by George Lawrence and edited by J. P. Mayer (New York: HarperPerennial).

Tomz, Michael, Joshua Tucker, and Jason Wittenberg. 2002. "An Easy and Accurate Regression Model for Multiparty Electoral Data." *Political Analysis* 10, no. 1 (Winter): 66–83.

Tomz, Michael, Jason Wittenberg, and Gary King. 2003. *CLARIFY: Software for Interpreting and Presenting Statistical Results*, Version 2.1, Stanford University, University of Wisconsin, and Harvard University, January. Available online at http://gking.harvard.edu.

Treisman, Daniel. 1997. "Russia's Ethnic Revival." *World Politics* 49, no. 2 (January): 212–49.

1998a. "Between the Extremes: The Moderate Reformist and Centrist Blocs." In *Growing Pains*, Timothy J. Colton and Jerry F. Hough (eds.), 141–76 (Washington, DC: Brookings).

1998b. "Dollars and Democratization." *Comparative Politics* 31, no. 1 (October): 1–22.

1999. *After the Deluge* (Ann Arbor: University of Michigan Press).

Tucker, Joshua A. 2002. "The First Decade of Post-Communist Elections and Voting: What Have We Studied, and How Have We Studied It?" *Annual Review of Political Science* 5: 271–304.

Umland, Andreas. 1997. "The Post-Soviet Russian Extreme Right." *Problems of Post-Communism* 44, no. 4 (July/August): 53–61.

Urban, Joan Barth and Valerii D. Solovei. 1997. *Russia's Communists at the Crossroads* (Boulder: Westview).

Vujacic, Veljko. 1996. "Gennady Zyuganov and the Third Road." *Post-Soviet Affairs* 12, no. 2 (April–June): 118–54.

Walker, Edward W. 2003. *Dissolution: Sovereignty and the Breakup of the Soviet Union* (Lanham, MD: Rowman & Littlefield).

Ware, Alan. 2000. "Anti-Partism and Party Control of Political Reform in the United States." *British Journal of Political Science* 30, no. 1 (January): 1–29.

Weber, Max. 1949. "The Ideal Type." *The Methodology of the Social Sciences*. Published online at http://homepage.mac.com/abukuma/weberian/weber/method/obje/objectivity_2c.html.

1990. "The Advent of Plebiscitarian Democracy," excerpted from "Politics as a Vocation" [1946]. In *The West European Party System*, Peter Mair (ed.), (Oxford: Oxford University Press).

Weiner, Myron. 1967. *Party-Building in a New Nation: The Indian National Congress* (Chicago: University of Chicago Press).

White, Stephen, Richard Rose, and Ian McAllister. 1997. *How Russia Votes* (Chatham, NJ: Chatham House).

Whitefield, Stephen. 2001. "Partisan and Party Divisions in Post-Communist Russia." In *Contemporary Russian Politics*, Archie Brown (ed.), 235–43 (New York: Oxford University Press).

Whitefield, Stephen and Geoffrey Evans. 1999. "Class, Markets and Partisanship in Post-Soviet Russia: 1993–96." *Electoral Studies* 18, no. 2 (June): 155–78.

Woodruff, David. 1999. *Money Unmade* (Ithaca, NY: Cornell University Press).

2003. "Khodorkovsky's Gamble: From Business to Politics in the YUKOS Conflict." PONARS Policy Brief No. 308, November.

Wright, Gerald and Brian F. Schaffner. 2002. "The Influence of Party." *American Political Science Review* 96, no. 2 (June): 367–79.

Yeltsin, Boris. 2000. *Prezidentskii Marafon* (Moscow: Act).

Zaslavsky, Victor. 1982. *The Neo-Stalinist State* (Armonk, NY: M.E. Sharpe).

Zimmerman, William. 2002. *The Russian People and Foreign Policy: Russian Elite and Mass Perspectives, 1993–2000* (Princeton, NJ: Princeton University Press).